China's Industrial Revolution

THE PANTHEON ASIA LIBRARY
NEW APPROACHES TO THE NEW ASIA

Other Asia Library Titles

The Japan Reader, edited by Jon Livingston, Joe Moore, and Felicia Oldfather
   Volume 1 *Imperial Japan: 1800–1945*
   Volume 2 *Postwar Japan: 1945 to the Present*

A Chinese View of China, by John Gittings

Remaking Asia: Essays on the American Uses of Power, edited by Mark Selden

Without Parallel: The American-Korean Relationship Since 1945, edited by Frank Baldwin

Chairman Mao Talks to the People: Talks and Letters, 1956–1971, edited by Stuart Schram

A Political History of Japanese Capitalism, by Jon Halliday

Origins of the Modern Japanese State: Selected Writings of E. H. Norman, edited by John Dower

China's Uninterrupted Revolution: From 1840 to the Present, edited by Victor Nee and James Peck

The Wind Will Not Subside: Years in Revolutionary China, 1964–1969, by David Milton and Nancy Dall Milton

The Waves at Genji's Door: Japan Through Its Cinema, by Joan Mellen

China from the Opium Wars to the 1911 Revolution, by Jean Chesneaux, Marianne Bastid, and Marie-Claire Bergère

China's Industrial Revolution

Politics, Planning, and Management,
1949 to the Present

BY STEPHEN ANDORS

PANTHEON BOOKS, NEW YORK

Library of Congress Cataloging in Publication Data

Andors, Stephen, 1938–
China's Industrial Revolution

  (The Pantheon Asia Library)
  Bibliography: pp. 323–32
  Includes index.
    1. China—Economic conditions—1949–   2. China—
Industries.   3. China—Economic policy.   I. Title
HC427.A787   1977   338′.0951   76-42161
ISBN 0-394-49250-1
ISBN 0-394-73293-6 pbk.

Manufactured in the United States of America
FIRST EDITION

My intention being to write something of use to those who understand, it appears to me more proper to go to the real truth of the matter than to its imagination; and many have imagined republics and principalities which have never been seen or known to exist in reality; for how we live is so far removed from how we ought to live, that he who abandons what is done for what ought to be done will rather learn to bring about his own ruin than his preservation.

Machiavelli, *The Prince*, 1532

What Marxist philosophy regards as the most important problem does not lie in understanding the laws of the objective world and thereby becoming capable of explaining it, but in actively changing the world by applying the knowledge of its objective laws. . . . When man in society devotes himself to the practice of changing a certain objective process at a certain stage of its development (whether changing a natural or a social process), he can, by the reflection of the objective process in his thought and by the functioning of his own subjective activity, advance his knowledge from the perceptual to the rational and bring forth ideas, theories, plans, or programs which on the whole correspond to the laws of that objective process; he then puts these ideas, theories, plans, or programs into practice in the same objective process; and the process of knowledge as regards this concrete process can be considered as completed if, through the practice in that objective process, he can realize his preconceived ideas, theories, plans, or programs into facts.

Mao Tsetung, "On Practice," 1937

Why is it that the communists always say they're for the working man, and as soon as they set up a country, you got guys singing to tractors? They're singing about how they love the factory. That's where I couldn't buy communism. It's the intellectuals' utopia, not mine. I cannot picture myself singing to a tractor. . . . Or singing to steel. (Singsongs) Oh, whoop-dee-doo, I'm at the bonderizer. Oh, how I love this heavy steel. No thanks. Never hoppen. . . . If a carpenter built a cabin for poets, I think the least the poets owe the carpenter is just three or four one-liners on the wall. A little plaque: Though we labor with our minds, this place we can relax in was built by someone who can work with his hands. And his work is as noble as ours. I think the poet owes something to the guy who built the cabin for him.

Mike Lefevre, Steel Worker,
Cicero, Illinois, in an inter-
view with Studs Terkel in
Working.

Acknowledgments

THIS BOOK BEGAN when I was a graduate student at Columbia University. It grew from the political and intellectual rebellion, excitement, and ferment generated during the last half of the 1960s. A good part of my early research was done in Hong Kong at the Universities Service Center in 1969, supported in part by grants from the National Science Foundation and Columbia University's East Asian Institute. I owe that experience largely to the efforts of a fine gentleman: the late John M. Lindbeck, who was the Institute Director when I began my work. My appointment as a Research Associate in Columbia's East Asian Institute in 1975 provided the time and facilities for me to complete the work I had been so involved with for more than five years.

I owe a special debt of thanks to many friends in the Committee of Concerned Asian Scholars who, though they may not know it, provided essential intellectual and moral support for my work. I am grateful to other colleagues who provided detailed and concrete criticisms of the early drafts. James Peck at Pantheon helped me turn a Ph.D. dissertation into a book. Deborah Bell and Ruthann Evanoff did the vital task of typing the manuscript. And it was the Chinese people who, in their words and actions, created the fascinating and complex reality which I hope is adequately described in the following pages.

STEPHEN ANDORS

Staten Island, New York
September 1976

Contents

Charts, Graphs, and Tables

Abbreviations Used in the Text and Notes

Chinese name and abbreviation	English translation
Chi-hua Ching-chi (CHCC)	Planned Economy
Ching-chi Yen-chiu (CCYC)	Economic Research
Chung-kuo Ch'ing Kung-yeh (CKCKY)	
	Chinese Light Industry
Chung-kuo Ch'ing-nien (CKCN)	Chinese Youth
Chung-kuo Ch'ing-nien Pao (CKCNP)	
	Chinese Youth Report
Chung-kuo Kung-yeh (CKKY)	Chinese Industry
Chung-kuo Mei-tan Kung-yeh	China's Coal Industry
Hung Ch'i (HC)	Red Flag
Jen-min Jih-pao (JMJP)	People's Daily
Kuang-ming Jih-pao (KMJP)	Illumination Daily
Kung-jen Jih-pao (KJJP)	Workers' Daily
Nan-fang Jih-pao (NFJP)	Southern Daily
Ta Kung Pao (TKP)	Impartial Daily
Ta Kung Pao, Hong Kong	

United States Government Translation Service Collections

Current Background (CB)
Extracts From China Mainland Magazines (ECMM)
Foreign Broadcast Information Service (FBIS)
Joint Publications Research Service (JPRS)
Survey of China Mainland Magazines (SCMM)
Survey of the China Mainland Press (SCMP)

Introduction

To UNDERSTAND OURSELVES by learning from others is not easy. The implications of such learning could be traumatic for Westerners in general, and Americans in particular, as their societies have dominated the history of the last two centuries and thus human perceptions of the future. About one hundred years ago, the first in a series of panics sent shock-waves through American society. The last quarter of the nineteenth century was rife with class, ethnic, and regional conflict as power rapidly shifted from rural to urban America and immigrants from Europe filled urban ghettoes. In Europe, Germany and France had recently concluded a bloody war, and alliances were forming in preparation for another. Increasingly open and violent competition began for economic advantage and military strength on a global scale. Conservative political forces attempted to consolidate and strengthen their rule.

For many intellectuals in China, an ancient, proud, and independent civilization, the tensions in the West paled to insignificance. Caught up in a tempestuous society, trapped and at first confused by an existential crisis of the old order, Chinese intellectuals were impressed with the "modernity" of the West; its wealth, unity, and strength. While many criticized Western belligerence and moral behavior, they also studied Western institutions and political philosophies in the hope of overcoming technological, economic, and military weakness.[1]

The image that proud Chinese intellectuals had of the West had not always been, even so grudgingly, one of admiration. Nor were the visions of the late nineteenth century reformers to remain unchanged. They evolved as national conditions changed, and as international politics and economics were transformed by war and revolutionary upheaval.

In the late nineteenth century, the turmoil in Western society indicated a certain kind of growth and development; in China, turmoil was a sign that the old order was dying. Now, many Western intellectuals have begun to talk about the decline of Western civilization, and to write about the possible or probable alternatives to "modern" society. There is not much optimism to be found here, and no wonder. To mention only some of the obvious problems which variously afflict the industrialized world is to describe a crisis of no small proportions.

Waste, pollution, and mindless growth gobble up limited natural resources. Alienation and anxiety result from gigantic organizations, complexity, and a dehumanizing division of labor. Technological developments and economic growth centralize power, create new elites, break down communities, and lead to rural squalor, suburban sprawl, and urban crisis. Manipulation, lying, and brutality are hidden behind the façade of *raison d'état,* and are justified by those with power and accepted cynically by those without. Persistent inequalities of wealth and all the other blessings of "modern civilization" lead to seemingly random, sometimes organized outbreaks of domestic and international violence. The threat of uncontrollable disaster haunts the popular imagination, as it preoccupies the concerns and plans of ruling groups.

China's Industrial Revolution

1 / Modernization in Historical Perspective: Capitalist Civilization and Developmental Convergence

WHAT HAPPENS to human communities as they become more "modern"? Who rules them? How are they ruled and for what purposes? What is a "modern" society like? Are all modern societies ultimately faced with the same kinds of problems—technological, economic, social, and political? Do technological and economic development inevitably shatter small communities by large-scale integration and interdependence, trivialize individual life by equating joy with consumption and work with service to machines and computers?

"Modernization" is an ambiguous term. As it is popularly understood, it means little more than "something like contemporary America, Japan, Europe, or the Soviet Union" in terms of living standards, industrialization, and urbanization. As used by academics and intellectuals it purports to describe both reality and a process. It can be understood as a descriptive norm toward which "less modern" societies develop or as an analytical tool to explain or predict sequences and relationships. However, in both its popular and academic use the notion has been closely linked with the particular development of European capitalist civilization and the subsequent spread of that system to global dominance. Modernization also has been identified with the evolution of society in Soviet Russia after 1917.

Like all civilizations, European capitalism was defined by a relationship between ideas and institutions. Fundamental premises concerning the nature and purpose of human existence were linked dialectically to the organization of common life.

There is perhaps no more useful way to examine the intellectual foundations of capitalism as a civilization than through the thought of three men whose work lies at the core of so much western social theory and practice. Thomas Hobbes, Max Weber, and Frederick Taylor provided a theory of human nature, a description of social development, and a blueprint for industrial-technological organization respectively, and these ideas have not only influenced major philosophers but shaped the thinking and experience of the most hard-headed, profit minded businessmen.

Thomas Hobbes (1588–1679) asserted that human nature was both rational and selfish. He defined human selfishness as the desire to accumulate possessions and the need for the physical security to protect one's person and the property by which an individual achieved social identity. Human rationality was defined as an ability to perceive that uncontrolled selfishness would lead to dangerous struggle and chaos. To prevent this result men formed governments whose sole purpose was to provide a civilized arena within which the pursuit and maintenance of property could take place safely. Hobbes had no concept of a common good or public interest, no concept of rationality that was not based on human possessiveness. Government was constrained by laws, but, since government alone had the sovereign power to use violence legitimately, it always held the trump card in any confrontation with the private desires of individuals or groups.

Because of human nature, community was sharply limited. Inequality of talent would be reflected in political, social, and economic arrangements; equality was solely a formal equality before the law whose very purpose was to maintain actual societal inequality.

Hobbes did not seem concerned by the possibility that the State (sovereign) would use its coercive power to deny liberty or the private fulfillment of property and security to individuals. Hobbes found kings to be "noble minded," and, in any event, in normal times they could be restrained by laws. Moreover, the sovereign had to have ultimate power to override private interests and to prevent chaos.

Hobbes's liberal intellectual descendants and later political practitioners disagreed with his optimism concerning kings. They did not, however, disagree with his views about human nature, rationality, and community. Adam Smith, John Locke, and the American founding fathers incorporated these basic Hobbesian views into a full-blown' theory and structure of capitalist political economy.

Adam Smith, unlike Hobbes, deeply mistrusted government and what he called the projectors in government who, whether in the name of virtue or for self-aggrandizement, always wound up interfering with the natural workings of human nature. He defined this nature essentially as did Hobbes, but he had far more trust in the competitive individual than did Hobbes, and this trust showed in his theory of political economy.[3] For Smith, the central institution in society was the marketplace. There the natural inclinations of human nature would find the greatest liberty, and provide the greatest economic efficiency and production as well. Since the market reflected human nature, it was both an excellent motivator and an automatic allocator of labor and resources.

The American revolutionary leaders shared this British liberal philosophical tradition and incorporated it into the system of government and economy that they fashioned. Like Smith, they were deeply pessimistic about centralized and arbitrary governmental authority, and they were more or less optimistic about people in society pursuing their "rational" private interests. The Americans, however, also agreed with Hobbes that law must limit the arbitrary power of the State but not its ultimate ability to regulate and override private interest. To reconcile these contradictions, they introduced a system of checks and balances which became institutionalized both within the central government and between the central and local authorities. In the nineteenth century, as the beliefs and institutions of capitalism emerged, the concept of rational self-interest played a central role in politics and economics. In economics, it was translated via the marketplace into the notion of profit where it was to have a profound effect on the location, size, and purposes of productive economic activity. In politics, in addition to its influence on notions of freedom and liberty, its most important impact was on the visions of equality and community. Equality meant equality of opportunity to compete; it was interpreted as a legal and procedural matter, not in an economic and social sense. Equality was *a means to achieve a natural order of inequality*, not an end.

Thus, in the liberal tradition the scope of politics was sharply limited. The production and distribution of life's necessities, as well as the organization and meaning of work, were private matters. The idea of a common interest in society by which humanity transcended the fears and insecurities which underlay the competition in the marketplace was viewed as dangerous nonsense. Politics thus lost its classical identification with problems of community and became instead concerned with the problems of the marketplace. Politics became synonymous with government, confined largely to matters of representation and regulation and quite far removed both spatially and temporally from the human relationships created in the daily world of production and work.

Most individuals, however, achieved identity and evaluated their lives in terms of the relationships perceived and created in their daily lives. Success or failure in capitalist civilization was not evaluated by one's individual contribution to the community, but rather one's contribution to the community was evaluated largely in terms of one's individual performance in the marketplace. Invariably, the measure used was cleverness or efficiency in possessing and disposing of labor, resources, and commodities, or buying and selling ideas, the demand for which had been shaped by the constellation of economic and political power created by previous competitive and accumulative activity. Such activity shaped the whole concept of human identity and human need. The marketplace had only one mechanism by which a common good could be reached, but it was not long before the contradiction implicit in the concept of a community based on rational self-interest revealed itself. The vision of community gradually retreated before the politics of procedure which recreated and regulated the marketplace. As economic development and technological change proceeded, the profit criteria, which shaped economic decisions, and the marketplace, which structured political concepts and human relations, took on a seemingly independent "systemic" yet more and more invisible existence, appearing to be part of modern society itself.

Beneath the civilization of European and American capitalism, therefore, lay all the fears and furies of the human spirit which in no way were pacified by a system based on competitive accumulation. Wrapped in the velvet glove of legal regulation and government by constraint lay the Hobbesian fist of state power, to be used should the competition get out of hand. And it did.

Contrary to the optimistic hopes of the nineteenth century liberals, competition in the marketplace tended to be self-destructive rather than self-regulating. The contest to gain the security that came with property and the capital that came with success in the marketplace gradually eliminated from competition those who would not or could not play by the rules of the system. By the beginning of the twentieth century, governments began to grow in power to prevent the collapse of a system increasingly threatened by destructive competition among economic behemoths on one level and struggle within a fragmented but increasingly angry population on another.

The development of monopoly and oligopoly, both the logical results of the underlying dynamic of the marketplace, transformed the earlier relationships, both social and economic, that had characterized the political communities in capitalist societies of Europe and North America. Supply, marketing, and investment decisions, once made by local factory owners or commercial entrepreneurs scanning a local market, were no longer the forces that shaped economic activity. Increasingly these decisions were taken on a much broader geographic scale, affecting the lives and consumption patterns of millions. Many local industries closed. Others, of relatively small or medium size, were assimilated into an administratively centralized structure where they became specialized parts factories or branches of a giant parent company. Localities, once relatively self-sufficient territorial units of production and consumption, gradually became more dependent on supplies and consumer goods made very far away. Many localities began to lose industry altogether as more profitable areas of investment and exploitation were envisioned by corporate managers scanning the labor and raw materials markets of a whole continent.[4] Marketing, supplies, and transportation became much more complex and interdependent. Urban centers became the production and administrative headquarters for far-flung corporate activities. Cities began to grow rapidly, attracting the rural poor and serving as the home bases for a new breed of manager who was often far removed from actual production sites. Capital investment flowed to where profits were highest, places with abundant cheap labor, raw materials, transportation, and communication facilities. As the urban-rural gap widened, society became more urbanized, but social inequality in the city set the stage for a massive move to the suburbs. In the United States especially, small farmers found it hard to compete with the larger and wealthier farms which were more mechanized and using current technology to increase output. In many areas rural poverty increased and became stubbornly entrenched, while urban centers began to decay after a period of very rapid growth.

Increasing centralization and interdependence of the whole economic system was accompanied by growing control for owners and managers over the pace, quantity, and quality of production in order to realize maximum profit and minimum cost through efficiency. Given these goals, management began taking power away from workers who, because of their skills and knowledge, often exercised considerable direct and indirect control over production. Frederick Taylor (1865–1915), an American, developed theories of "scientific management" which quickly became the way in which management sought to organize the production process by strictly controlling the time and content of every single step in a tightly supervised and minute division of labor.[5]

Technological and economic development, and the transformation of industrial organization and management was paralleled by bureaucratization of knowledge and education. The educational system reflected a growing demand for disciplined and skilled labor and for administrative and technical experts to be supervisors and coordinators on behalf of those who owned or controlled the means of production. Higher education became more universal and increasingly specialized. The acquisition of knowledge was treated as akin to the acquisition of property; as essentially a private possession which conferred economic advantage and the right to direct the labor process and literally control the bodies of other people.[6] The educated elite of earlier capitalism was now transformed into a highly differentiated and stratified educated population, the top echelons of which were to share power and the goals and values of the bourgeoisie ("human nature") described so starkly by Thomas Hobbes.[7]

Growing centralization and bureaucratization of government paralleled these trends in society.[8] Yet this was not at all what liberal capitalism was supposed to lead to. Hobbes's liberal descendants could not provide an adequate explanation of the evolution of modern society in European civilization. This was the task attempted by the great German social scientist, Max Weber (1864–1920).

Weber was clearly a product of European liberalism. He incorporated the basic Hobbesian notions of human nature into his conception of the Protestant ethic, as well as liberal ideas about rationality, the limits of community, and the purpose of social life. He hoped that political leaders would provide the unique blend of vision and talent necessary to assert rule over the ordinary person's narrower vision and parochial interests, but his elitist concept of politics was not simply an ideological premise. It was linked to the historical process itself, to "modernization," the key to which was bureaucratization.

Weber associated modernization with the growth and development of technology and economic interdependence brought about by the search for maximum production for maximum profit. In his view, modernization began a process whereby old communities, based on charismatic or magical authority and with human relationships based on traits of character, family, or personality, were torn asunder. In their stead there arose a different kind of society—one with a specific type of organizational structure whose *raison d'être* was efficiency.[9] This modern organizational form was called bureaucracy, and it drew power from "rational-legal" authority, law in the form of written rules and regulations that assigned duties and responsibilities. Bureaucracy, because it gave duties and responsibilities to offices and not to people, was to function like a well-oiled machine with interchangeable parts. The individual bureaucrat, highly trained in technical or administrative matters, was presumed to be impartial to special interests, economic or emotional, and motivated by the opportunity for a career, promotion to higher pay, more security and privilege, and more power over others.

Weber produced both a theory of organization and of modern society. It was a theory which set forth a system of human relationships, values, behavior, education and work which justified the destruction of traditional patterns of community and denied the prospects of any future form. It was, moreover, a theory of development in which people were more or less helpless and passive, except for a few political leaders who might be expected to present and pursue some vision of gentlemanly compromise.[10]

Weber, however, was not optimistic about even this modest vision of political community. "The question," he said in speaking of the purpose to which bureaucratic organizations would be put, "is always who controls the existing bureaucratic machinery."[11] Weber, answering his own question with a good deal of foreboding, postulated that a relatively few experts, technical and administrative, would ultimately control their own machinery. The technological and administrative demands of modern society could only be met by a few leading bureaucratic policy makers at the top of the organizational hierarchy. Functionaries, clerks, and workers were left to carry out orders whose purposes they could understand only partially at best.

The similarity between Weber's academic theory of modernization and organization and the practical, businesslike, scientific management principles of Frederick Taylor which were coming into vogue in the American business and corporate world at about the same time is quite striking. Both felt that administrative and technical experts had to wield power over workers assigned narrow and strictly defined duties and responsibilities if maximum production and efficiency was to be attained. Both accepted the idea that individual competition for personal wealth and privilege was the most certain way to motivate people to perform their tasks at peak levels of effort.[12]

Weber did not confine his theory of bureaucracy to the evolution of capitalist societies. He held that all "formally rational" systems, that is, those based on the goal of maximum output at minimum cost to those who owned or controlled the means of production, would develop into bureaucratic systems. He argued that the socialist alternative to capitalism (by socialist he meant state ownership) would not lead to greater equality and closer community as socialists argued, but rather would exacerbate the bureaucratic tendencies inherent in modern social and economic life. Instead of the relatively open dynamics of competitive capitalist bureaucracies, there would evolve the monolithic wall of a single state bureaucracy against which human freedom and creativity would be broken. As much as Weber feared bureaucratic rule, he thought it inevitable in modern society; for this reason he preferred the competitive capitalist bureaucratic system to a potentially, almost certainly, monolithic socialism. Weber's intention, both intellectually and politically, was to refute Marx.

In retrospect, Weber's work towers as a politically conservative, enormously influential, and monumental theoretical synthesis which combined an uncritical acceptance of liberal philosophical premises with a mild reformist outlook. Moreover, there was a logic in Weber's position that was inescapable, once his basic premises concerning human nature, rationality, community, and purpose in society were accepted. Even though Weber's organizational theory about the rationality and efficiency of bureaucratic organization has since been significantly modified,[13] his basic *political* conclusions about the structure of power and the goals of human activity in *modern* society have not been challenged in any coherent or consistent way. Since Weber wrote, neo-Weberians have pointed out that bureaucracy might not be as efficient or coherent as he had anticipated, but it certainly is as pervasive as he had feared. Experts and technicians might not rule alone over the bureaucratic organizations in modern society, but they are considered to rule in conjunction with, in cooperation with, or even in limited conflict with *political elites*[14] depending on the perspective of different analysts.[15] In Weberian tradition current political history is read as a twentieth century version of the eighteenth and nineteenth century liberal market-place. However, instead of free individuals competing for wealth, property, status, or power, now public and private bureaucracies and bureaucratic elites do the same thing. In this view, whether we name the future industrial, postindustrial, technological, or technetronic,[16] history is a record of struggle between elites, while the masses are the objects of one or another kind of benevolent or malevolent manipulation.

Management theorists trained in the business schools of the West have come as close to challenging Weber's organizational theory as is possible to do without actually rejecting Weber's larger theoretical and philosophical liberalism. These people were anxious to smooth over conflict between workers and managers and to increase worker motivation. The "human-relations" theorists, beginning with the famous Hawthorne studies of Elton Mayo,[17] and including the work of Maslow,[18] McGregor,[19] and others,[20] stressed that the rewards of cooperation, equality, and psychic satisfaction gained from a sense of belonging and contributing talents and skills to the group were potent forces in human affairs and were efficient ways to bring scientific and technological knowledge to bear on problems of modern industry and production. Such non-Hobbesian, non-liberal insights were never extended to challenge Weber's theories about the State or power distribution in society at large, nor did they challenge the right of giant private corporations to decide on the location, size, and purpose of productive human activity.

The most intellectually serious challenge to the Weberian-liberal paradigm of modernization and modern society did not come from the twentieth century business school professors and corporation advisers who developed the human relations theory of management. It came from Karl Marx, a man whose thinking has been oversimplified and vulgarized almost as much as it has been misinterpreted or ignored.

The Marxist View of Modernization

There is no doubt that Marx, like all of his European contemporaries, viewed European capitalism as the most advanced and modern form of nineteenth century society and economics, and there is little doubt that Marx believed societies such as China or India to be relatively backward. He clearly detested European imperialism and the brutality, hypocrisy, and exploitation that often accompanied it, but he still viewed it as a progressive historical force, one that shattered an essentially stagnant "Asiatic mode" of production and wrenched ancient civilizations violently into the modern world.[21]

However, Marx's attitude toward European imperialism did not mean that he viewed capitalism as an inevitable stage in the development of non-European civilizations. He held that societies must be viewed in specific historical context, that the external environment within which events unfolded and the concrete political, ideological, economic, and technological conditions under which class conflict took place in each society should also be considered. He rejected supra-historical or a priori schemes of historical stages which, he argued, served to mystify reality.[22]

Both Marx and Engels, however, had little or nothing to say about how modernization might occur without capitalism, or how socialism might evolve from a noncapitalist non-European historical setting.[23] Marx clearly felt that the institutions, human relationships, and values of capitalism were not necessarily universal, but that they would lead to what was universal: a socialist or communist society within which human potential could be fully realized. Marx wrote, therefore, about the relationship between capitalism and socialism in Europe, but his method and his vision were to have a more universal relevance.

Marx began with the premise that human nature and rationality were not what earlier liberal political philosophy had described them to be, that human nature could only be defined in terms of its potential. All humans wanted to be "truly human," to end their alienation from nature, from their own identity as beings both physical and mental, and from each other. To achieve this goal people *acted*, but their actions were always constrained by the actual circumstances in which they found themselves and by their own fears and ignorance,[24] what Marx called "consciousness."

To Marx, the classical liberal definition of human nature indicated that human beings had still not become "truly human." This human nature bore the stamp of the society in which it had grown, one where fear, poverty, and scarcity existed, and it was a "nature" compatible with and supportive of capitalism, whose institutions and class relationships perpetuated and justified it.

Like other civilizations before it, capitalism was a new but still imperfect and partial attempt to conquer fear, scarcity, ignorance and alienation. It was therefore transitory. Marx was much impressed with the technological and productive capacities of capitalism, and he viewed large-scale industrialization as laying the material foundations for a further, qualitative leap in the development of human civilization. However, capitalism by its very nature would soon be unable to utilize technology and industry in a way which served truly human needs.

Marx held that the right to sell one's life or labor time in the market and to receive wages and be able to purchase in the marketplace was an important step forward, one which opened society to creative human energy in a way that the arbitrary and often stultifying con-

straints of slavery or feudalism precluded. Yet this right was constantly
threatened by the vagaries of market cycles. Moreover, as technology
and the productive capacity of the economy developed, and as humanity's
knowledge and consciousness of its needs evolved, the limits of the
social relationships of capitalism would be revealed. The working class,
forced to sell the labor of its individual members on the marketplace
in return for the right to live and accumulate commodities, would
ultimately make a revolution, and take control over society to rule in
the interests of all-around human development.

The transition from capitalist to socialist, and then to communist
society, was to take place over a long historical period. Both Marx and
Engels believed that unequal political and economic relationships were
unavoidable and necessary counterparts of social organization until the
full development of communist social relations and communist men. In
Capital, Marx stated the need for some kind of authority in modern industrial society "whenever the direct process of production assumes the
form of a combined social process and not of the isolated labor of independent producers."[25] Engels more strongly stressed the need for
authority, discipline, and subordination as inevitable parts of industrial
organization.[26] Marx and Engels also spoke of the concept of "bourgeois
right," the desire for wages to be based on the value and difficulty of
work rather than on the needs of every worker, regardless of the division
of labor, and they envisioned an indefinite period of transformation,
both ideological and institutional, before this notion of bourgeois right
would be transformed into a commitment to human equality.

Marx could see that large-scale industrialization and urbanization
went hand in hand, but he and Engels envisioned a society in which
the inequalities between urban and rural life would disappear, where
technology would be used in a way that did not destroy the human
community or the natural environment. Though Marx was impressed
with the size and efficiency of capitalist industrial organizations, he did
not accept the political rule of owners, managers, or technical personnel
that these enterprises fostered.

Indeed, the political relationships of modern capitalism would not
change all at once. Marx instead foresaw rather close relationships
between the early forms of socialist economy and the influence of
specialists and engineers (no longer owners of property) because their
attitudes and functions had "developed on the lap of capitalist production," and changes in the educational system would not yet have had
an effect.[27] He projected that bourgeois specialists and technicians
would help to build a socialist society, through their contribution to material production.[28] In Marx's view, the need for such people would be
transitory. Their values and work styles would be outmoded by a host
of changes in the new society. Socialism and communism would create

"new men" where differences between workers and intellectuals, specifically managers and technicians in industry, would disappear.

Marx's vision of nonbureaucratic political power extended beyond the confines of the industrial enterprise itself. In writing about the Paris Commune, he stressed that power would not entail economic privilege and social inequality. Power was to be subject to the control of the people over whom it was exercised. "All posts," in the Commune, wrote Marx, were filled "by election on the basis of universal suffrage of all concerned, subject to the right of recall at any time by the same electors," and "all officials, high or low, were paid only the wages received by other workers."[29] Engels spoke of authority in terms of decision-making by "a delegate" representing a group of workers or "by a majority vote," but he noted the need for "a dominant will" that settles all subordinate questions whether this will be represented by a single delegate or a committee charged with the execution of the resolutions of the majority of persons interested.[30] Though Marx and Engels were much aware of the need for a strong state to protect the new order from attack and sabotage by internal and external enemies,[31] the relationship of the strong state to democratic control and the role of the state apparatus in the economic functions of planning and production in socialist society were left undeveloped and ambiguous.

In the absence of experience, neither Marx nor Engels attempted to foresee the concrete practical complexities involved in transforming capitalist society to socialism, and they said almost nothing about the relationship between noncapitalist societies and socialism. Late in the nineteenth century, however, Engels did touch on what was later to prove to be a central political problem in societies attempting to create a modern system. Jeremy Azrael describes Engels' warning:

> Writing in 1891, Engels warned Bebel: "If, as the result of a war, we come to power before we are prepared for it, the technicians will be our chief enemies; they will deceive and betray us to the best of their ability." And Engels was aware that the ability in question was bound to be considerable. To be sure, it might be possible to terrorize the technicians into formal submission, but the very conditions of backwardness that made terror necessary would make mere submission more or less irrelevant. Given such conditions it would be more than ever imperative for a socialist regime to launch a program of rapid economic development, and such a program could succeed if the technicians actively cooperated. Such cooperation, however, was scarcely likely in the case of men whose initial hostility was compounded by the regime's recourse to terror. Indeed, the problem of growth aside, it was far from certain that the use of terror would suffice to prevent rapid economic collapse. If terror was an effective weapon against overt sabotage, it was likely to be much less effective against covert "wrecking," the more so because the "armed workers" and their "acknowledged representatives" would probably lack sufficient edu-

cation to comprehend even the gross outlines of management procedures. In short, if for no other reason than the hostility of the managerial and technical cadres with whom it would have to deal, a premature revolution was likely to end in unmitigated disaster, with the attempt to establish socialism giving way either to a restoration of capitalism or to the consolidation of a bureaucratic superstate in which the managers and technicians would themselves play a prominent part.[32]

Engels' warning could easily have been written by Max Weber twenty-five years later. Yet to compare Marx to Weber and the liberal intellectual tradition is to sketch out two radically different views of how the world works and where it might be going. Marx saw history as class struggle and the collective drive of all humanity to create a truly human existence. He saw a highly dialectical interaction between political leadership and mass spontaneity which, in ever more egalitarian terms, transformed daily experience into a powerful force of collective consciousness. Those in the liberal Weber tradition, on the other hand, saw in history the inexorable laws of human nature rather than the potential of human aspiration. In this view a ruling elite guaranteed enlightenment which the masses were incapable of achieving for themselves and prevented the sloth and chaos which the people in their selfishness threatened to bring about; it established procedures to maintain the competition that guaranteed the achievement of other goals.

Marx and Weber also took a different view of the impact of technological development on modern society. Weber and the neo-Weberians foresaw increasingly mechanized and automated work that would lead in turn to a proliferation of administrative and technical groups. They foretold less meaning for creative work as a central focus of social life, and they looked with positive favor on the growing gap between work and private life.

Marx, however, viewed work as a continuous, primary focus of all human activity, and he did not envision a growing body of technical and administrative specialists to rule or manage the masses. With machines performing the necessary drudgery, Marx saw the possibility of combining mental and manual work in a new form of self and collective rule, one that would make use of creative imagination.

Weberians postulated that inequality between social classes was permanent, that possessiveness was a natural human instinct which had to be satisfied in visible social and economic inequalities if people were to perform their tasks in society at acceptable levels of efficiency. Education and position were the basis for the rise of a new ruling class and long periods of formal schooling were the only guarantee a society had for transmitting the knowledge necessary for the elite to manage a modern society and economy.

Marx dreamed of a classless, egalitarian society, one that would be a cooperative community. He argued that a time would come when intellectual and biological differences would become less important, as education became geared to participation in production rather than direction over it. Biological differences would not be justification for social or economic inequality. As humans evolved a higher morality, brought about by the end of scarcity and by the construction of non-capitalist relations of production, there would be no proliferation of new elites but a withering away of class rule altogether.

Finally, for Weberians theories of production were based on maximum profit (the "exact calculation" of costs and benefits) as the essence of rationality in a modern society. For Marx, however, this idea of rationality was only a product of capitalism; he envisioned a society where production for the needs of the whole human being would be the result of conscious, *political* planning. He argued that this method would produce a far more rational though ultimately very different social order.

History seems to have been much kinder to the conservative Weber than to the revolutionary Marx. Modernization in both East and West, capitalist and socialist societies has entailed bureaucratization and new embellishments have been added to the theories of bureaucratic rule. Neither Japan, which began modernization from a non-Western cultural and historical base, nor the Soviet Union, which began modernization from a specifically Russian and explicitly Marxist base, has been able to escape the logic of the relationship between the urbanization and bureaucratization of society and modern civilization.

Japan's modernization began in conscious imitation of the West. Confronted with the military and political threat of the Western capitalist powers in the last half of the nineteenth century, the Japanese rulers were anxious to match Europe's and America's strength as quickly as possible. Their model of modern civilization was, therefore, already in existence. It consisted of large-scale, urban-centered industrial growth, a system of universal education for training skilled workers and scientific, technical, and administrative elites for industry organized in a hierarchical division of labor and control for the purpose of profit; a strong central government (modeled on the Prussian state) which provided political and economic leadership and support to giant private enterprise, the marketplace, based on the mechanisms of price and profit, and the ethic of accumulation to allocate resources and determine growth, investment, and development. The Japanese quickly grafted all of these onto a tradition which was still influenced by the warrior-feudal ethic of personal honor, obligation, loyalty, and hierarchy.[33]

The result of this, in some ways radical but essentially conservative, late nineteenth-century reform was to consolidate the rule of a small oligarchy which used tradition to justify its position. The stage was then set for the evolution of a rapidly growing and expanding bureaucratic capitalism. Japanese capitalism was in many ways less democratic, more paternalistic, and more bureaucratic from its inception than its Western model. There was a more openly cooperative relationship between big government and big business than in Western European and American societies, where the government's commitment to giant private corporations was partially compromised by the individualistic, marketplace definition of democracy and by attachment to the ideological vision of competitive capitalism.[34]

The way in which aspects of Japanese tradition had been adapted to justify and legitimate the new capitalist-bureaucratic order of Japanese society created a Japan that differed from the West in some ways. Factory personnel policies, for example, were different, but far more important was the rise of Japanese fascism.

Recent Western observers assumed that because Japan was modernizing it would naturally become like capitalism in the west,[35] but this was largely a post–World War II view and one that both intellectually and politically was very uncomfortable with the reality of Japanese fascism. To explain this reality, it is important to see that the rise of Japan to the ranks of a world power was not the result of a revolutionary fervor which projected Japan as the creator of new values and institutions. From the outset, Japan's political leaders wanted to be similar to, not different from, the West, envisioning no other way to be free from Western military and economic domination. Japanese nationalism and Japanese modernization thus entered into an ambivalent relationship. As modernization occurred, nationalism grew but could not be based on anything unique in Japan's modernity. Instead, the virtues of economic and military power as the means to equal the West were stressed. References to traditional virtues and the glory of the Emperor lent Japanese society a tenuous sense of self-identity, one that was contradicted by its emulation of Western capitalism. If the social forms and institutions of modern Japan could not themselves be an integral part of Japanese nationalism and a source of pride rather than humiliation, and if they bred dangerous class struggle rather than social cohesion, they could be used in the service of another form of nationalism, one defined by expansion, glorified in the name of historical myths and symbols, and aimed at obscuring social conflict. The problem of fascism, the child of the marriage between tradition and capitalism, continues to be a ghost haunting Japan's participation in the global capitalist system.

The Soviet Union's modernization presents another matter. Here was a society whose revolutionary leadership took power with a dual goal—to modernize Russia and to create a socialist alternative to the bourgeois civilizations of America, Europe, and Japan, societies which at peace and at war had provoked a growing disillusionment and disenchantment with capitalist modernity. Unlike Japan, the Soviet Union was the first society to pose the issue of whether modernization could be separated from European capitalist civilization. Lenin rejected the idea of so-called orthodox Marxists that capitalism would have to run its course in Russia before socialism, and he projected, like Marx, a vision of a nonbureaucratic state where workers controlled the means of production and where equality and abundance ultimately progressed together through the process of revolutionary transformation into a classless society.[36]

Very quickly, the concrete problems of international politics, foreign policy, economic planning, and industrial and agricultural production impinged on the revolutionary optimism of the early Bolshevik leaders. In essence, and in spite of revolutionary rhetoric and some sporadic, isolated, and short-lived experiments to the contrary, Lenin adopted a fairly conservative program. Soviet development strategy aimed to copy the giant economic enterprises of the capitalist world, to build its heavy industrial capacity in urban centers, and to extract as much surplus from agriculture with as little investment or concern for the backward peasantry as politically feasible, at least until the task of heavy industrialization was well underway.

Moreover, in organizing production within the modern industrial sector, the Soviets, under Lenin's leadership, adopted the same patterns of control, authority, and incentive represented by the latest scientific management theories of Frederick Taylor. As one analyst of this Russian phenomenon explains,

> Whatever view one takes of Soviet industrialization, one cannot conscientiously interpret its history, even in its earliest and most revolutionary period, as an attempt to organize labor processes in a way fundamentally different from those of capitalism.[37]

In addition to imitating the advanced forms of capitalist industrial organization and control, the Soviets instituted a highly centralized system of planning to replace the oligopolistic marketplace of capitalism as the mechanism by which each enterprise and factory was integrated into the national economy. Scarce technical and engineering personnel were put in charge of daily production activities and they, along with high level administrative bureaucrats, some of whom were Communist Party members, were placed in key positions in the planning apparatus. Within every enterprise, workers were, at first, given formal rights to hold workers' congresses where they could comment on and make suggestions about the production goals and plant conditions. However, highly centralized planning together with the system of control within factories quickly made these workers' congresses progressively meaningless. The knowledge of the technical and administrative personnel gave them the power to make both day to day and long range production decisions. It did not take long for alliances to form between technical and managerial personnel at all levels. Moreover, a crude system of rewards and punishments contributed to the growing autonomy and power of the bureaucracy. This elite quickly and successfully opposed institutionalization and extension of the power of the early workers' congresses.[38]

The system of management and economic coordination that evolved in Soviet industry was called one-man management. One person at every level was given both power over and responsibility for the results of operations on that level. Material rewards, higher wages, and promotions were given to those bureaucrats and operations managers who fulfilled or overfulfilled the centrally planned goals, while sanctions, sometimes quite harsh, were applied to those who failed. This system resulted in a growing gap between workers and managerial-technical bureaucrats, for whom the pursuit of individual privilege and safety was primary. It began under Lenin, was intensified under Stalin, and was an important factor in gaining the support of the old intelligentsia for the Bolsheviks. As in Japan, the Soviet Union quickly began turning out large numbers of technicians, engineers, and, in the 1950s, business-management school graduates[39] to meet the needs of planned production. By 1940, those who had resisted the increasingly authoritarian nature of work in the USSR or who had resented the growing power of non-revolutionary technical specialists from the ancient regime had lost out politically to others who felt that these were the only methods that could guarantee efficiency and high levels of production.

During Stalin's time the ranks of the technical elite were swelled by the recruitment of workers into the institutes of higher education. In turn, they and their children became the chief beneficiaries of the privileged access to education which became a major factor in the social stratification of the USSR. By the late 1950s, 60 to 70 percent of the students in Moscow's institutes of higher education were from the families of officials or pre-revolutionary intellectuals.[40]

Even if a member of the Soviet technical-managerial elite was from a working class family or was a Communist Party member, as were many of the higher ranking managerial and planning authorities, all were constrained to act within the methods of control and communication which epitomized bureaucratic organization.

To suggest they might have done otherwise is to argue from the vantage point of hindsight rather than from actuality. The international environment was hostile and dangerous; Russia was a poor and relatively backward country with a large and mostly illiterate agricultural population; the political base in rural Russia was shaky. The Soviet

Union was also weak militarily. Military weakness aggravated political weakness, leading to an over-all strategy of development which emphasized urban-centered industrialization.

Thus, it was difficult for the Soviets to allow the revolutionary experiment to take precedence over short-term maximization of production. They had no precedents to follow. To experiment with new kinds of education or new forms of industrial management, even in urban areas where the Bolsheviks were politically strong, would have been a gamble with the very survival of the revolutionary government.

Increased production in heavy industry became the primary goal of Soviet development. This industrialization was then carried out on the model of the proven, liberal premises of the capitalist world. Lenin's theory of revolutionary leadership did not serve as an antidote to this. Though ambiguous about the boundaries between the elite leadership and the masses, it favored the former because there was little belief in the practical capacities of the latter. Even before the revolutionary seizure of power, the Tsar's secret police oppression put a premium on clandestine elite activity as opposed to open revolutionary mobilization. There was little to guide the Bolsheviks to achieve the goals of Marx.

The Soviet system evolved into a multibureaucratic one where a technical and managerial elite held power over workers in daily life,[41] but they themselves were subject to the power of the Communist Party which ruled in the name of those same workers. The party, with Stalin as its leader, wielded enormous police power and used Marxist rhetoric to justify itself, continuing to call itself revolutionary.

Both the Soviet and the Japanese development processes were affected by the global dominance of capitalist civilization. In Japan's case, this is obvious. But even with the USSR, it was capitalist values, institutions and military power that framed the alternatives and in crucial ways helped to define the historical reality within which the Bolshevik Revolutionaries were constrained to operate and upon which their visions and imaginations reflected. Yet, after October 1917 the world was never the same. The legitimacy and the inevitability of capitalism as the structure of modern society had been challenged.

Soviet socialism, though a heroic concept to many, was tragically flawed. Given the liberal premises concerning human motivation and purpose which could be traced much more directly to Hobbes than to Marx, and the gradual, though very pronounced Soviet acceptance of liberal ideas about the distribution and sources of human knowledge, the major organizations of work and education came to resemble counterparts in the capitalist world, and they became two major sources of inequality and privilege in Soviet society. Moreover, the Soviets almost uncritically accepted urban-centered heavy industry as the vision of a future socialism, which they intended to make real within decades. When this social reality was combined with the self-perceptions of Soviet political leaders as socialists and communists, their Marxist view of the future, and the particular experiences of the Leninist Party, then the growing gap between theory and practice, between ends and means, led to massive political repression, not to revolutionary development.

Eventually, reflecting the underlying philosophical and social realities, economic theory began to stress the profit motive as the best incentive for individual behavior and to recognize profitability of an enterprise as the key measurement for determining investment and growth priorities in national planning.[42] In Soviet socialism, urban-centered heavy industrialization was of crucial importance as was a highly paid, comparatively privileged, formally educated technical and managerial elite. The claim of the elite to rule on behalf of the working population bestowed legitimacy on these unequal political, social, and economic relationships.[43] Soviet Marxism talked more and more of class harmony rather than class struggle and the withering away of class differences. Soviet society became technocratic, organizational, careerist, and elitist, with loyalty to the bureaucratized Communist Party (which had become assimilated into the machinery even while it ruled over it) as the test of an individual's commitment to Marxism–Leninism.[44]

In the USSR there was little debate about the relationship of capitalist to socialist institutions.[45] Socialism was simply equated with loyalty to the Soviet status quo. In the West, however, the crisis of the 1930s, and resultant concern with the nature of modern society, had focused on the issue of capitalism versus socialism. After World War II and during the 1950s, however, the national and global strength of American capitalism and the ideological and organizational triumph of Weberian and neo-Weberian social science in American intellectual life reduced the debate to a mirror image of the non-debate of the USSR. The Weberians argued as before that socialism and capitalism were but forms of bureaucratic rule.[46] Intelligent and rational people, those who were not emotionally committed to ideological utopia or whose minds were not hopelessly ossified by outworn categories of thought, could make political choices between these two forms of bureaucratic society, but there was no other modern alternative. Only those societies painfully attempting to modernize might temporarily use the rhetoric of socialism as an ideology of national unity, but in Western "advanced" and modern society it was the era of the end of ideology.

The Soviets did not, however, speak about an end to ideology. They defended their institutions as being the embodiment of socialism and argued that Weber's theory of bureaucracy was itself an ideology that universalized the institutions and values of capitalism as if it were the natural result of machine technology.[47] In spite of their rejection of

Weber, only in their defense of Communist Party rule did the Soviet theoreticians differ significantly from Western ones. Their views on the organizational, educational, and existential imperatives of modern society were not that far from the Weberian and neo-Weberian theorists they rejected. Under these political and intellectual conditions, it was indeed difficult to talk seriously, intelligently, or for very long, about socialist alternatives to one or another form of bureaucratic society. On both sides of the Cold War, the issue of capitalism versus socialism degenerated into a debate over national loyalty.

All over the world, conditions had changed drastically with the conclusion of the War. The pace of rebellion in the countries of Asia, Africa, and Latin America quickened, though it was perhaps nowhere as pronounced as it was in China. The Bolshevik Revolution of 1917 had created a whole new international environment. European capitalism had spread into and then been weakened in many areas. Western values and institutions were frequently blamed for exploitation, oppression, and humiliation. European civilization had clearly lost its image of omnipotence and non-Western civilizations were provided with an alternative method of modernization. Unlike the Japanese, who in 1868 were confronted with the choice of copying Europe or eventually succumbing to it, the post-War national liberation movements were usually led by people with vague anticapitalist feelings and visionary sentiments.[48]

All of the political leaders of the Third World meant by modernization an increase in production, a raising of standards of health, education, and welfare, and capacity to utilize modern technology to make life better. Some looked from afar at Soviet socialism as the model for their modernization; others spoke of uniting their national traditions with a vague and confusing socialism, often ignoring both domestic and international political and economic realities. Still others spoke of a significant altering of their nations' relationship to the international marketplace, while some did not challenge capitalism or the existing hierarchy of the international political economy.

The effects of national liberation movements and the desire for independence and modernization that intensified in the Third World in the post-War years suggested that cultural, historical, and political factors were more favorable than they had been in 1917 to new and unprecedented forms of modernization that would not be heavily influenced by the philosophy or the institutions of Europe and America. There were also strong anticapitalist undercurrents in Europe.

China's revolution was very much a part of this global trend. China's revolutionary leadership was the product of an ancient society with cultural, political, and economic integrity and independence and a tradition which had influenced an entire group of societies in East Asia. Within two or three generations this largely self-contained civilization had been disrupted by a determinedly aggressive and often violent Western imperialism, and this was the immediate context within which China's communist leadership had matured.

Like the Bolsheviks more than thirty years before, the Chinese communists came to power from a basic Marxist–Leninist perspective. They were committed to the building of a modern socialist society. They fully accepted Lenin's idea that it was unnecessary and, in an age of imperialism, impossible to achieve this goal by relying on the Chinese bourgeoisie to lead the nation through a period of capitalist development. The very small Chinese working class was to lead this huge agricultural peasant society into industrial modernity. From the beginning, industrialization was to be an integral part of Chinese modernization, but it was to be done only on the basis of socialist goals.

The Chinese were in a better position to try to create the means to reach these goals than were the Bolsheviks. First, they could observe and learn from the Russian experience. Second, direct threat of military and political counterrevolutionary intervention in China was reduced (not eliminated) by the postwar weakness of Europe and by Soviet power in Europe, which focused American attention there. The possibility of Soviet military aid to the Chinese partially deterred those who counseled unlimited United States intervention in Chinese affairs, and Soviet aid mitigated the effects of the economic warfare launched by the United States after 1949. In addition, China's revolution had a firm political base with the huge mobilized peasant population. The tradition of guerrilla warfare offered only the comfort of a quicksand pit to potential invaders. The long years of experience and administration in remote rural areas had given many Chinese revolutionaries economic and political experience that was free from the exigencies of underground conspiracy and the influence of European capitalism which affected life in the urban centers. In spite of enormous domestic and international problems, circumstances were indeed better in 1949 for the Chinese Marxists than they were for the Russians of 1917.

China's modernization and relationship to the goals of socialist revolution have been the subject of many books and much thought. The Americans generally focus on the conflict between pragmatists, who are in favor of economic modernization, and revolutionaries, who are in favor of political revolution. When they do recognize the successes of Chinese development, even when methods contradict what liberal philosophy and Weberian theory prescribe as normal, they attribute these to peculiarities in China's tradition or to backwardness. Most serious Western analysts do not imply that the problems of technologically advanced capitalism can be better understood by looking at China's socialism.[49] The Soviets, for their part, generally search for the cause of China's deviation from "the normal historical process" of socialist development. The Soviets consider their own development to be the correct model. They use China's tradition and the peasant base of its revolutionary political power to explain why the Chinese have, in the Soviet view, an irrational anti-intellectualism which manifests itself in an anti-urban, anti-working class development strategy that can never lead to a modern socialist society.[50] Both the Soviets and the Americans believe that the outstanding characteristic of the Chinese revolution is the stubborn, irrational, and ultimately doomed resistance to the bureaucratic, elitist, technocratic urban life of advanced society. Yet, it is precisely such resistance that gives to China's modernization both its unique and its universal character. This book is about the patterns of and prospects for this resistance, and its meaning for all of us.

Definitions and Conceptual Clarity

In the following chapters, it will be important to understand the meaning of a number of difficult terms and concepts that will appear. The following definitions and clarifications are, therefore, offered to prevent unnecessary confusion.

1. In discussing Chinese modernization, it should be clear that the term modernization does not imply anything more than a process of technological change and development to deal with humanity's relationship to the natural world in ways which people define as an improvement over the past. A certain amount of industrialization and economic growth is part of this process, so, too, are better medical and health facilities and general living conditions. The focus of this book is on only one important aspect of modernization in China, the organization and management of Chinese industry. However, there is nothing in the term modernization here meant to imply that human relationships or ways and standards of living and consuming should parallel those associated with America, Europe, Japan, the USSR, or other countries of the industrialized modern world. These relationships and ways of living are precisely what is under investigation in regard to technological and economic development in China.

2. In discussing the organization and management of Chinese industry, the terms micro-management and macro-management may be used. Micro-management is concerned with the division of labor, decision-making, and power distribution within factories or industrial enterprises. Macro-management involves the planning and coordination of economic activity among factories and enterprises.

3. The factory is a unit which is usually involved in the production of a single item (for example, machine tools, trucks, sheet steel, steel

tubes, ball bearings, canned food, paper, textiles, etc.), although different products may vary widely in the complexity of their production. In China, however, a factory can be and often is involved in the production of miscellaneous items, spare parts, or sideline products for local use. A factory is always a unit of micro-management. The organizational boundary between a unit of micro-management and a unit of macro-management is the degree to which the focus of management is on coordination of production, and the degree to which management concerns allocation of what is produced. The boundary will not lie necessarily in the magnitude or the quantity of products.

The individual industrial enterprise can thus be and usually is a single factory and a unit of micro-management, though it is not always. Large integrated enterprises (for example, a steel company or a coal mining bureau or company) can be units of macro-management, but so, too, are the national ministries and the provincial, district, municipal, and commune level organs. These organs are responsible for coordinating economic activity within their assigned geographic regions and, depending upon the products, for new materials and markets in their locality, and they have varying degrees of autonomy and power to initiate economic activity.

4. Throughout this book, the terms centralization and decentralization are important analytically. These terms are used relatively and not as polar opposites. Thus, decentralization can mean that a lower level of authority has the power to initiate and carry out policy without permission from higher levels; that permission must be received before carrying out locally developed policy; that it can approve decisions made by higher levels; or that the local unit must be consulted before a decision is made.

5. In discussing management systems and procedures there will be frequent use of terms which refer to subdivisions within individual factories. The following are the most frequent and the most important:

a. The work team. This is the lowest level of collective organization in a factory. It is sometimes referred to as a work section, brigade, work group, or small work group, and all these terms are generally interchangeable. The work team usually numbers from three to ten people who have operational responsibility for a relatively narrow and well-defined part of production. They are organized around that activity (for example, a team on a large lathe or on a single sequence in one blast furnace).

b. The work shop. This is usually a middle level of production organization and coordination. It is made up of several work teams and may number from 20 to 400 people in large plants. The work shop coordinates the activities of the teams and is organized around a major technological division in the over-all production sequences of the factory (for example, an assembly work shop, a forging work shop, a spinning work shop).

c. Functional departments. While work shops and work teams are organized around production operations, functional departments concerned with administrative affairs (planning, designing, wage calculations and payroll, welfare and health programs, personnel) are what Westerners call staff management. Work shop and work team leaders are comparable to line management.

Functional departments exist at usually two levels in a factory (the factory level and the work shop level) and in an industrial enterprise which is also an organ of macro-management, they will exist at the enterprise level as well. Functional-department workers, no matter what their jobs, are the Chinese equivalents of white collar or mental workers. Shop and team workers are blue collar or manual workers.

When in 1948 the People's Liberation Army took power in North China, production in the war-shattered economy began again. The situation was chaotic in the factories and mines of the country, for it was here that the ancient traditional forces came in conflict with new and powerful factors deriving from a century of technological development, foreign imperialism, liberal reform, and Marxist revolution. This historical whirlpool whose power was harnessed by the revolutionary leadership also provided the dangerous context within which the Party first began to exercise political power. To understand what happened after 1949, it is necessary to take a look at the swirling currents before 1949.

2 / The Historical Setting

CHINA'S TRADITIONAL CIVILIZATION was a rich and varied one. To describe and isolate only those parts which have influenced the course of revolution and industrialization is no simple task.[1] There was a multi-faceted Confucian tradition; there were Buddhist monks and Taoist priests; landlords living in splendor, while peasants were mired in poverty; eighteenth century guilds and twentieth century factory labor; egalitarian flavored peasant rebellion and sharply hierarchical bureaucratic stability. Yet just as European capitalist civilization grew up inextricably related to a dominant liberal philosophical tradition, so China's traditional four-thousand-year-old civilization was dominated by the Confucian view of humanity and society. In both civilizations, those desiring fundamental change confronted the power of a predominant class whose political and philosophical principles became a coherent and generally accepted political ideology backed by the power of the state and by daily experience.

From the middle of the nineteenth century, however, the foundations of China's traditional civilization began to quake under the impact of domestic turmoil and external battering. Internally, massive peasant rebellions shook the Manchu empire created in the seventeenth century. The reverberations were felt throughout the Confucian oriented bureaucracy through which the Manchu Emperors ruled. Western and Japanese imperialism, while creating and perpetuating conditions which severely constrained industrialization, also acted as powerful catalysts for change.

Though the many-thousand-year-old Confucian ideology and the institutions of the once mighty Chinese empire had been badly shaken before the modern Revolution accelerated dramatically they still had helped to shape the political senses of revolutionaries immersed deeply in Chinese society and, together with imperialism, they provided the historical setting within which events after 1949 can best be understood.

China's huge agricultural economy, once technologically sophisticated and advanced by world standards, had by the middle of the nineteenth century become stagnant. There had been few significant innovations since 1800,[2] though agricultural technology had developed sufficiently to sustain a large population.[3] Small peasant farms were clustered in isolated villages and communication among them occurred within relatively independent marketing areas.[4] Towns and cities were commercial hubs, conduits for rural food and grain, and intellectual and political centers. The marketing areas created economic interdependence within the empire, and the shipment of grains brought them under the supervision of central authorities. Until the late nineteenth century, industry was largely nonexistent.

Towns and cities were the residences of government officials who performed political and economic functions. These bureaucrats had close connections with landlords and the richer peasants from whose ranks most of them came. They were scholars because they had studied the moral, political, literary, and philosophical precepts of Confucian classics and the body of scholarly commentary which had evolved over the centuries. The purpose of such study was to enter government service, and the classical education was the basis for competitive examinations which were the first step in pursuing a career as an official.

The first requirement for entrance into officialdom was literacy, and this was not a common attribute.[5] For a variety of reasons, the number of officials was far fewer than the number of educated or literate people, but it was passing the examinations, not literacy, education, intelligence, or creativity that was the chief means of upward mobility.[6]

Confucian teaching held that correct morality, correct values, and proper attitudes were the basis of political power and the most reliable guarantee for social stability. Men were able to rule because they were "virtuous" and behaved in accordance with their inborn moral nature. The virtuous man, the *chün-tzu* or "gentleman," revealed his inner nature in his behavior, and proper behavior generated respect from others and hence their obedience and submission. In this way, ethical power was translated into political power.[7] The attributes which gave certain individuals the capacity to behave as gentlemen and as leaders were considered to be inborn traits, unequally distributed throughout the population.

Natural and proper human relationships were, therefore, sharply hierarchical. Everyone had a proper place in society, and each station in life was understood by behavior which reflected an individual's inner and inborn virtues. Mencius, a disciple of Confucius, summed up the political implications of this value system in the following way:

> Great men have their proper business and little men have their proper business. . . . Some labor with their minds, and some labor with their strength. Those who labor with their minds govern others; those who labor with their strength are governed by others.[8]

When these hierarchical relationships were properly ordered and people behaved as befitted their station in life, then society was harmonious and prosperous. Thus harmony (li) was only possible when the appropriate relationships of inequality were developed.

The cardinal moral virtue of Confucian ideology, however, was not *li* so much as it was *hsiao*. Commonly translated as filial piety, *hsiao* actually meant obedience to those who are owed respect because of their position and the virtues associated with it. Superior virtues and capacities were therefore assigned to certain social and political positions. They were the property of males in general, of the father who was the head of the family, of the Emperor who was the head of the government and the state, and of the officials who were the Emperor's representatives.[9] Confucianism argued that the powerful and privileged were talented and virtuous, defined the specific talents and virtues it took to become privileged and powerful, and then completed the circle by defining specific positions and roles in the social order which were held by people of talent and virtue.

The mutual responsibility group (pao-chia) gave powerful support to Confucian moral and ideological authority. Begun by the early unifiers of the Ch'in Dynasty, whose Emperor, Chin Shih-huang, was a disciple of a group of anti-Confucian philosophers called legalists, this system held the family responsible for the public acts of its members. Though the legalist influence was quickly absorbed by the dominant Confucian ideology, the *pao-chia* system remained. When effective, it was able to exert enormous social pressure on each individual, inculcating the virtue of *hsiao* to the government and to the social order through the family. Failure to obey political authority and respect those in positions of power and privilege reflected on the family, particularly the father. Hence, in traditional China, the social order was protected by the official bureaucracy, and proper social behavior was more regulated by social pressure through family responsibility than by formal legal rules and an individualist ethic. Forces perpetuating the position of the upper class met in the Chinese family[10] more than in the courtroom and the marketplace, while in European civilization the family was not as central in maintaining political order.

To become an official in traditional China was no easy task. The literacy necessary to pass the examinations in most cases required economic security, ownership of land, or, at the very least, sufficient wealth in a family so that the labor of one son could be spared.[11] The system clearly favored recruitment of the rich, and it sustained a small privileged minority. In addition, the ideological hegemony of the Confucian bureaucracy was a powerful force throughout all levels of society. Even the poor hoped a family member would become an official. Ambitious individuals measured themselves by emulation of the scholar-officials. Emphasis on the life of the mind, disdain for manual labor, cultivation of a literary-poetic-philosophical life, and denigration of commerce, industry and profit were traits scholar-officials openly admired in each other.[12] Yet given their low official salary and the need to supplement it in order to lead a life befitting the gentleman, squeeze and the pay-off came to mark government's relationship with the populace more often than did the benevolent moral authoritarianism of the Confucian ideal.[13] As individuals used position to benefit their families and secure their own futures, nepotism and other forms of corruption frequently characterized official life.

The Confucian bureaucracy did perform essential tasks in the agrarian economy, coordinating, supervising, and controlling the productive labor of the tens of thousands of isolated peasant farms and villages. Without the bureaucracy, the Empire would have disintegrated, and there would have been no central authority. Production and distribution of goods would have been sharply limited.[14] Without the backbreaking labor of the peasantry and the skills of the small class of urban merchants and artisans, the bureaucracy and the central authorities would have had no material base for its privileged existence in the towns. The bureaucrats' monopoly of knowledge in political and economic coordination made them indispensable.

Subsistence agriculture put a premium on positions in society that would provide basic physical and economic security. Life was very hard in the countryside, and the extreme hardships and poverty of the peasantry were the ultimate realities underlying the system which Confucianism sanctioned and supported. Inner morality made gentlemen, and it made them deserving of the food, clothing, housing, and privileges that marked the gentleman's life and showed him to be truly civilized.

Important as the bureaucracy was to the political and economic system, its procedures did not make it efficient or creative. The primacy of personal behavior and individual morality in politics, rule by moral example,[15] meant that an official would not risk his privileged position by upsetting old routines, challenging entrenched privilege, or embarrassing his superiors.[16] An errant official could only be punished by a higher official or by a specially deputed advisor of the Emperor.[17] Relationships between levels of government depended on personal contacts, but because of slow communication and transportation these were not frequent. As a result, local officials had considerable latitude in dealing with the population, and they were always more concerned with their superiors impression of them than with local problems. Where wealthy landlords or rich peasants had high level bureaucratic connections as a result of family or school ties, the magistrate was careful not to antagonize them, in spite of his enormous power which often embodied in one person the functions of prosecutor, police chief, judge, and even coroner.[18]

Kinship groups, voluntary ad hoc associations, and craft guilds attempted to provide political protection and economic security. Most leaders of these were not elected and had position due to age, skill, or behavior. Guilds were dominated by master craftsmen who cooperated closely with government officials to protect membership and to maintain their access to local government projects. The guilds bestowed benefits, trained workers, and provided a strong sense of identity. Other organizations offered comparable services, and all depended on the power of leading members' skills, personality, and personal contacts with officials, and on the government's need for the services of the group.[19]

As long as the agricultural economy was able to support the town-based scholar-official class and the peasants, there was peace in the realm. The Emperor was considered a moral ruler, possessor of the mandate of heaven (t'ien-ming), who, under the Confucian code, provided for the masses.[20]

The political staying power of over 4,000 years of this emperor-led system was, from time to time, disrupted by massive peasant rebellion. When famine and flood destroyed agriculture and population growth pressed the food supply, *li* and *hsiao* were undermined. Natural disasters and the wake of suffering and starvation were taken as a sign that the Emperor had incurred Heaven's wrath by improper moral behavior, and moral bankruptcy in the Confucian tradition meant a loss of political legitimacy. It implicitly justified rebellion, not to set up a *new* order, but to re-establish the natural moral order.

The crisis was often of such scope that rapid, radical change was essential for the survival of a new government and the new Emperor. Thus, "revolutionary features marked the founding of every new dynasty."[21] But so long as the economic status quo remained and the Confucian ethics and principles dominated Chinese civilization, the scholar-bureaucrats were in charge.

The development of industry in China was accompanied by the rise of a middle class of entrepreneurs. But they had been inculcated in the values of the scholar-bureaucrat class. The early entrepreneurs in China

> felt impotent in the face of a competitor who seemed to hold all the advantages. Moreover, they had no real desire to be different, to oppose their own way of life to that of the ruling class. . . . Their ambition was limited: to find a position, if only a modest one, inside the ruling class. . . . Their consuming desire was that they, or their children, should become scholar officials.[22]

In addition, industrialization began while China was the political and economic arena for rivalries among various imperialist countries. The cities of the Northern and Southeastern coast of China, notorious as the treaty ports, became the centers for Western influence and technological modernization, but had negative, or only marginal, impact on the technologically backward and largely traditional rural sector.[23] Parts of the agricultural economy were linked to the vagaries and instabilities of the world market and modern manufacturing and technology was concentrated along the coast and along transportation networks. Transport grew, linking the internal markets and sources of raw materials to the treaty ports and through them to the global economy dominated by the capitalist nations. There was no balance between modern and traditional industry and agriculture, urban and rural. Even industry developed lopsidedly. Almost half of foreign investment was centered in Shanghai, and only 17 percent was in manufacturing.[24] Foreign firms dominated heavy industry, transport, producers' goods, and most financial institutions, and foreign pressures seriously hampered the development of an indigenous textile industry.[25] Most consumer goods in the cities, aside from a few important items like textiles, matches, and cigarettes, were imported. Luxury consumption, made up largely of foreign imports, became a drain on available capital for investment,[26] but it provided the means by which the Chinese bourgeoisie proclaimed their equality with their Western counterparts.

The political base of the post-1911 government, dependent on the support of warlords and urban and rural elites, was not strong enough to resist Western and Japanese imperialism, nor could the government afford to mobilize the masses whose strength would threaten its own base of domestic support. The bourgeoisie could find no political mechanism to support independent Chinese capitalist development. Rivalries led foreign powers to support one or another faction in Chinese politics, but none could use this conflict to establish its own hegemony. In the 1930s these troubles were compounded by Japanese aggression.

The development of modern industry in the last quarter of the nineteenth century, combined with foreign incursion and internal political upheaval, had created an explosive mixture. The coastal cities became centers for large-scale rural immigration as peasants, male and female, were recruited into the new factories and mines opened by Western, Japanese, and Chinese entrepreneurs. By the 1920s a militant and class conscious labor movement had developed, fueled by the abrupt changes in peasant life, now suddenly subjected to the pressures of foreign dominated, teeming treaty-port civilization. This labor movement was, not surprisingly, heavily imbued with nationalist sentiments.[27]

The labor force that was not assimilated into the modern sector often worked in small shops or in machinery repair and maintenance plants associated with mining and railroads. Chinese entrepreneurs often began these and people gained experience and learned technical skills working in them. Management also was trained here.[28] Though important as producers and employers, they remained small and were limited to light industrial machinery and spare parts. Moreover, the modern economy was subject to the economic and political chaos which plagued the whole society.

This limited though growing entrepreneural activity in China was not all the kind of production which, if mobilized and continued, could lead toward economic development. Much Chinese experience was not in manufacturing, but in business related to the operations and sales of foreign firms. In addition, the largest Chinese capitalists were not independent and did not want to be. Most nationally significant, non-agricultural business in traditional China had been run on the principle of official supervision and merchant management (kuan-tu shang-pan).[29] This system subordinated the profit and power of the nascent bourgeoisie to the political goals of Confucian scholar-officials who kept a sharp limit on economic activity. Even when entrepreneurs achieved legitimacy in the twentieth century, many merchants and businessmen used their wealth to provide their sons the liberal (literary or political) education of an official. As late as the 1930s, most university students were in political science and law rather than science, engineering, or business.[30]

The close, sometimes antagonistic relationship between private capital and government officialdom that had been institutionalized in the traditional *kuan-tu shang-pan* system continued in an altered form under the Nationalist regime. Many officials had become entrepreneurs in the waning years of the nineteenth century as they sought self-strengthening to resist the technological and industrial might of the West. In the Kuomintang years this developed into a full-blown system of bureau-cratic capitalism. Banks financed the business operations of favored government officials and their relatives and friends, while government officials used their positions to gain control over lucrative economic activity. Powerful bankers and businessmen supported the KMT govern-ment and enjoyed its support.[31] Such liaisons often involved lucrative criminal and rampant speculative activities that proliferated during this period of social disintegration and treaty port corruption.[32]

In sum, capitalism and industrialization were deeply affected by the Confucian social order and by imperialism. Chinese entrepreneurs were constrained by domestic and international politics. Social condi-tions worked against sustained investment. The structure of the market usually transformed those areas of investment that were not necessarily the most conducive to development into ones that were most profitable.[33]

Chinese businessmen and capitalists, uninterested in and often ig-norant of the technical and administrative aspects of modern industrial production, frequently hired others to run their factories while they pur-sued prestigious activities such as politics, education, theoretical science, and, later in the twentieth century, the military. Managers, hired to produce profit, were evaluated for results regardless of the means used to obtain them. They were the middlemen between workers and owners and their government allies. Loyalty to the owner was far more important than competence.[34] Administrators, therefore, had to delegate primary authority for operations to skilled, experienced workers known as gang bosses. Sometimes management would hire a professional labor contractor who, for a fixed price, would recruit workers and take responsibility for their behavior and performance. This policy was used prominently in foreign-owned companies, in Chinese companies with foreign experts as managers or technical specialists, among female workers, and in mines.[35]

Both the contract labor system and the gang boss system were open to grave abuse. In a poverty-stricken agrarian society where labor was abundant and cheap, females were considered as surplus, and since there were few or no laws regulating working conditions, female workers were especially abused.[36]

Management was far removed from the abuse, living in ostentatious luxury. If a manager was a foreign expert or a Chinese with technical skills, the disparity was intensified.[37] Even former workers turned labor contractors exploited the workers they hired.[38] Rich managers lived in fine homes in exclusive areas and came to work in sedan chairs and silk finery. In one typical case a German chief engineer at the Anyüan Coal Mine complex earned 2,000 dollars a month, while Chinese workers averaged six or seven dollars a month. Whether foreign or Chinese, managers often looked down on workers as crude, lazy, and stupid; they resorted to severe beatings, imprisonment, torture, and summary dismissals to enforce discipline under extremely dangerous conditions.

Even where personal relations were supposed to tie people together in society and at work, as in the craft guilds, growing commercialization worked to form new social relations. Guild masters became managerial entrepreneurs who allocated labor and contracted for apprentices and unskilled laborers. Guilds became fledgling capitalist construction companies whose managers, the guild masters, hired people for wages that were quickly returned to the guild in the form of membership fees. Pride of craftsmanship gave way to the search for profit, and guild masters colluded with government officials to get lucrative contracts. Brutality in enforcing the guild's monopoly over hiring and construction was common.[39]

Gang bosses and contract labor professionals were allied with the guilds and with clan associations and secret societies anxious to provide jobs and security for their members. Although they owed their position to personal relationships with the workers—a result of influence with management over pay and job allocation—they still worked for the owner's profit and by so doing insured their own rewards. Conflicts among workers over skills, kinship, or place of birth were aggravated by economic scarcity and job insecurity.[40]

Industrialization was largely confined to isolated islands within the huge agricultural economy. Interior industrial and mining centers were usually provincial attempts at economic and military self-strengthening initiated by reform-minded Confucian scholar-officials in the nineteenth century. Such, for example, was the area around Anyüan. There, the Hanyehping Coal and Iron Company, the largest Chinese-owned company, was started by several viceroys after the Taiping rebellion.[41] Anyüan was a comprehensive, though vaguely conceptualized development area which included heavy machinery, foundaries, and repair shops. This kind of local self-sufficiency was logical because the transport network was ill-equipped to supply modern industrial development, and the sources of machinery and supplies, most of which were imported, were far away on the coast.[42] Mining centers and railheads controlled by foreigners developed self-sufficient, comprehensive industrial areas for the same reasons. These modern interior enclaves, though few and far between, and linked to the world market and not the agricultural economy were of vital importance to industrial development after 1949.

As industrialization proceeded, the gap between rural and urban areas widened, and the industrial working class, laboring long hours under shockingly poor conditions for subsistence or below subsistence wages, was, during the decade of the 1920s, "galvanized . . . into a conscious and active movement of considerable significance."[43]

Under the prodding of strong Communist leadership the urban working class was organized into trade unions. Striking for higher wages, better working conditions, and against arbitrary dismissals,[44] workers fought the exploitation of the contract labor system under which the contractor could rake off as much as 50 percent of the workers' wages for himself. Workers resented the officiousness of foreign technical experts and the guildmasters' huge incomes, earned not by working with their hands but by managing and investing the workers' money while paying only apprentice wages to skilled workers in the guild. They were antagonistic to foreign-educated Chinese engineers and supervisors, and they were often highly nationalistic, leading or participating in boycotts of foreign goods. Many workers were former peasants, "frank, outspoken, and hot-tempered" with authorities who exploited them. In the leading ranks of the labor movement there was little left of *hsiao* and *li*.

Still, the labor movement as an urban political force was gravely weakened by warlord repression and by the nationwide white terror launched by Chiang Kai-shek in Shanghai in the spring of 1927. Beginning in the late 1920s and accelerating in the 1930s, the focus of the Chinese revolution changed to the rural hinterlands. There, under Mao Tsetung's leadership, the Chinese Communist Party spent nearly two decades mobilizing the vast peasantry; those well-disciplined soldiers were to take power in the cities in 1949. This experience was to have profound affects on the nature of Chinese industrialization and modernization. The crucial period was from 1937 to 1945 when the Communists were headquartered in Yenan, the capital of their liberated areas.

A small, poor city in the hills of northern Shensi province, Yenan's population lived in caves carved out of hard soil. Isolated from the busy cosmopolitan life of the treaty ports, Yenan offered sanctuary to the remnants of the Red Army which arrived in December 1936 after fleeing from Chiang Kai-shek's bandit extermination campaigns in south-central China. Though a good place to hide and recuperate, the poverty and isolation of the area presented the communists with severe problems. The most pressing was supporting new arrivals without alienating the local population whose participation and support was vital in strengthening the communists' political base.

In Yenan, therefore, the production and distribution of life's necessities were top priorities. Economics and politics were inseparable from the beginning. The guiding principles in Yenan were self-reliance and independence. After 1940 Yenan's poverty and isolation were compounded by the Kuomintang blockade of the communist-controlled areas, making self-reliance even more necessary for raising the collective standard of living and preventing the communist revolutionaries from becoming an unwelcome burden. Cooperatives and mutual-aid groups were started in both industry and agriculture. All available resources and skills were mobilized and creatively utilized. Simple, successful technology was developed. Workers and craftsmen used their own skills and ingenuity and locally available materials as there were no imported machines or highly trained specialists with formal academic credentials. Administration was kept to a minimum. Yenan military, educational, and governmental institutions became models of austerity and self-support. Participation in productive labor by intellectuals and officials was a consequence of necessity that was to have far-reaching political effect.[45]

As a result of the prevailing conditions in Yenan, economics, production, education, and the military became interrelated. Production units became relatively self-reliant economically and performed educational tasks and military training for the guerrilla army. Army units and schools were active in production, widely disseminating technical training and skill improvement. Lack of transportation and communication enhanced independence. There evolved a unique society organized around collective labor, shared hardship, and cooperation among equals. People worked in the service of the collective life: selfish activities were politically dangerous and economically defeating.

The economic imperatives of the Yenan period, and the practical aspects of production and organization that evolved from them, naturally influenced other areas of life. Attitudes toward authority were changed as legitimate power shifted from the traditional leisurely scholar-bureaucrat to the revolutionary cadre participating in the hard work of agriculture and industry.[46] The place of women in China's male-dominated society began to change drastically as female labor was mobilized for the support of the anti-Japanese war effort. Women became involved in the social revolution that was shaking the centuries-old grip of male supremacy and the traditions that supported the old system.[47]

Economics and politics also helped to shape military institutions and operations. The Chinese Communist Party and its Eighth Route Army could only fight the Japanese and the KMT blockade by using the advantages of terrain and mobilizing the local population, turning technological and material disadvantages to political and military advantage. Protracted guerrilla warfare with a technologically superior enemy made close relationships with the impoverished peasants imperative. There developed a markedly egalitarian and cooperative society with an attitude toward human relationships heretofore unknown in China, one which was later to be incorporated into the theory of the mass line.

Symbols of rank and office were foregone because by making leaders highly visible they endangered them; privilege was eschewed as it undermined the sense of solidarity and dedication necessary for survival under the harsh conditions.

The requirements of mass political mobilization and war strategy called for strong leaders and central authority, but at the same time tactical flexibility was needed to meet emergencies. The long-term strategic decisions of the Communist Party depended on the information that was being filtered up through a complex chain of military and civilian political hierarchy, and strict discipline helped to enforce important decisions and over-all direction. Leaders had to be willing to merge themselves with the hard life of the rural masses. This was an absolute requirement to acquire the information upon which to base future action. Moreover, leaders had to have the analytic capability to deal with the problems of economic and physical survival.

From 1937 to 1945 membership in the Chinese Communist Party grew from about 40,000 to over 800,000.[48] Many of the new members had not assimilated the intellectual or moral attributes of the guerrilla leaders because of previous social experience, ignorance, or illiteracy. Thus a great premium was placed on leadership training and ideology. As in traditional learning, political morality was the core of such training, but the Marxist value system and epistomological theory replaced the Confucian.

Individual character was the key to training received in Yenan as it had been in the education of Confucian scholar-bureaucrats. In the Marxist view, however, character was not regarded as the result of natural inborn qualities. Instead it was a function of class antagonisms in the society at large. The object was to foster proletarian-class character, a world view of collective interests taking precedence over individualistic ones, which accepted labor as the moral as well as economic basis of society. Combining a knowledge of the world with action to change was a moral and epistomological necessity. Conversely, individual bourgeois-class (exploiting) character had to be completely eliminated.[49]

Traditional social organizations were utilized to begin the process of revolutionary transformation, and local activists and natural leaders were encouraged and supported by centrally-trained political organizers and military leaders.[50] New organizations had to be created to shift the local balance of power from the old elites. Peasant associations, militia groups, women's groups and associations, trade unions, and youth groups were all heavily influenced by communist leadership, becoming important political factors in the base areas and guerrilla war zones.[51] A "three-thirds" system, whereby candidates representing the old KMT, the communists, and various mass organizations shared administrative power in the government was also important in institutionalizing and legitimatizing this shift of power.[52]

By 1945 the mass line was the over-all approach to political mobilization and administration, and its principles were stated by Mao in classic form:

> The two methods which we communists should employ in carrying out any task are, first, the linking of the general with the specific, and second the linking of the leadership with the masses. . . . But there is no possibility of testing . . . general directives and of making them more specific and concrete, and there is danger of them coming to nothing, unless the leaders, instead of contenting themselves with issuing directives, personally carry out the tasks on hand in concrete and thorough manner.
>
> Within each unit a leading group should be formed comprising a small number of active workers united around the head of a given unit, and this group should maintain close contact with the masses. . . . The activity of this leading group unless combined with that of the masses will dissipate itself in the fruitless efforts of a handful of people.
>
> In all practical work of our Party, correct leadership can only be developed on the principle of "from the masses to the masses." This means summing up (i.e., coordinating and systematizing after careful study) the views of the masses (i.e., views scattered and unsystematic); then taking the resulting ideas back to the masses, explaining and popularizing them until the masses embrace the ideas as their own, stand up for them and translate them into action by way of testing their correctness. Then it is necessary once more to sum up the views of the masses and once again take the resulting ideas back to the masses so that the masses give them

their whole-hearted support. . . . And so on, over and over again so that each time these ideas emerge with greater correctness and become more vital and meaningful. This is what the Marxist theory of knowledge teaches us.[53]

The mass line used personal contact and education to work on both leaders and led, allowing them to formulate goals and the means to reach them. Envisaged as a tool of revolutionary change and non-bureaucratic day to day administration, developed in rural China in times of great chaos, it was to be applied later to the complex problems of industry in urban China after 1949.

When the Chinese Communists formally took power over the entire country in 1949 the contradictions of the previous century were most clearly epitomized by the vitally important, small group of intellectuals.

Scholar-bureaucrats had scant technical knowledge. Assignments to county posts, the lowest official position, were short and officials had little opportunity and less inclination to learn from exposure to the peasants' daily life and work. The county level officials, however, were assisted by clerks, secretaries, and managers who lived permanently in the locality.[54] These important administrators formed an unofficial level of the bureaucracy and, like their official superiors, stood apart from manual labor. They were the experts, receiving their education mostly through practical experience. The literacy which qualified them for mental work came from formal schooling. This dichotomy between officials and experts demonstrates the unofficial system of practical education in traditional China that, while existing within it and dependent on it, was outside the scope of formal education.

Social upheaval brought new ideas to the intellectuals, who began to search for an answer to their confusion and for a way to make China the technological and military equal of the threatening and aggressive Westerners.[55] The impact of Western technology on intellectuals led to a broadening of the educational system.[56] It was not long before technology, engineering, business management, accounting, and economics became the subjects on which an increasing proportion of a growing but still very small group of privileged urban dwellers concentrated.[57]

As Chinese students went abroad—to Japan, the West, the USSR—foreign educators, specialists, technicians, and missionaries came to China, many associated with American universities or large foundations.[58] Many Chinese learned Western technology and business management methods from working in factories, banks, and commercial enterprises, Chinese and foreign.[59] Nankai University trained economists in Western, non-Marxist economic and business management theory; Nanking and Yenching Universities, in Western political and social science theory. The natural sciences, too, were offered here.[60] Many university graduates exposed to Western-liberal concepts were often criticized by the more conservative Chinese for their Western views.[61] However, these engineers, social scientists and economists trained by Western methods were to be crucial to the educational, political, and economic establishment after 1949, when trained technical manpower was at a premium.

Though revolutionary in that it helped to undermine the hegemony of the Confucian classics, Western education also increased the potential for social mobility by greatly expanding the curriculum of educational institutions. At the same time liberal philosophy accepted many of the traditional Chinese premises. There was a distinction between vocational and liberal or scientific education. Education for mental work, whether in industrial technology, liberal arts, or social science was of greater prestige than education for skilled manual labor or agriculture. Western educational philosophy reinforced the Confucian tradition that purely intellectual work was superior to manual labor. Therefore, even in modern industrial enterprises the mental-manual labor-gap often proved to be disruptive.[62]

The Western and the traditional Chinese educational systems were highly competitive. Both were based on the dubious idea that formal degrees constituted legitimate indicators of a person's knowledge and expertise, or that they should bestow power and privilege on those who held them, especially in relationship to those who had gained their knowledge through experience or practice. In both systems, there was a complex system of hierarchy among degree holders. For those who fulfilled all the formal requirements, education was seen as a guarantee of justice and equal opportunity.

The Yenan experience, however, had seeded another type of education—one that was to have profound impact as part of the general political mobilization that was to overturn the entire structure of old China. Wedded to the urgent need to solve the problems of mere existence by the use of technical knowledge was a commitment to a long-term educational process which had no less a goal than transforming the way the Chinese had traditionally related to one another. Marxist concepts provided the theoretical and moral basis for this philosophy wherein labor was not simply an economic necessity but a major source of human knowledge.[63] It was through labor that human beings related to one another and to the environment. Mao Tsetung's essay "On Practice"—explaining the unity of theory and practice, knowing and doing, mental and manual work—detailed this approach, becoming a major study document in Yenan's universities and the theme of the CCP's vast ideological education campaign of the early 1940s.[64]

From university down to spare-time literacy classes, education emphasized the importance of combining learning with participation in labor. Not only were students and teachers to participate in labor, but those who worked were to have education brought to them. At important universities like the Anti-Japanese Military and Political University (K'ang-ta), education not only stressed military technique and production but made application of theory a requirement for teachers and a central part of total education.[65] Students often acted as teachers for other students in small group study sessions, and cooperation among teachers and students undermined the traditional attitude. In combination with the common, austere standard of living in Yenan, education was immediately applicable to material improvement while transforming human relationships which then affected attitudes of the educated toward society.

The relationship between technical education and social transformation spilled over into the larger rural society and market towns. The social revolution and the educational revolution reinforced each other. Dissemination of technical information helped to overcome the ignorance and apathy of poverty, and in so doing helped to mobilize the people to change.

It was not until mass education became flexible enough to meet the needs of both production and warfare, however, that it really began to take hold,[66] becoming tied to basic productive units in the countryside, including industrial and agricultural cooperatives, work brigades, small factories, and militia units. Mass education was decentralized in terms of management and technical curriculum, with political education the cement which unified the whole system.[67] Educational centers were no longer limited to formal schools located in the urban areas or the larger market towns. Local labor heroes or peasants became the new teachers and they, not the dilettantish scholars, were elevated to the heights of social prestige.

When the Chinese Communists took power and began the process of reconstruction and industrialization, the situation was chaotic and fluid. This was nowhere more evident than in the factories and industrial system.

First of all, it was industry that was to pull China out of its weakness and backwardness, and make a new and modern China. This was the goal of every nationalist Chinese ever since foreign powers humiliated and exploited the once proud middle kingdom. The very commitment to a new and modern China was fraught with contradictions. At first, it meant little more than investing time, energy, and wealth in isolated projects, adding technical and scientific subjects to the Confucian classical education. Thus, the Confucian identity would be preserved and China would be strengthened. But this approach quickly proved impossible. Technological development and industrialization threatened core elements of the Confucian ideology and power. Some conservative Chinese gave up the vision of a new and modern China to preserve what they considered the very essence of Chinese existence, its Confucian value system and philosophy. But other intellectuals continued to search for a way out.

Some advocated and pursued a program of wholesale Westernization. Like their more radical contemporaries these Westernizers accepted the need for technological and industrial development and were thoroughly anti-Confucian. The radicals, however, like the old conservatives, remained extremely uncomfortable with the values and institutions of liberal capitalism which they viewed as undesirable and too closely associated with imperial power.

Many Westernized, Western-educated, or pro-Western liberals, and even some reform-minded Confucians, became important in education and business and a major source of technical and scientific knowledge by 1949. Most remained moderately pro-Western, though they opposed United States intervention in support of the Kuomintang after 1945.

The radicals—those whose dedication to a new China entailed hostility to capitalism as part and parcel of their hostility to Western and Japanese imperialism—had turned to the only revolutionary critique of Western society which offered possibilities for a more rational use of technology than was possible in the West. Marxism became the accepted creed of thousands of Chinese nationalist intellectuals, even while nationalism became the rallying cry of thousands of non-Marxist intellectuals. The anti-Japanese war from 1937–1945 obscured the contradictions between these groups. From 1937 to 1945 the pro-Western modernizers were given a reprieve. They could be nationalistic and pro-Western by joining the struggle against Japan. But from 1945 to 1949 this pro-Western group split into its component parts. The more conservative supported the KMT and its United States backers, the more leftist inclined to the Communist Party. Many retained their liberalism even while opposing the KMT, hoping that the United States Government would do likewise. Others, less optimistic about the United States, maintained strongly elitist and technocratic views of the New China they hoped to build; they supported the Communists because of the planning and technological modernization associated with socialism. These people had little use for the revolutionary goals set forth in Marxism, and only a superficial understanding of the Marxist critique of capitalist society.

Among the Marxists there were major contradictions. Marxist theory has always been vague concerning the practical tasks of socialist industrial management. The Soviet Union was the one country with experience, but it was far removed. Moreover, the USSR's relation to

Marxist theory was ambiguous and debatable. Important as it was to be after 1949, the majority of the CCP was not prepared to deal with this problem at the time. Their experience and expertise lay in mobilizing, leading, and articulating the forces behind the massive peasant revolt, and it was by no means clear how this experience was to be made relevant, if indeed it could be, to China's technological and industrial development.

The history of contradictory forces that faced the Chinese Communists in 1949 does not end here. China's Confucian bureaucratic past had endured for thousands of years and in China's industrial sector those with this view of the world worked alongside Westernized or Western-educated individuals, and both groups were only part of a wider society that included KMT police agents, communist labor organizers and political agitators, traditional gang bosses and labor contractors, and a working class that was often militant but just as often split by kinship, regional, or other ties.

Within the communist movement the strong influence of Leninist organizational theory and the notion of the vanguard party existed in ambiguous relationship to the Yenan experience. The Yenan experience was quite different from both the Confucian and Western-liberal tradition and in practice had given new depth to Leninist concepts of democratic centralism. The Yenan-born mass line was to emerge as an alternative to the Confucian, the Western, and the Soviet approaches to organization.

Underlying all of these contradictions were certain constants. The Chinese consistently related private morality and behavior to the public world of politics, and saw between the two an inevitable and dialectical interaction. Intellectuals, inevitably and centrally part of these political relationships in society, could not stand aloof from them. The public spirit was a higher order of morality than the private search for profit and there was and could be no happy coincidence between them.

In the Confucian heritage public spirit arose from a person's inborn character; it served to justify the political power, privileges, and wealth of those gentlemen fortunate enough to be able to cultivate this higher morality. For China's Marxist revolutionaries public spirit was acquired through struggle with the natural world and society and was emphatically not a matter of inborn character. It was possible for everyone and was to be the basis of the commitment to building a classless society. Though their definitions of public spirit were different, politics for all Chinese remained highly goal conscious and was understood as political economy, as the relationship of power to mechanisms by which people produced and distributed what they needed to live a "civilized," *human* existence.

By 1949 years of war and civil war had wreaked havoc on the economy and aggravated the sectoral imbalances of over a century of foreign influence. Japanese bombing and shelling and Communist-led guerrilla warfare against Japan had largely destroyed the transport system; the Civil War between the KMT and the Communists had taken care of the rest. Unsure of deliveries, supplies, and markets, businessmen could not invest or plan. Inflation was astronomical, and real estate speculation, foreign banks, luxury spending on imports, and hoarding were the main outlets for the capital possessed by the few wealthy Chinese. Many of these began to flee the country as the communist armies approached the cities. Shanghai, the largest city, the most important industrial center, and the main connection with the outside world, was beset by poverty, crime, starvation, prostitution, drugs, unemployment, and disease.[68]

Thus, in 1949 the focus of attention was clearly reconstruction of the economy. The conflict was in the means to this and longer term goals. In the industrial system, so crucial to China's modernization, the revolution was about to accelerate dramatically.

3/From Reconstruction to the Great Leap Forward: China's Industry in a Period of Transition

BY 1949 the massive peasant-based revolution had engulfed almost all of China. The Northern part of the country, both urban and rural, was rapidly occupied by the well-behaved and highly motivated peasant soldiers who made up the bulk of the People's Liberation Army. The heavy industrial centers of the Northeast, especially in the provinces of Liaoning and Heilungkiang, were under communist control by the end of 1948. In the South, remnants of the Kuomintang armies still held some cities and pockets of resistance continued in some rural areas. Chiang, however, was already making preparations to flee to Taiwan and it was simply a matter of time before the whole country would be governed by the communists.

By March 1949 the victorious revolutionaries paradoxically faced problems with which they had little experience. Political mobilization in rural areas required a thorough knowledge of local customs, class and clan structures, distribution of wealth, family relationships, as well as a knowledge of personalities and personal histories.[1] The Communist Party was experienced in rural China. It had had years of activity with a large number of locally-recruited activists and leaders.

By March the focus of revolutionary mobilization had to be changed. At the Second Plenary Session of the Seventh Central Committee of the Chinese Communist Party, Mao Tsetung noted that "the centre of gravity of the Party's work has shifted from the village to the city."[2] There were new problems in the cities, caused by a whirlpool of conflicting forces, trends, and personalities that made the complexities of rural society appear relatively simple.[3]

The capture of the cities presented the Chinese Communists with two sets of problems. First of all, international relations suddenly became of far greater importance than before. China's major cities were almost all located on the coast, and they were heavily populated. They imported large amounts of consumer goods and by 1949 were importing crucial amounts of food also. The years of war and civil war had caused a great population flux away from rural battlegrounds, and the inland agricultural regions were unable to feed the cities.[4] Moreover, the coastal cities paid for food imports and consumer goods either with loans from the United States and other Western governments and banks to the KMT government and business groups,[5] or by foreign exchange earned through comprador activity of Chinese firms selling Western goods inside China.[6] China's cities, therefore, had to be fed, and the population provided with a means of livelihood.[7]

When the Kuomintang began to blockade the east coast of China, using ships and planes from the United States, and when $75 million dollars in military aid for Chiang was approved by the U.S. Congress in September 1949,[8] the situation in the cities became potentially disastrous. United States indecision vis-à-vis continued support for Chiang on Taiwan between January and June 1950 finally ended on 27 June when President Truman publicly ordered the Seventh Fleet to patrol the Taiwan Straits[9] as part of United States military deployment for intervention in Korea. Ostensibly, the Fleet was to protect Chiang, but it also added a military component to the economic pressure (that had already been under way for nearly a year) against the new communist government.

In this international context, the relative urban inexperience of the Chinese Communist Party became all the more significant. The chief urban political rival to the rural-based Communist Party under Mao's leadership was the urban bourgeoisie, whose members possessed the literacy, technical knowledge, and business experience vital to urban production. The urban wing of the Communist Party was under the leadership of Liu Shao-ch'i. This group had been organized along very different lines than had the much larger rural-based Party. It had had to put much greater stress on secret underground activity and tight discipline, a political necessity in the cities where Chiang's secret police and military security operatives had penetrated the labor movement, and where a Chinese version of the Gestapo had had few scruples about killing any communist it could uncover.[10] Still, the urban wing could not supply the necessary trained cadres to deal with getting urban production going again. As these two groups began to work closely together for the first time there grew a potential for dangerous squabbling within the ranks of the party.

Another problem faced the victorious Communists. In Mao's view the urban middle classes were not merely political rivals. In spite of the fact that their talents were needed and would have to be utilized in the enormous tasks of reconstruction and industrialization, Mao felt that they were politically unacceptable as leaders. They were politically and intellectually oriented toward the West and their economic interests lay in establishing close ties with Western countries. Fearful of the mobilization of the Chinese masses, the urban bourgeoisie would only lead China once again into a dependent, exploitative relationship with the economically and technologically stronger West. As a result China's modernization and economic development would be thwarted, and China would quickly once again be foreign dominated, an arena for international competition. Therefore, in Mao's view, the working class and the party which represented its interests had to lead an alliance between the peasantry and intellectuals and businessmen.[11] Only then, Mao felt, could relations with the West be established on a basis of equality.

Aside from his concern with China's international position and its ability to develop an industrialized, independent, and modern economy, Mao was also concerned with revolution within Chinese society, and this was another reason for his rejection of the urban bourgeoisie as leaders in China's modernization. In April 1949 Mao began his essay "On the People's Democratic Dictatorship" which included the Marxist–Leninist definition of the revolutionary role of the Communist Party *after* it had assumed state power.

> We are the opposite of the political parties of the bourgeoisie. They are afraid to speak of the extinction of classes, state power, and parties. We, on the contrary, declare openly that we are *striving hard to create the very conditions* which will bring about their extinction. The leadership of the Communist Party and the state power of the people's dictatorship are such conditions. *Anyone who does not recognize this truth is no communist.* [Italics added.][12]

Mao, however, then went on to elaborate on the nature of the revolutionary aspects of the party's role. Membership in the Communist Party did not, he argued, automatically make one a communist. Rather, the acceptance of a revolutionary morality was the premise by which the individual party member could be judged and the standard by which China's modernization and economic development was to be evaluated. Mao warned those all over China, but especially in the urban areas, who were just joining the party:

> *Young comrades who have not studied Marxism-Leninism and have only recently joined the Party may not yet understand this truth.* They must understand it—only then can they have a correct world outlook. They must understand that the road to the abolition of classes, to the abolition of state power, and to the abolition of parties is the road all mankind must take, it is only a question of time and conditions. [Italics added.][13]

In the early years, the Soviets provided a relatively strong and absolutely vital international ally to help China smash the very threatening blockade of its eastern seacoast and the trade embargo led by the

United States. Soviet prestige in the communist movement could also help overcome whatever tendencies existed in the Chinese Communist Party toward enervating factionalism at this critical juncture in the party's history.[14] Moreover, the Soviet alliance deprived the Chinese urban bourgeoisie, so closely tied to the West and the major urban rival to the CCP, of its main source of international support. Finally, the Soviets' experience and reputation as the first society which had undergone rapid socialist economic development promised to the Chinese a path which led toward rapid production increases. In 1950, all this was perceived as entirely compatible with the revolutionary goals articulated by Mao in 1949.

All of these conflicts and complexities which faced the communists existed in concentrated form within the urban factories and industrial enterprises, for here were the central points around which production would be reconstructed. Here were conflicts and legacies left from previous foreign domination and management: British, American, German, and, in the Northeast, Japanese. Here the communists and Kuomintang had struggled for influence among the workers and in the trade union movement. Here peasant emigres from the recent battlegrounds of rural China mingled with skilled industrial workers. Here large-scale, modern textile mills, machine foundries, and iron smelters coexisted alongside thousands of tiny neighborhood shops for repair, parts, handicrafts, and nondescript undertakings of all kinds. Coordination, where it existed at all, was often chaotic. In the urban factories the bourgeoisie, always heavily influenced by a combination of Western and traditional Chinese values, who possessed most of the technical and business expertise in the country, faced the workers and Communist Party members who were to provide the revolutionary leadership but who were themselves products of vastly different political and general life experiences.

The task of this revolutionary leadership was to harness the talents of the bourgeoisie to production while beginning what Mao called the 10,000 *li** long journey toward socialism.[15] In Chinese cities which had long been exposed to the corruption, moral laxity, cynicism, selfishness, chaos, and greed which were typical of the urban treaty ports, this was no easy task.[16] Furthermore, in 1949 there were few revolutionaries or "reds" who were also "experts" in production, technology, or management. Ironically, while the question of state power had been resolved on the national level, inside the factories, which were to be the center of China's modernization, the struggle for power was just beginning.

---

* A *li* is about ⅓ of an English mile. But the Chinese notion of a 10,000 li journey signifies simply a very long journey of no specific length.

The Chinese communists had three main sources from which to draw for revolutionary leadership in the industrial sector. The first of these was the People's Liberation Army, which sent military representatives (who were also party members) to individual factories where they claimed the authority of the new government. As many of these people were not familiar with industrial production and management, they either relied on existing administrators and technicians or set up committees of skilled workers and willing technical personnel to restore production.[17] Although the source of leadership was the same, the management systems in various factories could differ greatly in the degree of authoritarianism and democracy.

The second source of revolutionary leadership was the urban-based Communist Party apparatus, members of which had led and organized clandestine labor activity during the civil war.[18] Many of these people were experienced workers.

The third source was comprised of skilled, literate workers who, with the blessings of the Communist Party, were quickly promoted to positions of leadership in the factories by the trade unions.[19] These workers were especially important as replacements for the old gang bosses, chiefs of secret societies and religious sects, and Kuomintang labor leaders. They helped to destroy the influence of the urban criminal underworld, formerly pervasive in many Chinese factories, which had often operated through those same gang bosses and sect leaders.[20]

Undercutting and replacing the leadership of the religious, criminal, exploitative, and anticommunist elements within the ranks of the working class was only part of the early struggle for power. The importance of the urban bourgeoisie increased because of widespread illiteracy and ignorance in the urban working class as well as among the veteran Communist Party cadres from the rural areas. In Shanghai alone, one of the most advanced industrial centers in the country, the illiteracy rate for all employees, including clerks and white-collar workers, was estimated at 46 percent.[21] Among blue-collar factory workers, this figure was much higher, probably near the 80 percent figure for industrial personnel in the whole country.[22]

During 1949 to 1950 the majority of China's industrial enterprises was in private or semiprivate hands.[23] Many people with administrative, business, or technical knowledge and experience, even if closely associated with the KMT, stayed on their jobs in urban business and government after 1949.[24] Although many middle-class Chinese trained in the West went with the KMT to Taiwan or emigrated to the United States or Hong Kong, many returned to China from the West.[25] Though this returned group of intellectuals was probably loyal to the new government, neither they, nor most other members of the Chinese middle classes, were Marxist revolutionaries in their attitudes concerning manual labor and class struggle. Even after 1949 many urban bourgeois continued to be influenced by the habits and values of traditional Chinese families and society, or were assimilated into treaty port life.[26] Throughout, a dilettantist attitude toward manual labor was often intensified by a high degree of status consciousness in interpersonal relations.[27] Antagonism toward the new revolutionary regime which had clamped down hard on nepotism, corruption, and private greed did not simplify matters.

Even as late as 1956, a major factory of China's northeast, presented as a typical negative example in the national press, had people who joined the party as a result of its intense urban recruitment drive in 1949 and who were guilty of flagrant acts of corruption and nepotism. The Shenyang Transformer Factory had a director of the organization department of the Plant Party Committee who sheltered and promoted his relatives, including his wife and his father-in-law. He tried to get his wife into the party and the Young Communist League even though she was clearly not politically interested or qualified and was found to have forged records in order to get money and benefits for her family.[28]

In 1949 almost all of the students in Chinese universities and higher level technical schools[29] were from the urban middle and upper middle classes.[30] Well over half (63 percent) of the members of this group who were university and technical school graduates in 1949 had majored in subjects that were essential for industrialization (engineering, social science, natural science, economics, business[31]), and they were quickly recruited into positions of power within key factories and into the party as well.

Major changes in the class background of students or in the substance of the pre-1949 curriculum did not get underway until 1951–1952.[32] By 1953 approximately 80 percent of the managerial personnel were of bourgeois background and 37 percent of these were pre-1949 graduates, returned overseas Chinese students, or factory owners.[33] Over one-half had been graduated from schools in China during or after 1949, but they had not experienced a much different education than had the bourgeois students of pre-1949 China. By 1953 only 20 percent or so of managerial and technical personnel was made up of urban Communist Party members,[34] promoted workers,[35] and communist-appointed factory directors (Ch'an-chang), vice-directors (Fu-ch'an-chang), party committee secretaries (Tang-wei shu-chi), and trade-union officials (Kung-hui-yuan). It was largely by means of this 20 percent that revolutionary political direction was to be maintained.[36]

Such political direction was not always strong nor guaranteed. The political influence of the bourgeois personnel resulted from previously acquired status and they often served as models for new urban and rural cadres. However, not all of these people behaved in the same way or held the same commitments and they faced workers and party members whose political sophistication, literacy, and skill varied widely. Moreover, it was by no means clear at this time just what it was that constituted revolutionary political leadership. Aside from speedily restored production, and the weeding out of corrupt, criminal, greedy, and actively anticommunist leaders, political leadership could be exercised in very different contexts. Even when workers' management committees of a broad and participatory nature replaced Chinese capitalists who had fled with Chiang or the Japanese or Western owners of major enterprises, the factory manager appointed by the military or party authorities retained great potential for concentrated power if circumstances required or permitted it.[37]

As a result, leadership consisted of technically and administratively qualified people of both worker and bourgeois background, who could be westernized, traditional, Marxist, non-marxist, or even antimarxist, urban or rural. In the crucibles of modernization, the factories of China, a diverse group operated under varied circumstances, with real disagreements and different perspectives regarding modernization and its relationship to the Chinese revolution.

The Early Development of Factory Management: Revolutionary Dualism and the Demands of Production

Two major approaches to the problems of revolution and modernization in China's factories emerged by 1953. Both were perceived as embodying the desirable political direction and the necessary technical and economic rationality. One system was to take advantage of the small, but dedicated, group of Chinese workers and Communist Party members with experience in administration and/or in industry. The other was to copy the "advanced experiences" of the socialist USSR. At the risk of oversimplifying what was obviously a very complicated situation which varied according to factory size, history, and location, these two systems can be described as the East China or Shanghai system, and the Soviet or "one-man management" system (yi-chang-chih).[38]

The East China or Shanghai System

The East China or Shanghai system of management evolved in the immediate aftermath of liberation. It was the nationwide system in the very first months, as military leaders and work teams were sent all over the country to establish political authority or to replace owners and managers who had fled. In the East China system collective leadership in the factory was exercised by a committee, while the factory manager was responsible for carrying out and organizing the production operations.

The committees could take many forms. Sometimes they were made up of technicians and owners who cooperated with the communists. Sometimes they were made up of military leaders and underground party workers. Often they consisted of large numbers of workers, especially in cases where workers had taken over plants when the former owners or managers fled.[39] Women workers in the textile mills were especially active.[40]

These management committees were responsible for getting production going in the plant. They made decisions regarding plans, personnel, organization, and welfare. From the beginning the whole committee was subject to the veto of the chairman of the committee who was also the factory manager.[41] As time passed the conflict between the manager and the committee became increasingly serious, especially if the Soviet system had been imposed on the earlier collective system.

In the early years, the management committees worked hard to create mass organizations in the plant and to mobilize workers for production as well as for political purposes. Trade-union and youth-league groups became important in the administration of the factories. They worked closely with the management committees to find and immobilize anticommunist elements among former owners, managers, and the old gang bosses who had disappeared into the rank and file. They helped draft and implement labor insurance regulations and other welfare measures. These were important to gain the support and confidence of workers cynical of the new authorities and often frightened of retaliation threatened by the toughs and "hit-men" of the pre-1949 leadership.[42]

Although not confined to East China and the coastal cities like Shanghai, this system of collective or committee management was still dominant when after 1953 the Soviet system of one-man management became official national policy with the formal beginning of the first Five-Year-Plan. Even before the plan started officially, Soviet influence in the heavy industrial centers of the Northeast had become pronounced. Because most of China's heavy industry had been dominated by pro-Chiang or by Japanese management, which had fled before the PLA advances, there was a leadership vacuum into which Soviet engineers and managerial experts stepped. In East China and in coastal cities, however, more local Chinese capitalists stayed to await the new authorities. In light industry, such as textiles, matches, cigarettes, and a myriad of small-scale firms which typified much of Chinese capitalism before 1949, communist authorities and newly recruited party members worked closely if not always cooperatively with the previous management.

Although a mass movement, known as the "five anti" campaign, began in 1952 to attack bourgeois owners and managers, it was designed to increase the power and participation of workers in management,[43] and not to establish the Soviet system which had, by that time, been implemented in the heavy industrial centers of the Northeast.

As production activities outside the former bureaucrat capitalist or Japanese enterprises evolved, both the party and the trade union became central to management. The Party Committee in the factory acquired the power of policy making and coordination which it had previously shared with bourgeoisie managers.[44] The trade union became heavily involved with welfare and labor insurance as well as training programs to improve workers' skills and chances for promotion to management positions.[45] It was also the intermediary between workers and the old technicians and engineers with whom the Communist Party was actively cooperating to utilize their expertise.[46]

A system of worker participation in operations and on-the-spot production management grew out of the old gang-boss system, once it had been thoroughly reformed and the old leaders either purged or reformed.[47] Former managerial and technical personnel were paid in accordance with their previous rank and experience, but, until the end of August 1955, Communist Party cadres, including newly recruited youth, workers, and labor union members, were on a system which provided them with daily sustenance and not much more.[48] Technical and engineering personnel were ranked by title and the authority to make decisions, both of which were based on length of formal schooling and practical experience.[49]

The East China or Shanghai system developed only within individual workplaces. It did not apply to the problems of economic coordination. It evolved where there was little Soviet influence and where Chinese capitalism had had its greatest independence and development. It envisaged a major role for the collective leadership of the Party Committees and the role of mass organizations like the Youth League and trade unions. It embodied significant worker participation because of its relationship to the old decentralized *operational* autonomy of the gang-boss system which the Communists had attacked and reformed but could not eliminate. It was also characterized by a certain equality and unity between the new managers and the workers, especially where the supply system of incentives was reinforced by mass campaigns to undermine the values and privileges of the urban bourgeoisie. However, as the economy began to recover from decades of war and as the problems of coordination and planning became more central in the task of socialist modernization, the East China system came under increasing pressure.

By 1953 another type of management purported to deal with precisely these problems. In the Northeast, Soviet methods promised not only efficient production within the factories and enterprises, but also a method for economic planning and coordination. It was a socialist form of management, hence revolutionary, or so it officially seemed to the Chinese leadership as the first Five-Year-Plan began.

The Soviet Model: One-Man Management and Socialist Modernization in the 1950s

Soviet influence in the industrial system was the result of a series of agreements of 1949–1950 which culminated in the Sino-Soviet Treaty signed in February 1950. Even before the first Five-Year-Plan had begun, major Soviet aid was present in the industrial centers, particularly in the Northeastern provinces of Heilunkiang and Liaoning. Liaoning alone was the location for over one-half of all the Soviet aid projects and the mighty Anshan Iron and Steel Complex was the center of this effort.[50] Other Soviet aid projects were scattered in other parts of the country and were key points of production in the FFYP.

The most direct and immediate effects of Soviet influence came from the presence of large numbers of Russian technical advisers and the training of many Chinese students in the Soviet Union. A minimum of 10,000, perhaps as many as 20,000, Soviet experts and industrial advisers worked in China during the 1950s, primarily in construction and planning.[51] At least 80,000 Chinese engineers, technicians, and advanced research personnel were trained in the USSR. Together these two groups, sophisticated theoretically, and formally educated, were an important segment of industry.[52] By 1956 over 200 complete industrial units were planned or already under construction and these projects were "set up down to the smallest operational detail"[53] under the close supervision and advice of the Soviet experts. Along with technology and operational blueprints, there now came *advice on how to manage* the industrial enterprises, as well as the knowledge to build and run the machinery.[54] The manager, workshop chiefs, technicians, administrative bureaucrats, and workers of one typical plant, went to sister plants in the USSR to study technology and management.[55]

By the end of 1953 the Soviet concept of industrial management had gained general, though only tentative, acceptance.[56] In spite of a major slogan of the times, "Let's be modern and Soviet,"[57] even at Anshan there were "still many cadres who (had) failed to realize fully how industry should be managed.[58]

A major appeal of the Soviet system was the close connection it embodied between what was called scientific management of each factory and tight central planning within the total industrial system. The two were integrated. Scientific management involved detailed work plans for each phase of production and administration. These plans were standardized, based on exact measurements of mechanical, technological, and human performances, and, once formulated as targets, were to be followed precisely. These targets were then sent to the higher level planning authorities, thus becoming the basis for the next sequence of plans, which in turn became the basis for new precision measurements and quota planning and so on.

The Soviet management system was organized around a production-territorial principle. In every plant there were three basic levels of organization: the factory, the work shop, the work team. The factory level was responsible for coordinating and controlling all activity within the plant, and it contained sections dealing with the functional matters of personnel, wages, quality control, supplies, storage, and communications with planning authorities and other plants. Work shops and work teams were organized around production and depended upon the technological or assembly sequences which were part of the process of manufacturing a given product. The number and size of work shops and work teams and the relationship between them depended mostly on the product and the technology used to make it. Work shops very often had functional or administrative sections to check on materials use and allocation, quality control, attendance, and similar matters.

The production-territorial organization of the plant was related to the factory's responsibility system,[59] which in turn was shaped by the principles of scientific management. The Soviet responsibility system was called the system of one-man management, and it worked as follows:

Usually, a control team made up of high-level management in the plant was responsible for seeing that production leaders and individual workers were carrying out their responsibilities, most of which were outlined and standardized in enormous detail by the measurements of scientific management. Daily production logs were kept by management for each worker, recording output for the day, rate of production (output per unit of time), and rate of material consumption.

The factory director was in complete control of the factory (limited only by his ability to administer and know what his subordinates were up to). One individual was responsible for and had power over each production unit, down to the work team or section. A strict hierarchy prevailed. Production coordination was established through the administrative sections at the factory and work-shop level. Each section had one section chief who was responsible for particular functions within the production units. Coordination between administrative sections and administrative and production leaders were handled by the leader of each functional section and production unit.[60] The administrative chiefs could not in theory give orders to work shop level supervisors. Administrative personnel were only to assist the production units. In practice however, it would become difficult to utilize this theory, especially when, for example, engineers belonging to the administrative technical section might make decisions which contradicted the shop-foremen that they were working under.

This one-man management system extended from individual factories into the planning apparatus. At every level of the planning bureaucracy, beginning with the central ministries, one person was responsible for getting accurate and comprehensive information upon which to formulate targets for his section and for reaching these targets.

Along with the production-territorial principle and the one-man management responsibility system, which the Chinese were slowly adopting, there was a corresponding incentive system. For workers on the production line, the scientifically determined output and consumption quotas computed by high level managers and experts in the administrative sections of the factory became the basis for a complex series of individual bonuses and rewards paid in addition to salaries. These quotas were also the basis for fines and other punishments.[61] Piece-rate wages also fit the control requirements of this kind of management in those industries where the production process lent itself to piece-rate wage calculations. This piece-rate incentive system caught on rapidly. By 1952 over one-third of all industrial workers were on piece-rate systems and by 1956 the percentage had climbed to 42 percent.[62] While over half of China's industrial workers were not on piece-rate systems, toward the end of the first Five-Year-Plan a significant portion of China's major factories were.

With the adoption of the Soviet management system the same kind of incentives came into effect for managers and cadres. In 1955 there was a general switch from the early supply system to a more formal and bureaucratically rational wage and salary system.[63] In industry non-laboring foremen would be considered cadres as would clerical personnel.[64] Administrative cadres, in government or party, were ranked in twenty-six grades with salaries ranging from thirty Yuan per month in grade 26 to 560 Yuan per month in grade 1. There were four additional noncadre ranks for service personnel. Technical personnel were divided into eight grades, followed by five grades of technicians and four grades of assistant technicians.[65] Administrators in industry were paid slightly more than those in government or party work, although it is not clear how this worked if a man were both a party member and a factory manager.[66]

In addition to ranking, grading, and salary incentives to get people to fulfill their responsibilities in the hope of being promoted, there were bonus payments to managerial and technical personnel at all levels of the industrial system when targets were met or overreached. It is possible that by 1956 these bonuses in terms of percentage of base pay were greater than they were for workers at the time.[67]

From the very beginning of the first Five-Year-Plan the Chinese clearly understood the two related aspects of the Soviet system for factories and for planning,[68] but they were not totally pleased for a number of reasons.[69] First of all, the system did not suit Chinese conditions technically, economically, or politically. As the transformation of the privately owned sector of the Chinese industrial economy began to pick up speed in 1954 and 1955, it became clear that the many small and scattered shops and factories in the cities would have to be amalgamated, have their operations unified, and have their structures rationalized. This frequently involved physical relocation of people and equipment and a merging of technical and managerial manpower from different plants into one new factory. In Shanghai, for example, there were over fifty small, scattered, privately owned electric clock and instrument factories. In forming the new Shanghai Tu Hua Instruments and Clock Manufacturing Plant, conflicts over value assessment and compensation arose as did problems concerning personnel and managerial authority. The question was, which managers, owners, and technical personnel from which of the old plants would have what responsibility and powers in the new set-up?[70]

To impose over this kind of conflict the tightly hierarchical and basically non-collegial atmosphere inherent in the one-man management system produced political and economic trouble. Since amalgamation was widespread in the mid-1950s, it caused unfavorable conditions for implementing the one-man management system.

Another reason why many Chinese capitalists and bourgeois technical personnel were disenchanted with the system was that they were still influenced by traditional Confucian ethics, ideas about authority, obedience, and discipline which came from inner morality rather than from external rule-bound constraints.[71] While these people would not be happy supporters of worker prerogatives which challenged their elite status, neither were they comfortable with the authority and decision-making of one-man management.[72]

A third reason for dissatisfaction was that scientific management required hard data for planning and judging the performance of individuals by which rewards and punishments were allocated. Hard and consistent data were also needed to predict output and consumption norms. Given old, broken down, or unreliable machinery and in some instances an inexperienced and unskilled labor force and uneven technical developments in different parts of the country and within different areas of the same industry, it became difficult to gather accurate information or to rely on the *general applicability* of the data that were collected even if they were accurate.[73] Without such data, planning and production within the factory system would be held back rather than promoted, while planning and coordination at the central, regional, and provincial ministry levels could be severely hampered.[74]

There were other reasons why one-man management was not whole-heartedly welcomed and why it generated opposition. Some Chinese technicians, engineers, and designers of industrial machinery and building had been trained in the United States or Britain and were either anti-Soviet or were wedded to American or British ways.[75] The plants which were helped extensively by Soviet aid were also key projects designated for rapid development in the first Five-Year-Plan; as such they attracted skilled workers and technicians from all over the country, but especially from Shanghai.[76] From wherever they came, however, skilled Chinese workers and technicians were often quite proud, and they did not always enjoy working under Soviet experts or following their suggestions.[77] In the case of the Shenyang Transformer Plant, opposition to Soviet experts took the simple form of changing blueprints and data, ignoring advice or taking it so literally that damage resulted to machinery, and plans for production were thrown completely awry.[78]

The one-man management system when superimposed on the older Shanghai system where Party Committees and trade-union committees had wielded power quickly generated potentially vicious conflict. Party Committee secretaries and plant managers, who were often party members, competed with each other for the honors, rewards, and promotions that came with the responsibility for meeting or exceeding the quotas of their factories. They also argued over who had the power to make which kinds of decisions, and in the process of fighting with each other they did not hesitate to use their position and influence as party members to get others in the factory to support one or the other side. The result was often chaos.[79]

The Chinese recognized the problems which the Soviet incentive system brought and which, in their view, reinforced some already existing relationships among people in the production process. The management–worker split grew wider from the control system and the realities of decision-making[80] and was exacerbated by the system of incentives based on quotas and differential bonuses. The competition for rewards and promotion among cadres led to a paralyzing factionalism, but this was only part of the problem with the incentive system. It was soon seen to be detrimental not only to the production process but to the planning process as well.

The system encouraged many factory directors and planners to seek low targets so that they could more easily be met or exceeded. It also led to concealing one's own mistakes or to covering up the mistakes of others if they might reflect on one's self. There was a tendency to report achievements where none existed or to listen to only good news and not bad news in order to be able to report that good news to higher authorities, hence gaining rewards or promotion. Not only did these things occur at the factory level[81] but at the municipal level Party Committees as well, which were supposed to be supervising the work of economic planning. They also occurred in the local administrative branches of central ministries which were responsible for planning.[82] The behavior that resulted directly from the incentive system (when it was linked to a bureaucratic planning apparatus) was clearly unacceptable to Chinese planners. It was furthermore a phenomenon that bore an uncomfortable resemblance to the behavior of that other group of administrative bureaucrats that had dominated China for thousands of years.

Finally, one-man management required a large number of people educated in skills that were not abundant in China, compared to skills that were already available. The Soviet system put great emphasis on management and leadership methods that were most likely to be found among the engineers and technicians, many of whom were of bourgeois origin. Even newly promoted and educated workers were subject to imperatives implied by the whole system of organization, control, and incentives. Many cadres rebelled against a system which was clearly threatening their own authority and status, but they also felt sure that such developments were a threat to the cooperative, egalitarian ideals of the revolution and socialism.[83] They argued that bureaucratic organizational structures and concepts of human motivation were threatening the revolution in the name of modernization and efficiency even while they prevented optimum levels of efficiency and inhibited modernization. In the prestigious heavy-industry sector, these bureaucratic ideas were threatening to become part of the daily routine of factory leadership, both party and nonparty.

It is easy to overemphasize the problems of one-man management and ignore the fact that during the period of the first Five-Year-Plan there was a rapid and very impressive rise in Chinese industrial output and capacity. Still, it must be remembered that Soviet industrial management and planning practices were a part of the general Soviet approach to economic development that the Chinese were following. This approach itself, not simply the portion of it concerned with industrial operations and planning, had contributed to other tensions and problems in Chinese society that, by 1957, were becoming increasingly obvious. The emphasis on heavy industry, the concentration of industry in urban centers, the investment of as little as possible in agricultural development and light industry consistent with feeding a growing urban population, and the tendency to ignore local and/or marginal resources, natural and human, in the quest for large-scale efficiency and concentrated development—all had brought China's agricultural production to the point where it had become an important constraint on further modernization in spite of drastic social and economic transformation in rural China. But since the development strategy and the management and planning process were related to one another, by late 1956 China, in spite of impressive gains in industry and important changes in agriculture, faced some hard political and economic choices.

In August 1956 the coalition of forces in China that opposed one-man management and Soviet planning procedures won the first battle in what had not yet become open confrontation. In fact, even in defending scientific management and the Soviet system in 1953–1954, the official party newspaper *Jen-min Jih-pao* (People's Daily) was decidedly luke-warm in its support, usually implying that criticism of the system was not unfounded.[84] In July 1956 a major report on the Shenyang Transformer Plant received national publicity as exemplifying all the negative characteristics of one-man management.[85] The leading cadres of the plant, including the Party Committee secretary, the plant manager, director of the plant Party Organization department, the first deputy director, and the chief engineer, were all demoted, expelled from the party, or otherwise punished. Since Shenyang was in the Northeast and the plant had a significant Soviet advisory presence, this article clearly indicated that the time of one-man management was limited.[86]

The official announcement came at the Eighth Party Congress in August 1956. Li Hsueh-feng, the Director of the Party Central Committee Industrial Bureau announced that henceforth the old Shanghai system, what Li called the system of "factory manager responsibility under leadership of the Party Committee" would replace "the one-boss system" (yi-chang-chih). In justifying this change Li made the following points against the arguments of those who were not happy with it.

1. Party Committee leadership would not necessarily lead to a separation of authority and responsibility, which in turn would cause uncertainty and inaction on the part of management. Responsibility for specific tasks and functions would be allocated and coordinated by the Party Committee.
2. Party leadership would assure the following of the mass line and circumvent bureaucratic tendencies. It would guarantee the making of realistic decisions based on actual observation thereby preventing the emergence of a privileged elite divorced from the production process and exercising power over it.
3. Party leadership would satisfy demands for worker participation in management.
4. Party leadership would replace the arbitrary, punitive measures of management, no matter at what level or by which authority, with persuasion, education, and administrative discipline.

5. Party leadership would see to it that management would be more realistic and flexible by taking into consideration the discussions of the workers at mass meetings.

6. Party Committees would improve their technical and professional quality. As 10 to 20 percent of industrial workers were party members by 1956 and the majority of factory leadership cadres were party members, it could be expected that factory management could easily carry out the political tasks of the party while also undertaking production responsibilities.[87]

Nonetheless, as the Soviet one-man management system was central to the over-all planning and coordinating of the national economy, it was not a matter affecting single factories in isolation. Since the same was true of quotas and standardized output and productivity norms which were the basis for incentives and controls at all levels of the system, a shift from one-man management to a more democratic, collective system could not only affect the division of labor within all factories but pose a major problem for the central planners as well. Early in 1957, though there was some indication that they knew a problem existed, the Chinese had no real idea of how management within factories was related to planning in the economy.[88]

Interestingly, the Soviets had begun facing similar problems at about the same time. Just when the Chinese were moving away from one-man management the Soviet economist E. G. Lieberman published an article on motivation and control in management under a decentralized planning and administrative system.[89] In February 1957 N. S. Khrushchev made a report "On Further Reforming Organization Work in Managing Industry and Construction."

The Chinese, obviously aware of trends in Soviet economic thought, familiar themselves with the economic problems of highly centralized planning, and anxious to move away from one-man management, published an editorial comment on this report in *Ta Kung Pao*.[90] The Chinese disagreed with much of what Khrushchev had to say but admitted he had raised some crucial points. These were: the relationship between politics and economics and the state and the party under socialism; the need to have a close relationship between daily administration and the over-all planning process so that the two would reinforce each other; the question of decentralization and local integration; the problem of motivation and incentives for management (the role of profit); financial controls; distribution of income; and statistical work.

The Chinese response was twofold. Actual operations and responsibility systems within the factories did not change, with the exception of the role of the Party Committee. Scientific management remained with the factory director being responsible for people following directions and fulfilling their assigned tasks.[91] The Party Committee now became the chief locus of power in the factory, responsible for two important activities. One was making all decisions that integrated the individual enterprise into the priorities of the national plan. The other was political leadership in the factory.[92]

On 18 November 1957 the second part of China's response appeared simultaneously in all the major newspapers of the country. It was a summary of a program to decentralize the planning machinery of the national economy, called the "State Council's Regulations concerning the Improvement of the Industrial Management System."[93]

The regulations set forth were to achieve two goals. The first was to decentralize planning by enlarging the powers of local governmental authority. Other than the large-scale enterprises for metals, chemicals, coal, power, oil, and precision machine-tools, all factories would be administered by suitable local government authority at the province level and below. Local government industrial bureaus responsible to the local people's committees would plan, allocate materials, and manage personnel. They would work closely with factory Party Committees and those at the administrative level. Local factory management was to be allowed more say in planning output and more power to determine and report on cost reductions, material, labor, and productivity quotas, and to experiment with new product lines and technical innovations. This was to increase local influence on the goals subsequently received from the state.

Goals consisted of four mandatory (chih-ming-hsing-ti) ones which could not be changed (except upwards) without permission of the State Council and eight which were not mandatory and could be changed by the factory without central permission.

The four mandatory goals set by the State Council were the quantity of main products, the total number of employees including staff and workers, the total wage bill, and profits. These mandatory goals, within limits, could be revised annually. Thus, by influencing the variables, especially consumption of raw materials and other inputs, enterprise managers could have significant impact on the goals for the following year. Decentralization in planning was designed to build in flexibility and adaptability, but it did not solve the problem of incentive for quality control, technical innovation, risk taking, and productivity increases for factories,[94] which was soon to become a major economic and political issue.

At the time of the decentralization order one-man management had been officially dead for over a year. The system of "factory manager responsibility under the leadership of the Party Committee" had attempted to put the party in charge of important questions of policy and coordination at the enterprise level in a way which would combine efficient production and technical decision-making with important political goals. These included active participation of workers in management and the elimination of the bureaucratic arrogance of technicians, engineers, and higher administrative personnel. Decentralization came at a time when the party had been made responsible for both the politics and policy of the enterprise. The factory manager at the head of factory responsibility system was to carry out the production goals or policy set by the Party Committee. The Party Committee was also responsible for proper revolutionary political relationships of all kinds in the enterprise. It was also responsible for economic and technical information necessary to the making of policy and for the factory manager's meeting of those policy goals in the course of daily operations.

Problems with Collective Leadership and Party Management

In the months before the Great Leap Forward the management system of "factory manager responsibility under the leadership of the Party Committee" led to much confusion about the crucial relationship between politics, policy, and operations. The operational system of one-man management was to be left intact by substituting collective decision-making for one-man management at the three levels of enterprise administration. Even in factories which did not have one-man management but had maintained systems of collective leadership, strict responsibility systems based on leadership by specialists in charge were advocated.[95] Although there was more collective discussion about operational problems and targets, the locus of authority for production operations remained, for the most part, unchanged. So, too, did the control and incentive systems backing up that authority.[96] This situation caused serious problems.

There was the difficulty of delineating decisions of a technical or operational nature, which were to remain the province of the factory managers and their staffs, and important matters of policy. In actual practice, the two often merged. Guidelines for general application could not be established since what was and what was not important varied from time to time and place to place. The Liaoning Provincial Party Committee held a work conference on this particular problem and posed the following answer:

> After all, which problems can be considered as important ones which require discussion by the Party Committee? Here, the meeting was of the opinion that as of now, there could not yet be a concrete set of rules. This is because our experience is not sufficient, and at the same time because conditions vary in different mines and factories and are constantly changing there are some questions that in one factory might be

considered important, and in another factory are not so definitely important. There are some questions that are not generally important, but may be so under special circumstances. Thus it is necessary to solve this correctly by considering the concrete circumstances at the given time. Generally, questions which involve enterprise production planning, economic and technical measures of central importance for carrying out state plans, questions of welfare for the broad masses of workers, important instructions and policy directives from higher levels, work arrangements over time, cadre policy (and cadre personnel problems) all should be discussed by the Party Committee.[97]

The party's involvement with important matters was no guarantee of revolutionary political leadership. In fact, some people failed to note any difference in factory management under the new system, except that a single manager and his staff of assistants was now replaced by the Party Committee and section chiefs had an increased role. An article in the *Jen-min Jih-pao* described the situation quite vividly.[98]

It began by saying that "as of now (January 1957) there is no one who does not agree in carrying out the system of factory manager responsibility under the leadership of the Party Committees in enterprises." The article said, however, that some people complained that party leadership didn't amount to much. Since not all party members had technical or professional knowledge, many party people had nothing to say when problems arose, and those that did said it in their capacity as managers and technicians. Therefore, the Party Committee's leadership was nothing new. While *JMJP* admitted the truth of this view, the only solution that it afforded was a comparison of the party to a critical theatrical audience, who watched the performance and then commented and judged its value. How to relate the human relationships postulated by politics to the process of industrial production and planning was still a long way from clarification.

To partially avoid the total irrelevance of politics to industrialization, large numbers of engineers, technicians, and educated youth were recruited into the party in 1956.[99] This by itself, however, could not solve the political problem. If well trained technicians—especially those who had worked in industrial enterprises prior to 1949 or who had been trained abroad—lacked the correct political attitudes,[100] cadres—who were either former workers[101] or who had been trained in China since 1949—did not always have the correct political attitudes either.[102] Some who were politically correct were technically lacking.[103] Organizational pressures and the detailed written rules and regulations of the responsibility systems, which outlined the work of every individual's position,[104] combined with the very human fear of appearing ignorant made many leaders more authoritarian just at the time they were supposed to be open to discussion and collective decision-making.

Power in Chinese factories in theory moved from the single factory manager to a horizontally coordinated system which, still dependent on expert decision-makers, remained authoritarian and centralized. The work teams held the same relative position in the decision-making hierarchy as before, and their performance was judged and rewarded on the basis of norms and quotas calculated by the experts in the functional departments of the plant. Basic level party leaders, unable to assert the primacy of revolutionary politics, found themselves trapped by this or had nothing to do. Party cadres at the work shop level or higher who had nothing to do were resented by workers as inspectors, while the daily routine of others was nearly identical to that of the plant managers, engineers, technicians, and administrative personnel.[105] Factory manager responsibility under the leadership of the Party Committee insured the supremacy of the party, but it was supremacy over a complex and sometimes confusing bureaucratic organization. In some places, this system differed from one-man management in name only.[106]

Factory Management on the Eve of the Great Leap Forward

The degree to which the system of one-man management was retained and the amount of confusion caused when collective party leadership was grafted onto it no doubt varied according to geographic region, industry, enterprise size, and local history. But even in those areas where the one-man system had not had great influence, the real meaning of collective party leadership was ambiguous because the meaning of politics was ambiguous. Bureaucratization and inequality had increased with the wage reforms of the mid-1950s and there remained a strong influence of the bourgeois technical and administrative personnel in almost all major enterprises.[107] In spite of local variations, however, some generalizations about industrial management on the eve of the Great Leap Forward can be made.

Chinese factories were generally organized similarly to the Soviet concept of production-territoriality with a complex administrative bureaucracy. Strict rules and regulations outlined in exhaustive detail the duties and responsibilities of all personnel. Though these regulations could not easily be changed, the degree to which they were followed varied. For example, regulations in force in the Chi Hsi Mining Bureau in October 1957 detailed the specific duties of the director-engineer of each coal pit (k'ang).[108] Four extensive written sections, containing thirty-two separate articles placed the pit director-engineer in a chain of command; nine articles outlined the scope of his responsibilities; and eleven more, the limits of his powers.

A 1957 study of a large-scale machine tool factory said it was typical of factory organization at this time.[109] The enterprise had twenty-four staff sections (functional departments involved with control, administration, and planning) and nine production workshops, with staff office personnel exercising control over production down to the work team level. The factory manager theoretically was responsible for production operations, but these in fact were the responsibility of a deputy manager for production technology who was also the chief engineer. The nine production work shops were under a production department head in the chief engineer's office who was assisted by a deputy chief engineer who in turn handled the technical details of production. The chief engineer was directly concerned with general operational problems. There were two other deputy plant managers, one for personnel and one for economic calculation and management. This complex structure was duplicated in medium- and small-scale machine tool plants with fewer staff sections according to circumstances.

It was this type of organization, with an enormous control and administrative structure exercising power over but not actually involved in production, that the Party Committee took over. The party replaced the factory manager and increased the lateral coordination between production leaders and staff leaders at the work shop level, but little else changed.[110] If one of the goals of politics was to reduce the gap between mental and manual labor, between workers and managers, it was clear that something else would have to be done.

The organizational structure and division of labor and responsibility which emphasized the functional gap between workers and managers was reinforced by the whole system of incentives. Worker participation in management was, in this organizational context, limited to workers' representative congresses (Kung-jen tai-piao ta-hui). These congresses were usually convened at the work shop level (which in a large factory could comprise hundreds of workers) and chaired by the trade-union secretary. Workers could listen to the reports of management officials, discuss them, and make suggestions. In theory, there was a broad scope of discussion which included everything from production plans, finance, technical development, and cadre behavior to welfare, medical benefits, and bonuses.[111] It can be assumed, however, that discussion centered mostly on matters of welfare and bonuses. Even then, the congresses had little real authority, and many trade-union cadres were quite unhappy with the power of the administrative cadres.[112]

Workers with special grievances could by-pass the congress and go to the manager who, at least in one case, held routine workers' reception meetings.[113] At these meetings, a form had to be filled out which became part of management's file for possible remedial action.[114] Often supervisory production workers and personnel attended the same meeting, but afterwards each person returned to his own activity.[115]

If workers' congresses did little to break down the administration-production dichotomy, the wage and bonus system did even less. On the eve of the Great Leap Forward factories depended on piece-wages or bonuses for worker incentives, and bonuses plus cash rewards for managerial staff and technical innovators. The result was increased inequality between workers and managers (party and non-party) and greater income stratification among workers. Although cadre gradings and the ranking system did not increase inequality, they did legitimate it.[116]

The new system of factory management did not end the conflict that often occurred between the Party Committee secretary and the factory manager under the old one-man management system. Conflicts still arose between these two due to confusion between policy (important matters) and operations (routine matters). Moreover, the strict division of production leaders and administrators in functional departments continued, often making realistic planning, which had to be based on accurate information and efficient communications, very difficult. This problem was exacerbated by traditional values and attitudes toward manual work.

The November 1957 decentralization of macro-management involved the party more in the work of planning, thus bringing to a focus the relationship between politics and economics. Decentralization was designed to increase flexibility and efficiency in economic planning and administration above the enterprise level, but it made the problem of coordination much more difficult and put the question of incentives in an even more central place than under the old centralized planning system. By giving the individual enterprise more room for maneuvering and fewer mandatory targets, decentralization allowed managers greater, legitimate ways to underestimate production capabilities while overstating supply and material requirements. With no other alternatives the pursuit of bonuses by management was the biggest incentive they had. In fact, the more a manager wanted bonuses, the smarter he became in order to get lower targets and more material. Decentralization in the context of one-man management authority and incentives increased the possibility that the gap between workers and management, which included many members of the Communist Party, would widen.

The dilemma on the eve of the Great Leap Forward was as follows: If a member of the Party Committee, which was now charged with over-all leadership of the enterprise, was not also an expert he found it difficult to become an integral part of the decision-making process; if he insisted on this prerogative, his presence became a hindrance to production. If he was an expert he became part of an internal and external decision-making process which made the political goals of the party more rhetoric than reality. In the first case there were inefficiencies

—technical and economic miscalculation and very poor coordination and communication. In the second case the result was the irrelevance of politics in spite of leadership by the party organization. This was the essence of what the Chinese began to call the "red and expert" problem. Moreover, any change in the way factories were managed and people within them motivated would have an impact on the newly decentralized, more flexible planning process. The Great Leap Forward was an attempt to deal with the political and economic problems posed by decentralization and the system of management which had tried to combine the responsibility and incentive systems of one-man management with the collective political leadership of the Communist Party. It was meant to unite politics and production, revolution and modernization with something far more radical than collective party leadership within enterprises run on the principles of one-man management.

4/Revolution and Modernization During the Great Leap Forward: "Politics in Command"

THE GREAT LEAP FORWARD, a truly awesome event, lasted for two years and ended by shaping China's modernization and the intensity of its political conflict irrevocably. Strategically, it was a grand-design in response to the economic and political problems that had surfaced during the turbulent years of reconstruction and the first Five-Year-Plan.

The main economic problem was agriculture. The rapid growth of industry during the FFYP period had not been matched by agriculture and, by 1957, agricultural insufficiency was an obstacle to further industrialization and economic expansion.[1]

In addition, within the industrial sector there were serious problems involving planning, coordination, and incentives for managerial and worker efficiency. In spite of industrial growth, planning and management were oftentimes extremely crude and cumbersome, wasteful and inefficient, which threatened further development.

The Great Leap Forward, an attempt to deal with these economic problems, can best be summed up by the Chinese slogan, Walk on Two Legs. Industry was to develop along with but separate from agriculture. Agricultural development was to rely on crude, locally generated technology and capital and collectivization in the new peoples communes. These units would develop irrigation, transportation, and manufacturing projects to serve agriculture. Thus, modern, large-scale, urban-centered industry could continue to receive the lion's share of scarce capital, technical knowledge, and equipment without these being siphoned off by the agricultural sector. Local industry would be developed alongside modern industry, light industry alongside heavy industry, and agriculture alongside industry in general. All human resources were to be mobilized for the development of all available raw materials. Skilled and unskilled labor would be utilized, women as well as men. Local authorities were to be given flexibility to make decisions regarding labor and resources as long as national plans were fulfilled. The Great Leap Forward, envisioned as a means of speeding up China's modernization, was to remove the constraints, both human and technical, of the carefully controlled industrialization of the previous years. Speed, however, was not its only purpose. It was an attempt to correct a serious and potentially disastrous imbalance in the economy.

As important as economic issues were during the Great Leap Forward, politics shaped the definition of these problems.

For one thing, the Chinese wished to maintain maximum independence and freedom in international relations. Given the economic issues of 1957, they might have adopted a different strategy. They could have continued the urban-centered, heavy industry focus of the FFYP and imported the food needed for a rapidly growing urban population. They could have imported consumer goods and agricultural technology in order to continue concentrating development on heavy industry. This, however, would have necessitated large-scale borrowing and credit in international financial markets, with concomitant long and short term debt. Since China had neither the export capacity nor foreign exchange reserves necessary to pay for a major increase of imports, to follow the development strategy of the FFYP would endanger China's international political independence.[2]

To have done so would have also benefitted the urban areas while leaving the poor rural areas largely untouched. Given the rural base of the revolution and the peasant support of the Communist Party, this would have been politically unwise, perhaps dangerous. It would have aggravated the existing urban-rural split, threatening further urban development with a swelling city population. Also affected would be that part of the revolutionary vision which had promised to eliminate the differences between urban and rural development and to do away with poverty and unemployment. Changes in rural Chinese society and the redistribution of rural wealth that had occurred since 1949 had eliminated the few rural rich (landlords and rich peasants) who might have been able to pay for the necessary agricultural technology to increase food supplies. Therefore, it was essential that China's international economic position not become dependent on imported and expensive capital and technology.

The political aspects of the Great Leap Forward involved more than rural China and national independence. A growing urban-based bureaucracy was becoming a drain on scarce resources while at the same time it was a threat to other revolutionary goals of socialism. Mao understood the dangers of bureaucratization. He had observed the upheavals in Eastern Europe in the wake of Khrushchev's secret speech to the Twentieth Congress of the Soviet Communist Party (in 1956, which officially began the de-Stalinization of the USSR and her allies).[3] Such bureaucratization was, moreover, a noticeable part of industrial development in China thus far. The educational system, also modeled on the Soviet pattern, was integrally related to this distribution of power within the industrial system, formally training engineers and technicians brought up to see themselves as an elite of the future.

And so, the Great Leap Forward proposed to deal with both economic problems that threatened China's modernization and political problems that threatened its independence and the goals of the revolution. It was a series of unprecedented experiments rather than well-thought-out, logically interrelated set of radical moves. Nowhere is this more evident than in China's factories.

The Great Leap Forward began slowly everywhere. However, it quickly gained an incredible momentum and reached its zenith by early 1959. It began to taper off after the meeting of the Communist Party Central Committee at Lushan in July 1959, but did not officially end then, continuing until the end of 1960, perhaps even beyond that.

The origins of the GLF in industry go back to the grass-roots criticism of the one-man management system in the early 1950's, when cadres at Anshan and other places urged the mass mobilization of workers and wanted to fight bureaucratic officiousness even while scientific management was being urged as official policy.[4] But a more direct cause was probably the "Hundred Flowers" campaign of 1956–1957.

This campaign involved everyone but its focus was on intellectuals. It was designed by the Communist Party leadership to release some of the tensions that had built up in Chinese society as a result of the rapid and tumultuous changes of the previous years. Mao said, "pus will always come out of a boil," and once the boil was lanced the pus did indeed flow. Not only did the Hundred Flowers campaign reveal pro-socialist or revolutionary antagonism to bureaucratic inertia, officiousness, and arbitrary behavior within the Communist Party and other institutions, it also revealed antisocialist and anti-Communist sympathies. While Mao obviously expected and was anxious to bring out the former, he was clearly not very pleased by the latter. The Hundred Flowers campaign turned into a major rectification campaign to combat bureaucracy within the Communist Party and to combat antisocialist attitudes and practices within the ranks of intellectuals in general.

The rectification campaign triggered the first steps toward concrete change in the hundreds of thousands of industrial enterprises. What set this in motion was a May 1957 directive from the Central Committee of the Communist Party which stressed the need for all administrative, managerial, and technical cadres to participate in manual labor.[5]

The call for participation in manual labor was not an arbitrary political whim. It had resulted from a serious dedication to antibureaucratic organization and from a theoretical analysis of bureaucracy that had been underway for some time and which became public in the mass media early in 1958.[6]

There were three problems. First was the division of labor into brain labor and brawn labor leading to a separation between workers and administrators. If not checked, this would lead to economic and status conflicts not much different from class conflict under capitalism. Since it was necessary to depend on a group of appropriately professionalized cadres, the best way to combat this was to have cadres participate in manual labor.

However, this led to the second problem. Because of attitudes from the old society, shaped by a traditional view of the world and of human worth, cadres were not always willing to labor. They looked down on manual labor and showed marked impatience with and arrogance toward workers' suggestions and questions.

Thirdly, it was difficult to overcome the tendencies toward bureaucracy if the workers themselves were unable to supervise cadres, because of a lack of knowledge or confidence, or both. A "low cultural level" of the workers intensified the problems caused by the division of labor and the old attitudes of administrative and technical personnel. Therefore, the way to combat bureaucracy was to have cadres participate in labor and allow workers to supervise or criticize the activities of the cadres through workers' congresses or wall newspapers, called *ta tzu-pao*. The division of labor and responsibility itself was not to be tampered with.

The Great Leap System in Embryo: May 1957 to April 1958

Even as this early analysis of bureaucracy was being publicized, events in factories throughout the country were moving fairly rapidly. Especially in Shanghai—and other areas where one-man management had to compete with the collective and more participatory traditions of the East China system—there was strong feeling that the fight against bureaucracy would have to go beyond formal representational workers' congresses.[7] Although an attempt was made to take workers' decisions more seriously,[8] and the powerful trade-union apparatus pushed hard for continuing these congresses as the main form of workers' participation in management,[9] the fight against bureaucracy became bolder and more imaginative.

In late 1957 a widespread movement began to focus on the middle-level managers of different factories. In planning sections, finance offices, wage offices, and inspection departments, people were sent down (hsia-fang) to production work shops where they became technical leaders, and the middle-level departments and offices were reorganized, reduced in size, or eliminated. The purpose was to force cadre participation in labor by reducing the amount of control and coordination exercised by middle-level management.

In one huge iron and steel plant, the Shihchingshan Iron and Steel Factory, about one-third of the departments and offices at the middle-levels of management were eliminated and the number of purely administrative workers reportedly was reduced by about one-half. Such drastic change was not unique.[10]

In the early part of the GLF the heavy industrial centers of the Northeast seemed to lag behind the rapid reforms in Shanghai and the Eastern coastal cities. In cities like Shenyang and Harbin many factories were holding their first workers' congresses as late as 1957. The rapid expansion of heavy industry in the Northeast during the first Five-Year-Plan and the relatively greater technological sophistication of that heavy industry made the question of technical education for workers a more immediate one than in areas where there was less shortage of skilled labor.[11] The importance of managerial and technical personnel from the old regime sharpened the militancy of workers outside the Northeast.[12] In the Northeast, in factories where one-man management was strong the labor directive did not always lead to more worker participation in management. In a rubber plant in Ch'angchün, middle-level managers sent to participate in labor took over the functions of the production leaders and the lower level staff bureaucrats in the work shops and reported directly to the factory manager and his assistants. The end result was more centralization and more confusion.[13]

By early 1958 change and ferment were at work in factories all over China. In February a directive of the Communist Party attempted to summarize and rationalize these changes and quicken the pace of innovation, to parallel changes taking place in agriculture with the creation of people's communes. The newest way to fight bureaucratization was called "planting experimental fields in industry."[14]

The Central Mining Machinery Plant of the Foushin Coal Mines was chosen as the model for planting experimental fields,[15] but other examples were reported in the press to suggest that the method was widespread.[16]

The Foushin plant was to solve technical bottlenecks in production and to promote cadre participation in labor. At first only factory level managers labored manually, but soon leading cadres from all the functional departments were. Participation in labor went from simple cleaning tasks to participation in technical and skilled production activities. This second type of participation quieted workers' fears that cadres participating in labor were nothing more than inspectors checking work.

But certain crucial problems remained. By itself, participation did not lead to better and more egalitarian relationships between workers and managers. Cadres had to change subtle aspects of their behavior and less subtle aspects of dress so that they would appear willing, both literally and figuratively, to get their hands dirty. Cadres had to learn to perform production activities; those from higher levels had to be sensitive to the feelings of basic level leaders. Finally, cadres had to begin to take part in the social activities of the people in the work teams to be accepted as equals and treated with confidence.

Planting experimental fields was part of "laboring with the shifts,"[17] another name given to cadre participation in labor in industry. As time went by, it became clear that the implications of this system were more far reaching than had been indicated at the beginning of 1958. As early as April 1958, important lessons were being learned that went beyond the experience of the Foushin model. It seemed that once the authority and daily routines of managers had been upset by cadre participation in labor, changes in both the organizational structure of the enterprise and in the content and definition of individual jobs were necessary. A report on the Shanghai #4 Cigarette Plant expressed this problem succinctly.

> In this factory, the factory manager and the secretary of the Party Committee personally led important cadres in the factory down to the work shops to plant "experimental plots" and the workers welcomed this while production improved also. *But because the whole management organizational structure and the content of work had not changed after the cadres went down, it was not three days before a meeting was called at the upper levels, and in each department there was a huge pile of reports with no one around to handle this.* Many cadres felt that if this "going down" were done over a protracted time, then the "experimental field" would not be planted well, and the work of the departments would not be done well, and laboring with the shifts could in no way be maintained. [Italics added.][18]

If cadre participation in labor was to mean change in the factory organization and responsibility systems, it would require change in the incentive systems used to motivate workers also. As long as incentives were the promise of bonuses or piece work premiums based on the quotas and targets calculated by cadres from the control departments of the factory, then the presence of these cadres participating in labor could be construed as a further means of control and discipline over workers' routines and rewards.[19]

The active and passive resistance of the cadres themselves had to be overcome. Cadres argued that the elimination or weakening of functional departments was not a suitable way to handle complex industrial organization and technology; that participation in labor, though a good way to be politically acceptable, would hinder cadres at the top from having an overview. It was not possible to be both red and expert. Sometimes those opposed to participating in labor slacked off, making the nontechnician, nonqualified party activists more responsible for technical innovations and reforms and thus making failure in these important efforts more likely.[20]

In spite of problems with the experiments, new models were constantly publicized. There was a momentous groundswell of experimentation and innovation at the grass roots level in mid-1958. At the Harbin #1 Machinery Plant finance and statistics, quota planning, labor allocation, technical control, and quality control were all made the responsibility of the production units. In other plants, the party rather than the factory manager and the functional departments became the chief administrative coordinator. Management emphasized face-to-face communication and on-the-spot investigation rather than use of telephones and messengers.[21] In one locomotive plant, this was called the floating office system.[22]

While organizational changes and experiments were being publicized, training and jobs were being transformed also, affecting educational institutions and philosophy. A huge effort to upgrade the technical skills and administrative capacities of workers and cadres was begun in 1957 and accelerated in March and April 1958.[23] Production leaders in work teams and work shops were given technical courses through on-the-job training or intensive education in secondary schools.[24] The stated purpose was to break down the division of labor and to facilitate the transfer of authority to production units.

Although problems existed elsewhere, the heavy industrial plants of the Northeast, where both technical and political factors were most resistant to change, typified the problem.[25] A Northeast model was therefore chosen to exemplify how to revolutionize industrial enterprises —the heart of the modernization of the country.

The Management System of the Great Leap Forward, Codified and Put into Practice as National Policy

On 26 April 1958 *Jen-min Jih-pao* reported that Wang Hao-feng, a Party Committee secretary of the Heilungkiang Provincial Party Committee, had made a speech to a meeting of industrial cadres in the province. Wang had mentioned five units being used as examples of the new management system. These five were representative of fairly complex, modern, heavy industry in machinery, metallurgy, construction, and heavy transport.

He began by stressing both the preliminary and the experimental nature of this experience. He noted that the new system, while not contradicting the idea of worker's congresses or worker's councils, went significantly beyond them; he linked the new system to the revolutionary goal of eliminating the difference between mental and manual work and between administration and production. But one had to be careful,

> Because the significance of this experience is very great, it is necessary to have sufficient knowledge. We are willing to state that in terms of over-all direction (fang-hsiang) this experience is entirely correct, but, because time has been short, it has not matured or been perfected in terms of concrete methods, and there are many problems which must be further studied and solved in practice.

The key to the emerging Great Leap Forward system was that small production groups would have additional administrative tasks, thereby lessening the importance of administrative departments and, by extension, that of purely administrative bureaucrats. Wang said,

> What is the nature of the small group? Is it a party, youth league, or trade-union group? None of these. It is rather more suitable to call it a production-management group of a mass nature. It is a kind of administrative organ. Its relations with party, union, and league should be resolved on these terms. Thus, it cannot substitute for party, union or league organization.

Three additional questions about small-group management were raised by Wang. One concerned the relationship of the size of the groups to the number of workers in the work shop teams,

> The matter of delimiting the scope of the small group should be solved in accordance with the special needs of production and what is of benefit to the workers. That is to say, whether the group is large or small in scope must be determined with what will benefit production and, at the same time, must be carried out while workers are on the job, but during time when they are not engaged in their skill. Thus each person's tasks must not be too heavy, and there must not be too many organizational levels in the organs of direct worker-management. I think that just one level of small production group is sufficient.

Another concerned the leadership of the group,

> On the question of the group leader, he should be chosen by the masses and confirmed by higher level.

The third was the question of internal responsibility.

> Division of labor within the group should be done according to individual specialties and expertise, under the principle of voluntarism. Everyone should have a job to do, no one should have too much to do, and not too much time should be taken with management tasks so that time is left for spare-time study and party activities.[26]

A closer look at how this system developed and operated was available through reports on the Chinghua Machine Tools Plant which became the model officially approved by the Communist Party Central Committee.[27] The changes in this plant occurred over a year and were impressive. The impetus for the reforms came from work shop production leaders after the May 1957 directive on cadre participation in labor. Labor participation for cadres at first was clean-up duty and grounds-keeping and was separated from "the command of the production system."[28] As cadre labor participation became more closely associated with production, a decentralization of power away from functional departments was required along with an increase in the administrative and managerial responsibilities of production units. The Party Committee in the Chinghua Machine Tools Plant decided to put almost all of the administrative and control work of the production teams directly under team management and in so doing they did indeed go beyond the old system of workers' congresses. Formerly, workers took an indirect part in factory management and results were difficult to evaluate. Now the team members managed team activities. They took attendance, recorded consumption of materials, scheduled and planned daily tasks, scheduled maintenance and check-ups, and did quality testing. Team heads were elected by workers and confirmed or officially appointed by management. (Management was defined as department heads, technical personnel, heads of party departments, and cadres above these levels.)[29] The result was a reduction of administrative and technical staff by almost 75 percent and elimination or simplification of over 50 percent of the number of forms used.[30] With paper work reduced, participation in production by management was more effective.

A more or less regularized system of cadre participation in labor developed. Cadres who were former workers and who had various skills were assigned to substitute for vacationing or absent workers or were given fixed production posts. Cadres of intellectual origin (presumably university graduates with no production experience) were assigned to fixed posts to be trained in an industrial skill. Technical cadres were to participate in labor where technical problems would be likely to occur.[31] Cadres in mid-level departments at the work shop level and work shop level union, league, party, or production chiefs were supposed to labor half a day every day. Leading cadres at the plant level were to labor one day per week. The system of management developed by the Chinghua Machine Tools Factory was called the "Two Participations and One Reform" System (Participation of Cadres in Labor, or Workers in Management, and Reform of Rules and Regulations that inhibited this.)[32]

In the weeks following the publicity given to the Chinghua Tools Factory, provincial and municipal level Party Committees attempted to adopt the Chinghua experience in their own localities. Reports from Nanking,[33] Canton, and Kwantung Province,[34] Wuhan and Hopei

Province,[35] and other areas[36] indicated a concerted effort to implement this management system rapidly.

By June, however, it was obvious that such major changes were not to occur without considerable opposition. An editorial in a Peking newspaper described things as follows:

> Direct worker participation in management is a new thing in enterprise management, and thus has a strong life and an unlimited future development. But precisely because it is a new thing, its significance and function have not been agreed upon by everybody, and there are rather big obstacles to pushing it forward. Today there are some management personnel, and even some leading cadres in enterprises who, when faced with a new thing, bring up all kinds of doubts.[37]

Nor were management personnel and leading cadres the only ones doubtful or hesitant. Some workers were unenthusiastic, either because of increased responsibilities or because cadre behavior intimidated them.[38]

Cadre hesitancy, however, seemed to be the major obstacle. The chief argument was bluntly stated: that the mass line style of management—which went back to the Yenan experience involving egalitarian human relationships, a flexible division of labor and responsibility, and enthusiasm generated by a cooperative and participatory spirit—was incompatible with the management of complex, modern industry, even though it might have been useful for peasant mobilization.[39] There were those in favor of one-man management and opposed to what they termed, with obvious distaste, the rural work style and the guerrilla habit of the mass line.

> Some cadres have failed to shake off the ideological effects of the remnants of bourgeois authoritarianism; in leadership work they still cling to some old procedures, obsessed with the thought of official grades, regulations and decrees, which, from their point of view, constitute the essential elements of regular leadership.[40]

The choice, however, was not, as opponents of the new system argued, between the order and regularity of one side and the chaos of the other. Rather, it was between two different types of order, what Li Hsüeh-feng had called "two fundamentally different methods of management," with different answers to three basic questions.

Would experts be dedicated to the egalitarian goals of the revolution including the elimination of classes or would they use their expertise to build reputation, power, and privilege? Would workers be trusted to make decisions or would specialized personnel make decisions for workers? Would mass production campaigns mobilize mass enthusiasm or would action be arbitrarily limited by rules and institutions alone?[41]

Do we need a fixed order? Of course we do. Is regulation good? Of course it is very good. Not being anarchists, we have never objected to order and never objected to regularization. The concepts of order, regularity, etc., have always borne a class brand. . . . Those objecting to "rural work style" and "guerrilla habit" condemn our comrades as "irregular" for launching mass movements. What are order and regularity in their eyes? They merely picture a leadership cadre sitting proudly in an armchair in his office, one hand holding a telephone and another wielding a pen to sign out orders. "He is tensely and systematically directing production." This merely means that "a superior just talks, leaving his subordinates to work," a "leadership cadre just talks, leaving the masses to work." Such order and regularity are nothing else but those bourgeois ideas with which we should break away in a thorough manner. . . . We don't want such order and regularity.

Insofar as Marxism-Leninism are concerned, the order and regularity needed for construction are nothing but the mass movement; i.e., the leader leaving his office to weld himself with the masses into one single piece, to consult with the masses on every issue and solve problems on the spot.

Whether we should regard the grade system, the dedication to regulation, etc., remnants of bourgeois authoritarianism—as the normal order or regard the "rural work style," the "guerrilla habit" and the mass movement as the normal order *poses two roads* of struggle in the sphere of leadership work. The normal order, cherishing the remnant or bourgeois authoritarianism with its multilayered structure and maze of systems, while admitting a "definite division of labor and an excellent order" unfortunately tends to fetter the activism of the masses in a most callous manner and inevitably smacks of bureaucratism to the detriment of the development of production. [Italics added.][42]

Planning and Economic Coordination
Above the Factory Level

As the system of management underwent rapid, drastic change, the entire planning and coordinative mechanism inevitably was effected. The central dilemma was that quotas and targets calculated by the mid-level departments, which served as crucial inputs into central planning, as instruments of control, and as the basis for incentives within the plants, were now all but obliterated. The changes in factory management during the early GLF facilitated the end of highly centralized planning, begun with the November 1957 decentralization order of the State Council. And while immediately afterward it was possible to continue planning based on previously generated quotas and targets, by the middle of 1958 this was no longer so. The offices and departments responsible for submitting the data upon which the quotas were based and for meeting these quotas no longer functioned as before. The decentralization order combined with the new factory management system made a new kind of economic planning absolutely essential if economic chaos was not to result.

Two things were needed. More extensive local or horizontal communication to supplement what remained of the still vitally important centrally-determined responsibilities of individual enterprises; and secondly, face-to-face communications and mutual cooperation to supplement the sharp decrease in data and statistics that formerly served to cement relationships and define responsibilities, and which had flowed out of and into the factory's control and planning apparatus. In both cases it was the Communist Party—with its extensive local organizational ties, its central or vertical integration, and its politically correct attitudes—that fit the requirements of the new system of planning. There were more local meetings of cadres from various factories; and the party took a greater role in settling disputes and contract suits. Municipal and provincial level Party Committees had to be directly concerned with economic realities and relationships within their jurisdictions.[43]

The involvement of the party at all levels became vitally important over the next few years. The evaluation of the new system became not simply a matter of theoretical relevance to the guardians of an abstract ideology but a question of immediate consequence to people occupying different roles at many organizational levels, having many different perspectives on practical problems. This potential split in the party, however, did not become apparent until after the Great Leap Forward had run its course and, in the process, had generated other fissures which added to the complexities of political conflict.

The Two Participations and One Reform System in Practice

During the last six months of 1958, factories all over China began to implement the two participations and one reform system that had been codified in May 1958. There is no accurate way to gauge the extent of this movement except to note that it was significant. Textile mills, steel mills, light and heavy machine and machine-tool plants, electric generating plants, and factories producing heavy transport equipment—all were involved, as were other types of factories.

Table 1 is a survey of the different types of factories that were reported in the Chinese press as having implemented the new system which gave workers more direct control over their daily activities as well as over longer range issues.

Table 1 Types of Management Power Decentralized to Production Units Within Chinese Factories April–November 1958

*Factory/Function	Insp.	Discp.	Safety, Hygne.	Repair, Maint.	Wages, Incntiv.	Tools	Matl.	Tech.	Pers.	Stat. Fin.	Welfare	Plng.
1. Chenkuang Machine Tool	x	x				x	x		x			
2. Ch'angchiang Electric	x	x	x					x	x			
3. Kwanghua Lumber	x		x	x		x	x					
4. Chungking Const. Mach.					x	x	x					x
5. Liu Li Ho Cement					x		x					x
6. Shenyang Hyd. Pump	x							x				
7. Lanchou Machinery			x			x		x		x		
8. Nanking #1 Mach.		x			x			x	x	x		
9. Amoy Glass						x	x	x	x			x
10. Nanking Electron Tube	x											
11. Chungking Hsinhua Prntg.		x							x			
12. Hsinhsiang Dyeing	x	x			x			x	x			x
13. Hunghsing Textile		x				x		x	x			

14. Chinhua Vehicle

15. Amoy Rubber Goods

16. Fukien Machine Tool

17. Nanking Tel & Tel

18. Chengfeng Textile, Sian

19. Peking Amal. Textile

20. Luta (Dairen) Mach. Tool

21. Shenyang Sungling Mach.

22. Harbin Pump

23. Harbin Rolling Stock

24. Huapei Radio

* Note following sources for factories corresponding to numbers:

1. NKJP, 5/12/58
2. Szechwan JP, 1958 n.d.
3. Peking, JP, 6/9/58
4. Szechwan JP, 6/3/58
5. JMJP, 12/4/59
6. JMJP, 5/9/58
7. Kansu JP, 6/6/58
8. NFJP, 5/7/58
9. Amoy Daily, 5/8/58
10. NKJP, 5/7/58
11. Chungking JP, 6/9/58
12. Hsia hsien JP, 5/30/58
13. Ch'angchiang JP, 4/4/58
14. TKP, 6/20/58
15. Amoy JP, 6/12/58
16. Fuchou JP, 5/24/58
17. NKJP, 5/18/58
18. Sian JP, 11/11/58
19. KJJP, 6/15/58
20. LTJP, 8/13/58
21. JMJP, 5/15/58
22. Peking JP, 5/8/58
23. KJJP, 5/8/58
24. Peking JP, 5/24/58

The degree and form of decentralization seemed to vary widely. The one common thread that runs through all descriptions was the rapid and progressive weakening of functional departments and a concomitant increase in the autonomy of production groups. Financial management was taken away from factory financial departments and given to departments more directly related to production or, where possible, to the production teams themselves.[44] These arrangements often meant that the banks and government departments which formerly had dealt directly with factory financial departments found it difficult to gain access to information for planning. Thus the task of economic control and co-ordination fell to the party at all levels. Many finance department cadres were abruptly sent down to production teams to help strengthen the teams' ability to record input and output and calculate costs.[45]

Other management functions were similarly rearranged, and cadres were sent to work in production teams or small groups. Planning of daily production schedules and operations was now done by the work teams as was tool management, daily job assignment, and discipline.[46] The production teams became more complex. Worker-managers were elected by the teams for separate tasks and confirmed by the Party Committees at the factory level.[47]

Even as this unprecedented experiment in worker control and participation in management swept over the nation, old problems persisted and new ones developed. In some factories, such as the Chen Kuang Machine Tool Plant in Nanking, the new work team managers bore a striking resemblance to the old gang bosses, and possibly could have been the same people. If they were not, conflict could result from the new leaders' attempts to establish themselevs with work-team members.[48]

The new management system also brought newly elected worker-managers into conflict with the old trade-union cadres, resulting in personal animosity. It was sometimes necessary to make basic level organization more complicated, by duplicating titles and positions to prevent the conflict from getting out of hand.[49]

Sometimes functional departments within a given plant were affected differently. Cadres in one department might have no problem with decentralization, while those in other departments might experience criticism and rancor from workers. Personal emotions of cadres sent down to production teams made individual background, education, and personality[50] important factors in morale during this time of rapid change.

The problems were perhaps most difficult when they involved technical controls and decision making. Technical innovation always affected future production capacity, and it required time, effort, and money, which in turn affected current production as well. As technical innovation at one time or another involved almost all departments, it was a crucial matter central to the success or failure of the experiment.

Prior to the Great Leap Forward technical innovation was handled by factory level technical departments working with financial, planning, and other factory level departments. In many factories the rules and regulations covering technical innovation were encyclopedic.[51] Most of these regulations had come from government above the enterprise level and were enforced through the relevant departments. Technical management required a constant filling-out of forms—reports, orders, requisitions, receiving slips—all of which had to be approved at the appropriate level before action could be taken.

Control of technical change was, therefore, always bureaucratic and very often irrational. Elaborate procedures were required before a screw could be requisitioned and changed or a pipe altered. Salaries for technicians and administrators were a major expense as were office supplies. To save both time and money many factory-level cadres had resorted to illegal practices or hoarding.

The Great Leap Forward attacked this problem in characteristically bold fashion. A system called the triple combination made its appearance at the end of 1958. There came the realization that, as production units became more central to the control process, the expert knowledge which had previously rested with the technical departments had to be transferred to the basic level groups. One way to do this was to regularize the *hsia-fang* of technical and engineering personnel and, in some cases, to make the *hsia-fang* post permanent. In this way the politically desirable cadre participation in labor would also become administratively and technically beneficial. Cadres working at a production post were able to help workers consider technical and economic factors and articulate them in proposals for innovation. At the same time cadres gained a better grasp of production realities, which improved their judgments and plans.

This led to the development of technical mutual-aid groups for the making of technical decisions.[52] In these, experienced technical personnel would consult with skilled workers. Eventually a big auto plant in Changchün created what became model technical design groups. These consisted of workers, engineers, technicians, and administrators. This "combination of leadership with the masses, labor with technique, and technical theory with production practice"[53] by November 1958 was called the triple combination. By December what earlier had been called the two participations and one reform management system had developed into the two participations, one reform, and triple combination system (liang-ts'an yi-kai san-chieh-ho). It was known as the constitution for industry (kung-yeh hsien-fa).[54]

As throughout the Great Leap Forward, shock-waves resulting from rapid, often drastic changes effected other transformations. The triple combination was one way to improve the management capacities of production teams and work shops. It also made cadre participation in labor viable and promoted the Great Leap Forward by mobilizing all kinds of talent and expertise. But the triple combination could not alone meet the demands for increased basic level technical and administrative knowledge required by the experiments in management and the new approach to development. The educational system in the country was therefore changed radically.

Massive programs began to train a much enlarged student population of all ages. Spare-time schools varying widely in quality and size were set up. By 1960 there were over twenty million people attending spare-time courses at all levels.[55] Factories all over China began setting up spare-time schools to train workers in technical matters to facilitate worker participation in management.[56] In Shanghai, Chengchow, Taiyuan, Chungking, and Tientsin they "sprouted like mushrooms after a spring rain." By August 1958 Shanghai factories alone had set up almost 1,200 spare-time middle schools, plus 197 spare-time colleges. Some plants reported that 60 to 70 percent of workers were enrolled.[57] In Chengchow's Textile Machinery Plant a complete system of education was set up for workers and their families, including a technical research section, a "red and expert university," and primary and middle schools.[58] In Taiyuan the trend was similar. Eighty-nine of the city's state and locally run enterprises set up schools, with worker enrollment reportedly varying between 75 and 97 percent.[59] Some of these spare-time schools and other educational efforts were specifically to provide skills such as statistics and simplified accounting that workers would need as managers.[60] Others increased the number of production skills of each worker in order to release others for management tasks and rotate functions.[61] In at least one major enterprise entire work teams were given technical training so that natural leaders would emerge without jealousies or resentments arising from those who were not trained.[62]

In training engineers and technicians, the full-time regular and specialized technical colleges, universities, and high schools emphasized the role of practical experience in production and work-study.[63] These programs were also designed to train workers with long years of practical experience and to train them for management at all levels.[64]

The program of training working class people for management positions began in 1956, immediately affecting all levels.[65] Rapid increase of engineering and technical cadres from the ranks of the workers was difficult. A 1957 survey of 900 men in the Chi-Hsi Mining Bureau in Heilungkiang Province found that work shift and section leaders had an average age of thirty-two and could read and write approximately on a fourth or sixth grade level, but 30 percent were totally or semi-illiterate.[66]

Most of the students of the Great Leap Forward generation became middle-level leaders rather than top-level managers. For example, in the Chungking Construction Machinery Plant by April 1958 nearly 75 percent of all technical personnel were promoted workers and the majority of work shop directors came from that category.[67] In the Shanghai #3 Steel Plant the spare-time technical school for workers trained twenty-four assistant group leaders and five furnace superintendents in four months.[68] What had begun in 1957 gained rapid momentum during 1958. Early in 1958 Shanghai factories were training over 5,000 workers (either on the job or in spare-time schools) to be grade three or grade four technicians in other industrial centers.[69] By May it was reported that most technical personnel of working class background (or from part-time work-study programs which for all practical purposes was the same thing) were work section chiefs, work shop directors, even heads of engineering and technical departments.[70]

The improvement of the administrative and technical abilities of the basic-level production units confronted old factory and middle level department cadres with a rapid increase in basic level, technically trained cadres with different class and educational backgrounds. These Great Leap Forward cadres challenged what had previously been almost a monopoly of expertise, and they posed a threat to old bureaucratic and elitist values and behavior.

Motivating Basic Level Cadres and Factory Level Leaders: The Problem of Incentives

The two-one-three management system, in addition to its other implications, focused the problem of incentives within the factories. By causing radical change in routines, responsibilities, and ˜self-images, it raised the question whether workers and cadres would be *willing* to accept new status and leadership and carry out new responsibilities.

The incentive problem was not an abstract moral or ideological issue but was connected to the distribution of power. If workers as a group were to participate in management and have increased control of the work teams, the incentive system could not be based on material rewards alone. If these were the only rewards offered for effective performance, and if the bureaucratic control system was weakened simultaneously, there was no guarantee that the workers, managing themselves, would do so to guarantee efficiency rather than large bonus payments. Under these conditions it would be in an individual's interest to obtain a higher bonus or a greater piece-rate premium. It would be easy and logical to seek large matériel allocation and low output quotas, to cover up mistakes, pursue quantity, ignore quality, and guard techniques rather than to share knowledge.[71] The use of material rewards as incentives was not politically acceptable either because it fostered and actually institutionalized antagonisms between workers and managers. Although such antagonism could be managed, it prevented the closing of the gap between production and administration, between mental and manual labor. The social effects of such incentives contradicted the political goals of socialism.

In 1958, as the Great Leap Forward management policy got under-way, a major attack was made, therefore, on worker piece-rate wages and bonuses on both economic and political grounds.[72] By 21 October 1958 over 400 factories in Shanghai had abolished piece-rate wages, including forty heavy industrial enterprises.[73] In Peking, of fifty-eight state and locally owned plants on piece-rate wages, fifty-one had ap-proved or were approving requests to end such wages while the others were sending requests.[74] This was a general trend.[75] The abolition of piece-rate wages was accompanied by a discussion of wage incentives which had included the wage-grade system.[76] The wage-grade system, which had replaced the supply system in 1955,[77] was not abolished.[78] Eight grades were maintained, the ratio between the highest grade and lowest being approximately three to one.[79]

The attack on the wage grade and bonus system was aimed less at workers than at administrative and technical cadres. Under the one-man management system the major incentives for cadres had been bonuses and the prestige and higher pay that went with promotion. Even though top grade skilled workers could earn over 110 yuan per month and a low grade cadre might earn much less than that,[80] the promotion to the top of the one-man management hierarchy could mean a salary of as much as 280 yuan per month.

Although this income differential was not wide by our standards, in the absence of any powerful alternative it probably did offer sufficient motivation for some cadres before the Great Leap Forward. If cadres had been prompted to optimum performance by grade, salary, rank, and status, it would not be logical to expect them to participate in labor on a long-term basis and to run their daily lives to emphasize participa-tion and equality, both of which were integral parts of the new system. For this reason in 1958 bonuses for party and non-party managerial personnel were abolished on a wide scale.

With the weakening of the incentive system which characterized one-man management the Great Leap Forward promulgated a new set of incentives more compatible with the two-one-three system. Material incentives, especially the wage-grade system and bonuses, were main-tained for workers, but the bonus payments now were based on the small groups' contribution to collective goals rather than on individual performance. Awards of money and title were still given for major inventions and technical improvements. There was a comprehensive system of labor and medical insurance and social welfare programs (hospitals, nurseries, sanitoria, clubs) funded both by the trade union and a special portion of the factories' total wage bill.[81]

Complements to material incentives became more important than before. These included emulation campaigns, work team and work shop competitions, titles and honors for good political attitudes and cooperativeness as well as for efficiency, and the liberal use of big character posters (ta-tzu-pao) for publicizing production statistics and criticisms of cadres.[82]

Worker participation in management brought about by the Great Leap Forward was itself an incentive, but the psychological fear of responsibility which came from fear of failure had to be overcome. In many factories, political work aimed at a change in workers' self-images by inculcating the feeling of being the master of the house (tang-chia tso chu-jen).[83] Worker participation and making workers multi-skilled was primarily intended to link production to administration, rather than just to redefine management or labor responsibilities while maintaining each as a separate sphere.[84]

Incentives for cadres as well were developed to fit the two-one-three system. The very challenge and increased autonomy presented by the decentralization of the economy was seen as a major incentive for cadres to perform well. As one observer expressed it:

> [The decentralization and the planned balance concept] seeks to become a powerful lever to prod the people at all levels in the country to forge ahead and bring into fuller play their positive influence.[85]

Cadre participation in labor was also to be a major incentive. By combining mental and manual labor, it would provide a more rewarding, less routinely dull daily existence,[86] and it would effect a moral and ideological view of labor as a positive value which would replace the pursuit of fame, wealth, and privilege.[87]

The Situation at the End of 1958

As the Shanghai Diesel Engine Plant was representative of the situation as it had evolved, a report on it is worth giving in detail.

Like many others in China, this plant had come under the Party Committee's leadership after the Eighth Central Committee Meeting in 1956, but the old one-man management system was not changed. The workers' congresses were mostly impotent and people had good reason to be cynical about them.

Although production plans were discussed at the lower levels, the important thing was [that the masses insure] implementation. Every day, every plan was arranged by the departments.

From the making of production plans to the finishing process everything was determined by departments. . . . Suggestions by the workers had to go through ten units, and thus small suggestions or requests for permission took at least three months and at most a year for action to be taken.[88]

The plant had a complex organizational structure. There were twenty-seven offices and administrative personnel and technicians comprised 26.4 percent of the employees. There were 133 rules and systems and more than 700 different forms. Technical cards, had to be filled out to requisition each and every spare part.

In the spring of 1958 this factory began to study the experience of the Chinghua Machine Tools Plant. It then reduced the power of functional departments and increased the responsibilities given to the small work groups or work teams. As a result, the teams decided on their own production operations, fixed working hours, gave job assignments, distributed wages, and managed tools. The workers elected their own group leader and managers and assigned them tasks. The work shop level had responsibility for sending monthly plans to the work teams and for holding discussions to insure that future plans would be based on workers' evaluations and dedication. The small-group leaders and activist workers took on the task, previously the monopoly of the trade union, of trying to maintain a high level of dedication by doing political work. Piece wages were replaced by hourly wage rates and when some workers' production level fell the activist workers urged them on.

Technical decision-making became chiefly the concern of the work shop, but it never was influenced by worker participation as much as other kinds of in-plant control, continuing to be a major problem, as the triple combination teams were not in early use here.

There was strenuous resistance to change from two sources, the cadres from those functional departments most affected and conservative workers. The question of technical control was the most difficult to solve because it consistently generated opposition from these sources. The cadres were not convinced that participation in labor was desirable from either a technical or a personal point of view. Objections were made on grounds of efficiency to mask the fact that some technical personnel were unwilling to learn to run machinery and take part in production on the shop floor. Ultimately, it was decided *not* to rely on a few experts and engineers working in isolation for technical control but to make technical control part and parcel of the production process through participation in labor. A key problem too was the competence of the basic level work teams in administration and technical control work and the function of cadres in improving it:

> Especially after power is sent down, how the small groups can be helped to manage well and how to raise the small groups' management level [are still questions that] require a lot of work. That is to say, after power is sent down, the cadres' responsibilities not only do not become lighter, but they are increased.

Thus, as the Great Leap Forward management system moved into its first full year of operation, three basic sets of problems had received the bulk of attention and publicity.

1. Where, and at what levels, control, coordination, and responsibility should be following the transfer of power over these functions.
2. How to improve the capacity of basic level production teams and individual workers so that they could take on management functions.
3. How to construct a system of incentives which would not contradict the new structure nor be unrealistic and generate opposition.

As 1959 began, it became clear that there was a good deal of difference of opinion regarding both the theory and practice of how to develop further the two-one-three system. The differences now, however, were not between the Northeast and the coastal industrial centers as before the Great Leap Forward. Now differences resulted from conflict among millions of people with varying skills and values who were in the midst of a major national experiment to reconcile socialist revolutionary principles with industrial development; to achieve organization without bureaucracy.

The Experiment Continues: Problems, Solutions, and Contradictions

The experiment did not progress smoothly or evenly. For example, not until the beginning of 1959 did some factories even begin to reform their organizational structures and simplify the role of functional departments.[89] But in those factories that had been in the vanguard, the experiment continued in order to solve new problems.

In the Chinghua Tools Factory, which had been the model of two-one-three management early in 1958, the chief problem was to delineate the powers of the small work teams and provide coordination in production.[90] Because the teams themselves had become overstaffed and the control systems of each team extremely complex, team responsibilities were lessened. Instead of duplicating the former bureaucratic factory structure at team level, the teams now began to focus on problems of operations. They set out their own work sequences for the month, based on the targets handed down by the work shop, and were responsible for daily work arrangements. The teams did some inspection of their finished work, but this was combined with inspection by cadres from functional departments. Teams were responsible for recording their consumption of material and for filling quotas they could now influence, but which were still determined higher up. By the beginning of 1960, some functional departments had begun to exert more control, especially in financial and technical matters, but there seemed to be a precarious balance between team level autonomy and higher level control. Basic level cadres had, in the meanwhile, continued to increase their specialized skills and technical knowledge. Cadre participation in labor had become systematized, with factory level managers participating less frequently than middle level cadres.[91] Workers had also shown a greater willingness to accept responsibility.[92]

The precarious balance was a major characteristic of other factories as well. In some cases, it tipped further toward the middle and upper levels of management than it did at Chinghua. For example, the Harbin Ballbearings Factory was a big plant with highly complicated, large machinery and many new, young, inexperienced workers.[93] Here worker participation in management at the team level centered around daily tasks arranged by the small group of people required to run one machine. Management in the factory, however, was divided into four levels, with the work section and work shop between the factory and the small group. The inspection of finished bearings was done by cadres from the inspection department, and, because the workers were relatively inexperienced, even scheduling and repair and maintenance work never went significantly below the work shop level. Workers controlled the scope and difficulty of direct production tasks in the small group, under the machine boss (chi-t'ai-chang) system. There was also a quarterly convention of workers' congresses.

By March 1959, even before the crucial Lushan Central Committee plenum in July, the two-one-three system had begun to show certain contradictions between what was now called professional management and mass management.[94] Theoretically, professional management was supposed to support and facilitate mass management,[95] but in practice circumstances determined the relationship between the two. In accounting and cost control, however, there was a harmonious effort to involve workers in recording their own use of materials because of its salutary effect on efficiency as well as because of politics.[96] Cadre participation in labor was becoming systematized on a wider scale, and the triple combination of workers, technicians, and cadres, though still problematical, continued.[97]

The year 1960 saw the emergence of a problem that had not received attention in the heat of early Great Leap Forward enthusiasm. It was manifested by unmistakable pressure, especially from party authorities above the enterprise, to revive the control functions of the functional departments. In June 1959, one month before the Lushan Plenum, a conference of CCP industrial-department secretaries from municipal and district party committees in Shantung Province stated:

> The meeting was of the opinion that the Party Committees of the enterprises must exercise unified leadership over the entire work of the enterprise, and when necessary, may also exercise leadership over certain important operations by means of "reaching the bottom with one stroke of the pole" (i.e., going directly to the source of the trouble). But because in modern enterprises techniques and equipment are rather complex, division of labor is minute, products are complicated, operation is continuous and cooperation is close among the different sections, it is necessary in the enterprise, simultaneous with the strengthening of the unified leadership of the Party, to institute and perfect a centralized command over production *and to set up or restore at once all the administrative offices that perform indispensable functions.*
>
> *The Directive of Combining mass movements with Centralized leadership and the directive of combining mass management with specialized management . . . must be followed in earnest; of these two "legs," the latter is more important.* [Italics added.][98]

Planning authorities above the enterprise level were becoming anxious to have the reliable data needed for interenterprise coordination and economic planning. Such data had previously come from functional departments. Clearly, this problem was one of the reasons for increasing difficulties. But confusion also arose from a contradictory attempt to exert more control over the increasing activities at the basic levels. It came from the enormous increase in the number of basic-level cadres with some technical and administrative expertise which challenged the monopoly of knowledge and the style of leadership of the functional-department cadres. It came from an incentive system which combined material incentives, even on the collective, team basis, with team participation in management.[99] And finally, it came from very contradictory attitudes toward the cadres' participation in labor that was absolutely essential to handle the complexities of organization and communication in a non-bureaucratic way. A mid-1960 report on the Chengtu Measuring Instruments and Cutting Tools Factory, considered an advanced example of the new management system, described these difficulties in detail.[100]

The Chengtu plant was a huge factory making precision cutting tools and measuring instruments. The time spent by factory level leadership on matters of interenterprise and enterprise-government coordination was considerable. Hence, the plant Party Committee was responsible for policy. Even so, it recognized the political significance of small group participation in management. In 1958 and 1959 the production teams were given responsibility in accounting, operations planning, even technical innovation and designing. A full-time technician was assigned a work post at the team level to help, and others on the team had responsibility for specific management functions. However, cadre participation in labor at the team level was not directly related to the job of coordination of team activities. Except for periodic triple combination trouble-shooting teams and factory-level cadres visiting production units to plant experimental fields, most interteam coordination and quota calculations were done by factory-level functional departments. Though these were numerically fewer than before the Great Leap Forward reforms, and though they were influenced by worker input more than previously, they operated through functional systems which had branches at every operational level, including branch factories, work shops, and the work teams.

The conflict between increasing team management activity and a growing amount of purely administrative coordination, divorced from participation in labor, was paralleled in the training of technicians and engineers. Like other plants during the Great Leap Forward, the Chengtu plant had, through spare-time schools at every level of education, involved over 99 percent of the workers in study, vastly improving the technical expertise of work-team chiefs, most all of whom had reached levels of technical competence nearly equal to work shop or factory-level cadres.

Finally, the basic-level work teams were operating under an incentive system that combined collective with individual bonuses, with the team itself determining how to distribute the collective bonus to individuals. There were also emulation campaigns based on target fulfillment, and there was the incentive that came directly from participation in management.

If the Party Committee saw any potential conflict in their factory, it gave no hint in the conclusion to its report:

> The rapid improvement in the capacity of workers in the management of the factory, and the emergence of large numbers of new administrative personnel will gradually narrow the gap between the workers and the administrators or technical personnel. With the elevation of the political consciousness and technical standards of the workers, the gap between mental labor and manual labor will gradually be eliminated, and the vestiges of capitalism—bureaucracy—will be eradicated.

The Role of the Party as the Great Leap Forward Fades

Through 1960 the problem of economic coordination gradually became central even though other problems were unresolved. The party and party-related groups (trade unions, youth league) were playing an ever increasing role at all levels of the industrial system[101] but within the context of growing contradictions over the nature and meaning of party leadership.[102] As participation and emulation campaigns were combined with small group or collective bonus payments, people either worked too hard or they did not work hard enough. The party and trade-union cadres were responsible for dealing with this, prompting people to work hard for the collective,[103] yet to be aware of situations where enthusiasm could lead to fatigue, accidents, or mechanical breakdowns.[104] It was not unheard of during the GLF for people to work around the clock, seven days a week, on an important innovation, often bringing food and bedding to the shop where workers ate and slept.[105] The hectic pace of the GLF had often required rearrangements of living accommodations and work-shift schedules for which the party became responsible.[106]

In addition, the Party Committee, as the chief policy-making body in the factory, became involved with determining appropriate labor norms and production quotas. These were partly the basis for the distribution of income within the factory either on a collective or individual basis.

The party's involvement with this aspect of management was paralleled by its crucial involvement with important questions of coordination above the factory level. This included the meeting of quality standards,[107] and popularization and promotion of innovations.[108] The party linked the enterprise with other enterprises and with higher planning and administrative authority.[109] It controlled the over-all use of enterprise capital and financial resources not under the unified control of the state, a job previously handled by the financial department at the factory level.[110] In addition to these functions, the Party Committee was to concern itself with personnel policies.[111]

Thus, not only did the factory-level party committee become responsible for guiding the implementation of the two-one-three management system within the plant, it also had to be responsible for the needs of other factories and to superior party organizations. And just as the Great Leap Forward management system posed a challenge to the elitist and bureaucratic values and routines of factory-level leadership, the decentralized planning system required new methods of leadership and new routines on the part of cadres above the enterprise level. When the old control systems were broken down, the party took over the prime work of coordinating the economy, and the stress on Municipal and Provincial Party Committees grew. As the GLF progressed and the importance of economic coordination became apparent in this critical transition period from the old to a new planning and coordinative system in late 1959, the enterprise level Party Committees were placed in a crucial position.

For example, to coordinate the iron and steel industry in Shanghai, the Municipal Party Committee set up a "unified control office . . . under the command of the Municipal CCP Committee Secretaries in charge of industry, while joint offices [were] also established in each major department of the economy."[112] Local Party Committees became responsible for initiating local construction or production projects and for adjusting the conflict between local needs and capacities of other areas and units.[113] Party Committees at the province level and in the larger cities were responsible for organizing interenterprise coordination and seeing that supplies were available and contracts were being fulfilled.[114]

In the absence of detailed plans from the center, and given the role of participatory planning and financial systems within the enterprise, this meant that the industrial control authorities in the Municipal and Provincial Party Committees were required to leave their offices much more frequently for on-the-spot checks. Such authorities had to take part in labor in order to gain a deeper understanding of what was happening in enterprises under the jurisdiction of their committees, since there were now fewer people at the enterprise level involved in communicating the necessary information. On-the-spot investigations and participation in labor within the factories were designed to replace the proliferation of paper work and reports, which was one cause of bureaucracy and which was used as justification (too busy to leave the office).[115] Indeed, as one detailed report on the activities of these control authorities put it,

> The work of raising the standards of industrial control is by no means a purely technical or operational question; rather, it is primarily, a question involving leadership style and management method.[116]

In short, the changing of management systems sharply affected the flow of communications between the enterprise and higher planning authorities, and although there was some realization of this before and during the GLF, the destroyed old system could not be immediately replaced. One result was a major though temporary dislocation of the economy. More important was that the party above the enterprise was affected differently and more consistently than the party organization at the factory level and below where conditions varied widely. The factory-level Party Committee was therefore in a potentially crucial political position between planning authorities and the people in its own factory.

Two systems of factory management had emerged during the Great Leap Forward. One was the system officially codified in 1956, called factory manager responsibility under the leadership of the Party Committee. The other, revolutionary system was called two participations, one reform, and triple combination.

While the two were in many ways the same, the 1956 system assumed that the party was capable of separating its political goals from the economic and technical tools of modernization. In the two-one-three system, policy, operations, and politics were to be unified and this logic led the party to assert control over the whole gamut of industrialization, not just over policy or planning but over operations and the human relationships at work.

The party's growing involvement with enterprise operations did not automatically mean an end to the influence of rationality and technical concerns. What it often did mean was a shift in the personnel who made the decisions for the enterprise. The technical and administrative competence of these newer decision makers was uneven, not nonexistent. It also meant a change in the distribution of power among the organizational levels of the enterprise, which had radical implications for the incentives that could be effectively employed as well as for the methods of planning and coordination that were possible in the larger economy.

The Great Leap never fully solved several problems. Incentives policy stressed material and participatory incentives and material incentives utilized both individual and collective rewards, with more stress on the somewhat less contradictory collective team bonus. Organizationally, the role of the functional departments and middle-level management was left ambiguous in relation to worker participation in management and cadre participation in labor, as well as to planners and coordinators above the enterprise. Personnel training involved a two-track educational system with full-time technical training at secondary and university level and part-work part-study or spare-time education closely attached to factories and mines.

All of these things were to lead toward the revolutionary socialist goals that were part and parcel of Chinese politics. They were to hasten modernization at the same time. The party's organizational leadership over factories was to guarantee this. The problem was, of course, that factory operations greatly influenced economic planning and coordination. The supremacy of politics could not be maintained only by dealing seriously with the factories, as difficult as that was, for the coordination and planning of a huge economic system also required major political choices.

Disagreements over how to solve the questions of management were open in the party as early as August 1959 when the communique of the Lushan Plenum noted that the main danger in the party was right opportunism among some cadres who wanted to negate the whole concept of the Great Leap Forward.[117] Over the next year, the problems and experiments with management and planning that have been traced in this chapter contributed to and were aggravated by this split in the party over the meaning of the Great Leap Forward. As the Great Leap Forward faded in 1960 and serious economic imbalances became evident in the economy, which offset the sporadic glory and amazing accomplishments of the previous years, Chinese politics had already begun a new phase.

5/Industrial Enterprises in the Aftermath of the Great Leap Forward, 1961–1963

CHINA WAS NEVER the same after the Great Leap Forward. Too many things had happened. Lessons positive and negative had been learned by millions who judged the social upheavals from widely differing perspectives. Forces had been unleashed which could not be brushed aside or ignored. The post-GLF period was therefore not an oscillation from radical, revolutionary to more pragmatic, conservative policy.[1] Neither was the post-GLF period simply a consolidation and perfection of the experimental forms of management and economic coordination of the GLF. Instead it was a period during which intense conflict developed, especially at the higher levels of Communist Party politics, a period of confusion for the millions working within the industrial system.[2]

By late 1960 severe crisis had begun to grip the economy. In this context of economic crisis evaluations of the Great Leap Forward became the central issues of political debate.

The crisis was characterized by trenchant imbalances between industry and agriculture which emphasized food and agricultural problems for both urban and rural populations. Severe bottlenecks in transportation had developed as construction and increased production outstripped the capacity of the transport network to handle the loads. New plants and factories did not keep pace with the availability of new sources of raw materials or with the increased capacity of old ones. New industrial and mining enterprises did not always produce adequate quality or quantity of goods to complement the increased capacity of older or newly built plants. In short, severe intersectoral imbalances were aggravated by severe intrasectoral ones and a crisis of major proportions developed.

The reasons for this crisis are many.[3] The three most frequently considered are:

1. a series of unprecedented natural disasters that struck agriculture and related industrial crops in the 1960–1961 period;

2. the growing Sino-Soviet conflict which culminated in the Soviet decision to withdraw all technical assistance from Chinese industry, with the departing technicians taking all their plans and blueprints and the directions for operation and assembly of complex machinery. Key industrial projects stopped in the midst of construction;

3. the policies of the Great Leap Forward—the attempt to develop agriculture along with industry, to develop local urban and rural communes based on agricultural and industrial enterprises, to mobilize all resources, including marginal human and natural ones, toward the goal of urban and rural modernization, to create forms of political participation which gave far greater power to workers and peasants expanding social equality.

An official policy of consolidation to slowdown the hectic pace of the Great Leap Forward was announced at the ninth Plenum of the eighth Central Committee which met from late 1960 into January 1961.[4] A central political issue in the years following this announcement was the answers people gave to the relative importance of these questions.

Was the crisis a result of the Soviet pull-out and the natural disasters, which had served to magnify the tactical but correctable errors of a basically sound approach to modernization and the building of socialism? Or was the Great Leap Forward an untenable strategy for socialist modernization? Did it cause the Soviet pull-out, leaving China without the technical and political expertise and experience necessary for further development?

Though these questions concerned the party they could not be posed that starkly for the millions of factory workers nor it seems did anyone in the party want a confrontation just yet. But there was evidence that the serious issues and differences concerning the philosophy and politico-economic structure of socialism preoccupied Mao and other leaders in the aftermath of the Great Leap Forward.[5]

Economic Consolidation and Political Ambiguity in Factory Production Relations and Macro Planning Methods

By February 1961 discussion of the two major problem areas of the industrial economy began to shift perceptibly. One was coordination of the economy and regulation of enterprise relationships. The other involved operational factors affecting quality, quantity, and variety of goods. The Great Leap Forward had defined operational control over production as a prime and central concern of politics and economic coordination as a matter of policy. Both politics and policy were to be under the guiding hand of the Communist Party, with politics in command. However, as the economic crisis worsened in 1961, economic coordination became the most important problem of politics, potentially affecting the very nature of state power. The revolutionary management system of the Great Leap Forward was now to be consolidated and perfected. Production operations were made the province of the factory managers and the Communist Party turned most of its attention to the vital matter of restoring balance to the economy.

Re-emphasis on the role of factory manager responsibility did not necessarily mean that consolidation of the Great Leap system was to mean abandonment of the system, although in practice, the line between consolidation and abandonment could be quite fine depending upon the individual factory. But there was a definite change of tone in important economic and political journals. In February 1961 Po I-po, a key party economic authority, wrote:

> Through accumulation of experiences in the past ten years in general, and in the past three successive forward leaping years in particular, we have formulated a complete system of enterprise management . . . closely coordinating centralized leadership with large-scale mass campaigns, leadership of the CCP committees with *the actual* responsibility of factory directors concerned. [Italics added.][6]

A *Jen-min Jih-pao* editorial of 22 February 1961 discussed the importance of consolidating the economy, of systematizing and popularizing the experiences of the two-one-three system, and of extending the responsibility systems to every work sequence, every machine. Then it came to the heart of the matter. CCP Committee leadership in the plant was to mean collective discussion-decision on all major problems, but:

> The collective leadership of the CCP Committee cannot replace the day-to-day administrative management of an enterprise. Nor is it necessary for the Party Committee to manage the daily routine affairs of the enterprise. . . .[7]

> To enable an enterprise to better implement the system of dividing labor under collective leadership, it is necessary to sufficiently enhance the functions of the various sections and departments in an enterprise.

After noting that an "unnecessarily large structure and excessive personnel" should be reorganized and retrenched, the editorial concluded:

> However, it would be a very poor method for the enterprise to completely tear down their original structure with the leading functionaries directing the hastily organized command posts, staff offices and work groups to guide production. The result would be an abolishment of the responsibility system among the sections and departments of an enterprise. The

sections and departments of an enterprise constitute the necessary structure for management of production.

This editorial marked the beginning of a whole series of articles in the Chinese press on the same themes: rebuild the functional departments, organize strict systems of financial, technical, and production control centered on those departments, and free the Party Committee from production operations management so it could focus all of its energy on important problems:

> Without a perfect system of responsibility of the factory director, or a system of command over day-to-day administration, the Party Committee will trap itself in daily routine, and be unable to concentrate force for solving important matters of policy or to step up the day-to-day ideological and political work of the Party. . . .[8]

The fact that production operations and the distribution of power within factories was no longer defined as a crucial aspect of politics was to have far-reaching implications. The Communist Party now turned its attention to problems of interenterprise coordination and economic planning. Both factory-level Party Committees and party organs above the factory level increased their involvement in the planning and coordination activity of the State. The enterprise-level committees were liaison with the planning authorities. They dealt with banks controlling credit for technical experiments, improvements, new equipment, and construction for expansion and with the flow of supplies.[9] The Party Committee within the factory had veto power over the plant manager, but only in exceptional circumstances if the manager's decisions threatened the factory's external commitments.[10] In addition, the party had responsibility for morale, welfare, and political education.[11]

Party Committees above the enterprise level also retained a central role in the economy in the aftermath of the GLF, especially since economic problems became directly related to political stability and legitimacy in these crisis years. Through participation of party members in a government economic organ,[12] or as a collective directly concerned with planning and coordination,[13] the party played a major role in general economic administration.

As the party's attention shifted to problems of planning, and as greater stress was placed on strengthening responsibility systems through the functional departments, a contradictory situation began to develop. Actually, the formal structure of industrial enterprises had not changed much, even in the most turbulent years of experimentation. With the exception of departments that were abolished, most factories were organized as they had been before. There were usually three levels: basic-level work teams, the work shops, and the factory. During the GLF, many control and supervisory powers of bureaucrats in functional departments had been given to work teams; others had been made the responsibility of production leaders in work shops. Administrative and supervisory personnel generally were required to exercise their authority while participating in the production process. For example, when a work team was given the responsibility for quality control the workers inspected and rejected or accepted their own work. Work teams given authority formerly held by the work-shop-level planning department decided on the pace of their production and hence output. Work shops given the powers of a factory-level planning department arranged their own interwork-shop coordination and sequence cooperation directly (through representatives from the work shops) rather than through rules and regulations created by factory-level planners.

In practice, however, the powers of the functional departments were reduced in degree rather than eliminated altogether. The re-emphasis on the role of functional departments at work shop and factory level was not, therefore, a denial of Great Leap Forward reforms. It was, however, difficult to draw precise lines and easy to cross from consolidation to abandonment. Three major areas of factory management—financial control, technical control, and general administrative supervision—showed this ambivalence clearly.

Workers, recording their own output and consumption levels, could participate in management through financial control and accounting, and cadres, translating raw production inputs into comprehensive costs, could participate in labor. During this interchange, both workers and cadres would become more aware of the technical and human reasons for poor or inefficient performance.[14]

During the Great Leap Forward, accounting was handled almost exclusively by the basic-level work teams and small groups. The results generally were uneven,[15] and by mid-1961 there were still serious problems in the accounting system.[16] The solution was to consolidate the system by strengthening specialized accounting while maintaining mass accounting. Specialized accounting was systematic; it was used to translate material input data into comprehensive cost figures which allowed top management to plan for the whole enterprise. Specialized accounting required a rudimentary grasp of mathematics; while much could be done by production workers with the time and the knowledge, some had to be performed at a higher level including more than one work team. Mass accounting, the recording of input and output, was done by work teams themselves.

One way to strengthen specialized accounting was with a financial section with special personnel in appropriate departments as well as in each production unit.[17] Another way was to reconstitute the specialized financial departments, abolished or drastically weakened during the GLF, making them independent of other departments and production units. By 1963 this was the usual approach to financial management. The re-established finance departments were staffed with "fine quality cadres . . . vested with powers to carry out supervision of the financial affairs of the whole factory"[18] under the factory manager and the plant Party Committee. They checked on the party and the plant manager by direct contact with the banks and had a principle role in the planning process.[19]

In addition to the factory-level financial departments, accounting was also to be done at the work shop and work-team level. Work-shop level accounting was considered specialized accounting because costs were calculated in money terms and balance sheets were drawn up by special financial sections or offices.[20]

Accounting at the work-team level was closely related to the matter of incentives.[21] The teams received targets from higher levels and their accounting was a check to see if these targets were fulfilled. Generally, there were five such targets: (1) output, (2) quality, (3) wages and attendance, (4) consumption of raw materials and semiprocessed goods, and (5) consumption of tools and related parts.

The mechanism for basic-level accounting was simple. Each team worker had a card called the Workmen's Job Record Card on which was recorded the worker's name, type of work, machine number, hours worked, overtime hours, number of finished products, number of rejects, and the number, length, and causes of work interruptions. For teams making more than one specialized product, an output schedule for the number of hours worked at each of the products was also included. These cards became the basis for team-made calculations of targets. Those responsible for these calculations were elected by the workers and had contact with the financial authorities who checked their work, sometimes doing the actual calculations. In such cases, work-team personnel were more communications links than accountants. Norms and quotas could be permanently revised only with approval of the functional department concerned (coordinating with the financial department) and only after timely suggestions had been made by the team. These changes could be used as targets of internal struggle for the team itself but were not allowed to affect other teams' activities or norms. Temporary variations from the norms were allowed in emergencies but were subject to approval by the departments.

As the financial departments at the work shop and factory levels increased their role in accounting, the other functional departments become more involved with quota management. Quotas depended on technical and engineering variables which influenced feasible running speeds, maintenance schedules, innovations, and the availability of supplies as well as on the mathematics of finance and accounting. The statistical work of these functional departments became part of the raw data for team quotas and norms, which were the basis of control and incentive systems.[22]

Although work-team-level accounting was marked by a growth in the power of middle- and upper-level management, there was still nothing comparable to one-man management. Workers could influence their targets and quotas by what they recorded on their job cards, by how hard they worked as a result of informal but powerful agreements among themselves, or by what they said at periodic sessions to discuss and estimate quotas and norms. Workers elected basic-level personnel for administrative duties. Over-all financial control at the factory level was handled by a special financial department.

The increasing power of middle-level and factory-level functional departments was also noticeable in technical responsibility systems, as these departments became more involved with quota management,[23] and exerted more influence over decisions regarding technical innovation, reform, and quality. The connection between daily operations and the knowledge required for production meant that technical control was central in determining the distribution of power among workers in the factories.[24]

During the Great Leap Forward, much of the control over technical decision-making was given to the work teams or triple combination groups. Higher-level managers and technicians acquired hard information primarily by direct labor participation. The triple combination groups encouraged suggestions for technical reform and innovation while also acting as a control. Important as these groups were, however, the atmosphere of euphoria that sometimes accompanied the GLF made it difficult for technicians to make any negative evaluations of workers' proposals without being accused of those political attitudes meant to keep workers the inferiors of technicians and engineers.

Naturally this led to problems, especially when workers' proposals were off the mark for technical or financial reasons. As one article expressed this problem:

> We must not confuse technical views with political views, or look upon technical views simply as constituting an individual's political stand and link them with political thought.[25]

Workers were to be encouraged to give their views on technical and administrative matters, but this had to be combined with strict technical control work, and such work was to be primarily the task of technical personnel working in departments at work shop and factory levels[26] and only secondarily of the triple combination groups. Like accounting and finance, the evolving technical responsibility system increasingly depended first on specialized cadres at the department levels and secondly on the raw information generated by the workers:

Chief Engineers, engineers, and technicians form the technical leadership force in industrial enterprises. They are primarily counted on for solving technical problems in production. Enterprise leaders must be good at listening to the opinions of the technical personnel and give scope to their role.[27]

Technical personnel were urged to work on triple-combination teams, but the teams were more a means of communication than a locus of decision-making.[28]

The trend of financial and technical management was repeated in general administration. The functional departments concerned with supplies, warehouse inventory,[29] inspection,[30] and repair and maintenance[31] all increased their power, while worker participation and basic-level leaders became less important. But worker participation by no means disappeared.

The New Power Distribution Between Functional Departments and Basic Levels

During 1961 to 1963 there were two contradictory tendencies. One was to continue the two-one-three system; the other, to undermine or negate the methods of the Great Leap Forward. A detailed examination of actual conditions inside some of China's factories shows a very mixed situation, and a good deal of complexity.

In the Yao Hua Glass Factory in Shanghai, for example, the Party Committee decided to put more stress on cadre participation in labor in order to rationalize the two-one-three system. It did not emphasize the role of middle-level functional departments, and it defended small group democratic management when it was coupled with cadre participation. The planning-department cadres were used as an example:

> After the cadres in this department entered the front line, helped the production small-groups set up a planning regulation position, and gave some of their power to the small-production group, thus establishing planning work on the basis of democratic management in the small group; the effectiveness of planning work was raised, daily reports on production came back only one-half hour after being requested from the shift, and, moreover, the figures were correct.[32]

In May 1959, various efforts were undertaken to make cadre participation in labor more effective. At first, three large groups of cadres left their offices and went to the work shops temporarily. But this did not work out well. Many cadres did not know what to do once they got into the shop, and many workers resented cadres taking over or temporarily replacing them because it meant loss of bonuses or other pay. The three large groups were then broken down into thirty small groups, each with four or five cadres and each cadre with a specific relationship to a work team. Since cadres came from many functional departments, this resulted in a surplus of managers on the teams and an irregular distribution of administrative and technical skills.

Some enterprises had mixed results from their efforts at readjustment. The Chinghsi Coal Mines[33] set up and maintained groups of worker-managers on the teams and mine shifts. More than one worker was responsible for each management task, lessening individual responsibility. Workers were not pressured to directly influence planning but there were quarterly workers' congresses for discussion of the monthly plans sent down by the leadership. Though some cadres moved their offices directly to the shaft sites, there did not appear to be much reliance on cadre participation in labor, though both the mining bureau and the individual mines had a system for it.

The Shanghai Smelting Plant[34] Party Committee continued to develop a system of direct worker participation in management and cadre participation in labor. Party members at all levels of the plant, working as leading cores within various units, were central to this system. However, direct worker participation in planning was gradually replaced by the convening of quarterly workers' congresses as the chief method of worker participation:

> We still regularly adopt the form of "reaching the bottom with one stroke of the pole" (yi pi-tzu tao-ti), and convene "four leaders' meetings" of shift-level leaders and small-group leaders of the whole factory. . . . These types of meetings possess the characteristics of administrative speed, shortness of duration, quick implementation, and broad representative character, etc., but they also have a definitely limited nature, and therefore cannot and should not be used to replace workers' representative meetings and can only be used as one form of effectively mobilizing the masses.

As work-team participation became less important, the role of the work-shop-party organs became more important and their relations with the technical units and persons at the work-shop level grew closer. At the small-group level there were small-group core groups (hsiao-tsu ho-hsin-tsu) with a party member as leader. These groups were responsible for ideological education and skill improvement. Statistics, planning, accounting, quota management, personnel management, safety, hygiene, and welfare—all came under the leadership of higher level functional committees, each of which had a representative within the small-group. The representatives were called the ten major officials (shih ta yuan) and were mainly responsible for implementing committee decisions. Hence, worker participation in management in this plant continued but was centered at the work-shop level, probably because of the technical requirements of smelting operations. Cadres at the work-shop level participated in labor more than did those at higher levels.

In the Chungking Yutienpao Coal Mines, the situation was incredibly complicated and confusing. The Party Committee took the lead in consolidating a responsibility system. Cadre management contracts[35] were made to specify each cadre's task in management. The responsibility system ran directly from the mine director to the shaft directors and specialized departments. Every cadre within every shaft had a special scope of responsibility and was directly under the shaft director. Thus, "the decisions of the Party Committee and the orders of the mine director" were carried out in this strict hierarchical way.[36]

The shaft-level cadres formed the link between the coal miners and the management of the mine. They met once a day to discuss production problems. The party branch secretary of each mining shaft acted as the over-all coordinator and morale booster for the miners, inspecting work surfaces in person, chatting with workers in the mess halls and with the foremen in afternoon meetings. He reported his findings to higher levels, received new instructions, and began the process again the following day.

Cadres above the shaft level were further from the workers lives, both geographically and psychologically. Willing to make inspection tours of the mines as part of triple combination teams, they were not, however, anxious to work in the mines, eat or live with the workers, but cadres at the shaft level did quite frequently participate in labor.

As cadres in the mine shafts began to participate more in labor and those above the shaft level continued to work in their offices, a communications gap developed. To bridge the gap, the middle levels were reorganized so that three main departments were left: administration, production and technology, and material supply. Some former mine-level cadres were made shaft foremen or party branch secretaries (the key men) at the pit level. The remainder of middle-level cadres was divided into three groups; one stayed on the surface to do administrative work, one went inside the mines to participate in labor, and one formed trouble-shooting groups which visited work sites in various mines. Personnel in each group rotated every three months. Some workers were promoted but very little power to plan the tasks of the day was given to the production teams.

The mine-level Party Committee now was confronted with a problem. From its perspective, the changes that had occurred meant that meetings of the mine-level cadres were not needed as frequently as before since many decisisons were made at the shaft level. But, without meetings to attend, time hung heavy on their hands. So, the mine-level cadres decided that: "When the top level called a meeting, *there had to be people to attend,* and those who came *had to have others take over for them."* (Italics added.)[37] The solution (!) was to reconstruct the middle level (surface level) of management by dividing the group of cadres at that level into two groups, one of which was to attend meetings (!). This system was then called the three-level, four-team, three-shift, and four-withs (san-chi szu-t'ao san-pan szu-t'ung) enterprise leadership and management system.

The Party Committee, not surprisingly, quickly simplified the Rube Goldberg-type system they had constructed. The new one was termed the "four-fix, three-guarantee, and one-reward system." The mine-level fixed: (1) the number of personnel, (2) the tools and materials, (3) the place of work, (4) the cooperative relationships for every work team. The teams had to guarantee: (1) completion of production, (2) safety, (3) fulfillment of cost quotas. If they did, they received bonuses. The teams recorded production and consumption on a daily basis. They were given responsibility for the use, maintenance, and safety of small and medium-sized tools and were allowed to help out other teams after the fixed cooperative relations had been fulfilled.

Bonuses were higher for underground jobs, and higher still for collective bodies than for individuals. Other incentives, such as honorary titles and letters of congratulation were utilized. Workers had little or nothing to say about quotas, and participation in technical innovation was almost nonexistent. The motivation for technical innovation was a system of cash rewards. Given the emphasis on material incentives, the attempt to have the work shifts evaluate their own performances (which was to be the basis of monthly bonuses) ran into trouble. Within six months, it had to be scrapped in favor of more control by the middle-level functional departments.[38]

The previous examples are meant to give concrete detail and a feeling for the complexity beneath the numbers on the charts which follow. The charts are an attempt to measure quantitatively the degree to which the Great Leap Forward management system was affected by the years of consolidation. Inevitably, the quantitative measures will give an appearance of precision where none is intended nor possible. It will be instructive, however, if the measurements are understood to be general trends. The sample is sufficiently large and inclusive of enough sizes, types, and products to allow a fairly accurate estimate.

Table 2 is divided into ten columns, each representing a specific management function. The names of the factories are listed at the left. For each factory and each function, three measures are used for the three major principles of the Great Leap Forward-management system: (a) worker participation in management, (b) cadre participation in labor, (c) the triple combination. It is assumed that the incentives of equality and participation, combined with collective material incentives and narrow income differentials flow directly from these three principles.

The three quantitative measures are: (1) a high degree of conti-

Table 2 The Evolution of the Great-Leap-Forward-Management System of "Two Participations, One Reform, and Triple Combination" in a Sample of 53 Chinese Industrial Enterprises: 1961–1963*

Name of Factory	Quality Control & Insp.	Discipline	Wages and Quotas	Repair & Maintnce.	Tools and Matl.	Technology	Pers.	Stat. & Acctg.	Prodctn. Plng.	Safety
1. Anyang Iron & Steel Iron Smltg. Plant				2a 2b				2a		
2. Tientsin Pharmaceutical						2a 3c 3b				
3. An Yuan Coal Mines	2b		2b	2b	2b	2b			2b	2b
4. Chungking Pesticide					3a			2a	3a	
5. Suchow Textile Dyeing								3b		
6. Liaoyuan Elec. Plant									2a	
7. Lanchow #1 Woolen Textile	3a		3a			3a		3a		
8. Canton Hsiin Te Sugar Refining								3b 2a		

Item	Codes
9. P'angfou Textile Dyeing	2a, 3b
10. Sian Agr'l. Mach. Plant	2a
11. Shanghai An Ta Cotton Txtl.	2a, 2b
12. Shanghai #2 Iron & Steel	2c, 1a, 2b, 2a
13. Hsin Mi Coal Mines	3c
14. Nankuang Coal Mines	3a, 2a
15. Tsing tao #2 Rubber	3c, 2b, 3a, 3a, 2a
16. Tientsin Cigarette	3a, 2c, 3a
17. Liaoyüan Mines	2b, 1c, 2a
18. Hofei Glass Factory	3a, 3a, 3a
19. Coking Plant, Shihchingshan Iron & Steel	2a, 2b, 3a, 2b, 3a, 2b, 3a

Table 2 (Continued)

Name of Factory	Quality Control & Insp.	Disci-pline	Wages and Quotas	Repair & Main-tnce.	Tools and Matl.	Tech-nology	Pers.	Stat. & Acctg.	Prodctn. Plng.	Safety
						Management Function				
20. Shenyang Elec. Motor	3a			3a		3a				
21. Tsingtao Iron & Steel	1a 1b				1a 1c				1a 1c	
22. Shenyang Smelting			2a 2c					2a 2c		
23. T'angshan Mines	1b 3a						3a		1c	
24. Chungking, Yangchiap'ing Machine Tool	3a		3a		1a			2a 3b		
25. Changchün #8 Rubber					1a	2a	3a			
26. T'aiyüan Mining Mach'ry.					2a 3b	2a 3b				

#	Enterprise	Codes
27.	Weifang Diesel Eng. Shantung	3a; 2a
28.	T'aiyüan Iron Smelting	1a
29.	Kwanghua Wood Products	3a
30.	Paotou Steel Smelting	2a
31.	Kwangchou Std. Instrument	1a; 2a; 3a; 3a; 2a 1c; 3a
32.	T'aiyuan Chemical	3a 1c 3b; 3a
33.	Chungking Waterwheel	3a; 3a; 3a; 3a; 3a
34.	Harbin Meas. Instrument & Cutting Tools	2a; 2a; 2a
35.	Shanghai Clock	2a 2b; 2a 2b; 2a 2b; 2a 2b
36.	Shihchingshan Iron Smelting	3a

Table 2 (Continued)

Name of Factory	Quality Control & Insp.	Disci- pline	Wages and Quotas	Repair & Main- tnce.	Tools and Matl.	Tech- nology	Pers.	Stat. & Acctg.	Prodctn. Plng.	Safety
						Management Function				
37. Tairen Machine Tool						1c				
38. Changchün Elec. Motor	2a					2a				
39. Changchün Shoe								2a		
40. Shenyang Transformer						1c 2a				
41. Kwangchou Machinery			3a 2c							
42. Tientsin Vehicles	2a			1c 2a	3a	3a 2c	1c 3a	2a	3a	
43. Shenyang Mining Machinery				1a						
44. Shanghai Steel						1c 2a				
45. Chungking Water Pump					2a 3b			2a 3b		

46. Tsingtao #9 Rubber					2a		2a
47. Hangchow Machine Tool				2a	2a	2a	3a / 2a / 2a
48. Shanghai Rubber	2a			2a		2a	2a
49. Shanghai Steel Pipe				2c / 2a			
50. Changchün Municipal Moving Machinery	1a / 1c	1a			1a / 1c		
51. Kirin Chem. Corporation	2b / 2a	2b	2b	2b / 3a	2b / 3a	3a	2a / 3b
52. South China Sewing Mach.			3a	3c		3a / 3a	1b / 2a
53. Wuhan State #1 Textile				2c / 2b		2b / 2c	2b / 2c / 2a

Grand Totals

	1	2	3
a	13	54	51
b	2	27	11
c	15	10	3

Table 3 Evaluation of Great-Leap-Management Continuity According to Industry at 53 Industrial Enterprises*

Name of Factory	Total Number of Instances				Number Ranked 1			Number Ranked 2			Number Ranked 3		
	a	b	c	Total	a	b	c	a	b	c	a	b	c
HEAVY INDUSTRY													
Anyang Iron Smelting	2	1	0	3	0	0	0	2	1	0	0	0	0
Anyuan Coal Mines	0	7	0	7	0	0	0	0	7	0	0	0	0
Sian Agr'l. Machine	1	0	0	1	0	0	0	1	0	0	0	0	0
Shanghai #1 Steel	1	0	1	2	0	0	1	1	0	0	0	0	0
Shanghai #2 Iron & Stl.	1	0	1	2	1	0	0	0	0	1	0	0	0
Shanghai Steel Pipe	1	0	1	2	0	0	0	1	0	1	0	0	0
Shanghai Rubber	5	0	0	5	0	0	0	5	0	0	0	0	0
Hsin Mi Coal Mines	1	1	1	3	0	0	0	1	1	0	0	0	1
Nankuang Coal Mines	2	0	0	2	0	0	0	1	0	0	1	0	0
Liaoyuan Coal Mines	1	1	1	3	0	0	1	1	1	0	0	0	0
Shenyang Elec. Motor	3	0	0	3	0	0	0	0	0	0	3	0	0
Shenyang Smelting	2	0	2	4	0	0	0	2	0	2	0	0	0
Shenyang Mining Mach.	1	0	0	1	1	0	0	0	0	0	0	0	0
Shenyang Transformer	1	0	1	2	0	0	1	1	0	0	0	0	0
Tsingtao Iron & Steel	3	0	3	6	3	0	3	0	0	0	0	0	0
Tsingtao #2 Rubber	1	1	1	3	0	0	0	0	1	0	1	0	1
Tsingtao #9 Rubber	2	0	0	2	0	0	0	2	0	0	0	0	0

* Sources for this information are the following (numbers below correspond to those preceding the name of each plant):

1. JMJP, 4/4/61
2. JMJP, 7/24/61
3. NFJP, 6/10/63
4. TKP, 5/22/63
5. TKP, 1/29/63
6. KJJP, 12/7/63
7. TKP, 7/29/63
8. TKP, 10/23/63
9. Anhwei Radio, 5/25/63
10. TKP, 2/21/63
11. TKP, 4/3/62
12. JMJP, 1/29/62
    KJJP, 7/24/62
13. KJJP, 5/31/60
14. JMJP, 1/30/62
15. KJJP, 8/3/62
    JMJP, 8/7/63

16. TKP, 6/19/62
17. JMJP, 3/11/61
    JMJP, 1/16/62
18. TKP, 5/9/62
19. SCMP #2695, p. 1
20. KJJP, 6/26/62
21. JMJP, 8/15/61
22. JMJP, 2/20/62
23. KJJP, 5/28/61
    JMJP, 1/17/62
24. TKP, 3/31/62
25. KJJP, 9/12/61
    KJJP, 5/17/62
26. JMJP, 6/1/61
27. KMJP, 10/19/61
28. KJJP, 6/23/61
29. KJJP, 4/27/62

30. JMJP, 8/23/61
31. NFJP, 3/13/62
32. KJJP, 9/14/61
33. JMJP, 7/7/61
34. KJJP, 5/10/61
35. TKP, 10/17/61
36. JMJP, 8/31/61
37. JMJP, 8/30/61
38. KJJP, 9/22/61
39. JMJP, 7/25/61
40. JMJP, 7/17/61
41. JMJP, 1/12/61
42. JMJP, 11/12/61
43. JMJP, 6/5/61
44. JMJP, 2/3/61
    KJJP, 2/22/62
45. TKP, 9/7/61

46. JMJP, 6/4/61
47. JMJP, 2/22/61
    JMJP, 6/4/61
48. KJJP, 8/16/61
49. JMJP, 3/2/61
50. KJJP, 8/22/61
51. JMJP, 10/20/61
    JMJP, 11/17/61
    NCNA, 1/30/61
    SCMP #2436, 1/30/61
52. SCMP #2687, pp. 8-12
    TKP, 2/2/62
53. JMJP, 1/7/61

It is not possible to know the precise date when Great-Leap-Management policies were either abandoned or introduced. While some plants may have abandoned the two-one-three system, or aspects of it in 1959, still others may only have adopted the same system in 1960, 1961, or even 1962.

115

Table 3 (Continued)

Name of Factory	Total Number of Instances				Number Ranked 1			Number Ranked 2			Number Ranked 3		
	a	b	c	Total	a	b	c	a	b	c	a	b	c
Tangshan Mines	2	1	1	4	0	1	1	0	0	0	2	0	0
Hofei Glass	4	0	0	4	0	0	0	0	0	0	4	0	0
Chungking Water Wheel	5	0	0	5	0	0	0	0	0	0	5	0	0
Chungking Water Pump	2	2	0	4	0	0	0	2	0	0	0	2	0
Ch'gkg Yangchiap'ng Mch. Tool	4	1	0	5	1	0	0	1	0	0	2	1	0
Taiyuan Mining Mach.	2	2	0	4	0	0	0	2	0	0	0	2	0
Taiyuan Iron Smelting	3	0	1	4	2	0	0	1	0	0	0	0	0
Shangtung Weifang Diesel	2	0	0	2	0	0	1	0	0	0	2	0	0
Paotou Steel Smelting	1	0	0	1	0	0	0	1	0	0	0	0	0
Hwangchou Std. Instmt.	7	0	0	7	1	0	0	1	0	0	5	0	0
Kwangchou Machinery	1	0	1	2	0	0	0	0	0	1	1	0	0
Harbin Meas. Inst. & Tool	3	0	0	3	0	0	0	3	0	0	0	0	0
Shihchingshan Iron Smltg.	1	0	0	1	0	0	0	0	0	0	1	0	0
Tairen Machine Tool	0	0	1	1	0	0	1	0	0	0	0	0	0
Changchün Elec. Motor	2	0	0	2	0	0	0	2	0	0	0	0	0
Changchün #8 Rubber	3	0	0	3	1	0	0	1	0	0	1	0	0
Tientsin Vehicles	7	0	3	10	0	0	2	0	3	1	4	0	0
Hangchow Mach. Tool	2	0	0	2	0	0	0	1	0	0	1	0	0
Changchün Mcp. Mov. Mach.	3	0	2	5	3	0	2	0	0	0	0	0	0

CHEMICALS AND DRUGS

Tientsin Pharmaceutical	1	1	3	0	1	0	0	1	1
Chungking Pesticide	3	0	3	0	1	3	0	2	0
Shihchingshan Coking	5	3	8	0	2	3	3	3	0
Taiyuan Chemical	1	1	3	0	0	0	0	1	0
Kirin Chemical	5	6	11	1	2	5	3	3	0

LIGHT INDUSTRY

Suchow Textile Dyeing	0	1	1	0	0	0	0	0	0
Liaoyuan Elec. Generating	1	0	1	0	1	0	1	0	0
Lanchow #1 Woolen Txtl.	4	0	4	0	0	0	4	4	0
Canton Hsun Te Sugar Ref.	1	1	2	0	1	1	0	0	0
P'angfou Txtl. Dyeing	2	1	3	0	2	1	0	0	0
Shanghai An Ta Cotton Txtl.	1	1	3	0	1	1	0	0	0
Tientsin Cigarette	2	0	1	0	0	0	2	1	0
Kwanghua Wood Products	1	0	8	0	0	4	1	0	0
Shanghai Clock	4	4	1	0	4	4	0	0	0
Changchun Shoe	1	0	7	0	1	0	1	0	0
S. China Sewing Machine	5	1	7	1	2	0	3	3	1
Wuhan #1 Textile	0	3	6	0	0	3	0	0	0
Totals	52	11		13	2	14	54	27	10

* In this table, an "instance" refers to a report on a particular management function, as indicated in the previous table. I am dividing the factories and enterprises surveyed into Heavy Industry, Chemical and Drugs, and Light Industry, in accordance with the criteria used in Richman, pp. 154–156.

Table 4 Continuity Factors Evaluated According to Management Function*

Function	Total No. of Functions	No. of times function described as									% of 1	% of 2	% of 3
		1a	2a	3a	1b	2b	3b	1c	2c	3c			
Quality Control & Insp.	16	2	8	5	1	4	0	2	0	0	31	75	31
Discipline	1	0	0	0	0	0	0	0	0	1	0	0	100
Wages & Quotas	8	0	2	5	0	1	1	0	2	0	0	63.3	75
Repair & Maintenance	13	1	4	5	0	5	0	1	0	0	15.2	70	39
Tools & Matl. Supply	19	5	6	6	0	4	2	1	0	0	31.5	52.6	42
Technical Problems	26	0	8	11	0	5	3	4	5	2	15.4	70	61
Personnel	11	1	2	8	0	3	0	2	0	0	27.2	45.5	72.7
Statistics & Accounting	23	1	14	6	0	1	4	1	2	0	81.7	73.9	43.5
Production Planning	15	1	7	5	1	3	1	2	1	0	26.6	73.3	40
Safety	7	2	3	1	0	1	0	1	0	0	42.8	57.1	14.3

* An examination of each management function was made and recorded, and often the management method for that one function was described according to more than one of the Great Leap principles. For example, the repair and maintenance function was described in the Anyang Iron Smelting Plant from the point of view of both the "a" and "b" principle of Great Leap management. Each description of one function is called an "instance." Thus, the number of "instances" given for any one function may be more than the total number of functions described for that enterprise.

nuity with the three principles, (2) some degree of continuity with the principles but not as a dominant factor, and (3) little or no continuity with the Great Leap Forward. Where no information was available on how management worked vis-à-vis one of the ten management functions, the space for that function in that plant is left blank. The chart has two groups of three factors, labeled 1, 2, 3, and a, b, c, respectively. In Group 1:

1. high degree of continuity with Great Leap Forward Management
2. some degree of continuity with Great Leap Forward Management
3. little or no degree of continuity with Great Leap Forward Management

and Group 2:

a. worker participation in management
b. cadre participation in labor
c. triple combination

A pairing of factors from Group 1 and Group 2 gives a continuity code. If for example, in the Nankuang Coal Mines, the Party Committee appointed all work-team leaders in 1962, this would compare to the Great Leap Forward principle of teams electing their own leaders. Thus under personnel management, continuity code 3a would mean little or no worker participation in management of this function in this mine.

The judgments about the degree of continuity are of necessity preliminary, based on somewhat fragmentary evidence, subject to personal interpretation. Tables 3 and 4 are thus qualified.

Tables 3 and 4 are taken from data in Table 2. The data from Table 2 are summed up as follows:

Worker Participation in Management:

1. Strong continuity—11%
2. Some continuity—45.4%
3. Little or no continuity—44.6%

Cadre Participation in Labor:

1. Strong continuity—5%
2. Some continuity—67.5%
3. Little or no continuity—27.5%

Triple Combination:

1. Strong continuity—53.6%
2. Some continuity—35.9%
3. Little or no continuity—10.5%

Of all the reported examples of worker participation in management, only 11 percent were ranked as being strongly continuous with the Great Leap Forward. Nearly half were evaluated as having little or no continuity, and the rest as having some, but not dominant, Great Leap Forward characteristics. In terms of cadre participation in labor, only five percent of the evaluated instances could be ranked as strongly continous with the Great Leap Forward, while over 25 percent showed little or no continuity, and nearly 70 percent showed some continuity.

The triple combination idea, however, showed strong continuity from 1961 to 1963, and probably accounts for some continuity in cadre participation in labor. Although the triple combination method could be used only temporarily for individual cadres, it was a regular system for a factory as a whole. In over half of the cases reported on the triple combination there was strong continuity with the Great Leap Forward; only 15 percent showed little or no use of this method while over one-third showed some continuity. It should be noted that the triple combination groups become less concerned with making policy and more concerned with providing information for the policy makers as worker participation in management changed and as cadre participation in labor changed.

The data from Table 3 are summed up as follows:

	% of Sample	% of Examples Ranked as 1	% of Examples Ranked as 2	% of Examples Ranked as 3
Heavy industry	68	90	59	57
Light Industry	23	3	26	22
Chemical Industry	9	7	15	20

Heavy industry comprised 68 percent of the sample, light industry 23 percent, the chemical industry, 9 percent. However, 90 percent of the examples ranked as strongly continuous with the Great Leap were from heavy industry, while the figures for light and chemical industry were 3 and 7 percent, respectively. The results of the other two rankings show similar proportions. Heavy industry contributed 59 percent of the examples of #2 rankings and 57 percent of the #3 rankings, both below the expected statistical contribution of 68 percent. Light industry contributed 26 percent of the #2 rankings (about as expected statistically) and 22 percent of the #3 rankings (again as expected), while the chemical industry contributed 15 percent of the #2 rankings and about 20 percent of the #3 rankings, both above their statistical contribution to the sample. These data lead to the conclusion that the Great Leap Forward, although undergoing significant over-all modifications, survived better in heavy than in light industry and better in both than in the chemical industry. Such a conclusion was also noted in an NCNA report at the end of 1961[39] and is indirectly supported by the following considerations.

The Great Leap Forward management system required politically motivated and technically-competent cadres willing to break with old routines in which a sharp division between production and administration had been institutionalized. The GLF system required a large number of trained, highly skilled, literate workers who were willing and able to assume the responsibilities and powers that it invoked. The best place to find both types was in modern industry where many cadres (at factory, department, and basic levels) were formerly skilled workers with the experience and confidence to participate in labor. They had also attended school on a part-time or half-work, half-study basis to get theoretical background. For example, the basic-level cadres at the Shanghai #1 Iron and Steel Plant were almost all former workers;[40] in Anshan,[41] Chungking Iron and Steel,[42] and in many Peking factories,[43] and the Machine Building enterprises of Shansi,[44] cadres were former workers whose attitude toward participation in labor probably would be positive. Of course, cadres who were former workers existed in all enterprises, but the skilled workers in heavy industry with experience in Shanghai, Tientsin, Dairen, and all of former Manchuria served as a base.

Light industry also had significant numbers of skilled workers to serve as a basis for recruitment of red and expert cadres which the Great Leap Forward-management system required, but two factors help explain why light industry presented more of a problem for Great Leap Forward management than did heavy industry.

First, much of light industry, especially textile plants, was closely related to pre-1949 management methods, with a higher proportion of bourgeois personnel. The heavy industry focus of the first Five-Year-Plan did not serve to expand light industry as quickly or as urgently. So, though skilled workers existed in light industry, not as many were utilized as cadres because expansion and growth were not as urgent. This resulted in engineering, technical, and management personnel in light industry remaining more homogeneously related to pre-1949 values and attitudes and less likely to accept the GLF revolutionary concepts of human relationships. Moreover, many of the workers were women, subject to other conservative, societal pressures and victims of a history of oppression and inequality in such vital areas as education.

Secondly, local industry had expanded rapidly during the Great Leap Forward[45] moving into areas where both workers and managers lacked experience and skill. Large numbers of part-time workers were assimilated into the local industrial work forces, many of them in light industry or chemical fertilizer plants; the limited time they had for learning skills posed a significant problem for the Great Leap Forward system.[46]

The chemical industry, which had grown as a complement to the needs of heavy industry, was rapidly expanded during the GLF, especially in fertilizers and pesticides and manpower requirements had to be met by workers with little or no experience and by cadres largely the product of highly specialized institutes of higher education.[47]

This social and educational polarity was not conducive to the Great Leap Forward-management system. As the period of readjustment got underway in earnest in 1961–1963, much tighter control from the top levels was necessary in enterprises where skills, experience, and literacy were lacking at the basic levels.

Table 4 evaluates continuity of the Great Leap Forward according to management function rather than according to industry. Here the data more clearly suggest the nature of continuity of Great Leap Forward systems. In quality control more power was given to functional departments. Although workers perhaps retained the right to make a preliminary judgment about quality, final decisions were made by cadres who now visited the production line rather than working as part of it. The determination of quotas was almost entirely removed from the basic-level work teams, primarily because quota management was integrally linked to the incentive system. Cadres from specialized departments became responsible for rational output, quality, and productivity targets, in consultation with workers as a means to measure intangibles such as morale and willingness to work.[48] In this way, political work for the Party Committee during 1961–1963 consisted largely of exhortation, morale building, and rhetoric designed to elicit maximum performance from workers who, increasingly rewarded for fulfilling targets and meeting quotas, had a selfish interest in *low* targets and easy quotas even as they were urged to contribute to the building of socialism.[49] Discipline became the concern of higher-level control organs, especially the Party Committee, rather than the function of the small work team.

Repair and maintenance work was scheduled and organized by specialized personnel; daily and minor maintenance was done by workers. Cadres from the technical departments drew up detailed and strict repair and maintenance schedules, but the actual repair and servicing was done by special mechanics from a separate work shop or by the machine operators themselves. Care and storage of tools remained largely in the hands of workers, but storage of and control over new and semi-finished materials was generally returned to special departments at the work-shop level with close relationships to middle-level departments such as finance and accounting.

Although technical decision-making was concentrated in the technical departments, there was a significant amount of interaction between workers and technicians and between technicians and basic-level cadres. The triple combination principle remained an ongoing system, and many technicians, especially in machine building enterprises, seemed to show a marked preference for this method of work,[50] although many technicians were spending more time in their offices.

Personnel management was usually removed from the province of the work teams and put under special departments of the Party Committee. Statistic and accounting work was recentralized, but workers continued to record quantities of input and output. Cadres exercised increased financial control over the small-group accounting units, with accounting at the small-group level being put under more control at the departmental level. The small groups retained the responsibility for shift change-overs and work sequence though not the regulation of work pace nor the assignment of individual jobs. In so far as workers' attitudes and comments had any influence on quotas, the incentive system was a crucial factor in determining how much worker participation in production planning would remain.

Safety management remained mostly the province of the work teams, with an occasional inspection visit by one or a group of cadres.

Clearly some management functions retained more characteristics of the Great Leap Forward System than others did. Tool and safety management and certain repair and maintenance functions remained largely under team control with significant cadre participation in these activities as part of scheduled labor at the basic levels. Technical problem solving continued to be strongly influenced by the triple combination in the course of daily operations, but innovation, design, and experimentation were almost completely removed from worker participation and became the province of specialized departments and personnel. Quota management, accounting, and production planning were put in the hands of the functional departments, although basic-level team accounting continued to be an important aspect of team work. In general, it seems that the management functions most significantly affected by the period of consolidation after 1961 were those which had impact on coordination and planning above the enterprise.

Cadre participation in labor was also mixed, persisting primarily as a means of gathering information for higher levels, being done for most management functions, though less so than during the Great Leap Forward.

Participation and Incentives

As ambivalence regarding power distribution grew, as more control over work-team decisions was vested in administrative and technical departments, there was major concern over incentives.

Distinction must be made between workers' congresses and worker control and participation in management.[51] Workers congresses can co-exist with a high degree of social, economic and political inequality; they are not able to alter class privilege, or attitudes, transform organizational rules or effect the acquisition of knowledge.

Beginning in 1961, workers' congresses and incentives were once again being openly debated.[52] By October, "the workers' representative conference . . . (was) . . . an important system for promoting democracy within an enterprise and for encouraging the worker masses to participate in enterprise management and administrative supervision."[53] These conferences were not only to "arrange tasks and mobilize the masses to fulfill production tasks."[54] Workers' congresses had essentially the same broad functions as before the GLF. These were to "listen to and discuss" the work report of the factory manager, to "investigate and discuss" enterprise bonus and reward systems, welfare and labor insurance programs, to "make decisions" about expenditures on these items. The congresses were to criticize cadres and send these reports to higher levels. The workers' congresses had the right to reject higher-level decisions once.[55] The congress was convened by the trade-union organization under the leadership of the Party Committee.

In practice congresses were concerned primarily with production and welfare. The agenda was made by the leadership, and the trade union had to be urged to take the congresses seriously and not turn them into an expanded meeting of cadres.

Workers' congresses meant that, for the great majority of workers, the frequency of participation declined compared to the Great Leap. They were held monthly, quarterly, on a trimester basis, or only once a year. For example, Anshan's Iron Smelting Plant elected representatives once a year and held full congresses once a quarter;[56] at the work-shop level, once a month. The Canton Shih Ku Mining area held congresses once a month,[57] the Tayeh Iron Mine in Wuhan, two or three times a year.[58] Participation in production management was often peripheral even when basic-level conferences were held once a week.[59]

Since the congresses were open to others besides production line workers, representatives on those congresses often were not workers but department-level functional cadres or work-shop-level leaders.[60] They had to operate within the existing power structure serving as a watchdog committee to see that resolutions were carried out.[61] Sometimes the representatives duplicated the activities of the trade union or youth league concerning discipline or morale. At meetings of the whole body of workers, suggestions or criticisms were accepted but had to go through existing channels.[62]

The discussions were usually limited to welfare and planned targets.[63] Suggestions for technical innovation, labor assignments and the exchange of information concerning new production processes or technical innovations were also considered.[64]

It is difficult to estimate the degree to which workers' congresses replaced direct participation or was a supplement to it. The Anshan Iron Smelting Plant reported that though congresses were held from 1958–1960 they became more important after 1960.[65] This was probably the trend in the rest of the country, but the crucial point is that workers' congresses as the main form of participation were part of the evolving incentive systems.

The Great Leap Forward did not abandon material incentives. Piece-rate incentives, wage grading, and bonuses had not been eliminated but were disbursed collectively.[66] What distinguished the Great Leap Forward incentive policy was the emphasis on political dedication to the building of socialism. Incentive would come from feelings of solidarity, mutual cooperation, and collective improvement rather than from individual competition and monetary rewards.

In 1961, Party Committees showed new interest in piece-rate wages. At first, the emphasis was on collective piece-rate bonuses, then on piece-rate wages to individuals.[67]

> The overwhelming majority of enterprises were under a system of some type of piece-rate or hourly wage, plus reward, for paying workers; the straight hourly wage without possibility of an added bonus was seldom used.[68]

By 1963 the wage-grading system was considered inadequate by some when compared to piece-rate wages. That year there was a wage reform allowing "bigger differentials based on skill and performance . . . as well as bonuses for managerial personnel."[69] There was more involved, however, than a return to individual material incentives.[70]

Even as renewed interest in material incentives emerged *Kung-jen Jih-pao* published a three-day series of articles for cadre and worker political study. The major themes were class struggle, collectivism, internationalism, the labor theory of value, and reliance on the masses. The articles called for the need to revolutionize political institutions and for courage, selflessness, determination, and for the fostering of revolutionary heirs; and they argued that public spirit was more important than selfishness.[71]

In 1962, this debate took on a much heavier theoretical tone. Disagreements about the role of material incentives in building a socialist society and on China's industrial development were still very much alive. The group which criticized material incentive upheld the two-fold character of reward for the amount and type of work, saying that it was still necessary, though unequal in its practical effects, and therefore a "bourgeois right." Moreover, it was premised on a bourgeois value system which considered some work to be onerous and which made arbitrary judgments about the value of different kinds of socially necessary labor.[72] This position argued that:

> (Distribution According to Labor) decides the equal rights of people to obtain consumer goods by the standard of labor and their unequal rights to actual standards of consumption. Such rights, which are equal in form and unequal in fact, are bourgeois lawful rights. Because such lawful rights are present, if we do not pay attention to ideological and political education, and if we enforce a wage system with great disparity in wage gradings, some people will evince such undesirable tendencies as being over-particular about pay, and laboring according to pay. Such tendencies are detrimental to socialist construction.[73]

Whatever the theoretical disagreements over incentives, the advocates and practitioners of individual material incentives had the temporary logic of circumstances and the evolving management system on their side. The generally tense, often chaotic, situation after the GLF made economic planners and administrators above the enterprise wish to exert tighter control. They wanted precise output and productivity data which they had previously obtained from the control departments within factories before the GLF. Increased control over production naturally reduced the participation, equality, and solidarity that had formed the basis for the incentives of the Great Leap Forward. Hence, individualist material incentives became more logical, but as they did, the need for further control became more pronounced, especially for output quotas and labor productivity norms which were the basis of the incentive system. Here, the selfish motives of individuals, which were the chief psychological basis of individualist material incentives, came sharply into conflict with high productivity. Moreover, the economic crisis and the psychological let-down after the euphoria that sometimes accompanied the Leap did very little to offset the emphasis on individual self-salvation that was an obvious, if only temporary, trend in Chinese society once again.

Thus, a vicious circle was set in motion. The more control, the more logic for individual incentives; the more logical individual incentives became, the more it was necessary to control quotas and norms which were the basis of incentive payments; and more management control made it more logical for individual material incentives to replace participation, equality, and solidarity and so on. The wage reforms of 1963 and a simultaneous promulgation of rules and regulations governing inventions and innovations evidenced this emphasis on material rewards.[74]

There was, however, not a complete reversal. In the post-GLF readjustment period there was only slightly more emphasis on individual piece-rate incentive payments. Bonuses were not overgenerous, averaging somewhere below the maximum allowed, which was 15 percent of a person's monthly standard wage. There was continued income inequality, but it was not widely disparate.[75] Though the 1963 changes raised workers' pay, there was less disparity between highest and lowest paid workers than under the 1954 system, which was officially in effect during the Great Leap Forward. There were lower maximum payments for technical innovations, and a raise averaging about 10 percent of the average monthly wage was accomplished simply by moving eligible workers up one grade in the eight-grade wage scale[76] without changing the range between grades one and eight. Emulation campaigns, model workers, cooperative agreements based on work-team initiative, and cadre and worker participation in triple-combination teams continued at many enterprises.[77]

Like the general management system, the incentive system in the consolidation period of 1961–1963 was an amalgam of the Great Leap Forward policies of politics in command and of earlier practices of control, one-man management, and material incentives. As the trend away from the policies of the Great Leap Forward gathered momentum throughout 1962, an intellectual and organizational confrontation was brewing—inside and outside the Communist Party which had become so integrally a part of the Chinese industrial system.

Industrial Management and the Emerging Political Confrontation

Evolving against the background of personnel changes brought on by the GLF, the growing professionalization and centralization of technical authority caused conflict between technical and production leaders and between higher and lower level technical personnel. One important discussion of these problems noted four major issues in regard to technical authority:[78]

1. Since the relationship between technical and nontechnical decision-making was not always clear in a factory where everything could be technically relevant, close coordination between technical and administrative personnel was required. Ideally, administrators should have technical knowledge, including members of the Communist Party.
2. Conflict between chief engineers and vice factory directors, emerged because both often had the same or similar responsibilities.
3. The relationship between the chief engineer and his work-shop-

level technicians, and the work-shop foreman was often antagonistic because the work-shop foreman could be a major source of
opposition to the chief engineer and his subordinates.
4. The relationship between technical personnel and workers was
   a major problem. If technical personnel now made all the decisions and consulted with workers at will, what then would become
   of the political impact of the GLF?

There were both organizational and political issues involved yet, the
conscious attempt to solve the organizational problems often ignored the
political implications. For example, one commonly advocated solution
in 1962 was to combine technical and administrative authority in one
person, who would then wear two hats:

> I believe that the factory director in charge of production management,
> section heads, and foremen should become respectively chief engineers,
> section engineers, and workshop engineers at the same time, for this would
> produce no contradictions in production management.[79]

In many cases the chief engineers were made vice-directors responsible
for all technical work,[80] with authority over technicians in special units
at each level. They were to brook no interference nor respond to any
other demands on their time.[81] As one article flatly expressed it:

> technical work in all enterprises must be done chiefly by technical per-
> sonnel, whose authority in the enterprises should be respected. Decisions
> made by them within the scope of their duties must be supported by the
> leadership.[82]

Aside from the fact that workers as a group would tend to lose
significant decision-making power under these conditions, there was
another far-reaching implication to consider. The increased emphasis
on technical and other controls at the department level indicated reliance
on only one sector of China's technically trained people. During the
Great Leap Forward there had been a rapid rise in the number of
technicians and engineers of working class or peasant background who
had studied at part-time, informal, or spare-time schools and an increase
in their employment at all levels.[83] Now, the emphasis changed; graduates of the formal, or regular and full-time, schools[84] were to provide
technical expertise and make decisions. Only when this was not possible
were part-time or spare-time school graduates used.[85] By 1962, 90
percent of the technicians had been brought up and educated since
1949. Most technicians and engineers were graduates of the full-time
track,[86] the majority from landlord or urban business families with a
more or less middle-class upbringing. The primary beneficiaries, therefore, of the trends in technical and other areas of management in Chinese
industry were precisely those students whose family or social back-

ground tended to make them prize the administrative, non-manual labor positions traditionally respected by the Chinese upper classes, and now once again assuming their organizational, if not ideological, legitimacy. For this reason, by the middle of 1962 there were latent schisms in the ranks of technical and engineering personnel which were related as much to values and attitudes toward manual labor as they were to issues of power, authority, and prestige.[87]

Contradictions were also beginning to develop in the administrative and planning area, and these were identified as crucial political-ideological differences. In December 1961 a conference of Communist Party secretaries in charge of work in industry was held at which a document—later to be known as "Seventy Articles for Regulations in Industry"—was discussed.[88] The "Seventy Articles" constituted an overall strategic approach essentially aimed at negating the GLF experiments and returning to one-man management. It was not the only position on these problems that had emerged. As polemics during the Cultural Revolution were later to assert, the Seventy Articles were put forth only a short time after Mao Tsetung had summed up what he considered to be the positive experiences of the Great Leap Forward in industry in a set of five principles called the Anshan Constitution.[89] Significantly, the Anshan Constitution was presented as a counterprogram to the Constitution of the Magnitogorsk Iron and Steel Works, the set of rules and regulations of the huge Soviet complex which presumably had served as a model for one-man management at Anshan when it was under heavy Soviet influence in the early- and mid-1950s. The five major principles of the Anshan Constitution were:

1. Stick to putting politics in command.
2. Strengthen party leadership.
3. Go in for mass movements in a big way.
4. Institute the two-one-three system of management.
5. Vigorously carry out technical revolution.[90]

Actually, however, the party disagreements over economic coordination and planning methods went beyond these five principles. It had become painfully obvious as a result of the GLF that the division of power and responsibility within plants could not help but affect coordination among them. The converse was also true: methods of coordinating the wider economy effected the division of power and responsibility in each individual plant.

Highly centralized planning, requiring a huge administrative apparatus, led to rigidity in implementation of plans and adaptation to unforeseen circumstances. Decentralization was to provide flexibility and reduce the size of the administrative bureaucracy, not to eliminate the importance of central authority in major investment decisions. On this there was general agreement. But decentralization did not in any way reduce the need to coordinate the activities of various enterprises, and it raised the matter of control and incentives. These were sharp and critical issues with multiple political and ideological implications.

There were two approaches to this dilemma. One saw the problem of economic coordination as both economic and political, advocating institutions based on concepts of value and efficiency which went beyond allocational or cost efficiency alone. Given decentralization of the planning process, Party Committees were to increase the flexibility to meet unforeseen demands or shortages by "diversified undertakings and multiple utilization" of facilities in their own factories.[91] Coordination of enterprises, and of enterprises with higher level planning authorities on local, provincial, or national levels, was to be through face-to-face bargaining. Questions of cost would be determined by using political and social criteria as well as those influenced only by the state of development and the structure of the economy.[92] At the same time, management, as a matter of political principle, was to exert every effort to be as efficient and economical as possible by using all locally available resources and labor. As an editorial in *Jen-min Jih-pao* put it:

> The running of enterprises with industry and thrift is not a question of method but of policy. It is not a question of management, but of political orientation.[93]

Under this system, management was supposed to serve the public first of all. Targets would be based on a conscious political inquiry rather than on prices which could more easily reflect previous imbalances and distortions in development, the priorities of far-away planners, or the ability to pay rather than need. Hoarding materials so that others had to do without needed supplies or the withholding of production in the hope that prices (and hence profits) would rise were all to be avoided on principle. Economic contracts between enterprises were to be established to concretize the targets that enterprises were given from higher authorities and to make more efficient use of excess capacity for pressing local needs.[94] In theory, these incentives would achieve coordination and economic activity would not become a process of self-enrichment and the justification for inequality in society.

The opposite position viewed the problem primarily as an economic one and stressed prices and the profit motive as the best guarantee for managerial efficiency and the main indicator which determined investment priorities for economic activity. This position was not seen as an abandonment of planning. It argued that economics and politics should be separated; that decentralization was to depend less on inquiry into local needs by local political authorities and more on the decisions of management, which would react according to the principle of profit maximization based upon prices determined by higher level planning authorities. Rather than factories to manufacture a broad array of parts and finished goods utilizing as many local resources as was consistent with the central planning priorities, under this proposed system economic coordination would be based on specialization and strict allocational efficiency criteria. Flexibility would be achieved through contracts between enterprises to be based on the prices of raw materials and other inputs of the production process.[95] Profits, aside from fixed amounts given to the central authorities, could be used as the managers saw fit. The party would see that managers did not use retained profits in corrupt or antisocial ways, as, for example, the purchase of a company car for the private use of factory officials on weekends. In both of these approaches, the local branches of the People's Bank, with the Party Committee and the financial departments would also help control the use of investment funds and profits.[96] But in the second position the banks would also be tied closely to administrators in large corporations or "trusts" as well as with local enterprises. The trusts would integrate all enterprises engaged in the manufacture or marketing of closely related products. The trusts would thus replace local governmental authority from the provincial level on down as the basic units from which national planning priorities would be produced. They would cooperate with national planners to determine the prices which would ultimately shape production patterns.[97]

Each of these concepts had a different image of economic administration. One, as an activist leader, competent in face-to-face communication, constantly making on-the-spot checks "at various levels . . . at regular or irregular intervals . . . deep into basic-level enterprise units to examine how their cooperation plans have been fulfilled and to discover existing problems on time."[98] The other, as a bureaucrat handling statistical reports, drawing up detailed tables and balance sheets from an office which had mostly telephone links not only with the enterprise but with the banks at various levels.

Given the tense economic situation of the times, and the pre–Great Leap experience with Soviet style planning and one-man management, it it not surprising that the higher level authorities would tend to fall back on the bureaucratic image as the way out of a potentially serious political and economic crisis. There can be little doubt that Soviet-style planning began to look very safe and far more reliable than the experiments of the Great Leap Forward. Based on nation-wide vertical integration and strict allocational efficiency rather than on both national and local development and mass mobilization of all human and natural resources, the Soviet system of material incentives and the profit motive would, however, exacerbate inequalities rather than reduce them by collective advancement. It tended to build up cities and neglect rural areas, intensifying cultural and developmental inequalities between urban and rural areas. It required a huge bureaucracy to administer the economy and coordinate the activities of closely related but widely scattered units of production. Such a bureaucracy would be likely to develop a vested interest in maintaining its privileged position in the society over which it ruled. These, at any rate, were some of the basic political-economic criticisms that Mao Tsetung made of the Soviet system and Soviet-style socialism.[99]

It was not easy for the Chinese planners to gamble on consolidating and perfecting the experiments of the GLF, since many of these experiments were at least partially responsible for the problems of economic imbalance that were now faced so uncomfortably.[100] For these authorities, economic coordination meant being busy with input-output tables, matrices of various kinds, and complex price calculations. To get this information, they demanded that enterprise-level management send up to them comprehensive statistical information concerning costs, utilization, and productivity quotas.

In turn, enterprise management would have to obtain this information, record it, analyze it, and send it on to higher levels. For planning authorities and industrial departments, the easiest figure to work with would be the enterprise profit index, for it gave them a basis upon which to give rewards to motivate managers, and it gave them an over-all economic indicator for comparing the most efficient use of scarce resources on a wide scale. For enterprise-level leadership, the most important source of information and control would be the specialized functional departments which handled quotas and figures. Coming in on a regular schedule, these figures were the substance of the enterprise's communication to higher levels and the basis of control activities and policy decisions.

As the substance and channels of communications thus developed, economic inequality would increase and workers would again become the political inferiors of technicians, engineers, and bureaucrats. They would take orders and fulfill the quotas and targets of the functional departments. Worker participation in management would atrophy as cadre participation in labor became more of a formal game than a relevant managerial activity, making sense only for middle-level management and below. Even here its importance would be questionable. Top-level enterprise management, including party members with other responsibilities would find participation in labor usually unnecessary, seldom useful, and rarely possible.

By the time of the Tenth Plenum of the Eighth Chinese Communist Party Central Committee meetings of September 1962, these issues represented the essence of class struggle in the industrial system. At this time Mao began to organize forces for a counterattack on the post-GLF trends, and initiated a process that had enormous resonance in Chinese society. It was ultimately to result in the major political upheaval of the Cultural Revolution.[101]

The confrontation was joined in September 1962 with an article in *Kung-jen Jih-pao*, followed by a long theoretical discussion of "class struggle during the transition period" in *Hung Ch'i*.[102] The *Hung Ch'i* article analyzed the stubborn power of the bourgeois class as flowing not from its hold on political power but on its cultural, ideological, and psychological reserves. This was possible because of two major characteristics of socialist society: (1) the need for expertise and its relative scarcity with the resultant tendency of experts to see themselves as a privileged group and (2) the force of bourgeois habits, morals, and ethics which held that personal privilege, power, wealth, and reputation were the proper goals of human activity. This theoretical discussion continued during 1963.[103]

Along with the tone of moral and ethical struggle in articles addressed to intellectuals generally, there was a major shift in emphasis on the economy and industrial management. This shift, signaled by a June editorial in *JMJP*, was quickly followed by a long discussion in *Hung Ch'i*.[104] Having observed the extreme importance of participation in labor and a "tendency which is in the budding state" to undermine the revolutionary nature of Chinese political institutions, the editorial then made the following points:

1. People's relationships in the course of production could be crucial aspects in the creation of new people and a new society. Productive activity not only prevented starvation, death, or hardship but had to help create these new people and this new society. Ownership did not determine the existence of classes under socialism, but the particular kinds of relationships between people in the course of daily production did. Cadre participation in labor was vital.

2. Participation in labor served important economic functions, reducing urban white collar bureaucracy which demanded consumer goods. This demand could cause pressure on limited consumer goods output and lead to inflation, loans, reliance on foreign aid, or luxury imports, all of which would exacerbate social and economic inequality, the urban-rural gap, and psychological and economic dependency. Hence, it was urged that enterprises:

> pay even more serious attention to the problem of the distribution of labor power in productive and nonproductive departments, and make great efforts to increase the number of productive laborers in a more effective way, so as to reduce the number of nonproductive personnel to the minimum.

Participation in labor would overcome bureaucratic management bringing unity, solidarity, cooperation, and a great willingness to contribute productively to the collective effort by generating an atmosphere in which nonbourgeois incentives could flourish.

The class struggle in industry, therefore, revealed a potential conflict between the enterprise leadership and higher level industrial departments or planning authorities on the one hand, and workers and many middle and basic level cadres on the other. Factory level management was in the center of the conflict and in the most ambivalent position.

Questions of attitude and not just organization were important because many cadres who did not want to participate in labor did have to and many cadres who did not have to participate in labor did, in fact, want to.[105]

The Communist Party was no abstraction divorced from the lives of the individual Party members who comprised it.[106] If the management system was ambivalent, so too was the party's position within that system. Party members were to master scientific knowledge and follow the mass line by more widespread use of triple combination teams,[107] but party organizations at the larger enterprises, except for cadres below the enterprise level, and in the planning and coordinative bureaucracy did not, it seems, require their members to participate in labor as stringently as did those in smaller plants.[108]

As part of the emphasis on class struggle beginning in September 1962, a socialist education campaign was launched throughout the country.[109] In industrial enterprises, the All China Federation of Trade Unions began a study of the heroic and selfless PLA soldier Lei Feng,[110] and factory histories were written and discussed in order to foster a spirit of struggle and collectivism, as opposed to comfort and privilege seeking.[111]

By the end of 1963 a nationwide movement to learn from the People's Liberation Army, was launched with the idea of making mutual help and equality a chief characteristic of relationships between leader and led. [112] While individual material incentives continued,[113] increased cadre participation in labor and worker participation in management generated greater reliance on incentives of emulation, pride, and cooperation.[114]

By 1964 it was clear that management problems would not be solved by the simple formula of "factory director responsibility under the leadership of the Party Committee." In fact, by 1964, the party's leadership in the economy and in industrial enterprises was as strong as it ever was, if not stronger. But the Party's organizational dominance could not hide the contradictions that, like the first signs of lava from a volcano that was soon to erupt, were bubbling to the surface of Chinese society.

6 / Ambivalence Becomes Confrontation: China's Industrial System from 1964 to 1966

THE GREAT LEAP FORWARD had been an attempt not only at more rapid economic and technological development, but also at redefining some of the principal relationships and crucial institutions in "modern" society. But the practical effects of the Leap had been very contradictory and the conscious attempt to find a socialist alternative to both capitalism and to the Soviet model of "socialism," exacerbated conflict within the Chinese Communist Party. The resultant debate was over nothing less than the meaning of modernization and its relationship to socialism or revolution. It became clear by 1964 that there were many who found the Soviet view persuasive; that modernization along Soviet lines was preferable to the uncertainty and imbalance of the Leap. And there were also many who felt that China could not modernize along Soviet lines, and that even if she could, the result would be far closer to capitalism than to any meaningful kind of socialism. The debate that developed openly in China in the spring of 1964 was on these issues, and within the next two years was to clarify the nature of the challenge that China's modernization was to offer to Western and Soviet perspectives on contemporary history.

Modernization as the Crucial Element

Writing in March 1964, Ma Wen-jui, the Minister of Labor, said:

> At present, our socialist state-operated enterprises consist mostly of modern enterprises, highly socialist in nature. We know that the production processes of modern enterprises are extremely complex and require coordinated efforts of hundreds, thousands, or even hundreds of thousands

of laborers. These laborers must utilize modern machinery and equipment; their division of labor is refined, and their working relationship is very close.[1]

Ma argued that, since modern industry required organization to make maximum rational use of technology, there was no real difference between the *internal* organization of capitalist and socialist industrial enterprises, except that socialist enterprise management paid more attention to "correctly handling relations among men" in the production process.[2] It followed that capitalist economies in general were not as rational as their factory organization suggested. The capitalist economy was marked by irrationalities and waste, while socialist economies, because they were planned, suffered no such shortcomings.[3]

Ma's analysis held that human relationships were shaped by the nature of society. In a capitalist system, the purpose of business was essentially the earning of profits, that this set capitalists in conflict with all the other workers—manual, administrative, and technical—because of the resultant unequal distribution of wealth.[4] The system of ownership in modern society determined the degree of class conflict and inefficiency in that society. Once the system of ownership was changed from private to public, the principle cause of class conflict in modernizing industrial society was eliminated. The most important task for management was production.

The basic task of State Operated Industrial Enterprises is first of all, in accordance with stipulations in State plans, to increase the social product to satisfy the needs of society.[5]

In Ma's view, the internal organization of socialist enterprises was not exactly the same as in capitalist society. There were three major systems of management.[6] For the first time in two years, the two participations and triple combination was mentioned as one of these systems. There were also workers' congresses and the system of "factory director responsibility under the leadership of the Party Committee." Ma saw the two participation, triple combination system and workers' congresses as management tools for smoothing over human conflict and making communications more efficient.[7] Workers and managers would remain essentially separate groups even in the long run, and in a socialist society the relationship between them was not part of the class struggle. Revolution was a matter of spirit and thought—the maintenance of good morale and a positive attitude toward one's work and position in the responsibility systems that were the concern of the plant manager.[8] Comradely . . . mutual aid and cooperation was to characterize the relationships between people in the plant,[9] while complaints could be aired at the periodic workers' congresses.[10] Incentives were to consist of individual material rewards, collective material rewards, political education on social responsibility, and emulation campaigns.[11]

Revolution Precedes Modernization

Ma's view that revolutionization was practically complete with the change in the system of ownership was challenged by those who argued that while "the success of a socialist enterprise demands modernization . . . revolutionization must precede modernization."[12] Revolutionization was more than a change in ownership, more than a prod to production. It included a change in the daily routines of the workers:

> Politics hangs in command (Cheng-chih kua-shuai) means that it must "hang" on the basis of production; political work must combine with economic work, the production struggle, scientific experiment, worker's livelihood, and cannot be carried out in isolation.[13]

The Party Committee was to be the link between politics and production, a guarantee that revolutionization would precede modernization. Whatever its precise meaning, the advocates of revolutionization, while very anxious to increase production, saw it as more than just a way to do so.[14] They were, in fact, willing to sacrifice some undetermined short range production goals if that was required.

> The leaders of some enterprises still regard the work of the revolutionization of man as a morphine injection for stimulating production; some comrades worry that persistence in revolutionization and class struggle would hinder the normal production of an enterprise; some comrades even grasp production only, take no heed of revolution, do no work on the revolutionization of man, and regard class struggle as unnecessary.[15]

The Debate Continues

As part of what was now obviously a growing and free wheeling Marxist debate, other articles interpreted the relationship between revolution and modernization differently.

One took a dim view of revolutionization, supporting trends of the past three years. In this view, the Party Committee would act as a kind of board of directors for the enterprise and the factory manager would be directly responsible for production. Technology more or less dictated the nature of production organization, and the mass line was simply a good method of leadership, one which could help smooth over conflict but not redistribute power. The division of labor must be strict, backed by written rules and regulations, not allowing job rotation or role exchange.[16]

Another article, using the USSR as a negative example of modern revisionism, insisted that "it is very dangerous for socialist industrial enterprises to talk only of modernization without carrying out revolutionization."

> The modern revisionists want only modernization but oppose revolutionization. Actually they also want to enforce the capitalist principles. They hold that modernization is omnipotent. As to man, he can only submit to and prostrate himself before the power of modern technology and be its slave. . . .
> Our viewpoint is fundamentally different from theirs. We want modernization, but we want revolutionization even more. The socialist industrial enterprises of China must not only be modernized ones. What is more important is that they must be revolutionized enterprises.[17]

Ignoring the prevalence of one-man management and Soviet influence prior to 1955–1956, this article extolled the role of Communist Party Committees in taking over Chinese industrial centers. However, in spite of its revolutionary tone this essay defined revolutionization as a process which accepted party leadership and helped workers to heighten their class consciousness and to rapidly increase production in the hope of promotion. Class struggle in the enterprise did not effect the basic relationship between workers and managers but was aimed at corrupt managers.[18]

Like many intellectual and theoretical debates, the discussion seemed to convey less substance as the arguments proliferated and were refined. Yet there was no doubt that there was a crucial issue beneath the surface. Another article clarified matters. *Jen-min Jih-pao*, continuing the theme of urging cadre participation in labor begun in June 1963, now expanded on it by urging the "working personnel of the *leading organs* of industrial enterprises" (no longer just the shop level or party branch level as was the case in 1963) and "their chief responsible cadres" to "maintain a firm grip on both upper and lower levels."[19] The newspaper focused on the middle-level control sections and departments. These departments, an editorial in *Kung-jen Jih-pao* said:

> Should not float emptily above, but should deeply enter the basic level, should not wait at the top in the doorway, but should go down to the door at the bottom, should not add to peoples troubles, but should create convenience for people, should not repeatedly delay but should do things determinedly and quickly.
> In all of this, if we don't clearly understand who serves whom, and don't strongly have the viewpoint of service, then none of it can be done. The revolutionization of department (or section) work relies on going

back to serving the basic level, to serving production, to serve the masses. This is the basic question in the revolutionization of section work.[20]

Once again, as during the Great Leap Forward, revolutionization was clearly concerned with the role of the functional departments and of the behavior and attitudes of management cadres above the basic level. And the same or very similar problems remained. One was the attitude of cadres toward manual labor.

> Some cadres, on hearing "serve the front line of production," immediately feel psychologically uneasy. They say some work is high, some low, some noble, some mean.[21]

Another, no less serious, was the practical question of daily routine and division of responsibility. Some argued that technology and modern production required management and a boss (chang) and, therefore, required functional departments to control and coordinate production.[22]

Revolutionization, therefore, could not be considered strictly a matter of thought or attitude but concerned the relationship between organizational levels and the distribution of power. Cadre participation in labor, one of the keys to revolutionization, required structural changes which were not fully understood even with the experience of the Great Leap Forward. An editorial in *JMJP* stated:

> If the cadres of industrial enterprises disassociate themselves from manual labor for a long time and place themselves in a special position, capable of rendering verbal service only without using their hands and indulging in an easy life without taking part in productive labor, then bourgeois thinking will take the opportunity to invade them, alienate them ideologically and emotionally from the working people, or even cause them to degenerate. This applies without any exception to cadres promoted from the working class. . . .
>
> *The contradiction between labor and the cadres' own regular work must be solved according to actual conditions. . . . The solving of the ideological question must also be followed with the solving of the question of method. . . .*
>
> *It must be admitted that in modernized industrial enterprises, it is impossible to organize the cadres well for participation in labor if no practicable measures and methods are designed to create the necessary conditions for the cadres to undertake labor.* Because even if there is some transient enthusiasm for labor, it cannot long endure. Modernized industrial enterprises in particular are characterized by production continuity, fixed production costs, complex techniques, strict management, and other features. How to accommodate these features and make cadres' participation in labor conducive to strengthening of management and increasing of production is indeed an important question. [Italics added.][23]

If revolutionization was based on continuing class struggle, as Mao had said, then the clear implication of these essays was that the basic relationship between workers and management in industrial enterprises was a key part of that struggle. Mao had seen potential conflict in this relationship as early as 1962 and had pointed it out in 1964. Early in 1965 he urged that the socialist education campaign be aimed directly at enterprise management.[24]

Part of this campaign was a series of articles on the relationship between exploitation and management which began to appear in the *Kuang-ming Jih-pao* in the form of an academic-theoretical discussion about the nature of exploitation in a capitalist society.[25] The central question posed by these discussions was, under what conditions could the work of management in modern industrial enterprises be considered exploitation? Since this kind of work was also done by capitalists, or at least by the managers they hired for the purpose, what then was the difference between socialist enterprise management, and capitalist enterprise management? If the manager's work was absolutely essential, if it could not, therefore, be considered exploitation, then why not admit that in modern industrial enterprises socialists used capitalist methods, thereby for all practical purposes obliterating the distinction between socialism-communism and capitalism.

By the end of 1965 the relationship between workers and managers was presented as a manifestation of the dichotomy between mental and manual labor, and the elimination of this dichotomy became an aspect of revolutionization. A major theoretical article in the economic journal *Ching-chi Yen-chiu* (Economic Research) flatly asserted:

> The problem of enterprise management is primarily one of relations between managers and productive workers. A socialist enterprise is different in essence from a capitalist enterprise. The important aspect of this difference lies in the relationship between managers and productive workers. In a capitalist enterprise, the managers represent the capitalist class; they are "rulers;" they abstain from manual labor and many of them do not engage in mental labor either; they are exploiters and oppressors who gain without labor and stand in opposition to the masses of the workers or the manual workers they rule. In a socialist enterprise, the managers are representative of the working class. They should take part not only in mental labor . . . but also in physical labor. [Italics added.]
>
> The existence of the difference between physical labor and mental labor does not owe its birth to the foundation of the socialist society . . . (Its) existence within the working class is both a manifestation of the lack of development in the forces of production and also a kind of manifestation of the class differences left behind from the old society. It is a remnant of capitalism in the socialist society.
>
> We must realize that if it is not overcome, or if it is allowed to develop further, it is possible that the difference will expand and even be transformed into antagonism anew. If managers and scientific and technical personnel, arising from the working class, become divorced from physical

labor, become fond of leisure and give themselves privileges, then bourgeois ideology will grow. If such phenomena emerge in large numbers, it will give rise to a specially privileged stratum to ride high over the masses of workers and peasants, provide a social foundation for the birth of revisionism and lead to the restoration of capitalism.[26]

This was not simply a theoretically interesting dilemma for continuing controversy and speculation amongst socialist or Marxist intellectuals. The experiments of the Great Leap Forward and the subsequent consolidation period had shown the nature of the problem clearly. Socialist management had real psychological and organizational implications. It was not an abstract intellectual matter to working people.

In September 1965 *JMJP* published a major editorial which surveyed industrial management's historical evolution in China and pointed out some of the implications that socialist transformation would likely have in the Chinese context.[27] The Chinese clearly saw themselves at a historic juncture with universal meaning. Industrialization and most of the systems of industrial management in China had been copied from modernized Western countries or from the Soviet Union, or were left over from pre-1949 Chinese factories. None of these were compatible with socialist modernization. A series of five major reforms had been enacted thus far:

1. Responsibility of the factory director under the leadership of the Party Committee.
2. Cadre participation in labor and worker participation in management.
3. Stress on ideological and political education for workers and administrative personnel.
4. Use of the triple combination.
5. Use of mass emulation campaigns.

Most enterprises had introduced some of these reforms "one way or another" but many others continued to adhere to their old regulations and systems, which led to bureaucratic domination by those at higher levels. In order to revolutionize management, there had to be a fundamental transformation of power distribution.

Some comrades who run enterprises stress "management" but ignore reliance on the masses and ideo-political work. Because everything is dependent on "management" by the higher levels, division of work has become more and more minute, and levels of control more and more complex.

Noting that control was only one aspect of management in industry, this editorial stressed the need to allow for socialist initiative and creativity by trusting and relying on the workers as a serious matter of basic political principle; one which took precedence over control by management.

Rules and regulations which assigned duties and responsibilities had to be overhauled, and organizational structure simplified. Administrative cadres could then be freed from routines which prevented emotional and political identification with the working class. But organizational change alone was not enough. Although without it nothing could be done, it was related to changes in attitude:

> Revolution in the management of enterprises first of all is a revolution in the thought of man. In the process of revolution, especially at the time when a revolution has just begun, there are bound to be people who don't dare make revolution or don't even think of it. Among these people, some fear the confusion in production, and some are concerned with their individual posts, fearing they won't be able to be the "boss" or an "official"; even more of them have . . . formed habits (of reacting to) things not in accord with the old ways.

> After enterprise management undergoes revolution, because overlapping management levels are reduced, and some departments which were too minutely specialized are amalgamated, some of the men who were factory directors or other "chiefs" and some administrative personnel may be sent to newly built enterprises; and some of the "directors" may be sent down to the shifts and groups to become workers.

Although neither the past few years nor the Great Leap Forward offered any panaceas, there was one principle presented as a premise upon which reform could proceed:

> *Attention should be shifted to the basic level, to shifts and groups and the worker masses.* This implies the basic approach, the common principle which should be acted upon immediately.

> If management of enterprises is not directed toward work shifts and groups and the worker masses for the purpose of serving production, if it is opposed to the worker masses and separated from them, making production workers bog down by the administrative machinery, *then bureaucratic, subjective and even metaphysical errors will continue to be committed even though administrative levels and administrative personnel are reduced considerably.* [Italics added.]

In turn, the middle levels of management were to be de-emphasized:

> Particularly after revolutionary changes in management have taken place, some enterprises have strengthened the independent operations of the work shifts and groups through the abolition of work shops and work section. Therefore, when leading cadres go deep into production and administrative personnel perform labor at the work-shifts and groups, the work-shifts and groups must be strengthened politically and organizationally so that everyone will handle production well with the attitude of being a master and undertake the work of mass management with initiative and responsibility.

Revolutionary Management Models During the Socialist Education Campaign: The Ta-ch'ing Oil Fields and the Tsitsihar Locomotive and Carriage Works

The debate in the national press was accompanied by detailed description of actual experiences at two huge industrial enterprises.

Both the Tsitsihar Locomotive and Carriage Works[28] and the Ta-ch'ing Oil Fields were modern enterprises representing two types of large-scale industry. Ta-ch'ing was new and had to recruit skilled workers as well as formally educated engineers and technicians. It was in an undeveloped part of the country where life could be lonely and difficult, where there was little in the way of consumer comforts. The Tsitsihar Locomotive and Carriage Works had a pre-1949 history and had, up until 1964, in spite of the Great Leap Forward, "mechanically copied foreign methods."[29] It was not specified whether the foreign methods were Western, Japanese, or Soviet. Tsitsihar was in an industrialized, economically developed area.

The reform of Tsitsihar began early in 1964. The plant had been operating according to unquestioned traditional assumption that the sole purpose of an industrial enterprise was to produce. Tsitsihar had been doing this fairly well for a long time and no one had even thought to change it. A voluminous number of rules and regulations had been codified and written down. There was the usual organizational breakdown into three levels of administration (factory, work shop, workgroup) with functional departments for planning, technical controls, finance, etc., at both the factory level and work-shop level. Bureaucratic red tape and inertia were commonplace. Departments were subdivided and overstaffed, and sometimes directives went through ten or more offices before action could be taken. There were almost 1,000 different forms to keep track of various material resources and human activities.[30] The organization of this factory was not unlike other complex organizations elsewhere. The majority at the bottom of the pyramid had to follow the rules made by those at the top, while those at the top were kept busy creating rules and control procedures. As time passed, this turned into a vicious circle.[31]

As the Chinese described it, ultimately the basic levels served the control departments. Workers went about their production tasks and were rewarded with bonus payments for meeting or surpassing quotas. They took little part, if any, in management coordination, since cadres at work-shop level and above did this in two meetings held for unspecified lengths of time every day. For these cadres, there were usually over seventeen meetings a week to attend.

Management was a two-layered tier: one layer watched the workers to make sure they didn't cheat or fall below quality and quantity standards, and the other supervised those who were supervising the workers. The work-shop level was the most crucial level,[32] because it had its own control departments and administrative offices as well as production responsibilities. Each work shop thus became a kind of "independent little kingdom." Competition for supplies could be covered up or aggravated by work-shop level material supply sections.[33] The factory level then became concerned about this "little black market" and tightened and complicated its accounting and control procedures.[34] Since inter-work-shop coordination was done at meetings rather than by work shops directly with each other, there was a natural tendency to proliferate forms and increase organizational complexity.[35] The equipment section of the work shop, for example, had to have enough fuel and electric power for its machines. To do this they had to fill out over 170[36] forms per month and send them to the planning section, which then dealt with the representative from the power section at an appropriate cadre meeting.

This affected the daily routines of leading individuals at all levels. The work-shop directors, most of whom were former workers, found themselves, like the work-shop director in a one-man management system, responsible for all matters "from the large ones like production planning, material supply, technical equipment and other things to the small ones like keeping pencils sharp."[37] The result was what one person called "three too manys and two too seldoms"—too many meetings; too many supervisory documents; too many papers to tear up; too seldom going back to the work groups to take part in labor; too seldom being concerned with human relations rather than rule-bound formality. Cadres in functional sections spent the day enclosed in their offices doing paper work.[38]

The revolution in management at Tsitsihar was called concentration at the factory level to serve the shifts and groups. What was involved was a drastic reduction of the administrative staff,[39] greater direct production coordination between work shops, more participation in production by factory-level administrators and technicians, and a greater reliance on emulation campaigns and collective efforts to raise output rather than on bonuses and other individual material incentives.[40]

But for all of its changes in 1964 and 1965, Tsitsihar was not far astray from the more "conventional" wisdom of the Great Leap Forward; thus, the same kinds of problems which had led to the contradictions of the post-GLF period resisted. In the Ta-ch'ing oil fields in Heilungkiang Province, a model was emerging that had begun to tackle some of these problems in unprecedented depth and detail.

The Ta-ch'ing oil fields grew from barren land into a major petroleum complex of global significance in less than ten years. Ta-ch'ing was, in a developmental sense, a revolutionary project, yet at the same time a new example of revolutionary factory management. It combined industry and agriculture along with residence in an unprecedented fashion.[41] The Ta-ch'ing development concept and the Ta-ch'ing methods of factory management made up the Ta-ch'ing model.

Ta-ch'ing's management system was a blend of organizational transformation and changes in attitudes toward work. Incentives and organizational transformation supported each other.

Management of the oil field complex was divided into two major groups called the "first and second lines" (Yi-erh hsien). The Party Committee was the leadership core of the first and second lines, and collectively, had the responsibility to see that first and second line management was carried out. Thus, the first and second lines equalled a new "division of labor responsibility system under the collective leadership of the Party Committee" (Tang-wei chi-t'i ling-tao hsia ti fen-kung fu-tse-chih). The old system of factory manager responsibility under the leadership of the Party Committee was replaced. For the people at Ta-ch'ing, the first and second lines were to be a revolutionary political concept consistent with the party's political role in leading China closer to a classless society. It united this concept of politics with production operations in a practical way (that is, in a way that contributed to production rather than undermining it). This was what was unique in the Ta-ch'ing model.

The first and second line management system worked as follows: all of the party members in top level management of the oil field made up the second line of administrative and technical leadership. This second line was not, however, second in its authority. It was responsible for over-all political leadership and the supervision of relationships between people involved in production. It was the main channel of communication between the oil field and higher level party and planning organs. The second line management group would spend a lot of time involved in production and mingling with workers to get a feel for the technical problems and morale situation, collectively discovering key problems for the first line cadres.

The first line was made up of groups of both party and non-party members who operated at all levels. Primarily daily production leaders, these were to provide information to cadres from the second line as well as to carry out the party's decisions on human relationships, welfare, living standards, and production.

The cadres on both the first and second lines were further divided into three groups. One group would do office work. Another group would be a trouble-shooting team in the field, travelling from place to place. The third group would "squat" or remain with the basic-level drilling teams. As often as possible, problems would be solved by informal meetings of the drilling team led by the team cadres or in cooperation with the trouble-shooters and roving members of the second line. Meetings with the office workers were held to a minimum, and many control and coordinating offices became unnecessary. Periodically, it was possible for cadres from the three groups to rotate assignments, but to belong to the second line required membership in the party and a high position in the oil field complex.

Because cadre participation in labor was basic to the communications network, and because office work, administrative, and technical control were often done on the production site, there were two aspects to the party's leadership responsibilities.

One was to strengthen the technical and administrative capacities of the basic level production units, i.e., the drilling teams, so that they could make decisions. The other was to create a situation where control by administrative cadres to get people to work hard and cooperatively was unnecessary.

The study of politics and ideology at Ta-ch'ing was therefore not the abstract study of political theory. It was a way to make "the thought of Mao Tsetung" a part of daily operations. The theory of knowledge, the methods of problem solving and analysis, and the spirit of experimentation embodied in that thought could then be used to help workers acquire a better capacity to handle problems, thereby realizing the key political objective of increased power for the working class within modern industrial enterprises.

Breaking down the barriers between workers and managers, improving the analytical and problem-solving capacity of productive workers, and conscious involvement in an important development project were the incentives for work at Ta-ch'ing. Improvement both quantitative and qualitative in the collective life would result automatically, and making people aware of this was the essence of the party's poltical work. This type of political and ideological work was to replace short-term individual gain or money incentives.

Political goals became a standard by which to measure the performance of the basic-level drilling teams. Taking a cue from the People's Liberation Army, a so-called five good movement was organized; work teams and individuals that were good at five politically admirable activities were given public acclaim and trophies of one kind or another.

The five good movement acclaimed those at the basic levels of production who were (1) able to analyze and solve production problems, (2) were organized around the leadership of talented and admired party members, (3) were willing to copy others' good experiences while experimenting on their own, (4) did not ask for unnecessary help from or create problems for the second line and (5) were helping gradually to bring up and train young workers for future leadership positions.

In addition to the informal but direct and frequent consultation of drilling-team workers with cadres from the first and second lines, there were other ways for workers to share power with technical and administrative leaders. The teams were given formally recognized powers, which were part of the oil field's written rules and regulations, to criticize the behavior and activity of leading cadres, elect their own team leaders, determine questions of equipment safety, repair and maintenance schedules. They also participated in accounting by recording their own input and output figures, in food management in the mess halls, and in the distribution of local agricultural production.

That the work team shared power with the cadres who also participated in the hard work of oil-well drilling and rigging was itself an important part of the Ta-ch'ing system. Because the dress, life-style, and mannerisms of cadres were similar to that of the workers and because the workers shared the cadres' power, the workers had a greater identification with leadership and the oil field as a collective, and were less likely to underrate their own capacities or fail to maximize production.

Revolutionization in Practice: From Theoretical Debate to Political Struggle

Both Tsitsihar and Ta-ch'ing had indicated the direction that revolutionization would take; both had revealed how complex and interrelated were attitudes, incentives, and organizational change. There was to be a focus on two-level management with elimination or contraction of middle level administrative control organs. The retrenchment of personnel which often followed these organizational changes could mean the loss of a job and reassignment to a new and unfamiliar factory, return to school, promotion to a factory-level management position, or "hsia fang" (send down) to the basic-level work-team.[42] These things changed the daily routines, surroundings, and associations (both personal and symbolic) of cadres at many levels, and these changes involved psychological and emotional feelings of self-esteem, prestige, and status. These changes, and the reactions to them, had impact on both party and nonparty cadres and depended not simply on what level of the organization one worked, but on one's attitudes about a whole set of propositions about general human relationships.

Closely related to status, prestige, and self-esteem were the practical organizational problems of cadre participation in labor. The Tsitsihar and Ta-ch'ing models were not the only ones presented as solutions to this presistent and crucial problem. The three fix and one substitution (san-ting yi-ting) model of the Chungking Water Turbine Works, whereby cadres at all levels fixed relevant times, posts, and duties of labor participation and learned production skills to substitute for a worker, was widely propagated.[43] So, too, was the half-day labor, half-day work of the Canton Chemical Works.[44]

As the socialist education campaign continued, attempts to make cadre participation in labor and organizational restructuring part of the revolutionization in management met with uneven results. Opposition came from work-shop level cadres,[45] but so did support for change,[46] and the reasons for both depended on such things as willingness to physically move one's office,[47] the capacity or willingness to interact personally with workers,[48] and one's attitude toward manual work which often, but by no means always, was a function of class and/or educational background, and previous routine in the organization.[49]

As cadre participation increased, so did direct worker participation in management, for the two depended on each other. In financial control and technical decision-making, significant changes began to appear throughout the country; as worker participation in management became broader, the nature of incentives also began to change. As *JMJP* had noted, "everything in industrial management is mutually related."[50]

In 1965, a decision by the Ministry of Commerce to popularize a new increase-decrease system of accounting began changes in financial management.[51] A fine balance was sought between control and complexity and maneuverability and simplification, with emphasis on the latter.[52] Workers were also given more control over the supervision of input and output quotas.

The Anshan Iron and Steel Mill became a model for revolutionizing financial management.[53] The system at Anshan actually involved transforming the bulk of financial control from its fixed office location into a roving group of cadres who scheduled visits to different production units. The roving group comprised cadres from the finance and accounting, mechanical and power, and planning departments. It was to translate the raw data of consumption of materials and power recorded by the workers into prices, or to calculate future plans and supply requirements. Enterprise level financial control depended on the roving cadres' direct contact with other departments and with production; it was this contact, rather than written communications and reports filtered up through a hierarchy of offices, that gave cadres the technical knowledge as well as the emotional insight that allowed them to make more realistic decisions on financial requirements and expenditures.

The Anshan Iron and Steel Mill used the image of skilled horsemen galloping over the wide northcountry plains near Anshan to symbolize this movement and flexibility. Called the Combined Itinerant Service Unit, the Wulan Shepherd Horsemen both in imagery and in reality was a far cry from bureaucratic office work. Since the change required

a break with old routines and the vested interests of functional departments, it met with opposition from those cynical about the changes,
who were unwilling to spend such active days, or who felt that leaving
their offices threatened their careers.

The Anshan experiment was represented as a means of carrying out
modern production in a way consistent with the goals of Chinese politics,
something that many years of factory director responsibility under the
leadership of the Party Committee was supposed to have achieved, but
had not.

> Efforts to revolutionize financial work did not begin today. Several years
> ago, central authorities repeatedly emphasized the three important view-
> points (the political viewpoint, the production viewpoint, the mass
> viewpoint) and called for the orientation in three directions (to face
> production, the masses and the basic units). Since then, we have done
> much along these lines and made much progress in thought reformation,
> in our work, and in our attitude and traditions. However, the thought
> revolution had not been carried out with thoroughness; *there had not been
> sufficient integration between politics and operations. . . . As a conse-
> quence, financial work, as a part of operations, had not served the ends
> of politics, the needs of production, or the masses too well*. It had yet to
> find a suitable form and methodology. [Italics added.][54]

As pressure began to mount to transform financial management,
there were noticeable changes regarding technical decision-making. The
triple combination teams popular during the Great Leap Forward had
never been abandoned, but in 1964–1965 there was a renewed emphasis
on them as well as an expansion of their scope of activity. Costs reported
to higher authorities as part of over-all production when workers were
taken off production to work on technical innovations or production
bottlenecks were lowered significantly, incurring less loss to the enterprise of profits retained for collective welfare or similar projects.[55] The
triple combination teams solved more sophisticated problems than
before, including the manufacture of precision machinery, autos, ballbearings, and diesel engines.[56] Cadres were urged to get out of their
offices to initiate triple combination projects,[57] while in many factories
rules and regulations were rewritten to facilitate worker suggestions and
participation in technical decision-making.[58]

Even though there was clear opposition to this turn of events,
particularly from technical personnel working at the factory level,[59]
worker participation became widespread in other areas of factory
decision-making, too. Through 1964 and 1965, work teams acquired the
authority to assess their own five-good workers.[60] In some cases, they
got more control over quality inspection, or the repair and maintenance
of machinery.[61]

A concomitant but subtle change in the policy toward incentives occurred. It was the difference between combining material with political incentives and stressing the primacy of political over material incentives. "Socialist countries," it was argued directly, "depended for movement not on those who toil for personal and material benefit, but on those who toil for the common interests. . . ." It was thus necessary:

> to integrate correctly the implementation of the principle of distribution according to work with the intensification of political and ideological education. The integrated relationship of the two should place politics in command and give *first place to intensification of political and ideological education. The two cannot be looked upon as of equal standing.* [Italics added.][62]

In late 1963 a campaign began which stressed the use of political incentives. A nationwide emulation campaign was also launched which involved intra- and inter-enterprise cooperation and competition.[63] A large-scale discussion on the nature and purpose of work and happiness was launched in the press,[64] and, early in 1964, another mass campaign to learn from the People's Liberation Army was begun; its themes were dedication to the collective well being, hard work, honesty, and frugality.[65] Foreshadowing what was later to be party opposition, there was by early 1964 evidence of direct PLA participation in factory political education.[66]

As these mass campaigns continued in the national press, there were other signs of change in incentive policy. By the middle of 1966, piece wages had been eliminated in a number of enterprises,[67] but a complex bonus system for individuals remained in effect for workers.[68] Bonuses for top-level management, however, were abolished in 1964 and income differentials were kept very narrow.[69] As individual material incentives became less prevalent, collective material security became central, with comprehensive health and disability programs becoming available to almost all full-time regular industrial workers.[70]

Increased political incentives and relatively egalitarian income disparity and standards of living did not end material incentives. For example, the wage-grading system remained in effect, and insurance payments received by workers were not only proportionate to income but were higher for members of the union than for non-members.[71] This could create antagonism between higher and lower paid workers or full-time industrial workers and part-time or contract workers.[72] Political incentives were themselves used to deal with such antagonism. Revolutionary rhetoric not backed by worker participation in management and cadre participation in labor could lead to cynicism and thus back to stress on material incentives and inequality.[73]

In reality, effective political incentives and political rhetoric reinforced one another in many ways. Personnel retrenchment meant many cadres in functional departments were no longer necessary to control or coordinate production.[74] Persuading people to pull up roots and move, to change jobs, or to go back to school could best be accomplished by political persuasion and appeals to collective and national priorities. In a poor country with great unevenness in economic development both regionally and sectorally, this was quite apparent.[75]

Renewed emphasis on political incentives did not end the concern for economic efficiency and productivity.[76] Paradoxically, however, the very success of worker participation in management, which led to big increases in productivity, often caused jealousies or resentment in other parts of a factory or in other factories—which only more political appeals could overcome.[77]

Increasing worker participation in management, combined with a greater role for basic-level production leaders, some of whom were former office workers or work-shop functionaries, caused some conflict between these new leaders and the traditional leadership, such as trade-union cadres. Trade-union leaders at the basic levels might not have been too happy about the two participations, and some suggested workers' congresses as appropriate substitutes which happily did not challenge the traditional political role of the trade-union organization.[78]

Opposition to revolutionization did not, however, come in its most serious form from these sources within the factories, not from functional cadres nor from organizations whose concept of political work was limited by their own group's past activities. The more serious opposition was from the Communist Party itself, especially above the enterprise level, since here was a power source with enormous influence on enterprises through the Party Committees.

The Role of Authority Above the Enterprise in Influencing Enterprise Management

By the middle of 1965 the socialist education campaign, along with the accompanying movement called the four cleanups[79] revealed that a major problem in revolutionizing enterprise management lay in the role and function of enterprise-level Communist Party organs. In so far as revolutionizing brought major changes in human relationships, the enterprise-level Party Committee was a key group, accepting or rejecting changes in procedure, routine, rules, quotas, and incentive systems. Still, enterprise-level Party Committees belonged to the powerful organizational apparatus which had become intimately involved in planning and coordination.

As early as April 1964, an overt attempt was made to prod party individuals and groups at all levels to take a more active and constructive role in leading the process of revolutionization. At that time, political departments were established in the industrial and communications system at every level of administration, as they had been established for years in the PLA down to the company level. In every industrial enterprise there was a political instructor (cheng-chih chih-tao-yüan) to see that the enterprise carried out the tasks of revolutionization by "learning firmly and effectively from the PLA."[80]

Even with the example of the PLA, the new political departments were too closely tied to the party to have much independent effect. Not only was the political official or instructor always a party member, but the political departments never set up a higher alternative organizational authority for the enterprise level Party Committee. Enterprise political instructors, like enterprise party committees, were subordinate to the next higher level party committee.[81] During the socialist education campaign even the PLA acted indirectly through PLA veterans, now civilians and party members.[82] Moreover, the conflict between the army's and the party's political role was very much part of the tension growing within the industrial system, even if difficult to discern.[83]

The Party Committee, as chief executive and policy-making organ for the enterprise, was not concerned simply with what went on within the enterprise but also with relationships between that enterprise and other enterprises and planning authorities at municipal, provincial, and national levels. In such a strategic position, confronted with conflicting demands for internal factory revolution and information needed by planners, the Party Committees at the enterprise level were subject to forces from above and below. The pressures from above were particularly relevant.

In February 1965 a major conference concerning industrial management and economic administration was held. Po I-po, then a vice chairman of the powerful State Council, gave the final report which included a good deal of verbiage concerning revolutionizing management, the need for cadre participation in labor, and the struggle between capitalist and socialist ideology. In this report, however, he touched on what was to be a key element in later political struggles—the question of method in coordinating and planning the economy:

> Remarkable results should be made this year in the revolution in planning, designing, and enterprise management, as well as in promoting coordination in specialization.[84]

"Promoting coordination in specialization" quickly became a major theme of a whole series of articles and reports in 1965, especially regarding the machinery and machine tool industry, but not limited to those.[85] The actual beginning of the movement toward specialization began earlier, either in late 1963 or mid-1964.[86]

The arguments in favor of specialization were made on both economic and political grounds. Economically, it was argued, specialization was more efficient—with high productivity from simpler job operations that could be more rapidly acquired. Specialization was said to use a lower rate of materials consumption and be easier to standardize and systemize. It eliminated the duplication of scattered production centers and lent itself to the tasks of economic administration above the enterprise level. Coordination for more specific problems of supply and marketing could be carried on via the development of large industrial corporations in certain lines of industry and between individual enterprises, even though widely scattered geographically. It was argued, finally, that specialization was inevitable in both developed capitalist and socialist economies.[87]

Politically, the argument in favor of specialization claimed that individual factories would be smaller, their structure less complex. Specialized factories were to be made from huge, or even small, integrated plants (called big, medium, or small and complex) which turned out whole products, and did their own designing, manufacturing, distribution, and made their own machinery. Specialized plants supposedly would have fewer administrative personnel, making it easier for cadres to take part in labor and helping to break down the divisions between worker and manager.[88]

All of the arguments in favor of specialization held that there was strong opposition from various enterprises, and they attacked this opposition in political terms, accusing it of selfishness and departmentalism at the expense of the common good.[89] The argument ran that the development of specialization, requiring more efforts at interenterprise cooperation, would make general interenterprise relationships more rational, though more complex and demanding of the time of economic administrators, including the enterprise-level party committees.

Opposition to publicity and pressure for increased specialization was not obvious throughout 1965. Aside from a few articles which indicated dissatisfaction at the enterprise level,[90] there were a few which claimed indirectly that specialization was not the answer to problems of modernization or revolution. A *JMJP* editorial, for example, said that specialization might be necessary in large cities but was less appropriate in medium-sized and small cities and still less suited to rural areas.[91] It also noted that the demand for specialization was new, contradicting the former policy of comprehensive plants of many sizes. Other articles observed the convenience of having designing workshops or chemical-testing facilities as integral parts of a factory, and the importance of building spare parts, carrying out development experiments, and testing and assembling machinery in the same plant.[92]

A speech by the vice minister of machine building defended the idea of comprehensive plants because they facilitated technical breakthroughs by consolidating the multiple abilities of building, experimenting, testing, redesigning, and so on. With obvious approval and significance, he said, "When I was in Yenan, a factory with slightly more than 200 workers had everything; it was 'small and complete'," and he urged that specialization take the form of standardization, but not necessarily be reflected in the division of labor between production units.[93]

Aside from the political rhetoric of its supporters, specialization had implications which were not ignored by its opponents.

First of all, on the enterprise level, specialization aimed to make many work-shop level managerial cadres into factory-level managerial cadres *primarily* concerned with questions of interenterprise cooperation and bargaining rather than with production. All arguments in favor of specialization claimed that the scope and complexity of interenterprise cooperation would greatly increase. They argued that simultaneously factory-level cadres would have more, not less, time for "facing the basic levels and serving production."[94]

The primary mechanism for coordinating the economy was to be the bureaucracy above the enterprise. The economic administrators would determine prices for all enterprises in a fairly large geographic region or in a vertically integrated trust and could then use the profit ratio among enterprises as a guide for further rational investment. Plant management would receive a bonus for successful efforts.

As a necessary comprehensive indicator to supplement complex input-output calculations for planning and coordination, the profit target was the logical choice for those who advocated specialization. Coordination would come from the decisions of nominally autonomous managers, whose actual autonomy was sharply limited by the predetermined price structure. Unless planning was to be abolished altogether, it would make little difference if those prices were determined by the priorities of the planners or by computerized input-output tables or by both. In any case, enterprise management could no longer rationally or realistically face the basic levels, whether in the factory or in the locality. Instead, it would be obliged to focus its attention on the economic authority above the enterprise. It was to this authority that management would give its detailed data and hard statistical measurement of worker performance and output, and from this authority would come prices, rewards, and possibilities for growth. The only alternative would be a market outside the confines of the plan, but this, of course, was not the ostensible purpose of specialization.

The political crux of the matter was that specialization would lead to a functionally necessary, privileged managerial elite on a national scale. The lowest rung of this structure was potentially enterprise level management. Or it would lead to a kind of bureaucratic capitalism consistently harassed by a bureaucratic government. As one commentator put it:

Acting in accordance with this blueprint . . . the socialist state of China would become a capitalist big boss granting credits to enterprises and allowing them to make money freely, while the state would collect profit in accordance with investment. Enterprises would become "joint-operated" companies, with the state and the directors or managers as partners sharing in the profits. *In such circumstances, the state and leading cadres of the enterprises would degenerate into a privileged strata.* . . . When the leaders of the enterprises had only bonus and profit in mind, in order to get more bonus and profits they would use their positions and power to exploit and oppress the workers mercilessly. [Italics added.][95]

Linked to the concept of specialization was the idea that large trusts were to be organized around production and marketing. Operating as middle-level liaison to integrate the enterprises into the nationally determined allocational priorities, the trusts would make primary investment decisions for enterprises under their control. Economic authority would be separate from local political and administrative power, and the needs and priorities of these localities could be by-passed if they conflicted with nationally determined cost-efficient planning priorities and the profit goals of the vertically integrated trusts.

Further industrialization and modernization would thus occur mostly in those regions already having an economic infrastructure, trained manpower, and known raw materials. These would usually be urban areas; the peasantry would be a pool of cheap labor for the growing cities and industries. Under this plan, the peasantry and the rural areas would bear the brunt of modernization's dislocations and government itself would begin to lose its revolutionary identity and purpose, becoming instead a self-perpetuating arbiter of permanent inequality and conflict.[96]

The push for specialization and the accompanying trust system became strong in 1965 just when the revolutionization attempts of the socialist education campaign were beginning to take effect. Enterprise-level Communist Party Committees had little awareness of the intensity of the clash taking shape above them, but they were factors in the struggle.[97] A polemical article on Liu Shao-ch'i and the Vice-Premier of the State Council, Po I-po stated the situation clearly:

In compliance with Liu Shao-ch'i's intention, Po I-po cried "it is necessary to learn experience from capitalist countries in the promotion of the trust for the purpose of promoting the socialist trust." From 1964 onward, he himself presided over the experimental running of 12 national trust enterprises.

He said, "Monopoly must be exercised over the enterprises. The power of command over personnel, finance, material supply and the processes of production, supply and marketing in enterprises must be concentrated in the trust." He cried that "the exorbitant taxes and miscellaneous levies of local party and government administrations must be abolished." *His aim was to place the enterprises above the local party and government administrations in the name of leadership "enforced under one head."*

The report of the party group of the Ministry of Coal Industry on the running of the trust on an experimental basis stated ". . . *We suggest the formation of the party committee of the China Coal Company for assuming all-embracing responsibility toward the Central Committee, for exercising unified leadership over Party, CYL, trade union, production and construction work in enterprises and business units and for enforcing dual leadership by the Party Committee of the Company mainly but in conjunction with the regional and municipal committees."* Their object was to seize Party and government power. . . .

Counter revolutionary revisionist Chang Lin-chih (Vice Minister of Ministry of State Farms and Land Reclamation) remarked even more barefacedly, *"This means taking over power from the Party."* [Italics added.][98]

It would be a gross oversimplification to accuse the advocates of specialization of being conscious promoters of bureaucratic capitalism, but there can be little doubt that they saw a relationship between economic coordination and management at the enterprise level. The advocates of specialization justified themselves in terms of both revolution and modernization. A vice-mayor in Tientsin's municipal government said:

According to the principle of specialization and coordination, dividing up a large factory into several small ones and readjusting the relations between factories is aimed mainly at reforming production relations and the superstructure. Once this reform is instituted, the productive forces will be further liberated. This will powerfully advance the revolutionization and modernization of enterprises. *Moreover, it will further promote revolutionization of the industrial administrative leadership.* [Italics added.]

While readjusting and splitting factories, we should organize "small but specialized" and "'middle sized but specialized" factories according to separate trades, readjust the relations between those new factories and the old factories from which they are detached. We should establish specialized companies.[99]

The opposition supported a different purpose for the enterprise,[100] different relationships between enterprises and society, and different relationships between management and workers. Therefore, they rejected economic coordination which relied on manipulation of prices and the pull of the profit motive, and they rejected much but not all of the trusts and specialization.

The opposition argued that a planning system should be flexible enough for constant readjustment due to shortages or unforeseen bottlenecks. There had to be a guarantee that individual flexibility did not undermine the plan or provide license to acquire personal wealth and privilege. The answer lay in both ideological commitment and organizational context.

Management, as a matter of political commitment and principle, was to fulfill planned targets for major items as efficiently as it could, using local initiative and materials for technical innovations as far as possible. Even if shortages of materials were anticipated, there was to be no stockpiling, hoarding, nor reduction of targets. Multipurpose enterprises were to be built to facilitate self-reliance. If all else failed, readjustment of targets could be made, the users of an enterprise's products being notified accordingly. Hence, the pursuit of profit was to have no place in socialist planning, and, therefore, could not be the basis for evaluating and rewarding the performance of an enterprise. Instead, hard work and service to the plan and to the local community would characterize the goals of a socialist enterprise.[191] Local industries would have to meet local needs, which could not be defined *solely* in terms of cost efficiency.

Once the broad targets for major items were fulfilled, the enterprise management could structure its operations to fulfill local needs by turning out subsidiary products for the local rural or urban population, or it could undertake other functions such as recreation, housing, or medical facilities. Decisions would not be based on profit (which depended on purchasing power and price) but on a *political* desire to produce high quality goods or deliver services in great demand.

The ideal of the revolutionary modernizers at this time seemed to be an integrated, multi-purpose enterprise of any size or a geographical location organized around productive labor. Administration was to coincide with a local political subdivision to bring the production of goods and services under the control of the local political authority to be more responsive to local needs. Still, the goals and targets of the national plan had priority. For this reason, rural-urban residence points combining industry, agriculture, and services were to be developed. Urban centers were to take advantage of the natural historical industrial development pattern of urban China and to progress by making small self-reliant neighborhood plants or groups of plants an important part of urban industry.

For the management of such as these, the central focus of their attention, therefore, would be down into their enterprise's production and other activities in which they were urged to participate at first hand. They would not—and this seems to be a key point—be oriented exclusively toward getting hard data on worker productivity nor would they be under pressure to treat people as they treated machines. Nor would the complex needs of interenterprise specialization with impersonal, long distance communications for orders, materials, price checks, parts, etc. be the sole focus of their daily schedule. Their goals would not be based on the profit target and the profit motive as a mechanism to ease the complexity of specialization and hence the potential for self-aggrandizement would be minimized even though they were given a good deal of flexibility. Thus, the Ta-ch'ing Oil Fields became the model of revolutionary modernization:

We build an enterprise in order to add to the ramparts of socialism. . . . Therefore, socialist industrial enterprises not only add to the country's production, but they must also develop the socialist ramparts in an overall political, ideological, and economic sense.

If we do things according to foreign conventions, then in making industrial and mining enterprises, it would be necessary to build tall cities, or to enlarge cities, and necessary to build up wealthy areas with tall buildings, using walls to keep out the peasants, thereby seriously separating ourselves from the masses and enlarging the differences between worker and peasant, and city and countryside, endangering the worker-peasant alliance. This would be unbeneficial to constructing socialism and would prevent us from reaching communism. From the beginning, Ta-ch'ing oil fields have done things resolutely different from these foreign conventions.

In 1958, Chairman Mao visited the Wuhan Steel Works, he pointed out: Large scale enterprises like the Wuhan Steel Works can gradually develop into comprehensive, united enterprises, which apart from making many different parts of iron and steel products can also operate some machinery enterprises, chemical enterprises, construction enterprises, etc. In this kind of large enterprise, there can be a little bit of agriculture, commerce, education, and military, in addition to industry. When leading comrades of the Central Committee came to Ta-ch'ing for inspection work, they also pointed out: The construction of this drilling area has guaranteed the worker-peasant alliance, the unity of city and countryside is beneficial to production and convenient for living. The living quarters of workers and employees are spread out, not bunched up together, and it's not necessary to build big cities. The households are well organized, participate in labor and develop production.

We respect the directives of Chairman Mao and the Comrades of the Central Committee in carrying out the building of this mining area. As of now, Ta-ch'ing is taking first steps to build a new mining area with unity of city and countryside, workers and peasants, and politics and industry.

Ta-ch'ing is not making concentrated urban centers, but dispersed residence units (chu-min-tien). Now, three workers towns (kung-jen-chen) have already been constructed, as well as several tens of central residence points (each with 1 or 2 hundred households). Each central residence point together with 4 or 5 surrounding residence points has become a livelihood base; there are machinery stations, agricultural technology research stations, primary schools, half work-half study middle schools (for industry and agriculture), bookstores, health clinics, nurseries, restaurants, sweetshops, work shops (tso-fang), stores, barbershops, bathhouses, shoe stores, tailor shops, post offices, savings associations, banks (ch'u-hui), and many other places of production, livelihood, education, and health which benefit production and livelihood.[102]

The party's role was also quite different in the Ta-ch'ing model. Rather than being part of a geographically dispersed, bureaucratically oriented managerial elite whose base was in large trusts or corporations which were national in scope, the Party Committee at Ta-ch'ing was oriented almost wholly toward the local area. Governmental administration was coterminous with the mining district, and the oil field Party Committee was also the Party Committee of the mining district and local goverment. Thus, production and other activities of the enterprise were under local political leadership, with Ta-ch'ing's relationship to the nation being its delivery of oil and petroleum and its role as a model for enterprise management.[103]

By April 1966, it was evident that the struggle [which had become focused and polarized during the socialist education campaign] had served to split the Communist Party and the whole industrial and communications system as well. At a national conference for leading cadres in industry and communications, held in Peking and attended by almost every party and nonparty official involved in industrial management from municipal level on up. The final communique was only able to note, in spite of the Ta-ch'ing example, that "a complete set of experiences in managing enterprises has not yet been summed up."[104] Among the delegates to this meeting, Liu Shao-ch'i and Teng Hsiao-p'ing were reportedly very active, as was Chou En-lai, who delivered a major speech.[105]

Behind the struggles and arguments of this high-level conference were the enterprise Party Committees and managerial staffs who were the prizes. And in back of them were the hundreds of thousands of workers and employees, men and women with different educational experiences, family histories, skill levels, and life experiences. It is against this enormously complex background that the organizational and ideological power struggle of the Cultural Revolution erupted in the late summer of 1966.

7 / Politics, Planning, and Management in the Cultural Revolution: The Rebellion Begins and the Issues Are Clarified

Major Themes

ON 8 AUGUST 1966 the Central Committee of the Chinese Communist Party adopted and publicized sixteen points concerning the Great Cultural Revolution.[1] This may be a convenient way to date the beginning of this major political upheaval, but it is also misleading. The Cultural Revolution was not the product of a decision but of the process described in the previous chapters.

As the currents unleashed by the Great Leap swirled together with those of managerial and bureaucratic conservatism, a major debate about the modernization process, its forms, and its logic had become the focus of political conflict. What was at issue was not revolution or modernization but profoundly different visions of modern society and sharply divergent ideas of individual identity. Ultimately individual attitudes toward authority, responsibility, and purpose were enmeshed with perceptions of the possible and desirable within the human community. The result was a confrontation with some of the classic and universal dilemmas of politics.[2]

These basic political issues were manifested in disagreements over the scope and depth of worker participation in management, cadre participation in labor, and incentives for working. The political and organizational consequences of technology and industry which, in the West, were assumed as the universal givens of "modernity," were very soon to become the center of highly charged debate and sometimes violent, often confusing struggle.

The Cultural Revolution, which had all through 1966 been going on in artistic and academic circles moved into China's factories in June.[3]

A proclamation issued under the auspices of the All-China Federation of Trade Unions specifically asked Party Committees to take the lead in organizing discussions on selfishness (szu) and public spiritedness (kung).[4] Party Committees were urged to implement the two participations, one reform, and triple combination system and to unite operations and politics.[5] The basic level Party Committees led the early stages of the Cultural Revolution,[6] although they were watched and guided by higher levels.[7] By the beginning of August, the issues of worker participation in management, particularly in regard to technical controls and innovations, was a central concern once again as was the very delicate question of incentives.[8]

The sixteen-point declaration of August 8 had, moreover directly raised the always explosive issue of organizational authority. Specifically, it said that:

1. The Cultural Revolution was aimed principally at a small group of capitalist roaders *in the party.* (Point IV).

2. The party organization was not to be the only group responsible for the Cultural Revolution. Cultural revolutionary groups were to be set up in all units including industrial and mining enterprises. Members of these groups were to be elected as in the Paris commune (lists of candidates drawn up by the masses, full discussion, elections, and representatives subject to criticism or recall after a discussion and vote). (Point IX).

3. Generally speaking, scientists, technicians, and working personnel in general were not to be the subjects of attack, but they were to be subject to criticism with a view to strengthening their socialist commitment or transforming their lack of it. The principle of unity-criticism-unity would be used in these cases. The main targets were not necessarily party organs at the enterprise level. In urban enterprises, the results of the socialist education campaign and "the four clean-ups," which accompanied it, if satisfactory, should not be disturbed. (Points XII and XIII).[9]

For the next few months the Cultural Revolution in industrial enterprises proceeded very slowly and carefully. Factories were urged to carry on with production while continuing with or beginning the kinds of reforms necessary to implement the two participations and triple combination. Red Guards and revolutionary students were specifically urged to remain outside of the factories; workers and functionaries were to remain at their posts.[10]

By November, however, there were growing tensions. A meeting of a central-level group called "the Cultural Revolution Small Group of the CCP Central Committee," at which there was obvious participation by student groups, decreed that no reprisals against rebel workers by factory-level leaders were to be made. The enterprise-level Party Committee was denied participation in important decisions, and a new kind of triple alliance made up of a revolutionary committee, a revolutionary leading group, and a revolutionary representative congress was given legitimacy to administer the factory. Outside pressure on enterprise Party Committees began to grow as representatives of revolutionary student groups were cleared to establish contact with workers inside enterprises. Workers and technicians could also visit other plants and schools to exchange experiences, but only after work.[11]

By the end of 1966, a *Jen-men Jih-pao* editorial reported that there were a "handful of people in power within the party who take the capitalist road . . . in industrial and mining enterprises."[12] It said that support for the Cultural Revolution was not optional or a trifling matter. Party members were specifically forbidden by a Central Committee directive from hiding behind the party banner to avoid criticism, forbidden from using their administrative powers to manipulate or repress Cultural Revolution organizations.

What had started as a careful attempt to free enterprise-level Party Committees from control by the municipal and provincial levels had evidently not succeeded. Enterprise Party Committees, many of which had been integrated into the larger coordinative mechanisms and planning structure and had been using management methods consistent with that structure, showed themselves to be stubborn and clever guardians of their positions. In the words of the *JMJP* editorial:

> It should be noted that many of our industrial and mining enterprises are seriously influenced in varying degrees by capitalism, revisionism, and even feudalism in the fields of political ideology, organizational leadership, and production management.
>
> Collaboration between bourgeois roaders in the Party, landlord, rich peasant, and counter-revolutionary bad elements, and unreformed bourgeois elements have, in some enterprises, *doggedly opposed* Chairman Mao's correct line. Therefore it is absolutely essential to carry out the Cultural Revolution in industrial and mining enterprises, and to do this, *serious struggle is necessary.*[13]

Serious struggle there would be. A 1967 New Year's Day joint *Hung Ch'i* and *Jen-min Jih-pao* editorial signaled the official opening of the new phase in the Great Proletarian Cultural Revolution by noting that it "must go from the offices, schools, and cultural circles to the factories and mines, and the rural areas as well." The editorial warned that "any argument against carrying out of a large-scale proletarian revolution in factories and mines and the rural areas is incorrect."[14]

The Shape of Early Conflict: August–December 1966

Prior to the editorial there had been indications of turmoil. Before the official spread of the Cultural Revolution to factories and mines disputes over technical authority and technical decision-making were sources of open conflict. Opposing each other were the "bourgeois technical authorities" and the "revolutionary technicians."

Bourgeois technical authorities were criticized for relying too heavily on Western or Soviet technical conventions and designs and for being afraid to experiment and opposed to all workers' suggestions for innovation.[15] Revolutionary technicians, conversely, were cooperative, daring, creative, and innovatively competent.[16] The bourgeois technical authorities were accused of monopolizing knowledge to hinder innovations which did not originate from their own ideas. They were unwilling to use their knowledge to help workers to innovate because they wished to boost their own reputations.[17] The revolutionary technicians refuted the idea that knowledge was private property to be used for wealth and personal promotions. They advocated a broad use of the triple combination.[18] They seemed mostly to be younger technicians and some workers.[19] Conflict within the organization was not, therefore, a simple matter of the party vs. non-party people. This distinction was meaningless in many practical everyday decision-making ways.

The Party Committee secretary and the factory director had usually developed a similarity in function and daily routine. The director was usually a member of the factory Party Committee or Party Branch.[20] When this was not the case, the Party Committee secretary became the de facto factory director, while the director then became a de facto deputy, serving in a technical or administrative capacity.[21] The Party Committee or Branch was, in theory, the nucleus for decision-making, but it rarely met more than once a week, and often no more than once a month. Though the Party Committee was elected by all the party members in the plant,[22] and in smaller factories sometimes comprised all the party members of that factory,[23] the day-to-day experience of most members was as workers or functionaries. Many basic level party leaders were not even on the factory Party Committee.[24]

Since the Party Committee met infrequently, the Party Committee secretary usually acted for the Committee, making decisions and presenting them for formal approval to the committee. Though individual members might disagree they were hesitant to challenge these decisions because of group pressures, fear of upsetting plans, or a desire to please the secretary, an influential person in promotion decisions.

All factory-level management, therefore, was split along two lines, one according to organizational position and the other according to attitude; and these divisions were by no means congruent to one another. When the January Revolution began and power seizures became the order of the day, these conflicts took on added complexity.

The "January Revolution": Who Is the Enemy?

In January 1967 the Cultural Revolution entered a new phase with power seizures by rebel groups against enterprise authorities.[25]

The authorities were not at first clearly defined, though all had some formal administrative power or exercised formal technical control.[26] In the beginning then, all cadres were not attacked; nor were any non-cadres attacked. Administrative and technical managers at the factory and work-shop level bore the brunt of early rebel activity, but not all technical and administrative cadres were attacked or prevented from working.[27]

The early power seizures revealed complex political alliances. Those attacked fought back, calling in reinforcements or being sent help by their allies.

A popular tactical maneuver was economism. This strategy aimed to buy off the rebels—bonuses and wage increases were suddenly forthcoming, and other money was distributed. Travel funds for the ostensible purpose of exchanging revolutionary experience were issued, but the ultimate effect was to undermine rebel leadership, cause chaos in production, or alienate potential support for the leaders by getting them out of the factory.

This money came from the factory's circulating or enterprise funds.[28] Usually, circulating funds required permission from higher authority or banks, but enterprise funds were under the direct control of the Party Committee and/or the director.[29] In disbursing funds, the highest level of factory administration necessarily worked with the municipal or provincial Party Committees and the banks.[30] By the end of January economism had become the main weapon of the hard-pressed power structure.[31]

There were other indications that management was being influenced by or was in collusion with municipal and provincial authorities. Withholding supplies needed for production was another tactic employed against those who had seized power.[32] Another, even more direct link between enterprise management and higher level party authority was the personal relationships which had evolved into webs of political influence.[33] To illustrate, a report by a Red Guard group at the Chukiang Paper Mill in Kwangtung Province is instructive.

Rebels at the mill were angrily criticizing the Party Committee secretary who had recently been transferred from the Canton Paper Mill.

The former deputy plant manager at the Canton mill was a fifty-four-year-old man, a veteran of the party's heroic long-march in the mid-1930s. He had obvious connections to the central-south regional CCP bureau headed by T'ao Chu. Under T'ao's tutelage, the long-march cadre had been promoted to Party Committee secretary of the Canton mill, the old Party Committee secretary being transferred to Chukiang. When a work team arrived at the Chukiang mill, sent by the central-south bureau, it criticized the work-group leaders and section-level supervisors but not the new Party Committee secretary or the factory director. In this way, the promoted long-march cadre was guaranteed his post at the Canton mill while the party member in the Chukiang mill was protected, until the rebels seized power.

Similar liaisons between work teams sent by higher authorities and key cadres at the enterprise level were reported at the Shihchingshan Power Plant in Peking and the Yangshupu Power Plant in Shanghai. In Peking, there was a close relationship between the municipal Party Committee and an enterprise-level cadre.[34] In Shanghai, there was a tie between the political department of the CCP East China Bureau of Electric Administration and the factory manager.[35]

The Rebel Leadership

The power seizures which began in January were aimed largely at factory-level management, but they had been preceded by months and in some cases a year or more of power struggles.[36] Most of the early rebel leaders were workers and cadres directly involved in full-time production, active critics of the factory leaders before power was actually seized. In later power seizures, outside impetus and leadership played a more important role. By 1968 rebel leadership within the plants broadened, but only after the issues had been clarified.

Outside influence in the early stages, aside from the work teams sent by higher authorities to quiet things down, came from Red Guards and the PLA. PLA influence, however, only became important after March 1967,[37] while the role of the Red Guards began in October 1966, at first being limited to helping rebel workers articulate their grievances.[38] Many rebel workers were extremely hostile to all forms of intervention from outside the plant.[39]

The following list of factories was gleaned from the public media in China and includes a brief description of who rebel leaders were in the early stages of power seizure.[40]

1. Chungking Municipal Mining Machinery Plant—workers and Red Guards.[41]

2. Nanchang Steel Plant—minority of workers, evidently skilled.[42]
3. Shanghai Steel Tubing Plant—workers; technicians seemingly neutral.[43]
4. Peking Stamp Printing Plant—workers; technicians seemingly split.[44]
5. Kweichow Hunghsing Tractor Plant—workers.[45]
6. Kweichow Provincial Machinery and Equipment Company—workers, two deputy managers; technicians and engineers split.[46]
7. Changtung Lathe Plant—workers, plant manager.[47]
8. Shanghai Huangpu Instrument—leading cadres at work-shop level and work-shop managers.[48]
9. Tsinan Lathe Factory #1 Branch—workers and some cadres.[49]
10. Chungking Hungyen Machinery Factory—worker-engineers and some workers.[50]
11. Kweiyang Cotton Mill—workers, work-shop level leaders (not necessarily work-shop chiefs), some work-shop-level technicians.[51]
12. Ch'angchiang Machine Plant—workers, cadres at all levels.[52]
13. Nanking Foundry—workers, deputy factory director, cadres; some cadres undecided.[53]
14. Canton Auto Assembly Plant—low-level party members, model workers, production group leaders.[54]
15. Canton Power Plant—workers, section and work-group leaders at work-shop level and below.[55]
16. Shanghai #7 Enamelware Factory—workers and basic-level leaders from work-shop level on down.[56]
17. Tsingtao Internal Combustion Engine Plant—deputy work-shop head, some workers, and the factory manager who was also a CP member.[57]
18. Harbin Farm Machinery Repair Plant—acting Party Committee secretary, workers.[58]
19. Shanghai Tungfanghung Shipyard—technicians, lower-level party members, workers.[59]
20. Harbin Hsin Feng Finishing Plant—workers, deputy plant manager, other middle-level cadres, including work-shop Party Branch secretary. Cadres from deputy section chief and above seemed to be the pivotal elements in the power struggle and many were sympathetic to rebels.[60]
21. Soochow Tungfanghung Silk Weaving Mill—eight veteran workers with from twelve to forty years experience.[61]
22. Kailan Coal Fields—worker technicians and engineers promoted during Great Leap Forward.[62]
23. Peking #1 Lathe Works—workers and section level cadres at work-shop level of worker background.[63]

24. Shanghai #17 State Cotton Mill—thirty hard-core rebels, including seven lower level CP members.[64]
25. Wuhan Municipal #2 Machinery Works—workers, deputy Party Committee secretary, two other high level cadres.[65]
26. Harbin Bicycle Plant—workers, deputy plant manager, CP member for thirty years (Yenan cadre), and a PLA man demobilized. Middle- and upper-level cadres were the focus of struggle between rebels and Party Committee.[66]

Although many of the early rebel leaders were full-time workers and cadres, a number of contract workers (ho-t'ung-kung) or auxiliary workers provided support and perhaps leadership for rebels[67] as they were discriminated against compared to regular full-time workers.[68] Moreover, these contract workers might have had fewer qualms about attacking the factory's leadership than regular or model workers. Many workers were clearly ambivalent, even negative, toward the rebels, being at first either unwilling or unable to challenge what they knew to be powerful authority or to dissociate themselves from the Party Committee's leadership which had, 'in the name of the whole CP, brought enormous improvement in their lives.[69] Very often model, or five-good, workers were caught in precisely this predicament; being informal—if not formal—leaders their support for the rebels was all the more pivotal.[70]

The analysis of rebel leadership and conservative opposition, thus clearly suggests that more was at issue in these early power seizures than a simple struggle between haves and have nots, a contest between a conservative, full-time industrial labor force assimilated into modern factory life and a somewhat more militant and certainly more jealous "underprivileged" group of marginal people in industry who supported the rebellion against management. Distribution questions were only part of the problem, but the issues of authority and morality were more important ultimately.

Authority concerned not only who had power but how it was used. This was the issue behind the major conflict between bourgeois technical authorities and revolutionary technical personnel where what mattered was not simply the relative position of two power-seeking groups, but a decision-making method and a work style. Officiousness and snobbery were more than marginal concerns of many rebels.[71] Technical decision-making was not the only issue either. Favoritism in personnel handling and apple-polishing for job assignments were equally resented. Arbitrary controls over work-shop communications and regimentation of the pace of production, based on quotas made by functionaries in factory offices, antagonized enough people to fuel the rebels' spark.[72]

The twin issues of morality and purpose were manifested in disagreement over factory incentives. Some workers rebelled in the expectation that power seizure would lead to increases in wages, promotion to a higher salary grade, or added bonuses.[73] This was obviously the reason for the preliminary successes of the economist strategy, but it seemed less a motivation of rebel leaders, who were interested in changing behavior or acquiring power, than early rebel followers.[74]

Other rebels were concerned less with individual self-enrichment and more with the relative distribution between workers and managers. They attacked privileges both on and off the job. Typically, when power seizures occurred, they were followed by behavioral or organizational change, not just economist demands.[75] Yet the links between distribution and morality, brought together in factory incentive systems, were to remain an issue that took a good deal of attention throughout the year.

Power Seizure Case Histories

Examples that illustrate the nature of rebel leadership, the issues that motivated them, and the tactics used by factory-level management to defeat them are described below.

The Shanghai Glass-Making Machinery Plant[76]

This was a medium-sized urban factory employing about 1,200 people, requiring a moderately skilled labor force. It was typical of Shanghai plants owned by Chinese capitalists prior to 1949. The former owner was the factory manager, and he had befriended some members of the plant Party Committee. This plant had perhaps never fully implemented one-man management, but there were certainly differences in life style and standard of living between workers and managers—not surprising in a large cosmopolitan city like Shanghai.

The rebels in this plant were unhappy about the privilege differential. Rebel leaders were basic-level work-team leaders; skilled workers and technicians on the teams and in the work shops supported them, although when the time came to assume authority on management committees many workers hesitated because they feared reprisals or from lack of confidence. After the power seizure, a factory-level revolutionary committee was elected to manage production. At least four factory-level technical leaders were relieved of their posts and sent to labor in work shops. The strength and militancy of the work-team leadership, the gap between workers' and cadres' routines and privileges, plus the difficulty of getting the workers to take authority, makes this an interesting case.

The Kweiyang Cotton Mill[77]

This plant was located in the southwestern province of Kweichow. The nature of cotton spinning made the work shop a production but not a managerial necessity. Still, the work-shop levels of staff management had become very powerful, and this was resented by workers who felt that coordination between work shops could be more directly achieved. Rebel workers also resented the officiousness of many middle-level control cadres. When the plant Party Committee tried to protect the old management system of work-shop-level staff sections, the Party Committee came under attack. It is also possible that the conflict in this plant involved male-female relationships since the cotton industry traditionally employs a large female labor force while management tended to be male. At any rate, the Kweiyang mill sharply curtailed the power of work-shop-level control departments and increased direct contact between factory-level management and production by having cadres participate in labor more frequently.

The Peking Kwanghua Wood Products Factory[78]

A medium-sized factory administered by the city and employing about 2,240 people, this was built wholly after 1949. As one-man management operated on every level, rebels were antagonistic to formal leaders all the way down to the team level. The requirements of one-man management generated scientific production quotas based on statistics and time frames. The cadres who gathered this data had no first-hand production experience and were oriented toward the factory-level cadres who in turn had close relationships with the Peking municipal Party Committee. But not all cadres liked this situation, and some no doubt resented the factory-level cadres use of the factory automobile for personal use and the comparative luxury of factory level offices as much as the workers did. The worker rebels were joined quite early by cadres in functional departments who became members of the new revolutionary committee.

The T'aiyüan #1 Thermo-Electric Power Plant[79]

This was a key electric generating plant in central Shansi Province. It is significant because the rebel leaders immediately split into factions and cadres were not noticeable in any of the rebel groups—in fact, the army later had to play a large role in reconciling workers and in getting cadres to join a reformed management structure. The chief difficulty and probably the cause of factionalism was a very tight system of control, which was resented by many workers, was combined with a complex system of bonuses and awards, which was *not* resented by other workers. The difficulty of showing the interrelationship between the control system and the incentive system makes this factory's experience with the power seizure an instructive one.

The Harbin Boiler Plant[80]

This was a large factory in the northeastern industrial heartland, employing approximately 5,000 people. The functional departments at the factory level exercised tight control over production, but the rebels—made up of production workers and basic-level cadres from the workshop level—took over these departments. Many functional-department cadres remained loyal to the factory-level management, but many others sympathized with the rebels. However, none of the department chiefs supported the rebels, and because of this many other cadres refused to join their ranks. Finally, the department-level cadres who joined the rebels formed with the workers a factory-level coordinating body, which restored some semblance of order to production but was not an effective management group. Plagued by unwillingness to take responsibility or mistrust of everyone who previously had had responsibility, the rebel workers were prevented from effective leadership. Leading cadres, especially the plant Party Committee, maintained a stubborn hold on legitimacy which frightened opposition or threatened to neutralize it. Though there was a willingness to challenge authority, some rebels did not have the experience to be immediately effective, while still others did not have the will to make a clean break with power and legitimacy.

The Peking #2 Machine Tool Plant[81]

This large plant, closely connected to the Peking municipal Party Committee, had a skilled labor force. The rebels were not intimidated by the early efforts of the municipal Committee to put down the rebellion through the dispatch of work teams. The Party Committee was itself split. Not only did basic-level cadres join and lead the workers who rebelled, but ten out of the seventeen members of the Party Committee sympathized with the rebels. Pressures to cooperate with the work teams were formidable and had more effect on the dissenting members of the Party Committee than on the rebels. Although most rebels were young or apprentices, many were older, with both skill and experience. The Party Committee temporarily succeeded in creating splits in the rebels ranks by the use of economism, but the issues of rebellion were clearly not economic, and economism served only a temporary purpose. The real dispute was about the skilled workers participation in technical innovation and control procedures and the personal relationships between functional-department cadres and workers.

The Loyang Tractor Works[82]

This huge industrial enterprise, begun as a Soviet aid project in 1953, came into production in 1959, during the Great Leap Forward.

The power struggle here reflected early dissatisfaction with the strict control systems of Soviet technical and managerial advice. Since the Loyang Plant was a key project in China's economic development, many of the most skilled and experienced workers from the Northeast and Shanghai came to Loyang. Even before the project was completed these workers strongly resented the controls they were subject to, but there also was the added factor of hurt pride that came from working under highly trained, sophisticated Soviet and foreign-trained Chinese technicians with formal educational credentials and superior or paternalistic attitudes.

The resentment of Soviet aid personnel and Chinese technicians, trained in the West or copying Soviet models, erupted in 1958 during the Great Leap Forward. Workers became involved in technical innovations, a process which gathered tremendous momentum throughout 1959. Eighteen skilled workers were promoted to engineers. The triple combination of workers, technicians, and cadres was used frequently and widely, involving technical personnel, who had been workers but not graduates of technical institutes or universities, or who had previously worked only in big office buildings that were both functionally and geographically separated from actual production and from the peasantry for whom the tractors were designed.

There was opposition, however, and during 1960–1964 tighter technical controls were instituted. Many technical innovations were scrapped, and the eighteen worker-engineers all were removed from their posts. The office of the chief engineer became the central focus for all decision-making on technical innovations and reforms. The renewal of hostilities between the skilled workers and worker-engineers and those in favor of centralized control by people with formal academic credentials began in 1964 and continued with great intensity following January 1967.

The early power seizure stage of the Cultural Revolution in China's industrial enterprises, therefore, generally grew out of some workers' discontent with the authority patterns of management. There was significant support for the rebels from other workers and other lower level cadres and some, but much less, support from the cadres at the middle level and above who were part of the control apparatus being attacked. In organizational terms, the power seizures were aimed at the party committees and functional departments at the factory level and at work-shop level sections of those functional departments.

In personal terms, however, this dichotomy was not always so clear, since cadres in functional departments and sections as well as cadres in positions of leadership in production accustomed to working with those functional departments came under attack.[83]

For all but a few cadres[84] at middle level and above, party or non-party, the first stages of the Cultural Revolution created a mixed and anxious situation which was inherent in the issues that affected people with very different family backgrounds, educational experience, and expectations. The result was that the power seizure stage of the Cultural Revolution uncovered many conflicts, both personal and ideological, that had developed over the years of rapid and uneven social change and economic progress.

After March 1967 the Cultural Revolution began to spread to factories and mines which had not previously experienced power seizures but which nevertheless contained the same kinds of cleavages which had generated power seizures elsewhere. By March 1967 factionalism[85] —a result of confusion as to what the issues were and how to remedy a situation that many now agreed was bad—was spreading. Sometimes it was based on disagreement over whether any issues existed at all. But everyone could agree at this point that something was happening, and that the chief focus of attention was the Communist Party.

The Role of the Army, the End of Factionalism, and the Beginning of "Struggle"

As the Cultural Revolution became a mass movement and spread, the party itself was attacked and the pace of the movement in many places began to outstrip its capacity to resist or to set up alternate leadership and authority to the Party Committees. But not all enterprises were able to seize power from the Party Committees. In this context, the People's Liberation Army served several roles.

It was an alternative source of authority and legitimacy for rebels within enterprises at the crucial municipal and provincial levels of government and party organization.[86] PLA teams sent to industrial enterprises after March 1967 were authorized by a Military District or provincial level military commands, a clear indication that they were bypassing provincial and municipal level party and government authority.[87] Thus, during ideological turmoil the PLA became a source of administrative coherence and symbolic legitimacy.[88]

The army also served as a political broker between the rival factions within industrial enterprises. It was extremely important in bringing cadres at middle and higher levels back into administrative and production activities through the formation of what were called revolutionary great alliances between workers, cadres, and PLA representatives.[89] In addition, the PLA was an instrument of political propaganda. It tried to clarify issues concerning authority, incentives, and leadership, and it attempted to relate these to specific individuals or groups so that judgments could be made about the revolutionary qualities of any person being considered for a position of leadership.[90] In the early stages PLA representatives often took part in organizational reform to prevent the Cultural Revolution from turning into a mere purge.[91]

Finally, the PLA acted to keep production going especially in factories where factionalism or attacks on cadres were so severe as to threaten to paralyze operations and coordination.[92]

Although some factories had power seizures, had established revolutionary committees, and had begun managerial reform quite early in 1967, in most plants, even with the PLA present, these changes were preceded by many months of factionalism and confusion.[93] By late 1967 factionalism (but not necessarily the confusion) had been ended by the formation of revolutionary great alliances which often included a representative from the PLA. If no PLA representatives were in the plant, then the third representative in the alliance was from the militia or a mass organization. The uneven formation of revolutionary alliances, from which were elected members of the revolutionary committees, indicates that conditions in individual factories were the determinants of the pace of agreement, not simply directives emanating from higher authorities.

The general directive to form the revolutionary alliances seems to have come from Mao in early 1967.[94] By September the city of Hangchow, for example, reported that 90 percent of all factories and enterprises had formed great alliances.[95] In Tientsin, it was reported that over 800 factories and enterprises had formed great alliances on 21–22 September alone.[96] In Peking by the end of the year, 90 percent of the 800 big or medium-sized enterprises had formed great alliances,[97] and in the plants where the PLA was present the figure was 99 percent.[98] In other cities like Shanghai,[99] Anshan,[100] Canton, and Tsingtao,[101] similar reports were made.[102]

The Formation of Revolutionary Committees

The revolutionary alliances were actually emergency measures to be replaced by revolutionary committees which would then begin serious organizational and ideological transformation. The establishment of revolutionary committees proceeded unevenly, the end of 1967 and the first four months of 1968 being the major period of formation. Although the general directive to form revolutionary committees (as opposed to the earlier revolutionary alliances) came from Mao sometime in late 1967,[103] the date of establishing the revolutionary committee varied in each enterprise according to specific situations. Therefore, before investigating the substantive issues in the conflicts common to all enterprises, it would be instructive to analyze the factors specific to individual factories, such as size, location, and historical development, for influence regarding the intensity of the conflict.

Table 5[104] lists industrial and mining enterprises by type. Whenever possible, size, location, and relevant historical data are included. The dates on which revolutionary committees were established are also listed. On the assumption that these dates vary according to the intensity and complexity of struggle over substantive issues and reform measures the table is an attempt to relate these to type, size, location, and history of each factory. Because of the incomplete nature of the data, the conclusions drawn can be considered only hypotheses.

From the samples in this table, it is possible to draw the following tentative conclusions.

Figure 1 below illustrates the relationship between the date of

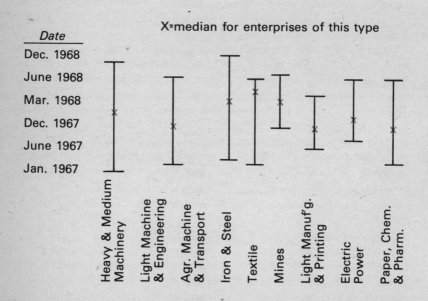

Figure 1 Establishment Date of Revolutionary Committees Related to Type of Factory

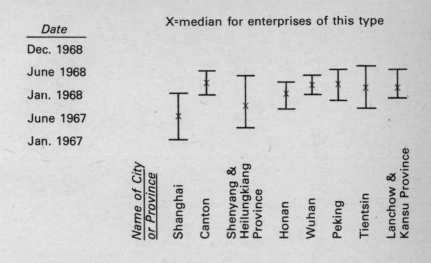

Figure 2 Establishment Date of Revolutionary Committees Related to Location of Factory

establishment of revolutionary committees and the type of factory. The establishment of revolutionary committees did not seem to be influenced very much, if at all, by the category of factory or industrial enterprise. In the nine categories under consideration (Heavy & Medium Machinery, Equipment & Machine Tool; Light Machinery & Engineering; Agricultural Machinery & Transport; Iron & Steel; Textile; Mining Enterprises; Light Manufacturing & Printing, Electric Power Stations; and Paper, Chemical & Pharmaceutical), there emerges no pattern of revolutionary committee establishment based on category, and the time-spread in almost every category runs roughly from April 1967 to April 1968, with the median around the end of 1967 or the beginning of 1968.

Location, which would include such things as economic infrastructure, degree of urbanization or previous industrialization, North China, coastal China, etc., does seem to have some influence on the establishment of revolutionary committees. Not only is it obvious that local authorities exercised a good deal of influence on the rate at which revolutionary committees were established, as noted by the significantly shorter time spans on Figure 2, but the degree of previous industrialization tended toward earlier revolutionary committees. Shenyang, for example, had revolutionary committees as early as March 1967, Shanghai as early as January 1967, while Lanchow, a comparatively new

Table 5 Establishment of Revolutionary Committees According to Location, Size, and Relevant History of Factory

Name of Factory	Location	Size	Date Oprtnl.	Relevant History	Rev. Com. Estblshd.
HEAVY EQUIPMENT, HEAVY & MEDIUM MACHINERY & MACHINE TOOL					
1. Hutung Shipyard	Shanghai			PLA in plant	10/67
2. Ch'ang Chün Crane Factory	Changchün, Kirin			PLA in plant	4/67
3. Lanchow Chemical Machinery	Lanchow, Kansu			PLA in plant	10/67
4. Wan An Machine Bldg.					1/68
5. Tsingtao Foundry Machinery	Tsingtao, Shangtung			PLA in plant	1/68
6. Lanchow Ch'ang-fang Machinery	Lanchow, Kansu				10/67
7. Ninghsia Machine Tool	Ninghsia-hui Autonomous Reg.			PLA in plant	8/68
8. Shanghai Machine Tool	Shanghai			Pre-1949 US & KMT interests; expanded during GLF	9/67

	Location	Workers/Scale	Date	Notes	
9. Shanghai Heavy Machinery & Equipment	Shanghai	6,000 workers		A few Soviet experts here, but began in present form in 1958	1/67
10. Wuhan Heavy Machine	Wuhan	Large scale	1958; const. began 1956	A Soviet aid project; PLA in plant	1/68
11. Changchiang Machinery	Nanking				4/27/67
12. Hungtung Machinery	Nanchiang, Kiangsi				1/15/68
13. Lanchow General Mach.	Lanchow, Kansu				2/25/68
14. Changcheng Mach. Tool	Ninghsia-hui Autonomous Reg.				3/16/68
15. Shanghai Construction Machinery	Shanghai				3/28/67
16. Harbin #1 Machinery	Harbin				4/16/68
17. Huhetot Lathe Plant	Inner Mongolia				9/67
18. Peking #1 Machine Tool	Peking	4,000 workers	1958	Pre-1949 origin; present plant began during GLF	1/68

Table 5 (Continued)

Name of Factory	Location	Size	Date Oprtnl.	Relevant History	Rev. Com. Estblshd.
19. Hankow Machine Tool	Hankow			PLA in plant	12/67
20. Wuhan #3 Machine Tool	Wuhan			PLA in plant	12/67
21. Loyang Mining Machinery	Loyang			PLA in plant	12/67
22. Canton Chemical Mach.	Canton			PLA in plant	2/68
23. Lanchow Petro-chemical Machinery	Lanchow			PLA in plant	1/68
24. Tsunyi Yungchia Gen'l. Elec. Equipment Plant	Kweichow				
25. Kweichow Diesel Engine	Kweichow				3/67
26. Tientsin Regulator Valve	Tientsen				2/68

27. Chengchow Electric Cable	Chengchow, Honan		PLA in plant	12/67
28. Chengchow Diesel Engine	Chengchow, Honan		PLA in plant	12/67
29. O-Mei Machinery			PLA in plant	2/68
30. Hung-chou Machinery				1/68
31. Shanghai #2 Textile Machine	Shanghai			4/67

LIGHT MACHINERY, MOTOR, & ENGINEERING FACTORIES

1. China Clock Factory	Shanghai	1941	Pre-1949 militancy; joint operated to 1956	2/67
2. Shanghai Diesel Pump & Motor	Shanghai	7,000 workers / 1957	Pre-1949 US & KMT operation; head of plant was a Kung (4 families)	9/67

Table 5 (Continued)

Name of Factory	Location	Size	Date Oprtnl.	Relevant History	Rev. Com. Estblshd.
3. Shanghai Truck	Shanghai	1,030 workers & staff	1958	Pre-1949 British auto repair began to produce trucks in 1958; self-reliance, very low level of technology in beginning	12/67
4. Tsingtao Ssu-fang Rolling Stock	Tsingtao	Large			2/68
5. Changchün Auto	Changchün, Kirin	23,000 workers	1957(?)	A Soviet aid project; PLA in plant	3/68
6. T'ao Chuang Coal Mine Chiaochuang Mine Bureau	Shantung				1/68
7. Lungyen Iron Mines	Lungyen				1/68
8. Tachungi Colliery, Chihsi Mine Bureau	Heilungkiang			PLA in plant	10/67

LIGHT MANUFACTURING AND PRINTING

	Location	Notes	Date
1. Hsiangtung Hygiene Matl.	Tientsin		9/67
2. Canton Gen'l. Flashlight	Canton		4/68
3. Peking Arts & Crafts	Peking	Originally many handicraft co-ops; began manufacturing in 1958	11/67
4. Hsuanhua Brick Factory	Changchia-kou		12/67
5. Red Flag Cement	Nanking		2/68
6. Shihchiachuang Cement Pole Factory	Hopei		11/67
7. Mutanchiang Cement	Heilungkiang		7/67
8. Shanghai Sluice Gate	Shanghai		6/67
9. Hsinhua Printing Plant	Hunan		3/68
10. Hsinhua Printing Plant	Kwangtung		4/68

Table 5 (Continued)

Name of Factory	Location	Size	Date Oprtnl.	Relevant History	Rev. Com. Estblshd.
ELECTRIC GENERATING PLANTS					
1. Hsiku Thermal Power	Lanchow			PLA in plant	10/67
2. Chingpohu Elec. Plant	Heilungkiang				2/68
3. Hangchuang Sub-station, Chiangsu Hsüchou Electric Bureau	Kiangsu			PLA in plant	4/68
PAPER, LEATHER, PHARMA-CEUTICAL & CHEMICAL					
1. Lup'ing Hsien Leather Plant	Chengtu, Szechwan				1/68
2. Tungfanghung Paper	Chianghsi				1/68
3. Chianghsi Paper Mill	Canton				3/68
4. Canton Paper Mill	Szechwan				4/68
5. Chengtu Pharmaceutical					4/68
6. Tientsin Chemical	Tientsin				1/68

	Location	Notes	Date
7. Shanghai #2 Chem. Fibre	Shanghai		4/67

IRON AND STEEL INDUSTRY

	Location	Notes	Date
1. Peking Steel Wire	Peking	800 workers	late 1967 — A rope-making plant prior to GLF; Soviet aid project; PLA in plant
2. Hangyang Steel Rolling	Hangyang		11/67
3. Shihchiachuang Iron & Steel	Peking		12/67
4. Shenyang Smelting	Shenyang		3/67
5. Shanghai Multiple Steel Tube	Shanghai		4/67
6. Penki Iron & Steel	Penki		6/68
7. Shanghai #2 Steel	Shanghai		11/67
8. Wuhan Iron & Steel	Wuhan	Very lge. vertical integration	11/68 — Const. began in 1955; Soviet aid project; PLA in the enterprise

Table 5 (Continued)

Name of Factory	Location	Size	Date Oprtnl.	Relevant History	Rev. Com. Estblshd.
9. Wuhan Steel Rolling Mill	Wuhan	1,500 workers	1953	In 1953 was a very small plant in marshy area; developed bigger during GLF; very bitter struggle here.	late 1967 or beginning 1968
TEXTILES					
1. Tientsin Colored Cloth	Tientsin				1968
2. Tsingtao #9 State Cotton	Tsingtao				1/67
3. Peking General Knitwear	Peking			PLA in plant	11/67
4. Tientsin Szuhsin Yarn	Tientsin				2/68
5. Shanghai #32 State Textl.	Shanghai				1/68
6. Tientsin Linen	Tientsin				5/67
7. Lanchow #1 Woolen Textile	Lanchow			First RC in Lanchow factories	10/17/67

	Location	Size	Year	Notes	Date
8. Chengchow #6 State Cotton	Chengchow			First RC in Honan Prov.	10/17/67
9. Szechuan Ctn. Print & Dye	Szechuan				2/10/68
10. Anhwei Cotton Textile & Dye	Anhwei			PLA in plant	3/2/68
11. Kiangsu "Aug. 1" Linen & Weaving Mill	Kiangsu				4/1/68
12. Anhwei Silk Textile	Anhwei				2/6/68
13. Shanghai #2 Print & Dye	Shanghai				1/67
14. Peking #2 Textile	Peking	5,300 workers 2,400 looms	1955	PLA in plant; Chinese machinery; 70% women employees	2/15/68
15. Shanghai State Silk #1 Plant	Shanghai	2,400 workers	1957	Active innovation during GLF	11/67
MINES					
1. Tienshuaifu Coal Mine, Penki Mining Bureau	Liaoning				4/68
2. Penki Coal Mine Bureau	Liaoning	Large scale			4/68

industrial center, did not have any committee until October 1967. However, this is not construed as a crucial variable. Peking, because of the strength of the old municipal committee, and in spite of previous industrialization, was later in establishing revolutionary committees, and the same can be said for Wuhan. The significance of location seems to point more to the importance of local political power than to the degree of urbanization or industrialization.

Finally, plants located in minority areas seem to have established revolutionary committees relatively late.

Size seems to be important. Large-scale factories had revolutionary committees established as early as January 1967 and as late as March 1968, but the data I have indicates that the largest (over 5,000 workers) plants did not as a rule establish revolutionary committees until the beginning of 1968.

Another variable closely related to size is the amount of Soviet aid and managerial advice. All the large-scale plants for which I have data, except the Shanghai Heavy Machine & Equipment Factory, had a significant Soviet presence. The Shanghai plant, with only a few Soviet experts helping for a very short time, established a revolutionary committee in January 1967, but the Changchün Auto Vehicles Plant did not establish one until March 1968. In the Peking Steel Wire Plant the revolutionary committee was established in late 1967; though this was a Soviet aid project, it was a medium-sized plant with only 800 workers as of 1966.[105]

Aside from the fact that the Soviet aid projects seemed to have caused a good many problems for the establishing of revolutionary committees, other factors are illuminating.

Most plants for which there are data and where the PLA was present established revolutionary committees early, usually by the end of 1967. However, there were enough exceptions to show that the PLA did not impose an administrative solution to the problem. The history of the enterprise—when it was built (during the Great Leap Forward, before 1949), from what origins it developed (combined from several small plants or many handicraft co-ops, built from scratch, or evolved from a distantly related manufacturing process)—all had effect. Generally speaking, those Shanghai plants with a pre-1949 history, influenced by the KMT, the U.S., or Britain, tended to earlier revolutionary committees than other Shanghai plants but all were established before the end of 1967. Plants begun during the Great Leap Forward and later expanded, and those extant in 1958, expanded during the GLF, and continued as important industrial enterprises, seemed to have had bitter struggles, establishing revolutionary committees late in 1967 or early 1968, for Shanghai, Peking, and Wuhan factories covered in the investigation.

In short, the establishment of revolutionary committees depended more on political, organizational, and historical factors than on economic, geographical, or technical ones.

The Issues Are Clarified: The Mass Campaign to Criticize the "Seventy Articles" and the "Trust System"

By the middle of 1968 the effort to establish revolutionary committees merged into a mass campaign for struggle-criticism-transformation.[106] Intended to clarify the issues of the Cultural Revolution, it was characterized by criticism of two theoretical and related approaches to management and economic coordination: The Seventy Articles for Industry,[107] and the trust system. Active factors were Mao's descriptions of the "revolutionary line" and Liu Shao-ch'i's identification as the chief supporter of the "bourgeois line."[108]

The Seventy Articles, purported to outline the duties and responsibilities of enterprise managers, party and nonparty, to insure strict technical control and guarantee party leadership over responsibility systems which closely paralleled one-man management. This was considered to be revisionist.

Direct criticism of the program began early in June 1967 when eighty revolutionary organizations in Peking set up metropolitan liaison stations to coordinate enterprise criticisms of the Seventy Articles. The criticism spread rapidly from Peking to other cities, and a full-blown mass campaign followed.[109] Even Anshan, the model for Mao's Anshan Constitution, was influenced by the revisionist principles of the Seventy Articles,[110] a program whose influence was subtle, uneven, and pervasive. The rationale for the mass campaign lay precisely in this. Many factories in Shanghai, for example, claimed to be unaware of the Seventy Articles, while other factories claimed to have heard about but rejected them. Thus a member of the Shanghai Municipal Revolutionary Committee insisted at a mass rally in June:

> The seventy-article industrial program was put into effect on a trial basis in Shanghai in 1961 (and) it was boycotted by Shanghai's broad masses of workers, staff members, and revolutionary cadres. However, China's Krushchov and his ilk and their agents in Shanghai used suppression and forcefully implemented it. *Its bad influence was widespread and deep. Therefore, all the localities, no matter whether they have or have not tried this program, should carry out thorough criticism and repudiation of it.* [Italics added.][111]

There were four major issues at stake:

1. The organizational problem: The Seventy Articles advocated control over workers by rules and regulations, to be enforced by inter-

mediate-level control supervisors or work-shop-level administrative personnel separated from production. According to the Seventy Articles, "authority in enterprises was centralized under senior engineers, accountants, and plant managers."[112] These people made final decisions based on reports and figures submitted by staff subordinates.[113]

For example, the Ai-Min Confectionary Factory was suggested as a typical case worth serious study. The plant was small, about 200 workers, but it had six functional departments and a work-shop-level administrative office. Altogether, thirty-eight people, or 17 percent of the work force,[114] were administrative cadres. There was a strict hierarchy; requests for spare parts or tools went via the team leaders, work-shop chief, division chief, and the factory director. Administrative personnel often had nothing specific to do, except look busy. Workers got quite angry.[115]

In the Kweichow #9 Chemical Industry Construction Company, there were 800 pages of rules covering 755 regulations. In nearly thirty offices and sections, one-third of the employees worked as administrative personnel.[116]

In the Shanghai Printing Ink Factory, with nine sections, two special offices, and administrative offices at the work-shop level as well, 104 full-time staffers accounted for 20 percent of the factory's personnel.

In the Shanghai China Clock Factory, the triple combination technical innovation method of the Great Leap Forward was subverted in 1960 by the institution of extremely complicated forms. From its beginnings, one technical section staffed by six or seven people, the plant had developed three big sections (technology, equipment, and inspection) and a habit of passing the buck when it came to accepting responsibility.[117]

2. The educational background and political attitudes of technicians and engineers: Informal as well as formal authority gravitated toward experts who had graduated from full-time universities in China, the USSR, or the West. These people insisted upon the machinery, technology and management methods of the already industrialized countries. Impressed by their importance and wisdom in relation to the unschooled workers, they were attacked for elitism, for slavish or comprador mentality,[118] and for practical incompetence.[119]

The Shanghai Machine Tools Plant illustrates how this expert in command system functioned.[120] A large-scale complex manufacturer of precision grinding tools, it had a technical force of over 600—45 percent former workers and 55 percent university graduates of which only 5 percent were pre-1949 graduates. Among the university graduates, there was a split. The older ones since 1960 had had authority and the younger ones had to impress this power structure with their own individual competence in order to get promoted.

The impatient younger technicians, of university and worker background alike, joined workers rebelling against the control of the technical authorities. One-tenth of college graduates were familiar with advanced technological theory, having done graduate work in China or graduated from colleges outside of China. The former workers numbered about 250, but only a minority had received formal education up to several years at secondary technical schools. About 25 of these people, however, were able to do advanced independent designing of high-grade precision machinery.

Former worker-technicians were better able to understand practical difficulties in designing. They were more creative and innovative than the college graduates, especially in their willingness to challenge foreign designs and procedures. Moreover, the extended period of formal education seemed to foster political attitudes of elitism and careerism. Major innovations in the plant had originated not from this group, but through the combined efforts of workers, former workers who had become technicians, and some leading cadres.

In the Kiangsi Motor Vehicle Plant, the plant manager was accused of relying on foreign models and imported equipment. Innovation was difficult because workers were unwilling to challenge experts who cited foreign descriptions of the state of the art.[121]

In the Shanghai #1 Steel Mill, a technical innovation to make high-grade silicon steel for power generating equipment was monopolized by capitalist roaders and reactionary technical authorities. After two years in the laboratory, several hundred experimental heats, and considerable expense, the results were inferior to existing material.[122]

In these and other examples—the Kweiyang Coal Mines,[123] the Seamless Steel Tube Plant at Anshan,[124] the Mutcanchiang Textile Plant in Heilungkiang,[125] and the "555" Clock Factory in Shanghai[126]—the attack on experts in command was not on technical rationality nor on all technical personnel and engineers, but on authorities accused of lack of creativity, pompous incompetence, and elitist attitudes often related to educational background.

3. The organizational problem and the problem of experts who monopolized technique and control of production was accompanied by a third criticism: the incentive system of the Seventy Articles, with its emphasis on piece work and individual bonus payments.[127] Since before 1960 and even during the height of the Great Leap Forward, the main principle of incentives policy was to "combine putting politics in command with material incentives."[128] A June 1967 editorial in Shanghai's *Chieh-fang Jih-pao*, however, called this revisionism:

Material incentives mean introducing the economic principle of capitalism into socialist economic life in order to develop bourgeois individualism.

Can putting politics in command be combined with material incentives? They are diametrically opposed principles. One puts the public interest in first place; the other puts self-interest in command. There will be a decisive battle between the two. [Italics added.][129]

The editorial pointed out that this incentive system created a privileged stratum which formed the base for a revisionist betrayal of the revolution. Echoing, but simultaneously developing, earlier arguments, it was now pointed out how this particular incentive system would support experts-in-command and a multiple-level control apparatus.

For example, in the Shihchingshan Steel Works in Peking, operational observation teams were formed. Made up of over 100 job analysts, these teams stood at every work site collecting data for time and motion studies which were used as the basis of calculating bonuses and piece rates. The total number of detailed job analyses reached over 100,800.[130]

Still another attack on the incentive system came from those who claimed that the bonuses and rewards were distributed unfairly, favoring those in a higher position. One report from the Yangshupu Power Plant in Shanghai noted:

Take, for instance, the rates of awards for different grades of workers and staff as laid down under the system of "awards for safe operation" (a system that had been in use in the plant since 1954 and attacked during the Great Leap, but reinstalled after 1960). The rate of awards for ordinary workers whose wages were low amounted to only 15% to 20% of their wages; yet for engineers or shop directors whose wages were fairly high, the awards ran as high as 45% to 50% of their wages. In some cases, the awards even exceeded the average monthly wage of a veteran skilled worker.[131]

Finally, the incentive system of the Seventy Articles came under attack because it inculcated the corrupting values of consumption and competitiveness, instead of fostering dedication to the collective welfare and a spirit of cooperation.[132]

4. The Seventy Articles management system was also attacked for the role it gave the Communist Party to play. Assigned the task of meeting the production goals of the enterprise and communicating important data up to the planning authorities, the party was also the most powerful organizational force in Chinese society and particularly its industrial system. In standing guard over the organizational, attitudinal, and incentive systems characteristic of the Seventy Articles, and in concerning itself only with the production responsibilities of the enterprise as these were defined in economic targets, the party would in effect forget that human relationships in production operations were the essence of revolutionary politics.[133] As one observer has written, "It became the duty of the terminal party organizations to eliminate party

control over enterprises."[134] Perhaps more accurately, the purpose was not to eliminate party control, but to enforce it over a non-revolutionary system.[135]

The degree to which the party actually implemented the Seventy Article management system depended on three things. One was the administrative and coordinative context of the enterprise and the degree of collusion between enterprise-level Party Committees and those economic or political authorities in higher-level organs who were committed to the Seventy Articles.[136]

Second was the degree of enterprise-level obedience and discipline to higher-authority directives, regardless of their political content, substance or implications.[137] Third was the degree to which the enterprise-level party organization understood higher-level politics.[138] Whether a conscious accomplice or an unconscious tool of higher authorities, the enterprise-level Party Committees were in a key position to influence enterprise-level management systems. Not only did the Party Committee make and enforce formal policy, shape incentive systems, and appoint personnel, it also influenced the whole structure of informal authority.[139]

The Critique of the Trust System of Economic Coordination

Criticizing the Seventy Articles was only half of the problem, because this system was designed to fit into a wider planning system using the party as a key integrative mechanism. The wider context was crucial. It was called the trust system, and in criticizing it the Cultural Revolution brought to a head a debate that had been growing more urgent since 1957. The attempt to create trusts, begun in 1963,[140] was part of this conflict.

As a result of the Great Leap Forward, the task of economic coordination became of paramount political as well as economic concern. The Seventy Articles specifically mentioned the task as one for Party Committees at each enterprise.[141] From January 1961 at the Ninth Plenum of the Eighth Central Committee when the party became officially involved in the coordination process to 1963, when the so-called trust system was officially presented, the enterprise-level Party Committees were pulled in different directions over how best to coordinate and integrate the economy. As the task of coordination was economic as well as political,[142] the party became involved with economic organs on the municipal, provincial, and ministerial levels,[143] and became part of the channel of communication in financial institutions: the banking system above and the accounting system within the enterprise.[144]

During 1961–1963, a series of articles was written on economic coordination, concerning the role of profit, the allocation of resources, and the use of contracts between enterprises. Two related issues were discussed: the question of specialization in industry and managerial motivation at the enterprise level.[145] However, it was not until the trust system was attacked during the Cultural Revolution that these three issues were discussed as a definite body of macro-management theory. The argument evolved as follows.[146]

First the trust system was attacked for treating industrial enterprises solely as units of production. Industrial enterprises, because of human relations, were also units of political and class struggle, where the fight against special privilege and inequality had to continue if the revolution was to be successful. Enterprises were urged to become "schools of Mao's thought" rather than merely producers. To simply increase wages and well-being rather than also focus on political and social equality at work would reproduce or create anew a class structure and ultimately contradict the goals of communism.

The trust system would create a new privileged stratum as it had in the Soviet Union and the Soviet bloc countries. In order to avoid the complexity of highly centralized planning, the trusts would employ decentralization at the national level only. Each particular industry would be highly centralized, with the headquarters of the trust responsible for purchasing and allocating materials and marketing finished goods. At the production end each enterprise would be evaluated according to profits based on assigned prices.

The trusts would plan production and marketing according to the profit criterion, and individual managers would be rewarded in proportion to profits earned. Party organs were to supervise relations between enterprises or between trusts. Former central-level ministers would form a board of directors for each trust.

The contours of the new privileged stratum begin to emerge. Using government or party organs as a pork-barrel authority to be persuaded or threatened into making favorable decisions for allocating men and material, the managers of enterprises and the officials in the trusts, whether party members or not, could easily form alliances with government officials and planners, thus adding political backing to an already economically privileged group. Their monopolistic power in economic and political sectors guaranteed ultimate if not total safety from competition for scarce raw materials and machinery. Enterprise-level management would be oriented upward for rewards as well as orders in this vertical-integration pattern. Motivated solely by profit, enterprise management would be pressed to link productivity norms and quotas to a system of bureaucratic control. The end result was to cast workers in the traditional role of labor in bourgeois society, that is, a controlled, fragmented person working for extrinsic rewards. Plant-level management—high-level engineers, administrators, and party personnel—would form the lowest level of the new privileged stratum.

The third criticism of the trusts was that they coordinated the economy on the principle of vertical integration, with unacceptable economic development consequences. Vertical integration was an attempt to calculate, at the national level, by means of the trusts, the regions, industries, and enterprises in which it would be most economically rational to invest. The profit target became the measure of economic rationality because it supposedly gave the trust officials automatic cost-efficient indices for investment decisions.

Vertical integration, using prices based on centralized national calculations of efficiency, and the resultant profits of enterprises as the determinant for investment and allocation, would lead to regional imbalance and numerous isolated pockets of poverty and under-development. Those regions already built up and utilizing abundant resources would continue to grow, while poorer, underdeveloped regions would lag behind.

It was said that vertical integration would also lead to local imbalance between industry and agriculture, as it did not allow much chance for local agricultural mechanization through local industry or resources. Because investment and development decisions were to be made on a comparatively centralized and geographically wider basis, it might appear to efficiency-minded planners that local resources were not worth developing. Vertical integration was attacked for not fully and efficiently exploiting marginal sources of raw materials, or utilizing waste materials adequately because of short-term cost.

The transport and communications demanded by national vertical integration were, it was argued, unnecessary, undesirable, and unavailable. Specialization on the local level was easier to coordinate with a strong local planning authority rather than with a large nationally based bureaucracy. Additionally, small, non-specialized operations were better able to overcome shortages or to adapt to transport and supply bottlenecks.

Another complaint against vertical integration and centralized development of industry and specialization was that it unnecessarily prevented people from relying on their own efforts, and fostered a sense of dependency on others.

One major point ran through all the criticisms of the trust system. This was the need to stress planning over profits. Not only was the pursuit of profit unacceptable because of its tendency to build on the best and cause serious political and economic imbalance, but profit was thought to corrupt psychologically. When the trust institutions of co-ordination and planning were combined with the personal values of profit, the result could only be human beings who were incapable of performing effectively in a planned system. The combination of planning with a profit based incentive system would lead to graft, speculation, stockpiling, raising prices, and corruption between government officials and economic authority. The trust system would lead to ownership by the privileged class manipulated by the highest levels of party authority. Ownership, of course, would not be based on legality but on bureaucratic control and economic inequality.[147]

The Role of Liu Shao-ch'i in the Mass Campaign

The mass campaign, begun in mid-1967, to criticize and repudiate the Seventy Articles and the trust system clarified the issues in the vast power struggle that was now shaking Chinese society. But, the remaining problems were formidable. There was the task of analyzing and evaluating each enterprise's implementation of what had come to be called the capitalist road, and identifying those responsible for capitalist road management. Another problem was to change the management and planning system so that the economy could function in a rational manner but to ensure that the values and behavior of "capitalist roaders" would not grow and develop. The first of these indicated prolonged debate because personality could easily be confused with ideology. In this connection, Liu Shao-ch'i became politically vital. If he did not exist, it would not be an exaggeration to say that the Chinese would have had to invent him.

Liu was defined as the highest authority figure in an organizational network with individuals at varying levels of conscious commitment to the Seventy Articles and the trust system. If degree of consciousness was to be seriously considered as a means of evaluating cadres, production would decrease in proportion to the increase in the number of personal, trivial, and contradictory attacks. It was difficult to evaluate cadres because they may have been subject to routines and job assignments that personally they found distasteful. By blaming Liu and a few of his agents in provincial and municipal organs for whatever implementation there was of the capitalist road or revisionist management, the factory level cadres would not have to face the problems of defending the purity of their intentions, only the results of their actions.[148] It is much easier to change one's behavior than to defend one's moral purity.

There was another purpose in focusing attacks on the person of Liu Shao-ch'i and on his policies. The attacks on Liu focused on a series of speeches he had made in Tientsin in April and May 1949.[149] What emerged from an analysis of those polemics was a composite picture of the capitalist roader. Thus the criteria upon which criticism of cadres was based was clarified.

Liu was accused of being both personally and politically attracted to capitalist methods and, as a consequence, of putting capitalists in positions of authority, and of allowing them into the party, and of liking them socially. However, an attack on Liu for favoring the managers or technical personnel of the old regime could not be taken seriously or literally after nearly twenty years during which they had become a distinct and relatively unimportant minority. What mattered was that the values attributed to this minority were still very much alive in the structure and methods of enterprise management.[150]

Liu's role in the Cultural Revolution did not eliminate the need to evaluate the performances and intentions of individuals nor to further transform management and planning. It did, however, objectively limit the disruptive potential inherent in a movement that openly made individual behavior and morality the subject of political debate.[151]

8 / "Taking Stock of Class Ranks" and "Better Troops and Simpler Administration"

THE CAMPAIGN OF mass repudiation against the Seventy Articles and the trusts created a paradox. The differences between socialist and capitalist as abstract categories became clearer, but the difficulty was to find the enemy, or, in the Chinese phrase, the capitalist roaders. Few individuals were totally good or totally evil. Discovering enemies was also connected to organizational transformation.

> If we carry out only the task of taking stock of class ranks, without imple-menting the policy of better troops and simpler administration, we will inherit only the huge and unwieldly old administrative structures, leaving untouched the soil for the growth of revisionism and keeping a hotbed for the restoration of capitalism. . . . Therefore, the policy of better troops and simpler administration is a major question concerning what line the revolutionary committees at all levels are implementing and what road they are taking; it is a question of fundamental importance to the pre-vention of and fight against revisionism.[1]

The phrase taking stock of class ranks meant a criticism of those who had made mistakes and job dismissal for those who persisted in opposing the transformation of management and organization.

"Who Are Our Enemies, Who Are Our Friends?"

The early stages of the Cultural Revolution defined the enemy as certain cadres. But as taking stock of class ranks developed as part of the struggle-criticism-transformation campaign that the Cultural Revolution had become, it seemed that all kinds of people were potentially vulner-able to criticism for non-revolutionary, or even anti-revolutionary, behavior and attitudes.

Comparatively high level enterprise cadres who had become pre-occupied with modernization and had forgotten about revolution were criticized. Using the previous and the proven as guides to action, they no doubt thought they were contributing to economic development and industrialization and to revolution as well. Hence the paradox. Their dedication to industrialization had led to conservative managerial policies,[2] reliance on foreign technical designs and machinery,[3] and reliance on university graduate technical personnel.[4] But these cadres also had a deep commitment to their jobs and when they were criticized for conservatism they became resentful and alienated. As the former Deputy Director of the Peking General Knitwear Mill said, in what was a mild understatement:

> In the Proletarian Cultural Revolution, the masses criticized and repudiated me. I could not understand this and was dissatisfied.[5]

In fact he became deeply demoralized, refused to assume responsibility and told his children, "never become a cadre."[6]

Other cadres attacked for nonrevolutionary attitudes had showed interest in personal advancement and no interest in manual labor. They were accused of talking glibly and toadying to authority,[7] of assuming official airs of superiority,[8] or of losing their personal relationships with former co-workers.[9]

These two groups of cadres came from all social and family backgrounds,[10] making social and family background by itself not an adequate way to understand the causes of conflict.

Up to the time of the Cultural Revolution, China's educational system had been a two-track system.[11] The full-time, formal track was similar to those in the West or the USSR—kindergarten, primary, junior, and senior middle schools. It included vocational schools, college, and post-graduate work. The other track began with part-time, basic literacy classes and went to spare-time higher education, usually at the workplace, with a few possibilities for post-graduate work and research.

The great majority of industrial cadres were graduates of specialized vocational schools of either track for at this level the two overlapped.[12] University graduates "tended to be employed as department section heads, vice directors, workshop chiefs, and their deputies in research, design and development work, and as engineers."[13] When the Cultural Revolution officially began over one-half of the full-time university graduates were from pre-1949 bourgeois families.[14] Differing social backgrounds of people thrown together at similar levels of authority and responsibility was a source of potential conflict. In addition, full-time university graduates of whatever background usually had different attitudes from worker-engineers towards work and position.

For example, in the Shanghai #2 Iron and Steel Works a former worker engineer had graduated from the Shanghai Work-Study University. A technician graduate from a full-time university resented that he was graded lower than the former worker. At every opportunity he humiliated and embarrassed the worker and showed his superior grasp of theory. The worker was good with machinery and had an excellent knowledge of practical matters, but his ability to theorize or express himself abstractly was not as well developed as the university graduate's. The two were in constant conflict, the university graduate gaining the favor of management since the worker-engineer supported the Cultural Revolution rebels.[15]

The Shanghai Machine Tools Plant became the most famous model of this type of conflict. Former workers and graduates of the work-study track's senior and junior technical middle schools were superior both technically and politically to the graduates of full-time universities.[16] However, higher level cadres were full time university graduates, Chinese or foreign; they held controlling positions in experimentation and technical innovation. The worker-technicians resented them for being arbitrary and high-handed, for wanting status more than technical innovation.[17]

In addition many of the worker-technician cadres who had supported the Cultural Revolution had been promoted during the Great Leap Forward, only to be subsequently discriminated against.[18] Even if these people were not active rebels in the beginning, it is clear that they were to be regarded as reliable allies against the technical and engineering personnel from the full-time, formal educational track.[19]

The expansion of all education during the Great Leap Forward[20] had guaranteed a pool of people with some advanced technical or vocational training who later found themselves without much responsibility or authority, particularly in technical innovation and decision-making. There was less trouble in plants where promoted workers had kept the positions and responsibilities attained as a result of the Great Leap.

For example, in 1961–1962 the Shanghai #17 State Cotton Mill had promoted eighty-six technical cadres trained during the GLF: eight to engineers, sixteen to master technicians (chi shuai), and sixty-two to technical personnel (chi shu yüan).[21] By 1967 the mill was a prestigious model for the Cultural Revolution in seizing power and in handling production without bourgeois authorities.[22] That almost eighty percent of the party members were of worker or peasant background and still came into conflict with rebels was attributed to their pre-1949 oppression of older, senior cadres. These cadres interpreted the revolution in terms of greater comfort and privilege for themselves and enforced strict control in a hierarchical fashion by pushing material incentives. Younger cadres were pressured by the system and by higher authorities,[23] but, since many had recently been promoted, it was not difficult to win them over to the side of the rebels or to assimilate them into the new management structure.

There were frequent reports of cooperation between older worker-technicians and younger student-technicians in rebellions against bourgeois authorities,[24] but, as in the Shanghai #17 Cotton Mill, conflict between pre- and post-1949 generations was a factor which showed in several ways. One was that workers rebelling against control over technical innovations frequently had the cooperation of revolutionary technical personnel, usually young technicians.[25] Another was previous Kuomintang affiliation. Often, anyone old enough to have been associated with the KMT came under attack. In the "February Seventh" Rolling Stock Plant at Changshintien, Peking, many cadres at the work shop and factory level had been workers before 1949. They had had to join the organizations which the Kuomintang set up to compete with Communist influence. By 1966, many of these people occupied important positions which they owed to members of the former Peking Municipal Party Committee and to influential party members in the municipal government which administered the factory.

The chief criticism of these men was their attachment to material incentives and support of management methods consistent with this system. Rebellion began among younger workers in the work shops and spread slowly and confusedly. During the period of criticizing and purifying class ranks, it was discovered that many of these cadres had former KMT connections and the young rebels assumed they were either actual or potential KMT agents. With the PLA in the plant, extensive discussion and debate ensued; ultimately a very lenient policy toward cadres was adopted.[26] What ostensibly were criticisms over former KMT membership were more likely convenient excuses for criticisms based on divergencies between generations and disagreement about the nature and purpose of work, or simple personality conflicts.

In other enterprises, however, older cadres who had not been workers and who had been former KMT members or former capitalists were criticized much more severely, often being removed from their positions.

In the Wuchang Carriage Factory the chief enemy turned out to be a former member of the KMT who had become a CP member. He had tremendous influence in technical decision-making and recruited into the party those prone to continue making decisions without involving workers.[27] In the Shihchiachuang Printing and Dyeing Mill the chief engineer had been a major in Chiang K'ai-shek's army and a member of the KMT. He and his two deputy engineers were singled out as the capitalist roaders. They had decisive say in regard to wage increases, technical questions, and the promotion and transfer of cadres. They had shaped the process of technical innovation so that workers had little chance to participate.[28] A similar report came from the Shanghai Tractor Plant.[29]

Aside from the older cadres who were former KMT members, cadres of landlord or bourgeois families were frequently isolated as capitalist roaders, especially in plants privately owned before 1949. Like former KMT members, many of these were important to technical management.

In the Suchow Monosodium Glutamate Factory the capitalist roader was the chief technician, a former landlord.[30] In the Ai Min Confectionary Plant some of the leading cadres in charge of labor protection, marketing and supply, industrial hygiene, and designing had been capitalists before 1949.[31] In the Tientsin Weighing Equipment Plant the main problem was the influence of pre-1949 capitalists on the Party Committee's judgement of the capabilities of workers.[32] In the Shanghai Tool Factory the former capitalist management still played a part in production management and was accused of corruption. In the Shanghai Switches Factory two former capitalists were made deputy factory managers, eight were made work-shop directors or the heads of functional sections.[33]

It is not realistic to attribute careerist and elitist attitudes[34] solely to former KMT membership or pre-1949 capitalism. Though these could be meaningful, more relevant was the dichotomy between older cadres, of whatever class background, and younger cadres and workers, as the "February Seventh" Plant's experience makes crystal clear.[35] Of course, since the overwhelming majority of cadres were trained after 1949,[36] including those pre-1949 workers who had become cadres,[37] generational differences must be understood and related to education and family background.[38]

It was therefore not easy to determine who the enemy was. In 1967 and early 1968 the issues of the 1966 rebellion became public during the mass campaigns against the Seventy Articles, the trusts, and the personal attacks on Liu Shao-ch'i. By mid-1968 the Cultural Revolution was focusing criticism on attitudes to and methods of decision-making. But these essentially clear intellectual contrasts were clouded by the practical realities of generational conflict, educational background, and individual values.

Personnel Turnover in Enterprise Management

Though criticism was acrimonious and confused, few cadres in the end were actually dismissed; many, however, were transferred or demoted temporarily, and there was an influx of new faces into factory management.

Information on this subject is incomplete, but trends can be deduced by the data presented below.

Table 6 lists seventy-four factories showing the make-up of revolutionary committees until early 1969,[39] coded as follows to designate the pre–Cultural Revolution position of each member:

a=Party Committee Secretary or Party Branch Secretary

b=Plant Manager

c=Deputy Plant Manager or Deputy Party Committee Secretary

d=Technical or Administrative Cadre, work-shop level or above, or other than a, b, or c

e=Workers, including basic level team leaders, but not former cadres in d

* Denotes CP member where identified as such

Table 6 Personnel on Factory Revolutionary Committees, 1968–1969

Name of Factory	a	b	c	d	e
1. Anshan #1 Steel Smelting Plant		b			e
2. Changchiak'ou Hsüan Hua Brick Factory				d	e
3. Chengtu Thermal Electric Plant		b			
4. Cholu Coal Mine, Hopei			c		
5. Fengch'eng Coal Mine, Liaoning					e
6. Harbin Agricultural Machine Repair Plant	a (acting)				
7. Harbin Bicycle Factory			c		e
8. Harbin Boiler Plant				d	
9. Harbin Electric Generating Plant			c	d	
10. Harbin Mutanchiang Cement Factory					e
11. Hsingt'ai Boiler Factory			c		
12. Hungkung Mining Bureau			c		
13. T'angchiachuang Mine, Kailan Coal Mines of T'angshan	a				
14. Kiangsi Paper Mill				d	
15. Kiangsi People's Steel Plant				d	
16. Kwangchou Paper Mill	a				
17. Kwangchou Auto Plant	a				
18. Kwangtung Heavy Duty Machine Works			c		
19. Kweiyang Cotton Textile Plant			c		
20. Loyang #1 Tractor Plant					e
21. Lup'ing Leather Plant					e
22. Nanch'ang Iron and Steel				d	
23. Ch'angchiang Machine Plant, Nanking					
24. Nanking Foundry			c		

Table 6—continued

Name of Factory	1968–1969 Members of Rev. Comm.			
25. Nanking Rolling Stock				e
26. "2-7" (Feb. 7th) Rolling Stock Plant, Changhsintien, Peking	b	c	d	e
27. Peking General Knitwear Mill		c	d	e
28. Peking Kwang-an Forging Plant				e
29. Peking Kwanghua Wood Products Factory				e
30. Peking Lightweight Aluminum Plant		c	d	
31. Peking #2 Machine Tool Factory		c		e*
32. Peking Pei Mu Carpet Factory				e
33. Penki Iron & Steel Company Coking and Chemical Plant				e
34. Penki Iron & Steel Company, Lutien Coal Mines			d	
35. Shanghai Boiler Factory				e*
36. Shanghai China Clock Factory	b*			
37. Shanghai Chiuhsin Shipyard		c		
38. Shanghai Kohsin Electric Motor Factory	a			e
39. Shanghai #2 Iron & Steel Works				e
40. Shanghai #3 Steel Mill	b*			
41. Shanghai Machine Tools			d*	e
42. Shanghai #1 State Cotton Textile Plant				e*
43. Shanghai #2 State Cotton Mill				e
44. Shanghai #17 State Cotton Mill				e*
45. Shanghai #32 State Textile Plant				e
46. Shanghai Seamless Steel Pipe Factory	b	c	d	e
47. Shenyang #2 Agricultural Machinery Parts Factory	a			
48. Shenyang Northeast Machinery Factory			d	
49. Shenyang Smelting Plant		c		e
50. Shenyang Transformer Factory			d	
51. Shenyang Tungfanghung Wood Processing Plant		c		e
52. Shihchiachuang #3 State Cotton Textile	a		d	
53. Shihchiachuang Weitung Garment Factory			d*	e
54. Ta-ch'ing Oil Fields			d	e
55. T'aiyuan Mining Machinery Plant				e
56. T'aiyuan 126 Textile Plant, Shansi				e
57. T'angshan Porcelain Company	a			
58. Tientsin Colored Cloth Factory	b			
59. Tientsin #14 Colored Cloth Factory	a			
60. Tientsin Dry All Battery Factory	a			

Table 6—continued

Name of Factory	1968–1969 Members of Rev. Comm.		
61. Tientsin Hsingtang Hygiene Material Factory	a		
62. Tsinan Vehicles Plant	b	d	e
63. Tsinghai Plastic Factory			e
64. Tsinghai Shanch'uan Machine Tool Forging Plant			e
65. Tsingtao Chemical Fertilizer Plant	b		
66. Tsingtao #1 Furniture Factory		d*	
67. Tsingtao Internal Combustion Engine Plant	b*	d	
68. Tsingtao #8 Textile Mill			e
69. Tsingtao #9 Textile Plant	a		
70. Tsingtao Steel Mill			e
71. Tsitsihar Vehicles Plant	a		
72. T'unghua Rubber Goods Factory	a		
73. Wuhan Iron and Steel Company	b		
74. Yingt'ai Boiler Factory		c	

Only general tendencies can be observed.
(1) Many factories elevated workers with no former management experience to the level of factory managerial authority.[40]
(2) Many factories reassigned old cadres (those who had held management positions before 1966) to the revolutionary committees. Category d, middle level managerial personnel, was the most frequently held leading position on the revolutionary committees. Party Committee and Party Branch secretaries reappeared on 19 percent and factory managers reappeared on 13 percent of the sample revolutionary committees. However, on none of the revolutionary committees did the plant manager and the Party Committee secretary reappear together.[41]
(3) The deputy factory managers outnumbered the factory directors and Party Committee secretaries as reintegrated cadres. This group, usually younger than the director or party secretary group,[42] appeared on 23 percent of the sample.

Altogether, 64 percent of the sample, by the time of the 9th Party Congress in April 1969, had reassimilated old cadres onto new revolutionary committees and 35 percent had assimilated top level management.

There is every indication that these trends continued after the 9th Party Congress. Widely publicized examples emphasized that all but a small number of former cadres were to be reinstated or given new, though perhaps lesser, responsibilities.

In the Changhsintien "February 7th" Rolling Stock Factory, one eyewitness reported that by the end of 1967 almost all senior cadres were reinstated except the Party Committee secretaries who had lost their posts.[43] A Red Guard newspaper was negative about similar developments in Canton.[44] In the Shihchiachuang State Cotton Mill #3 eight out of nine top managerial cadres were reinstated, and seven of the eight were made leading persons.[45] The Peking General Knitwear Mill reinstated the former Party Committee secretary, Deputy Party Committee secretary, and a Deputy factory manager[46] and allowed nine out of eleven former plant Party Committee members (ten including the secretary) to remain in the party and in positions of responsibility. While only one of the former Party Committee's eleven members was in a leading position on the mill revolutionary committee, only one was expelled from the party.[47]

The tentative assessment is that large numbers of workers were assimilated into managerial positions at the factory level, compared to pre-Cultural Revolution patterns. Many younger new cadres rose from the ranks of worker-technicians and engineers.[48] Also, large numbers of former managerial cadres maintained positions similar to those they held formerly, but there was some attrition among this group. By and large, it seems that many of the new cadres were also young cadres.[49] The tensions and conflict that quickly grew up between the "new" and the "experienced" or between the young and the old only underline the importance of both groups.[50]

Organizational change within the enterprise was, however, not only a matter of new faces in factory management bodies but of linkages between the factory and the planning and coordinative apparatus. Table 7 describes these linkages in terms of personnel.[51] Abbreviations are at the end of the list.

The sample of fifty-seven people is divided into two main groups:[52]

1. Managerial staff (including workshop directors, engineers, factory level party and nonparty management: thirty-eight
2. Workers (including basic-level leaders, model workers, apprentices): nineteen[53]

Of the thirty-eight managerial personnel, twenty-two were on the list only because of positions held before the Cultural Revolution; of the remaining sixteen, twelve held positions on revolutionary committees in locations other than the one in which they accumulated their industrial experience and had not held previous positions in government.[54] Only four of the managerial personnel (or about 10.5 percent) of the sample held positions in government both before and after the Cultural Revolution.

It seems that a significant portion of managerial personnel held positions on revolutionary committees above the enterprise after the

Table 7 Linkage of Industrial Enterprises with Higher Level Management Organs as Seen Through Individual Representatives

Name and Position In Industry	Govt. Position Before CR	Govt. Position After CR
1. Sang Wen-Kuo, worker, anti-revisionist steel plant, Heilungkiang	None	Member, Heilungkiang PRC
2. †Wei Feng-Ying, lathe operator, Shengyang Northeast Machinery Plant 1960; 1966, engineer, same plant	1964 NPC Deputy and member, NPC Presidium	1969, V. Chairman of Liaoning PRC; member, 9th CC of CCP
3. Wang Wen-hsing, veteran worker, CP member, Tientsin Weighing Instruments Factory	None	1969, member Tientsin
4. Teng Tzu-p'ing, worker in Tientsin	None	1969, member Hunch'iao Dist. RC, Tientsin
5. Wang Fu-Yuan, veteran worker Tientsin	None	1969, member Tientsin MRC
6. Sung Hsing-lu, mgr. Hsifang Locomotive Plant, Tsingtao 1957	1959–1960, Secy., Tsing-tao MPC	Not Listed
7. Li I'ch'ing, PC Secy., Wuhan Iron & Steel Co., 1960	1965–66, Secy., CCP Central-South Regnl. Bur.	Not Listed
8. Li K'o-tso, Dep. Plant Mgr. & Chief Engr. Peking Agr. Machine Plant 1962	1964 NPC Deputy, from Peking	Not Listed
9. An Ch'ao-chung, 1958 Depty. Plant Mgr. & Chief Engr., Shihchingshan Iron & Steel	1964 NPC Deputy, from Peking	Not Listed

Table 7—continued

Name and Position In Industry	Govt. Position Before CR	Govt. Position After CR
10. Feng Kuan-chih, 1958 Mgr., Kwangchow Paper Mill	1965 Dep. Dir., Ind. & Commun. Political Dept., Kiangsi Prov. PC	Not Listed
11. Liang Yen-pin, 1963–66 Party Br. Secy., Hsianfan Cotton Txtl. Plant, Hupeh	1964 NPC Deputy, Hupeh	Not Listed
12. Hsing Tzu-t'ao, 1957 Mgr. Harbin Elect. Appliance Plant	1965 Secy., Shengyang Mun. PC	Not Listed
13. Chang Hung-shu, 1958 Mgr. Harbin Rolling Stock Plant	1960, Dep. Dir., Industry Dept. of Harbin MPC; Vice-Pres. of Harbin	Not Listed
14. Li Peng, 1966 Mgr. Fouhsin Electric Plant	1960, Dir. Cadre Div., Kiangsi, PPC	Not Listed
15. Ch'en Yu-sheng, 1965 Mgr. Hangchow Boiler, previously a worker and engineer here	1964, NPC Deputy from Chekiang	Not Listed
16. Nuang Jung-ch'ang 1965–66, Dept. Chief Engr., Chungking Iron & Steel Works	1964 NPC Dep. from Szechwan; 1964 member NPC Nationalities Comm.	Not Listed
17. Chang Wen-chin, Workshop Dir. Chungking I & S Smelting Plant	1964, Deputy to NPC from Szechwan	Not Listed

#			
18.	Chang Che-min, 1957 PC Secy., Harbin Linen Txtl. Plant	1965, V. Chm., China Civil Engr. Society	Not Listed
19.	Ma Heng-ch'ang, 1958–59 Chief Mech. Model Worker, Tsitsihar #2 Mach. Tool	1964–65, NPC Deputy from Heilungkiang	Not Listed
20.	Han Ning-fu, 1960 Dep. PC Secy., Wuhan Iron & Steel	1964–65, V. Governor, Hupei Prv. People's Govt.	1967, resp. person, Hupei PRC
21.	Chai Fent-t'ing, Dir. Tatungk'ou Coal Mine, Chishi Mining Region, Heilungkiang 1964	1964, NPC Deputy from Heilungkiang	Not listed
22.	Tang Ying-pin, 1965, engr., Shanghai Chiangman Shipyards	1964, NPC Deputy from Shanghai	Not listed
23.	Sun Mao-sung, Model Worker, Harbin 1962	1964, NPC Deputy from Heilungkiang	Not listed
24.	*Chang Chen-yüan, 1959 engineer, Tientsin Hsinkang Shipyards	No previous position	1967, member of Peking MRC
25.	*Wang Ching-wu, 1964 PC Secy., Yupei Cotton Textile Plant, Hupei	No previous govt. position	1968, member SC of Harbin MRC
26.	Yang Ch'ang-chien 1966 worker in Shenyang Smelting Plant; 1968 Dep. Dir., Rev. Comm. in same plant	No previous position	1969, responsible person Liaoning PRC
27.	†Hao Chien-hsiu 1965–66 model worker, Tsingtao #8 Cotton Txtl. Plant, 1968 member factory RC	1964 NPC Deputy from Shantung; Member, presidium, NPC member 9th YCL Cent. Comm.	1968, member Shantung PRC

Table 7—continued

Name and Position In Industry	Govt. Position Before CR	Govt. Position After CR
28. *T'ang Wen-lan, 1966 worker Shanghai #17 State Cotton Textile Plant	No previous govt. position	1968, member Adm. Bur. of txtl. industry
29. Wang Hung-wen, 1966 worker and CP member, Shanghai #17 State Cotton Mill	No previous govt. position	1968, member CC of 9th CCP Congr.; memb. stdg. comm. Shanghai MRC
30. †Yang Fu-chen, 1966 worker & labor model, Shanghai #1 State Cotton Textile Plant	1964 NPC Deputy from Shanghai	1968, mem. CC of 9th CCP Congr.; mem. Shanghai MRC
31. *Chang Ming, 1959 mgr. Shanghai #2 State Cotton Mill	None	V. Chm. Kweichow PRC
32. Liu Hsi ch'ang, 1966 worker, Peking Kwanghua Wood Products Factory, 1968 member factory RC	None	1968, member SC, Peking MRC; mem. CC 9th CCP Cong.
33. *Keng Cheng, 1959 PC Secy., Harbin Electric Meter Factory	None	1968, member SC, Hopei, PRC
34. *Liu Hsin, 1958 Plant Mgr. Honan Hsinhsiang Metallurgy Plant	None	1968, member SC, Heilung-kiang PRC
35. Chih Ping-yüan, 1957 Dep. Plant Mgr., Chief Engr., Shenyang Mining Mach. Plant	Deputy to 3rd NPC in 1964 from Liaoning	Not Listed

36. Chang Pai-fa, 1963 model worker in Peking	1964 Deputy to 3rd NPC from Peking	Not Listed
37. Sun Mao-seng, 1960 model worker, Harbin #1 Machine Plant	1964 Deputy to 3rd NPC from Heilungkiang	Not Listed
38. *Wang Chih-yu, 1960 worker, Harbin Steam Turbine Plant	None	1968, member SC, Mongolia PRC
39. Meng Ch'ing-ch'un, 1959, model worker, Anshan Steel Mill	1964 Deputy to 3rd NPC from Liaoning	Not Listed
40. Sun Yueh-chi, 1957 Deputy Dir. in Kailan Coal Mine Head Office	1964 mem. of KMT RC of 4th Chinese People's Polit. Consultative Conf.	Not Listed
41. Ma Hsüeh-li, 1959 workshop foreman, Wuhan Heavy Machinery	1964, Deputy to 3rd NPC from Hupei	Not Listed
42. Wang Ch'ung-lun, 1966 worker, Anshan General Machine Repair Plant	1964 Deputy to NPC from Liaoning member, budget comm. NPC	Not Listed
43. *Hsü Chin-pao, 1962 Deputy Party Branch Secy. Wuhsi Petro Refinery, Kiangsu 1960, worker in same plant	None	1968, member SC, Heilungkiang PRC
44. *Liu Wen-yüan, 1960 director Liengyan Coal Mine, Kwangtung	1964 alternate memb. of CC of 9th YCL Congr.	1968, member Inner Mongolia PRC

Table 7—continued

Name and Position In Industry	Govt. Position Before CR	Govt. Position After CR
45. *Yang, Chia-chün, 1960 Dep. PC Secy., Yenchou Zinc Plant, Kwanghsi Auton. Region	None	1968, resp. person, Chekiang Prov. RC
46. *Kao Yang, 1959 Dir. East Anshan Iron Mine	1962–66 Minister of Chem. Ind. 1964 Dep. to NPC Liaoning Prov.	1968, Min. of Chemical Industry
47. *Wang Feng, 1966 mgr. Peking "2-7" Railroad Car Plant, Changhsintien; 1967 Chm. of Plant RC	1958 alt. mem. of CC of KMT RC in Chinese People's Pol. Consultative Conf.	Not Listed
48. Hsu Ch'uan-heng, 1963 Dir. of Lu An Mining Bur. Shihkochie Coal Mine, Shansi	1964 Deputy to 3rd NPC from Shansi	Not Listed
49. Yang Ch'un-lu, 1965 Workshop Dir., Yuchuaniou Limestone Pits, Shihchingshan	1964 Deputy to 3rd NPC from Hopei	Not Listed
50. *Yüan Chen, 1958–1964 Co. Mgr. and PC Secy., Anshan Iron & Steel Co.	1964 Sec. of Anshan Munic. Party Comm.	1970, V.Chm. Shansi PRC
51. Meng T'ai, 1960 Deputy Mgr. Anshan Iron Smelting Plant	1964 Dep. to 3rd NPC from Liaoning	Not Listed

52. Ch'en Mao-li, 1962 Dep. Plant Mgr. & Engr., Wuhan Iron & Steel Co. Smelting Mill	1964 Deputy to 3rd NPC from Hupei	Not Listed
*53. Wang Feng-en, 1962–67 Dep. Chief Engr., Shengyang Transformer Plant	1964 Deputy to 3rd NPC from Liaoning	1968, V. Chm. Liaoning PRC
54. Ch'en Hai-shan, 1958 Dir. Fuhsin Mining Bur. P'ing An Coal Mine	None	1969, member SC of Heilungkiang PRC
55. †Wang Hsiu-chen, 1966 worker, Shanghai #3 State Cotton Mill; 1968, Dir. Mill RC	None	1969, member Shanghai MRC, mem. CC, 9th CCP Cong.
56. Wang Chin-hsi, Dep. Dir. Oil Drilling Dept., Ta Ch'ing Oil Fields 1966; 1964, model worker; 1967 member Ta Ch'ing Rev. Com.	1964 Deputy to NPC from Heilungkiang	1969, resp. person, Heilungkiang PRC; mem. CC of CCP Congress
57. Li Feng-en, 1959–66 Dep. Plant Mgr. & Engr. Wuhan Iron & Steel Co. Iron Smelting Plant	1964 Deputy to 3rd NPC from Hupei	Not Listed

†—woman
*—not certain same person holds both positions
CC—Central Committee
CCP—Chinese Communist Party
CR—Cultural Revolution
PC—Party Committee
PRC—Provincial Revolutionary Committee
MRC—Municipal Revolutionary Committee
RC—Revolutionary Committee
SC—Standing Committee

Cultural Revolution (42 percent of the sample), but only 10.5 percent held positions before and after, and 31.5 percent held no previous government position and assumed power far removed from the influence of former colleagues.

The situation with workers is different. Of the nineteen in the sample, three held positions both before and after the Cultural Revolution. Of the nine who held positions before the Cultural Revolution, six were not on post-Cultural Revolution revolutionary committees. However, ten of the nineteen came to their positions after the Cultural Revolution, having held no previous government position, accounting for 52.6 percent of the sample. Comparatively speaking, while there was a large turnover in both worker and managerial personnel in the sample, there seemed to be a comparatively greater influx of new workers into positions of governmental authority. Before the Cultural Revolution, workers made up 23 percent of the total number of government representatives and managerial personnel about 77 percent.[55] After the Cultural Revolution, workers made up about 48 percent and managerial personnel about 52 percent.

Of the three workers who held posts both before and after the Cultural Revolution, all were women. Only one woman came to a position after the Cultural Revolution who had not held a position previously. Men showed a higher percentage of turnover. While 75 percent of the women in the sample remained in positions of governmental authority, only 10 percent of the men did. This limited survey reveals no instance where a woman from a factory who held a position in government before the Cultural Revolution did not hold one after the Cultural Revolution as well. It seems likely, therefore, that the women engaged in political activity above the grass roots level remained confined to previous activists and that new women workers did not appear as often as new men workers in positions of government.

Before the Cultural Revolution, factory personnel were represented in government by membership in the National People's Congress and through it on municipal and provincial People's Congresses. This was true of all workers and all but fourteen of the managerial personnel. Of these fourteen only eight can be considered to have occupied important positions, the remaining six being represented on the largely symbolic CPPCC (Chinese People's Political Consultative Conference) or one or another professional or functional association.

Sung Hsing-lu, the manager of the Hsifang Locomotive Plant in Tsingtao in 1957, was by 1959–1960 a secretary in the Tsingtao Municipal Party Committee. He was not listed on any revolutionary committee by 1960. Li Yi-ch'ing was the Party Committee secretary of the Wuhan Iron and Steel Company in 1960 and by 1965–1966 was a CCP secretary at the important regional bureau level for Central-South China. He was not listed on a revolutionary committee. In 1958 Feng

Kuan-chih was the manager of the Kwangchow Paper Mill and by 1965 had worked his way through the bureaucracy to be the deputy director of the Industry and Communications political department in neighboring. Kiangsi Province. He was not listed on a revolutionary committee. In 1959 the manager of the Harbin Electrical Appliance Plant, Hsing Tzu-tao, was by 1965 a secretary on the Shenyang Municipal Party Committee. He was not listed on a revolutionary committee. Chang Hung-shu, manager of the Harbin Rolling Stock Plant in 1958, was by 1960 deputy director of the Industrial Department of the Harbin Municipal Party Committee and a vice mayor of Harbin. After the Cultural Revolution, his name did not appear on a revolutionary committee. Han Ning-fu was in 1960 a deputy Party Committee secretary at Wuhan Iron and Steel, in 1964–1965 a vice governor of the Hupei Provincial People's Government, and in 1967 was listed as a responsible person on Hupei PRC. Kao Yang, in 1959 the Director of the East Anshan Iron Mine, became minister of the chemical industry in 1962 and remained at this post through the Cultural Revolution. Yuan Chen, from 1958 to 1964 the company manager and a Party Committee secretary in the Anshan Iron and Steel Company, was also a Party Committee secretary of the Anshan Municipal Party Committee. In 1970 he was vice chairman of the Shansi Provincial Revolutionary Committee.

Five high ranking party and government cadres with backgrounds in industrial management did not appear on revolutionary committees anywhere in the first few years after the Cultural Revolution. Two of the three who did were in areas other than where they had held power. Others from industrial enterprises who appeared on revolutionary committees had no previous government or party post on the municipal or provincial levels. Their new positions were generally in places other than where they had accumulated their industrial experience.

Two preliminary conclusions flow from this analysis. The Cultural Revolution saw a marked influx of workers and new cadres from factories into organs of local government. People who had represented factories before the Cultural Revolution on local or provincial peoples congresses (with the exception of women) were largely replaced on the revolutionary committees. Secondly, the revolutionary committees saw an increase in worker over management representatives on the organs of local and privincial government. People with backgrounds in management who had subsequently been promoted into the government, were for the most part removed from their powerful positions. Those who had not previously been the recipients of fairly rapid promotion generally appeared in rather striking numbers on revolutionary committees. They had apparently been transferred more frequently, appearing on revolutionary committees far from their original place of managerial responsibility.

These changes in personnel linkages between factories and the planning apparatus were important. Local authority now involved more people directly engaged in factory work. Direct and more personal contact between enterprises and government, as illustrated by these personnel changes, was the antithesis of the system envisioned by the "trust" method of macro-management. As contact became more personal, the need for detailed written communications, based on staff reports of functional departments within the factory, became less necessary as a means for providing information to planning authorities. Factory level managers would therefore have more time and more inclination to "face production and the basic levels." The Chinese thus set about institutionalizing direct linkages between production and government and this facilitated revolutionary reorganization within the enterprises.

Changing faces, therefore made little difference in the absence of this kind of fundamental change. Different people could occupy the old positions, sit in the same offices, give the same orders, demand the same routine of management.[56] Thus, the establishment of revolutionary committees, the dismissal of former high ranking officials, and the assimilation of large numbers of new cadres was only the beginning. An editorial in Shanghai's *Chieh-fang Jih-pao* connected the transformation of factory management to a much broader revolution in education and economic development, to what it called the need to establish the leading position of the working class in society. It stressed that this be done carefully and logically under the assumption that in autumn of 1968 there was still a long way to go.[57]

General Patterns of Organizational Change: Revolutionary Committees

While the complex question of membership on revolutionary committees was being decided throughout 1968, the direction of change in many factories had already been established. Middle-level managerial control organs were merged or abolished, staff cadres being put to work in production units, and emphasis was placed on direct communication between the levels of factory organization by means of cadre participation in labor. These trends continued during the organizational transformation of industrial management, called "better troops and simpler administration," that followed struggle and criticism.

The old system of factory director responsibility under the leadership of the Party Committee, which had been in effect even during the experiment of the Great Leap Forward, was now abolished. In its place the revolutionary committee assumed leadership while the party recuperated from the shocks received during the height of the struggle and power seizures. Though the party was soon to be rebuilt, for the time being it took no formal part in the new management systems, which after all were not really all new. There was cadre participation in labor and greater decentralization of control functions to the production units; functional departments decreased but were not eliminated. In other ways, however, the collective management work of the revolutionary committees was new.

The members divided work between personal investigation of conditions in production and planning and coordination. Either the committee would be permanently divided with periodic job rotation, or everyone would be given a permanent assignment. Everyone participated in labor. The committee was also responsible for morale and discipline. Participation in labor was to create feelings of solidarity and become an integral part of a politicized incentive program emphasizing participation in production and collective material advancement. Bonuses and piece wages were eliminated.[58] Following are some illustrations of how the new system worked in practice.

1. The Peking General Knitwear Mill[59] was a clothing plant built in 1952 employing about 3,400 workers. It was a national model in transforming management. The revolutionary committee had nine members and a staff of twenty administrative cadres; before the Cultural Revolution there had been about 700 administrative cadres. Sixty percent of the workers were women.

There was a twenty-person factory-level management group, ten concerned with production and ten with politics; and a nine-person revolutionary committee divided into three sections: production, politics, administrative coordination. At any one time, five of the nine were stationed in the office for administrative coordination. The others were two-person teams, one in the production section, the other in the political section. The political staff was responsible for incentives and motivation. The production staff helped workers to solve immediate production problems by improving their skills and ability. To this end they studied Mao's theory of knowledge and analysis, as described in "On Practice" and "On Contradiction," and his concept of struggle and service as described in "Serve the People," "In Memory of Norman Bethune," and "The Foolish Old Man." The four cadres in the political and production staff were participating in labor full time.

The revolutionary committee members rotated jobs so that no one was engaged only in office work, gaining most information through first-hand observation and participation rather than through reports, graphs, charts, and lists. Staff members who were not on the revolutionary committee attended periodic management meetings.

2. In the Ningyang Chemical Fertilizer Plant[60] in Kwangtung Province, the revolutionary committee set up three main sections on the

factory level, a political work team, a grasp revolution and promote production team, and a rear services team. Staff was reduced from seventy-three to sixteen, the excess being sent to the work shops.

The committee managed the plant by direct communication with production through participation and on-the-spot observation. The five members who headed new offices would rotate visits to the production floor where they made decisions collectively but quickly. Control over production by the middle levels was thereby short circuited, engendering some opposition.

3. In the Shanghai China Clock Factory[61] the revolutionary committee had eleven members, seven in work shops who attended factory level management meetings only on important questions. The other four worked regularly in the work shops. Staff was reduced by 34 percent due to diminished need for information previously supplied by the middle levels.

There were indications that complex enterprises were having difficulty developing systems that allowed revolutionary committee cadres to participate in labor, and be the direct links essential for shrinking bureaucracy.[62]

Revolutionary committees in all factories had the same responsibilities.

1. Technical management and decision-making.
2. Financial control, cost analysis, economic efficiency.
3. Incentives that guaranteed discipline and motivation which did not require a large control apparatus.
4. Macro-management, including the economic relationship of the enterprise to other enterprises and to higher planning authority. Crucial in this respect was the system of economic integration within which the enterprise functioned.

Technical Management and Control

Triple combination teams were now used in operations, designing, and research at every level. The idea was to eliminate the vertical chain of command, requiring tight controls on innovations, and the voluminous rules concerning repair and maintenance schedules. Administrative technical personnel became active in production units. What was not clear was what proportion of time cadres would spend in production or what the schedule and composition of triple combination teams would be. Some examples of triple combination teams in practice indicate the variety possible.

1. In the Peking Peichiao Timber Mill the trial production of new items, maintenance work, and new technology were taken out of the hierarchical chain of command and put under the authority of triple combination teams. Three-in-one technical innovation groups were set up in every workshop, but it is unclear how long and for what purposes the group lasted, or whether membership was permanent.[63]

2. In the Tientsin Textile Machinery Plant control procedures concerning technical innovations had contained as many as fifty-six separate steps, while most of the designs and innovations came from the drawing boards of engineers and technical departments. As a result of the triple combination teams, proposals made by workers for innovations and improvements went almost directly to the revolutionary committee at the factory level. Workers on the group were experienced and skilled and exercised "general direction and overall production planning." The technical personnel spent less time in their offices and more time in production where they gained experience and listened to the opinions of the workers. Their designs became more relevant and their solutions to problems more practical.[64]

This substitution of triple combination teams for a strict and hierarchical division of labor in designing and innovation was repeated in other cases.[65]

Financial Controls, Economic Efficiency, and Cost Analysis

The previously controversial meaning of efficiency was now interpreted as encompassing social benefit, local developmental needs, and educational side-effects. Since "the notion of 'efficiency' or 'rationality' . . . has no meaning until the underlying basis of social values is comprehended,"[66] what remained was the problem of lowering costs once this concept of efficiency had been established.

In this regard, the Cultural Revolution brought no major change. A report on a "new" system of financial management at the Dairen Dyestuffs Factory, published in *JMJP* in late 1970, showed some of the trends that had developed during the Cultural Revolution.[67]

The new system of accounting had already been tried with some success before the Cultural Revolution; there was a system of three-level quota management and two-level cost accounting; quota and norm determination, the raw data for planned targets, stressed direct participation by workers at the level of the work team; cost accounting, which translated consumption and output into comprehensive prices, stressed the role of professional accounting personnel or statisticians at organizational levels where composite figures could be calculated.

The big difference with pre-Cultural Revolution accounting was the degree and kind of supervision and increased emphasis on worker participation. Supervisors were triple combination teams of workers, administrative cadres, and accountants. These teams led discussions of quota and norms at the basic levels and were a communications link between them and the work shop and factory levels, which then sent data to higher levels where targets were calculated. In this way, workers influenced the future pace of their work. Face-to-face supervision and communication replaced impersonal methods. The work teams kept records of their own material consumption and output, with strict accounting of raw materials and semifinished products.

Control was increasingly exercised by triple combination groups, or by individuals in different production units in direct contact with production workers. Coordination was done at the factory revolutionary committee level. Simultaneously, more responsibility for keeping records was given workers, including data that could affect quality control and utilization norms.

The Crane Workshop of the Shenyang Locomotive and Rolling Stock Plant reported quality inspection by workers in conjunction with those specially in charge. The previous accounting system whereby "six persons in charge . . . sat in the office (and) press(ed) for statements busy at the abacus and the books" was replaced by one bookkeeper at the work-shop level, one bookkeeper-worker in each work team, and a great deal of individual worker responsibility.[68]

Incentives and the Cultural Revolution: Material Incentives

The elimination of piece wages and bonuses began in the earliest stages of the Cultural Revolution, even going back to the later stages of the socialist education campaign. In 1966 individual piece-rate wages had already been eliminated in some places and little use was made of collective piece-rate wages. Bonus payments to workers had been eliminated in 20 percent of one sample of thirty-eight enterprises.[69] By 1971, however, bonus payments had been eliminated at most plants.[70] The decision to end piece wages and bonuses was made at the factory level.[71] The wage-grade system was maintained, again becoming controversial, but wage differentials were not large enough to become a major factor in motivating people to work on a daily basis.[72]

An eight-grade wage system remained unchanged, with grades

fixed according to skill, length of experience, and political attitudes.[73] Seniority was increasingly a factor in determining a worker's grade after 1968[74] because older workers and basic level cadres had previously earned more with bonus payments and had to be pacified for the rapid advance of younger people during the Cultural Revolution.

Although engineers, technicians, and administrators continued to be paid on a different grade scale than workers, the wage differentials did not change greatly. The figures in Table 8 represent a sample of wage rates and, where available, wage and income differentials (the two being synonymous, except for former capitalists whose income derived from sources other than wages) in some industrial enterprises before and after the Cultural Revolution (1966 and 1969 respectively).[75] Figures are in Yüan per month.

Table 8 Pre- and Post-Cultural Revolution Wage Distribution in Chinese Factories

Date	Name of Factory	Highest Wage	Lowest Wage	Average Wage
1966	1. Shanghai #19 Cotton Textile	200	39	78
1966	2. Shanghai #9 Sung Sing Cotton Textile	100	50	78
1966	3. Shanghai Wei-Ming Battery	120	37	78
1966	4. Shanghai #3 Mach. Tool	126	42	75
1966	5. Shanghai Forging & Pressing Machine Tool #3	115	38	75
1966	6. Shanghai Truck	140	41	72
1966	7. Shanghai #3 Steel	120	50	71
1966	8. Wuhan Iron & Steel Co.	180	38	70
1966	9. Shanghai Heavy Machine Tool	210	42	70
1966	10. Tientsin Jen-Yi Woolen	122	30	67
1966	11. Canton Machine Tool	140	—	67
1966	12. Wuhan Heavy Mach'ry.	150	37	66
1966	13. Shanghai Pharmaceutical #3	174	40	66
1966	14. Canton Chem. Fertilizer	200	46	65
1966	15. Peking Clothing	110	36	65
1966	16. Tientsin Shoe	84	37	62.5
1966	17. Nanking National Chem. Fertilizer	170	34	62
1966	18. Peking Coke and Chemical	150	34	61
1966	19. Hanchow Machine Tool	108	33	61
1966	20. Canton Lan Yang Elect. Appliance	135	40	60

Table 8—continued

Date	Name of Factory	Highest Wage	Lowest Wage	Average Wage
1966	21. Nanking Machinery	120	—	60
1966	22. Peking Pharmaceutical	138	30	60
1966	23. Peking #3 Cotton Txtl.	150	—	60
1966	24. Peking Wool Fabric	130	36	60
1966	25. Peking Wool Carpet	135	38	60
1966	26. Wuhan Paper	170	35	54
1966	27. Wuhan Diesel Engine	110	37	52.5
1966	28. Wuhan Diesel Engine	190	38	52
1966	29. Peking Steel Wire	98	34	52
1966	30. Peking #1 Machine Tool	180	34	52
1966	31. Wuhsi #2 Silk Reeling	100	41	52
1966	32. Hangchow Silk Reeling Dyeing & Weaving	110	—	50
1966	33. Soochow Cement	100	—	50
1966	34. Tientsin Watch	150	34	50
1966	35. Loyang Tractor	205	30	49
1966	36. Wuhsi Red Flag Mach'ry.	87	39	48
1966	37. Hangchow Clothing	69	30	48
1966	38. Tientsin North Lake Instrument	96	32	47.5
1967	39. Wuhan Heavy Machine Tool	—	32.5	50
1967	40. Kunming Heavy Machine Tool	205 (?)	30	52
1967	41. Shenyang Heavy Machine Tool	—	37.5	74
1968	42. Shanghai 555 Clock Factory	100	40	70
1968	43. Wuhan Steel Rolling Mill	165	33	—
1968	44. Peking #2 Textile	105	—	60
1968	45. Peking Steel & Alloy Wire Works	Same as before Cultural Revolution		
1968	46. Double Rhomb Clock & Meters	Same as before Cultural Revolution		
1971	47. Hsinhua Printing Plant	170	36.5	55
1971	48. Shanghai Machine Tool	—	—	65
1971	49. Nanking Film Projector	—	—	45
1971	50. Northwest China #1 Textile	—	—	70
1971	51. Soochow Embroidery	—	—	40+
1971	52. February Seventh (2-7) Rolling Stock	—		60+
1971	53. Shenyang Machine Tool	140 (?)	—	—
1971	54. Anshan Mine (?)	108 (?)	—	—
1971	55. Chengchow Textile (?)	188 (?)	—	—

In the immediate aftermath of the Cultural Revolution there was, however, some indication that an informal trend developed to lower the salaries of the highest paid personnel.[76] This was reported in the Shanghai Docks Area #3, Hsinhua Printing House, Changsha, the Double Rhomb Clock and Meters Factory, and the Wuhan Steel Rolling Mill among other places.[77] In general, however, the impression is that the differential of wages and salaries based on rank was not great. The gap between the highest paid skilled worker and the lowest paid unskilled worker was about three to one.[78] When the salaries of administrative and technical personnel are considered, the differential could rise to 4 or 4.5 to 1. Usually, the discrepancy was not this wide.[79]

High salary was not always a result of high position. In one survey, workers were the highest paid in eight out of thirty-eight enterprises, and in two other plants they shared this position with technical or administrative cadres.[80] In the Peking #2 Textile Plant a skilled worker received a higher wage than the plant manager.[81]

Wage differentials seemed to change very slowly toward greater equality. Even with continued wage inequality, however, the elimination of bonuses and piece wages meant that daily work had no immediate impact on income.[82] Although the elimination of bonuses and piece wage incentives triggered strong debates about reforming the wage-grade system,[83] there were other strong incentives operative, since production in industry continued to rise impressively.

Non-Material Incentives

The Cultural Revolution put emphasis on cooperation and collective esprit as motivating factors for both workers and managers. Large-scale, detailed discussions were held to revise rules and regulations to maintain discipline and order without a control apparatus to supervise every detail.[84] Rules and regulations formulated with worker participation were strictly and eagerly obeyed because they were realistic.

In addition, attempts were made to change the division of labor to improve efficiency and to make work more interesting.[85] The triple combination teams especially in giving workers a greater impact on technical innovation fostered a feeling of greater control over their daily lives rather than being, as workers described themselves, "living machines,"[86] or "talking machines."[87] The feeling of esprit caused all to work hard to solve problems, often in competition with other teams.[88] Workers also participated, though to a lesser degree, in quality inspection,[89] quarterly planning,[90] wage-grading,[91] and accounting. The benefit of participation lay in generating confidence and willingness to improve as well as in making more realistic plans. A positive self-image was an essential part of the learning to improve later performance.[92]

Cadre participation in labor was a major incentive during and immediately after the Cultural Revolution. This increased productivity by eliminating unnecessary staff workers[93] and it had the important psychological effects of changing workers perceptions that people in offices did little work that mattered, though they seemed busy.[94]

Cadre participation in labor, therefore, made workers feel that everyone was pulling a fair share and that people in positions of authority did not have unfair privilege. The need to combat the cynicism that could negatively affect morale probably accounts for the de-emphasis on special clothes or titles for managers,[95] or the use of factory automobiles for any but urgent business.[96] The need to see just patterns of distribution led to worker opposition to arrogance or official airs.[97] Though these themes were not new, the attack on this kind of behavior must have provided a positive incentive to potentially cynical workers.

For cadres, participation in labor meant "a thoroughgoing revolution in their thinking, in work, in their style of work, and their everyday life.[98] A major incentive for cadres—aside from the satisfaction that came from accomplishing challenging tasks—was the feeling of solidarity.[99] As one cadre in the Peking General Knitwear Mill said, "Now the masses understand me and they see my heart. Our cross consciousness is greatly enhanced."[100]

Macro-Management and Economic Integration

All of these trends in factory management were taking place as a concept of economic integration, and planning to support them was finally, after years of argument and debate, emerging in greater clarity. Two characteristics of the evolving system stand out: decentralization and despecialization.

Decentralization was not new, but what does seem to be new, although this was foreseen in some of the rural industrialization and urban commune programs of the Great Leap Forward, was the way in which decentralization was combined with various administrative and governmental levels of economic despecialization. This created a multi-layered system of relatively more independent localities and enterprises than those which would be linked together in a vertically integrated economy.

Despecialization was to make use of local production links, both industrial and agricultural. It was characterized by the building of numerous small-scale enterprises in rural areas with links to larger nearby plants. These small plants processed agricultural produce or served local consumer needs.[101] Sometimes this brought agriculture into what previously was a purely industrial or urban environment.[102]

A second aspect was the idea of multiple production and independent machinery design and manufacture to make the enterprise or locality relatively self-reliant. Factories and localities were, within limits, to build their own equipment or get it from nearby enterprises if possible. The Shanghai Diesel Pumps and Motors Plant, the Shanghai Heavy Machine Building Plant, the Shanghai Waitung Truck Factory, the 555 Clock Factory in Shanghai, the Peking Double Rhomb Clock Factory, the Wuhan Steel Rolling Mill, the Wuhan Tractor Factory,[103] the Fuchun River Smelting Plant,[104] all are examples. Other plants were to utilize waste materials or industrial pollutants for manfacture or to supply the locality with needed material.

A third aspect of despecialization was reduction of complex interregional, intercity, and interenterprise planning and coordination. Standards were usually national or provincial[105] and widely needed consumer goods were distributed nationally, but manufacturing operations were locally coordinated by enterprises,[106] or by municipal, county, or commune-level revolutionary committees.[107] Other decentralized, despecialized units included submunicipal-level economic systems[108] or commercial trusts subordinate to the planning authorities and not using profit as an investment criteria or to motivate managerial staff.[109] The economy thus depends both on large key enterprises and central planning and on horizontally linked *local* specialization and coordination. Vertical integration in planning and nationally based specialization is limited.

After the Cultural Revolution enterprises became places to train people as well as produce goods. Education and its relationship to production were an important result of the Cultural Revolution. A system of factory-administered schools was revived and expanded, and between industrial enterprises and educational institutions new and direct relationships were established.

The chief function of these schools was political: to give workers the knowledge and the confidence that they needed to wield power in technical and administrative decisions. For example, the Shanghai Machine Tools Plant ran a "July 21" University with a two and one-half year course. There were also part-time schools at lower levels and three-in-one combination designing groups and experimental departments.[110] Other factories, including the Chinghuo Dyemaking Plant in Shanghai,[111] the Peking Instrument Factory,[112] and the Peking #1 General Machinery Plant,[113] followed this trend, which began in 1968 with a campaign to change the educational system in order to make the enterprise a central part of it.[114]

The Party's Role in Post-Cultural Revolution Management

The old party organization had been the chief target of much of the Cultural Revolution, even though a number of party cadres were active in the early power struggles and later became members of the revolutionary committees. Before the Cultural Revolution the party and management theoretically formed a dual structure, the party being responsible for politics and for broad policy decisions and the management responsible for operations. This distinction broke down in actual practice, and what happened was that the party and management, for all practical purposes, become indistinguishable. The Cultural Revolution finally acknowledged this reality, and both the management system and the party's relationship to it were changed. Politics and production were to be inseparable. Politics was to be applied to production, shaping human relationships, defining purposes, and providing incentives for hard work.[115]

Politics was the relative position of production line workers and technical and administrative staff, and any managerial system which subordinated workers was bad politics even if the Party Committee sanctioned it. Politics meant breaking down the mental-manual labor gap and eliminating classes and privilege. This was the direction management had to take. The triple combination, cadre participation in labor, and worker participation in management were steps in this direction, as was despecialization and the transformation of the educational system. The Party was to lead this modernization process rather than one which put workers in a hopelessly subordinate position. Before the Cultural Revolution there was no clear understanding or coherent presentation of the many relationships involved, many of which reached far beyond the confines of individual factories and even the industrial system.

The party was quickly redesignated as the leading organ in China's modernization. The Party Committee was to be the nucleus of the revolutionary committee.[116] However, the party now was connected to all aspects of modern industry, not a separate bureaucracy that made politics either dysfunctional or irrelevant. The new system was called single line leadership (yi-yüan-hua ti ling-tao).. The transformation of social and economic relationships and incentives that had begun on a large scale with the Great Leap Forward continued to develop tortuously, though with the Cultural Revolution more rationally and comprehensively. By 1970, the transformation was not yet complete.

9/ "One Divides into Two": China's Industry Since the Cultural Revolution

AS DID THE GREAT LEAP FORWARD, the Cultural Revolution left in its wake a China that would never be the same. Once again, a truly enormous social upheaval had disrupted the patterned routines of daily life. New experiences had shaken old values and generated new ones— things could never return to the status quo ante. In that turbulent three-year period, officially begun in August 1966 and ended formally with a declaration of victory and a call for unity at the Ninth Party Congress in April 1969, the Chinese had developed a coherent theory to reconcile the political with the technical and economic aspects of revolutionary socialism. By the beginning of 1970, although the dust of revolutionary battle had not completely settled, the main outlines could be clearly discerned.

Basic to this theory was a political insight concerning the relationship between power and morality. Within the industrial enterprise context, morality was applied to incentives.

The word for incentive is *tzu-chi*, which has the connotation of inciting or provoking into action; behind the definition is a morality or state of mind embodying one's inclinations even in the absence of external stimuli which is only a trigger for doing what one is anyway predisposed to do.

This predisposition, according to Marxists, did not come from basic human nature. The argument was that morality, the basis of incentive, must be a product of social relations and experiences, that these must underlie the incentive structure even as it must support the network of social relations and experience that shapes morality. Two important principles of organization result from this dialectical view.

First of all, incentives based upon the principle of self-aggrandizement were in logical contradiction to a participatory politics. People motivated by self-aggrandizement could not govern themselves for long. That industrial organization was itself political because of the unequal power distributed to the levels of administration put the question of incentive at the center of the problem of socialist management. Since cadre participation in labor was the only alternative to bureaucratic communications with a large control apparatus, cadres had to be willing to do hard, dirty work. Those motivated by self-aggrandizement or privilege could not be expected to labor.

As incentive could not rest secure on simple morality but had to be constantly reinforced by tangibles, participation in management was enhanced when workers saw cadres participate in labor. The idea of everyone doing a fair share, working hard, with none unduly privileged was a potent antidote to selfishness. Without tangible evidence of equality within the plant, all rhetoric about it was meaningless, possibly counterproductive. By accepting responsibilty for others' well-being, everyone had to perceive that same concern for equality in the actions of others, or the result was injury to self-esteem. In the realization that nobody liked to look the fool, the new egalitarian-based theory tapped a major source of ego incentive. It is in this sense that material incentives were attacked as reflecting an inner value system which prized personal possessions and power. The question of incentives could not be seen as a technical or economic matter, but was the subject of extensive political debate about the purpose of life and work.

Morality in industrial organization and justice inside and outside the factory were not the only points. Power was dependent on knowledge. Along with material distribution and morality, there must also be a broad dissemination of technical skill among workers. The idea that differences in human capability and skill should be reinforced and perpetuated by the educational system, and that technical knowledge was communicable only to a relatively small elite was rejected as being fundamentally incompatible with socialist industrial organization. The Cultural Revolution therefore linked factories with technical education, whether by participation on projects in triple combination teams or by formal classes in schools run by or linked to factories.

Organizationally, the management system was two-level, with a great deal of control over daily operations given to people actually engaged in production. Communications were face to face and participation in labor by leading cadres was essential to the incentive system as well as to communications. The middle level of control and coordination was reduced consistent with the actual knowledge of workers as well as the technical necessities of production. Production people had opportunity to acquire skills or improve them so they could make technical decisions and keep accurate records. They had authority to supervise quantity, quality, and intensity of their daily labor, provided they did not enrich themselves. The revolutionary committee, the highest level of authority, with a core of Communist Party members, rotated labor assignments with office work. The CP members were responsible for running the plant and its educational functions, for connecting the enterprise to the larger economy, and for insuring that worker and cadre participation continued. The relationship of this kind of factory management to a coherent theory of economic coordination and planning was a crucial development in the Chinese understanding of the problems of socialism. There was three aspects to this macro-economic theory. One, the industrial enterprise was to be redefined. It was *not* to be simply an economic unit for production and profit. Efficiency was a matter of political principle and morality, but management was expected to pursue other goals: cooperation with other enterprises even if this caused losses; satisfying local needs and providing services such as day care, entertainment, sports, medical care, and education. The industrial enterprise was to be central to society, with labor as the moral basis of the socialization process and the core of education. It was to train people in technique and educate them in terms of values.

Two, a balance was struck between centralized planning and decentralized operations. Centralized planning was to coordinate loosely and allocate strictly. The central plan set specific targets for quantity, quality, variety, and profit. Within the plan, local enterprises would have the flexibility to respond to local needs or varying circumstances in terms of operations planning and supply problems, and they could arrange economic and other relationships with other factories or units providing the planned targets were fulfilled. The central plan was limited to major enterprises and products, while the local political body had the authority for meeting local needs not covered by central plans. In general local planning authorities, being closer to local production units, would serve as the basis for what was conceived of as a locally, or horizontally, integrated system, one that depended on in-person visits and personal observation more than it did on detailed statistical information which originated in factory control departments and which, therefore, enhanced their importance in the daily work of the plant.

Three, despecialization and self-reliance were to mobilize marginal sources of raw materials and develop poor and technologically underdeveloped areas. Despecialization was a way of calculating the costs of development to encompass more than profit. It therefore opened up locations and opportunities for industry that would not have been considered otherwise. The purpose of despecialization was to create relatively self-reliant economic localities and regions with strong ties and responsibilities to the central authority. It was to foster creativity by the demands it put on people to innovate in order to improve their own lives, and this was seen as positive education for future projects. Within regions and localities, however, specialization was encouraged where appropriate.

Despecialization, by emphasizing the local development of many types of industry, undermined further the foundations of bureaucracy. By cutting down on the needs for long-distance communication and distribution of resources over a broad geographical area, despecialization was to diminish the functional necessity of an administrative bureaucracy. Moreover, by limiting profit to the measurement of efficiency *within* enterprises and eliminating it as a basis for reward in the form of promotion, bonuses, or new investment, despecialization was to defer selfish behavior among administrative planners. Not only planners but enterprise managers were able to calculate costs altruistically and to spend less time on paperwork. Both were encouraged and better able to spend more time investigating local conditions and periodically to participate in production rather than responding only to the plans of far-away administrative bureaucrats. By shaping the values and behavior of local leaders, despecialization was to engender models at all levels of society who, in their individual lives, embodied at least partially those values which could be emulated collectively. It thus influenced the over-all class structure and the politics of the whole society.

These general and mutually supporting theoretical principles of industrial enterprise management on the one hand and economic planning and coordination on the other that had been articulated and illustrated by the Cultural Revolution provided the context within which events unfolded in Chinese industry after the Cultural Revolution. Though by 1970 revolutionary theory was clear, the scope of its practical applicability was still at issue. During the Cultural Revolution the implementation of the theory in practice and the development of practice into a more sophisticated understanding of theory had gone on unevenly all over the country. Heavy machine tool factories and knitting plants were models; so, too, were huge steel complexes, auto and railroad car plants, and oil fields. Factories in Shanghai, Peking, and Ta-ch'ing were models. But not until the end of 1972 did some plants even begin organizational reform and redistribution of internal power.[1] The years following the Cultural Revolution were filled with continuing experiment, and many contradictions remained operative.

Technical decision-making and financial control were two areas of concern. During the Cultural Revolution there had been an upsurge of worker-initiated innovation and grass roots creativity as cadres working in the technical and cost accounting control apparatus were attacked for monopolizing skill, knowledge, and technique to oppress the workers and constrain their enthusiasm. Triple combination teams were widely praised for pathbreaking innovations, creativity, and efficiency,[2] and there can be no doubt that workers had a central role either on triple combination teams, on factory-level revolutionary committees,[3] or in designing offices.[4] In that first year following the Cultural Revolution many rules and regulations were pushed aside as incompatible with the new experiments and distribution of power. This included technical control procedures and labor and material cost accounting for innovations and experiments. This caused concern over technical controls, cost accounting, and rules and regulations generally, not easy issues to deal with. Some, opposed to the Cultural Revolution, wanted production to falter and so they tried to undermine discipline, coordination and efficiency by joining or creating ultraleft or anarchistic groups.[5] Many workers, especially the young, were not at all happy with the discipline of factory work nor did they appreciate that technical innovation was serious, often difficult business, capable of causing enormous waste if not done carefully with a good technical understanding. So, early in 1970, older workers with highly developed skills, whose attitudes toward work and authority were not as rebellious and romantic as the younger workers, were given an increased role in factory life, usually on triple combination teams. Emphasizing the importance of frugality, discipline, and the hard work of mastering skills, the role of the veteran workers was increasingly stressed and continued to be at least until the spring of 1973.[6]

Aside from the political difficulties resulting from the sometimes euphoric attitudes of younger workers or from the questionable motives of alleged ultraleft or anarchistic groups, there were intellectual problems. There were still those who confused efficiency and cost accounting with profit in a market economy. In 1970 a far-ranging discussion of the idea of profit in a socialist society concluded with the idea that profits were an important measure of efficiency and cost accounting and could not be ignored; but they had only a limited role to play in a socialist society. They could not determine the purpose of an enterprise's activity, the rate or direction of technical innovation, depreciation, obsolescence, or intra-enterprise relationships, nor could they be an excuse to hoard supplies or withhold cooperation.[7]

Rules and regulations were essential in running enterprises. Although it was necessary to destroy many old systems, it was vital that new systems be created immediately. All rules and systems had political implications because they distributed power and responsibilty to specific groups and individuals. The problem was to create rules and regulations on the principles of two participations and triple combination of the Anshan Constitution[8] without making workers the permanent inferiors of a techno-bureaucratic elite.

This was to become an issue of vital and far reaching importance in the post Cultural Revolution period. The whole question of the proper role of technicians and engineers who possessed what was still undeniably scarce and vital knowledge in the developing economy was still to be solved. Not only did some factories have sophisticated methods and machinery and others quite simple ones, but the relative skills of the labor force varied. Even within factories there were highly-skilled and unskilled workers. Workers on triple combination teams could easily see themselves as "part of the elite now"[9] as one essay put it. The educational transformations of the Cultural Revolution designed to destroy a major source of energy for the reproduction of a class of technocratic-bureaucratic rulers[10] were still only in their formative stages.

Thus, with a good deal of justification the Chinese claimed in March 1970 that:

> The formulation of the revolutionary principle of "two participations, one transformation, and triple combination" is a great pioneering act in the history of the international proletarian movement. In theory it enriches the Marxist-Leninist doctrine of continuing the revolution under the dictatorship of the proletariat, and in practice it solves the question of "the working class must exercise leadership over everything."[11]

Yet, they would shortly have to admit that these questions had, in practice, been solved only in a preliminary way.

Workers stated the problem openly. When, they asked, does the creation of rules and regulations turn into the "supervision, control, and suppression" of Liu Shao-ch'i and the management systems of "experts running factories" that had been criticized so soundly during the Cultural Revolution? What in fact was the difference, in practice, between new rules and regulations that conformed to the two participations, one reform and triple combination, and those that violated these principles?[12]

As the Cultural Revolution became recent, but meaningful, history, and as the pace and momentum of production in industry quickened, the contradiction between the factory's role as a school for class struggle and technical education on the one hand, and its role as producer of material wealth on the other, intensified. Pressures for higher output and new productivity quotas again raised the bothersome issues of control and incentives.[13] There were additional pressures to assimilate technical and engineering personnel who had been criticized and demoted during the Cultural Revolution into technical decision-making jobs.

Both of these issues were, by 1971, crucial matters which touched on the foundations of the two participations and the changes that had been legitimized by the Cultural Revolution. Could workers take part in determining quotas and norms, both of which directly affected the daily pace and intensity of work as well as the eventual output of the whole factory and its role in national plans? What would worker participation mean if this proved to be impossible? What were to be the rules and regulations governing safety, repair, and maintenance, and who was to be responsible for carrying out these tasks? What were to be the rules and procedures governing technical innovations and controls, and how would these influence the frequency and importance of cadre participation in labor? What, in fact, did it mean to urge, as it was urged in the press during the spring and summer of 1971, that old technicians and intellectuals be brought fully into plant activity;[14] or that they be given strategic leadership positions as part of "strengthening the production command system" as was urged in March 1972, on the anniversary of the famous Anshan Constitution?[15] How could the technical training of workers proceed, as was absolutely essential to make the two participations work, if the pressures of production made cadres hesitate to let their most productive and skilled workers off to go to school, or if workers lacked adequate preparation, or if the factory lacked proper facilities to provide opportunities for all those willing and able to learn? What was the meaning of the two participations if workers who were trained wanted no part of physical labor, or if those who wanted to take part in physical labor saw no use in the study of technology?[16]

By the spring of 1972 there was far greater stress in the national media on the importance of control, discipline, and leadership and much less emphasis on worker innovation and spontaneity. It is also clear that the technical personnel who had been so thoroughly criticized during the Cultural Revolution were once again wielding significant authority in many factories,[17] and that great importance was placed on statistics,[18] on efficient and productive quotas and norms requiring intensive labor,[19] and on technical controls in general.[20]

Yet, it would be misleading to read these obvious trends as clear-cut contradictions of the Cultural Revolution. For one thing, tighter controls by expert cadres working on their own or through technical departments, rather than on triple combination teams, seemed to occur where there had been insufficient time to provide adequate technical-scientific education for workers, mostly in the chemical or electronics industries, where educational requirements wre high, or in rural areas or in newer factories, where skill and educational levels were low,[21] though other industries were obviously affected. Furthermore, not all advanced-technology industries were affected, especially where workers had a high level of education.[22]

In addition, there was a tendency for the technical personnel to play larger roles on triple combination teams and to become important leaders in those groups, but there is little or no evidence to show that these groups were replaced or supplanted. Cadre participation in labor, including technical personnel participation on triple combination teams continued unabated for the most part.[23] This was the distinction between rational and oppressive systems.[24]

Perhaps most importantly, all of the control systems that were operationalized after the Cultural Revolution were made up after a comprehensive consultation with workers. Included in this were productivity, labor, and input-output norms and quotas,[25] but regulations concerning repair and maintenance schedules, shift changeovers, responsibilities of production posts, the division of labor, and technical innovation were also drawn up in this way.[26]

In general, during the first two years after the Cultural Revolution new contradictions only superficially resembling those of the 1961–1963 period of consolidation appeared. By the autumn of 1972, however, there was no small debate about how far and in what directions one could go in correcting what were noticeable problems of discipline,[27] efficiency, and productivity without at the same time re-imposing the old control patterns and political domination of a bureaucratic technocratic elite.[28] But the situation was clearer than following the GLF.[29] Workers promoted to positions of technical or administrative responsibility were suspicious of bourgeois intellectuals,[30] and rank-and-file workers insisted that they be consulted regarding rules and regulations concerning operations planning, target formulation, quality control, and the descriptions of job responsibilities.[31] The triple combination groups remained the organizational form through which technical personnel were reassimilated into the managerial system,[32] and worker participation in accounting, quality control, and quota determination remained.[33] All of these trends grew stronger with the gathering momentum of the campaign to criticize Lin Piao and Confucius (P'i-Lin P'i Kung).

The old question of incentives was a continuing contradiction. The Cultural Revolution had condemned the principle of individualistic material incentive though it had made it clear that unequal distribution, based on a wage grading system as well as collective improvement in material living standards would be maintained.[34] In the post-Cultural Revolution period, this policy did not change, though it was part of a controversy begun in 1970–1971 and continuing through 1975.[35] In a 1972 wage reform the lowest grade workers were moved to grade 2 salary levels, but there was no significant change in the differentials between grades. There was, however, a lowering of pay of the highest paid technical and administrative staff in some plants.[36]

The controversy was not so much over long-term distribution of wages as over the relationship between material incentives and worker participation in management. Immediately after the Cultural Revolution, there was no doubt that incentives were to be political, not material. In concrete terms this meant that the calculation of quotas and norms was to be completely severed from bonuses and piece wages. Workers were to take part in planning and calculating their own norms and quotas, and because this was to be based on a clear understanding of how one's individual work contributed to collective goals, this participation itself was to be a prime mover for hard work and efficiency. Moreover, these norms, drawn up in open discussion and based on actual experience and the intangible but extremely important will to work hard, carefully, and creatively, were to serve as targets for emulation, competition, and cooperation. By severing norm and quota management from an individual material incentive system, and by putting the calculation of such norms, including their readjustment up or down, under the control of workers, there would be no economic reason for more proficient workers not to help other workers. There were no penalties for not reaching norms nor bonuses for surpassing them, though respect and honors went to those groups or individuals who did surpass the norms and who taught others.[37]

There were two essential, though tacit, principles required if this participation was to function as part of the incentive system. One, workers had to have some control over the changing of norms. Two, when norms were revised upward they had to feel that, as a consequence, they did not suffer in comparison with other workers and especially with the management of the plant, which was responsible for communicating targets and, hence, revised norms to the workers. If their position worsened, the sense of justice and solidarity upon which the incentive system rested would be seriously compromised.

As industrial emphasis shifted back to production, the problem of incentives intensified. This had little to do with the relative short-term effectiveness of participatory incentives in stimulating production, for there was evidence to indicate that production in 1970–1971 rose steadily in those factories which had severed quota management from material incentives.[38] Rather, the workers' sense of justice and control over norm calculation, both of which were essential to making participatory incentives work in the long run, tended to be compromised by the rush of events. There is evidence that, as production responsibilities increased for factory-level management, they tended to ignore worker suggestions for costly technical innovations which were necessary from the workers' view to make norm increases less onerous.[39] Cadres participated in labor less frequently, partly because labor was becoming more difficult, and therefore less appealing, and partly because they got caught up in busywork.[40] In one classic case, it was not until cadres in a brick factory went to the production floor and began lifting and moving some of the eighty tons of brick that each worker had to handle daily, that they supported workers' suggestions for innovation.[41]

As the scope of technical innovation narrowed and as cadre participation in labor became more problematic, the increases in production, which were reflected in increased quotas and norms, seemed more and more to be borne by workers, not cadres. Moreover, planned increases in production were communicated down to the factory with less willingness to discuss these plans and revise them based on workers' suggestions.[42]

These problems with participatory incentives made some factory-level cadres begin to stress technical control and the objective capacities of machinery using political enthusiasm and mass mobilization only sporadically, when particularly heavy tasks were set.[43] Logically, as participatory incentives became less central material incentives were linked to crude output figures.[44]

It must, however, be stressed that there were contradictions in incentives policy. There was frequent cadre participation in labor under extremely harsh conditions[45] and worker pressure on cadres to participate in labor.[46] There were attempts to change the division of labor by teaching workers to do the jobs of other workers, thereby being able to substitute for those who had to attend important meetings.[47] Mass-based technical innovation and triple combination teams also continued.[48]

Many of these issues came to a head in the city of Hangchow in 1975. There, during the heat of July and August, labor unrest broke out, ultimately involving workers in about twenty-five factories and eventually leading to the intervention of the People's Liberation Army. Under harsh working conditions, exacerbated by extremely hot weather, and compounded by an intense production schedule, workers began to perceive *unjust* inequality in their daily lives. Complaints about the heat were backed up with complaints about eating facilities and sanitary conditions. In the cotton-textile and silk weaving industries, many of the women workers complained about the lack of nursery and child-care facilities, and the lack of public transportation for getting to work, especially on the night shift. And because female workers in Hangchow were still responsible, it seems, for preparing meals at home and doing other forms of housework when they came home from work hot and tired, or had to go to work on the night shift, their husbands complained and then brought their troubles to work with them the next day.[49]

This large-scale though unofficial strike took place during a nationwide campaign to "Study Marxism and the Dictatorship of the Proletariat," right after the P'i-Lin-P'i Kung campaign, both of which were aimed at increasing working-class confidence, skill, and willingness to exert authority. It was also evident that the harsh working conditions and intensive production schedule were not always accompanied by cadre participation in labor. The result was to make relative privilege that much more obvious, and, given the natural as well as the political and ideological climate that summer, that much more unacceptable. The Hangchow Summer demonstrated that a perception of equality or *just inequality* was absolutely necessary to a political incentive system. Wages were not the issue in Hangchow, nor was the right of workers to rebel. For the PLA did not smash the strike with force nor mediate for higher wages. It broke the strike by demonstrating that collective welfare was crucial and that cadre participation in labor, even under extremely harsh working conditions, was certainly possible, and absolutely essential if workers were not to see themselves—correctly—as being exploited. Yet in the developing economy, it was clear that collective welfare and participation in labor were not yet to extend to the traditional male-female division of labor in a family. Part of the PLA's political role in Hangchow seemed to be to persuade *wives* to have things arranged at home so that (male) workers would be happier![50]

Worker participation in management and cadre participation in labor, both of which continued to lie at the heart of post-Cultural Revolution organizational structure and incentive systems, continued also to be influenced by the way in which events unfolded in the larger society. There is no doubt that the campaign to criticize Lin Piao and Confucius which began in June 1973,[51] and became an open issue in the mass media in December 1973,[52] and the subsequent campaign to study Marxism and the Dictatorship of the Proletariat were both important in consolidating and supporting the two participations and triple combination system by their attack on intellectual elitism and the concept of "labor as a commodity."[53] But aside from these ideological and study campaigns, there were the fundamental institutions of economic coordination and education which, like national wage and distribution policy, provided a long term organizational and material context within which revolutionary factory management evolved.

By the end of the Cultural Revolution, levels of economic and political authority above the enterprise were no longer the strong supporters of bureaucratic-technocratic planning that they had been after the Great Leap Forward. Not only had the political implications of this position been fairly well spelled out and attacked, but so too had the economic problems it presented. The polemics of the Cultural Revolution, however, in revealing controversy about this problem, should not obscure the fact that in practice the economy had been, throughout the 1960s, increasingly integrated by using the concepts of decentralized operations and centralized allocation of major resources and projects. Planning and development had largely proceeded on the premises of despecialization which led to growing, though limited and regional, self-sufficiency and development of small-scale rural industry.[54] The organs of supra-enterprise authority had some experience in this kind of economic coordination and planning, enough to present a realistic alternative to the bureaucratic-technocratic approach that had been, in its Soviet form, the only model that planners had had to look back on after the Great Leap Forward had shaken things up.

The post-Cultural Revolution period at first gave enormous impetus to the macro-economic concepts of planning and development that had been summed-up during the intense polemical atmosphere of the preceding three years. Rural local industry grew even more rapidly than in preceding years, and now anticipated a major increase in the development of self-sufficient localities related to agriculture.[55] Urban industry continued to stress the importance of local, especially municipal self-sufficiency, and to cut back on long-distance transport and highly complex allocation plans for factories widely separated from one another. Municipal authorities took an increasingly active role in opening up local resources to serve nearby industrial enterprises,[56] in arranging for coordinative and cooperative relationships among factories in the city which had been assigned special tasks,[57] and in arranging for technical cooperation between factories.[58] Urban enterprises continued to cultivate horizontal or local connections,[59] even while maintaining vertical responsibilities for central plans and targets.[60] These horizontal connections included relationships with other large factories,[61] with local small-scale parts or supplies factories,[62] with agricultural areas and communes,[63] and with factories in other industries or trades.[64] Air and water pollution were recognized as problems affecting local communities, and in utilizing waste and residue, factories increasingly sought to establish ties with research institutes, schools, and local governments, including communes which used the waste as fertilizer.[65]

Not only was the immediate post-Cultural Revolution period marked by continued and increasing integration of industrial enterprises with other industrial enterprises in the same locality, but the trend toward enterprise self-sufficiency continued in places where such a policy seemed appropriate. The recycling or reprocessing of waste into raw material used to start up small-scale neighborhood factories was one way this was done.[66] The manufacture, in one plant, of machinery, spare parts, and other items needed in the production process was another way, especially in rural or newer factories which were far away from supply sources.[67] Large technologically advanced plants, in addition to meeting nationally determined plans, were to help local factories to get started by providing them with machinery, parts, or technical training and knowledge.[68]

By late 1971 the emphasis on local integration and self-reliance had, however, begun to create problems for central planning and allocation. Not only had some rural local industry grown to a point where it began to affect labor, supply, and consumer markets outside of the locality in which it had begun,[69] but some urban factories had begun to ignore centrally mandated responsibilities in their rush to meet local needs.[70] Nevertheless, this did not mean an abandonment of the politics of local integration and despecialization. By 1973 municipal authorities still remained important in the tightened central training process and this process had not become impersonal and bureaucratized. Municipal authorities, whether from the planning or the financial sectors of economic administration, were very active in personally checking on economic efficiency and costs of operations,[71] and were busy spreading technical knowledge,[72] discussing and making arrangements for economic cooperation,[73] and finding models to stimulate the economic and technical performance of other enterprises in the city. Indeed, it seems that the constant search for models by means of on-the-spot investigation became the central task of urban administrators.[74]

In providing concrete examples for other enterprises to emulate, model enterprises substituted for more technocratic and bureaucratic methods of evaluation and control. Yet, administration by models[75] created problems of its own. Not the least of these was that in their anxiety to become a model—a vital goal in management's incentive to work hard—some factory leaders evidently tried subtle forms of bribery on municipal level officials. One such form was to provide municipal planners with trial products or free samples of new products for testing purposes so that the planners would be persuaded to acclaim the innovation as the result of excellent management.[76] Even if motives were not of the purest, post-Cultural Revolution coordination and planning continued to provide an administrative environment consistent with the two participations, and it continued to support the spatial development and orientation consistent with the vision of revolutionary urban-rural, industrial-agricultural community development centers that, by 1975, were increasingly institutionalized as part of China's revolutionary development.[77]

The macro-economic context, though still filled with contradictions, offered a more satisfactory and consistent guide for revolutionary factory management and over-all development after the Cultural Revolution than it did after the Great Leap Forward. In a similar way post-Cultural Revolution education provided support, though not always of consistent strength, for the redistribution of power away from a technocratic elite and toward workers—the heart of revolutionary political conflict within the factories.

Educational reforms were crucial for teaching technical skills to workers and inculcating a Marxist value system. These goals of the educational system were, as implied by both the GLF and the Cultural Revolution, to be reached by linking education with production. The Shanghai Machine Tools Plant's "July 21" Worker's College became the model for reforming higher education. By 1973 there were over twenty-three factory-run universities in Shanghai, plus ten more worker universities at the *Ch'ü* level and one at the municipal level.[78] By 1974, there were thirty-four factory-run universities in the city.[79] Other cities reported similarly impressive but not spectacular results. A 1971 survey of the Northeastern industrial base put the number of factory-run colleges in Shenyang, Luta, and Fouhsin combined at thirty-six,[80] and another report put the number at fifty at the end of 1973, but included Anshan and Fuhsün in the total.[81]

The number of workers involved in these factory-run colleges was not large, but they did occupy strategic positions within factories.[82] The first class graduated from the Shanghai Machine Tools Plant in 1971, and it numbered fifty-two students who had completed the three-year course, some of whom could design their own machine tools independently.[83] There were 2,305 workers enrolled in the fifty factory-run universities in the major industrial centers of Liaoning,[84] and similar programs were carried out in Southern China where graduates of the factory-run colleges occupied important positions in the factory power structure.[85]

Factory-run colleges were, however, only part of the post-Cultural Revolution educational system. In addition to full-time colleges, there were part-time colleges giving crash courses on specific technical problems, usually relating to immediate production needs or new production processes, and there was no way to calculate the number of these.[86]

Regular colleges and universities also established ongoing relationships with factories, either by sending students to learn particular subjects,[87] or by having teachers go to teach.[88] Skilled workers also came from factories to teach at universities. Until May 1973, for example, Peking factories and mines had established one or another kind of tie with eleven of the institutes of higher education in the city, and at Tsinghua University there were over twenty part-time lecturers who were workers from nearby factories.[89] Nor were universities the only schools involved in these efforts. More important in terms of numbers were the relationships between secondary and primary schools and factories.[90] The triple combination teams and spare-time technical training classes were another way to spread technical knowledge. From 1968 to 1973 in Shanghai alone over 2,800 of more than 3,000 enterprises had some kind of technical education programs which involved over 207,000 workers.

As impressive as these efforts were in strengthening the foundation for future revolutionary political struggle, there were still contradictions. Not only might worker graduates of factory-run universities occupy higher positions than graduates of factory-run or factory-associated middle schools, but there was no guarantee that new worker-cadres would not believe themselves to be a new elite.[91] There were unresolved organizational and educational problems in the new system. How were admissions to the new colleges and universities to be determined? What standards should be used to judge quality? In what way was traditional academic excellence, understood as mastery of theory, separable from revolutionary excellence, understood as linking theory with practice? How could the drive for sophisticated technical knowledge for the working class be reconciled with the fact that many working class people grew up in an environment not conducive to acquiring verbal and other skills needed for intensive study?[92]

How were science and engineering schools to locate factories with appropriate technology to link theory and practice, especially in smaller cities and rural areas? What about the teaching of highly advanced, theoretical natural sciences—nuclear physics or molecular biology, for example, where the link between theory and practice was in the laboratory rather than the factory?[93]

Yet, these contrasts did not lead to a return to two-track education from the pre-Cultural Revolution period. In 1975 the link between theory and practice, even if only in the laboratory, remained the foundation of education. Full-time universities maintained close ties with factories either through admissions policies or by direct contact.[94] In many industrial and mining enterprises this relationship went beyond the technical and scientific to include political and philosophical study.[95] In the campaign to Study Marxism and the Dictatorship of the Proletariat, the level of discussion on Marxist concepts in the factories was quite sophisticated. Such education had a direct bearing on concepts of interest which lay at the core of political struggles.[96] The worker theorists who came out of these courses, though less than 10 percent of the work force,[97] were important political allies of workers acquiring technical skills at factory-run and factory-related schools. In 1975 the number of these schools increased dramatically. By July Peking reported 135 "July 21" Worker Colleges, with an enrollment of 10,000 people.[98] In May Shanghai reported 260 factory-run Worker Colleges in operation and noted that over 3,600 graduates had gone to various factories over the past few years. In Shenyang the number of factory-run colleges went from eight to twenty-eight and since about 1973 had graduated 930 people.[99] Much of this upsurge came in 1974–1975. By March 1975 there had been only 150 worker-technicians graduated from the Shanghai Machine Tools Plant,[100] and 52 of these had graduated in the first class of 1971.[101]

Events in China often give the appearance of moving with amazing rapidity, at least to people viewing from afar. To a large extent this is true. Clearly the evolution of political relationships within the industrial enterprises, the trends in economic planning and coordination, and the evolution of the educational system were all accompanied by enormous experimental activity and a good deal of disagreement over the scope, depth, and pace of development. Yet, in another sense, the contradictions of this period were not, in substantive terms, vastly different from the issues after the Great Leap Forward and during the Cultural Revolution. Certain problems continued unchanged and others faded and in different ways kept cropping up almost as if, nothing had changed. Yet, a close examination shows that the balance of societal and individual forces tipped slowly and ponderously in favor of a revolutionary political principle, which mandated transfer of power to the working people. The appearance of rapid and fundamental change melts away when the revolutionary principles of the Cultural Revolution or the Great Leap Forward are examined in the light of the post-Cultural Revolution. Yet, revolutionary transformation has been no illusion.

Conclusion: China's Revolutionary Industrialization in Historical Perspective

THE CHINESE APPROACH to modernization is, in some ways, not at all new. Modernization means industrialization and economic growth. It means building factories, roads, rail systems, and mines. It means the exploitation of natural resources, energy, machinery, and technology in order to mechanize the work process, automate it if possible, and to increase agricultural yields. It means the search for better health and more education to meet the needs of an increasingly complex and sophisticated economy and technology. As it did in the West, Japan, and the USSR, modernization in China promises to profoundly transform the lives of a largely rural, agricultural population living in a still poor, technologically backward society.

Work in China's industry is not all that different than elsewhere. Work in a big steel mill is always hot and sometimes dangerous; work in an auto assembly plant is terribly noisy; work in a mine is dirty and hazardous; and serious health risks can exist in plants making asbestos fibers or producing polyvinyl chloride for plastics. Industry in China, as elsewhere, has a tendency to pollute the air and water. These realities are a part of China's modernization and working-class life, as they were and are for others.

Yet, things are not all the same in China. The idea of modernization, the relationship between agriculture and industry, is different from other modern societies. Industrial location, land utilization, and development all are different. Food growing and distribution are geographically linked with industrial centers. The production of goods and services has become the focus of community life, recreation, education, and residence.

The division of labor and dissemination of learning is perhaps as advanced as anywhere in the West. In so far as the Chinese by no means reject material incentives altogether in the form of inequality which reflects notions of distributive justice but emphasize instead the importance of small-group autonomy and the effectiveness of participation and cooperation as substitutes for money, they are very close to the human-relations management theorists in the United States. They have equaled the most progressive and democratic experiments taking place in various corporations of western Europe.

In important respects they have gone further by emphasizing the importance of values, institutions, and distribution of wealth outside the factory to support and enlarge the scope of worker participation within it; by linking the question of power in factories directly to a revolution in education; by using the triple combination teams to reinforce this distribution of power; by making cadre participation in labor a major psychological foundation for organizational solidarity and an incentive for management to support technical innovation and efficient administration.

In the general political ethos and in mass political study campaigns, goals to transcend personal acquisitiveness and to give meaning to the responsibility of participation have been articulated.

The Chinese have recognized that technical innovation is itself a major goal for workers, and they have provided a way for workers to participate in this vital activity; in educational reform and triple combination teams they have discovered a way to proceed that does not ultimately rely on a technocratic or bureaucratic elite.

Thus, what in the West are still essentially short-lived and usually isolated experiments in response to growing and dangerous worker apathy or boredom are, in China, the stuff of everyday life. And though the degree and intensity of these new forms of organization varies widely from place to place and time to time, there can be little doubt that the general model is one which the world will have to deal with from now on.

The Chinese have also achieved insight into the nature of planning and economic coordination and the relationship between coordination and factory management that is unprecedented in any modern economy either of the market or the planned variety. By emphasizing the direct influence that methods of planning have on class structure, and in trying to limit the impact and need for bureaucratic administrators divorced from productive labor and from the local communities over which they exercise power, the Chinese have indeed made an unprecedented contribution to what people can perceive as possible in a modern, highly complex and inter-dependent society. The willingness and capacity of local government to tackle air and water pollution early in the industrialization process is one result. So too is local government regulation of intraurban economic relationships and urban-rural or urban-suburban relationships. Food is increasingly provided to urban areas from agricultural areas close to or even within the city; the urban areas provide technical knowledge, skills, and hardware to the rural areas to increase agricultural output.

These trends in occupational, geographical, and sectorial relationships are unprecedented in the history of industrialization. In moving toward production-centered communities where the relationships between industry and agriculture, work and administration, work and residence, and urban and rural are increasingly close, the Chinese process of development is in many ways the reverse of how the concentration of population and the division of social labor have proceeded thus far in other modern societies.

In observing the nature and intensity of conflict within China's industrial sector, it seems that whether or not this revolutionary approach to modernization works well, partially, or not at all is less dependent on technological than on social or historical factors. Education, the history of a locality, including the family background of workers and cadres, the age of workers but not their sex, and the date or origins of an enterprise—these seem to be more important than the difficulty or sophistication of the machinery or technology being utilized or the size of the factories being considered. It should be realized that different types of production sequences and coordination lend themselves to different degrees of participation, and different sized localities and different geographical and climactic conditions make differences in the functions of local government. But these differences will also change as technological innovation proceeds, general education improves, and economic development continues.

It is clear, however, that this theory is a much varied part of practical reality all over the country. If workers in a steel mill have no say about how fast they have to move to get a good heat, they can participate in technical innovations, safety planning, and quota management. This does not mean that they "sing to the bonderizer," but it does mean that they can have some control over how hard they will work, and that is important. If workers in a highly-automated tractor plant cannot participate in interworkshop coordination, they can have important say in production pacing on the line and in technical innovations. If workers in a cotton mill cannot participate in quality improvements, or check on quality of finished cloth, they can certainly participate in technical innovation and in other kinds of quality inspection as production progresses. And if the big, old cities like Peking and Shanghai rely on nearby suburban communes for fresh food and produce, in other areas, like Ta-ch'ing, industry and agriculture are more closely related.

Thus conflict in China's industrial sector was particularized according to the history of each plant and locality—the types of cadres who worked there, the educational and skill levels of the workers, the perspectives about the nature and purpose of work that people brought with them. In one plant there could be a worker with a middle-school education who believed strongly in working-class leadership in socialist society and, in the same plant, a worker with the same educational background whose parents were poor peasants and who was happy just to have a steady income and good welfare benefits. Needless to say, their attitudes about revolutionizing management would not be the same.

The political conflicts in Chinese industry were and are both the cause and effect of attempts to revolutionize the modernization of China. The issues that divide people are not difficult to discern: the matter of worker participation in management and cadre participation in labor; the question of how best to utilize the technical and scientific knowledge that is so scarce in China and yet so vital for modernization; the question of incentives; the problem of training and recruitment of the labor force at all levels of industrial activity; the issue of sectoral balance and the relations between industry and agriculture, rich and poor, technologically advanced and technologically backward areas, and the matter of investment priorities—whether to develop fast the already developed or to use the already developed simultaneously with an attempt to exploit marginal or undeveloped areas.

The Great Leap Forward seems to be a crucial turning point. Yet, it was such an ambivalent experience on a national level. People had been rapidly promoted and quickly trained and their experiences with participatory management made them ambivalent toward the consolidation of the 1960–1963 period. Part-time schools and work-study education existed alongside full-time universities and regular, academic-oriented high schools. Peasants went to school together with urban intellectuals from middle-class family backgrounds with traditional attitudes toward manual labor. Workers whose parents had been illiterate found themselves the potential members of a managerial elite. In some areas, there was a long history of foreign occupation and oppression. In other factories, Soviet influence was very strong. In still others, there was a history of Chinese bourgeois ownership, and, in still others, American or western European influence was dominant. Mass campaigns and concrete organizational changes in factories were unevenly implemented in scope and in depth. In some places there was much change, in others, very little. In some, the two participations and triple combination system worked comparatively well; in others there was confusion based on inexperience and lack of training and understanding.

The Great Leap Forward had left an ambivalent legacy of theory as well. The system of two participations, one reform, and triple combination was based on the assumption that the party could solve the contradictions between people's attitudes, values, and routines and the need for efficient productivity. The party was to assert the primacy of politics in human relationships and to lead the process whereby the status and privilege and knowledge gaps between workers and administrators would vanish. But until the uniting of politics with operations could be reconciled with economic coordination and planning, party leadership in the Great Leap Forward merely fractured the party along the same lines that existed in the society as a whole. People at different organizational levels had different perspectives and, because of the uneven, heterogeneous nature of people's experiences, family backgrounds, education, or place of socialization, even people at the same levels had varying views on the same problems.

In this sense, the Cultural Revolution was a different but equally complex phenomenon. There had been six years of more or less bitter debate and contradictory experience with the decentralized and despecialized economic planning and coordination methods to offset the influence of the Soviet planning model. There were many people who were products of the Great Leap Forward's experiments in education and management, so that by the time of the Cultural Revolution there was a comparatively more educated, experienced, and larger working class. There were more younger people whose experiences did not predate the bad old days of preliberation China, some of whom took the revolutionary goals seriously and others who only wanted the secure, traditional position urged on them by well-meaning parents in a society where urban security was still a big step above rural poverty. There were lots of engineers and technicians who had been from working class or peasant background, and there were more workers from rural families.

Everyone had experienced changes. The stated revolutionary goals and values of the society were not equally understood nor consistently implemented, but they did serve as the context within which all these conflicts existed. After the Cultural Revolution, these values and these goals became the objects of massive study campaigns often led by the same people who had come to the forefront of struggle during the Cultural Revolution.

In retrospect it seems clear that the Chinese learned from their own history and from the history of others. The realization that the key to revolutionization lay not simply in the organizational leadership of the party but in uniting politics with actual production operations and uniting production operations with an appropriate planning system came only after years of turmoil and experimentation. Yet if this realization has been made, and a theoretical approach has been put into practice, a number of by no means insignificant problems remain nevertheless.

It is, first of all, very clear that, although the two participations is a reality, there are still differences between workers and managers. Not all workers, moreover, participate in management to the same extent and most do little more than attend periodic workers congresses or record their own input and output figures. Workers on triple combination teams or on revolutionary committees at various levels, however, do participate more in important managerial decisions concerning planning, technical reform and innovation, and intra- and inter-enterprise coordination.

Chinese technology has not reached the point where boring, repetitive, or dangerous work can be automated, and yet, as workers do become more aware and educated, problems concerning health, safety, and working conditions may become more important, especially as worker participation in management continues. Demands for investment in welfare and for technical innovations can cut into demands for investment in present production, and the precise drawing of this line promises to be a point of future political debate.

The system of enterprise management and planning requires a work force that is well-educated and capable of making decisions, and it is based on an assumption about the willingness of human beings to strive for greater equality. In a country which is still poor, where knowledge and education are still uneven, and where demands for improved living conditions are not always demands for unnecessary luxury, there will be strong tendencies for the educated or political elite to begin living in comparative comfort and/or privilege. These pressures can be assumed to exist alongside those working in the opposite direction, but the issue of incentives promises to be a continuing point of conflict.

In the economy as a whole, despecialization and decentralization can lead to the aggravation of inequalities for localities less favored with human and natural resources. If local development proceeds too far, it can disrupt national planning and coordination. There will, therefore, continue to be tension regarding localities and the central, regional, or provincial planning authorities. In so far as these differences are more pronounced at a fairly low level of economic and technical capability, they can be expected to diminish as China becomes richer and all localities begin to exist well above poverty levels.

This, however, is not yet the case. If the fine balance between central planning and coordination and local autonomy and orientation tilts too far in either direction, it could lead to tighter central control, to the point where such control would begin to effect negatively the way in which enterprise-level management could or would be willing to participate in labor. Worker participation in management could also be negatively affected as factory-level management was constrained to act as simply another level of control in an administrative apparatus needed to prevent inequality from becoming so pronounced as to lead to dangerous political conflict. Thus, the fight against bureaucracy can be expected to continue and be closely related to the level of economic development in the national economy, and to the question of incentives and morality. It does not promise to disappear in the near future.

Finally, there is the problem that the definition of efficiency, as containing both political and social priorities as well as a calculation of economic costs based on the given state of technological, human, and natural resource development, can lead to waste and planning errors. It is not always clear how to evaluate the trade-off between political and economic costs in the short and long run, or to see all the many ramifications of one set of priorities being chosen over another. This planning problem is not unique to China, but the fact that these issues are handled by public debate is. It promises to make politics at all levels of society rather contentious at times.

In comparing the course of China's revolution and modernization with the Western capitalist countries, Japan, and the USSR, one cannot help but be impressed with the enormous strength and progressive weakening of capitalism as a civilization. In the nineteenth and early twentieth centuries, in spite of national rivalries and wars, this civilization brooked no rivals for global supremacy, and its existence defined the limits both of political vision and political action for people confronted with its values and institutions. Only political leaders from a proud and independent historical tradition in its own right, and able to mobilize the huge and insulated peasantry in a country as physically large as China was, were able to provide the resistance that allowed for the development of a noncapitalist alternative. This resistance was part of a Western tradition, too, one that went back to Marxism and to the Bolshevik Revolution which was the first major practical attempt to transcend the horizons of western European bourgeois civilization.

The revolution and the modernization of China gathered momentum slowly and ponderously, and the enormous weight of China's own history which acted as a buffer against the West and the ideological and cultural appeal of capitalism, also acted to shape the speed and form of social and economic transformation. In some ways tradition and revolution reinforced each other and hastened modernization also; in other ways revolution and tradition clashed and slowed the pace of both modernization and revolution.

We in the West tend to ignore China's revolution or reject it. We focus on China's poverty or population, confining our perspective to the exotic or to struggles for power at the top levels of government. There is no doubt that these struggles are important. But Mao Tsetung was too much of a Marxist and too aware of Chinese history to see the problem of revolutionary succession only in short-run terms of personalities and leaders. If the changes that have been described in these chapters are any indication of the situation in the rest of Chinese society outside of industry, then the very historical inertia created by institutions, values, and interests that has made the revolutionary transformation so filled with conflict and so difficult may now work to make an attempt at counter-revolutionary restoration no simple task either. But China's contribution to a new global socialist civilization is not yet a self-generating historical reality.

Appendix A

Table 1 Percentage of Engineering, Technical, and Managerial Personnel Working in Chinese Industrial Enterprises Who Were of Bourgeois Background as of 1953, Based on Educational Statistics of 1949–50 and Including Pre-1949 Graduates of Chinese or Foreign Educational Institutions

Field	Voc'l.-Scndry.-Tech.-Student Enrollmt.	Voc'l.-Scndry.-Tech. Grads.	Univ. Students	University Grads.	Total No. of Engr. & Tech. Personnel in Chinese Industry in 1953
SCIENCE			7,000[d]	1,468[d]	
ENGINEERING	21,400[a]	7,000[b]	30,300[d]	4,711[d]	
FINANCE & ECON.	14,800[a]	1,600[e]	19,400[d]	3,305[d]	
TOTALS	36,200	8,600	56,700	9,484	
TOTALS	44,800		66,184		

GRAND TOTALS			110,984 as a percentage of		210,000[e]

PERCENTAGE of engineering, technical and managerial personnel in Chinese industry in 1953 of bourgeois educational and family background   53%

---

[a] Orleans, p. 46.
[b] Orleans, p. 47.
[c] Computed from Orleans, pp. 46–47, taking % of students *graduating* in finance and economics to be same as % of enrolled students in finance and economics.
[d] Orleans, pp. 74–75.
[e] Orleans, p. 165.

Table 2 Estimated Number of Surviving Pre-1949 Graduates in 1953 from Higher Education Institutions in Fields Relating to Industry[a]

	Engi-neering	Science	Finance & Econ.	Total All Fields This Age Group[b]	Sur-vival Rate[c]	Total Sur-vivors
1928–1932	2,977	1,820	1,699	6,496	.793	5,151
1933–1937	5,499	4,347	3,030	12,876	.845	10,879
1938–1942	7,796	4,008	3,378	15,182	.891	13,527
1943–1947	15,418	5,638	10,840	31,896	.932	29,727
Totals	31,690	15,813	18,947	66,450		59,184[d]

[a] Excluding 1948.

[b] Orleans, p. 171. I added every five-year interval to get these totals.

[c] Survival rates are extrapolated from rates used by Orleans based on ages equivalent. His rates are based on ages as of 1960, mine as of 1953. See Appendix A, Table 1, n. 3, in Orleans, p. 169.

[d] Since 1948 totals are excluded, the total should be higher, but I assume this figure to be about equivalent to the attrition rate due to emigration and other political factors.

The figure of 80 percent arrived at in the text was achieved by assuming the following: Of the number of people enrolled in school on the levels concerned (senior technical-vocational secondary school and above), almost all were of bourgeois family background. Some of these people left with their families as the communists came to power. Others migrated in the first year or two, but before 1953. An additional proportion of students were probably not from bourgeois background, although no figures are available. Moreover, obviously not everyone with the educational background used in these calculations automatically assumed positions in China's factories after 1949. Some were teachers, doctors, research scientists. Some of the communist cadres without educational criteria did have practical experience with machinery during the Revolutionary Civil Wars, and were able to assume managerial positions. Moreover, workers often were quite technically competent and were given administrative responsibilities, and were rapidly promoted to positions of authority. Moreover, it can also be assumed that some managerial and technical personnel in China's factories in the early years were secondary school graduates of bourgeois family background, but with long revolutionary service, and hence "proletarian" class background in ideological and political terms. All of these factors, I estimate, would tend to reduce the percentage of bourgeois personnel in China's factories as of 1953 to about 75–80 percent, as an arbitrary, though approximate, figure.

Appendix B

Chart 1 The Organizational System of a Large-Scale Factory (1957)

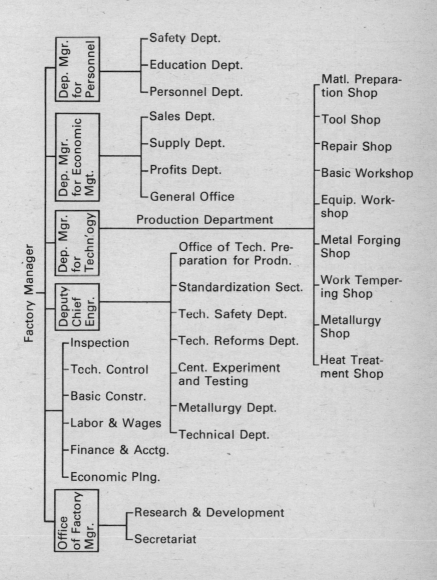

Chart 2 The Office of the Factory Manager

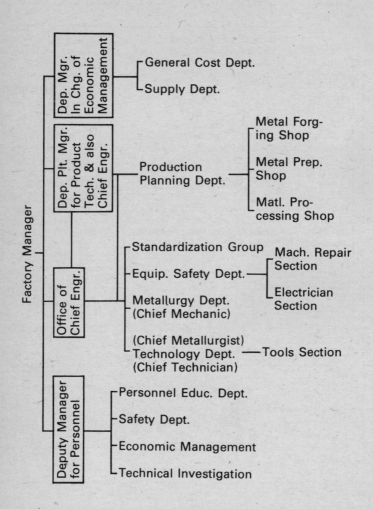

Chart 3   The Office of the Chief Engineer

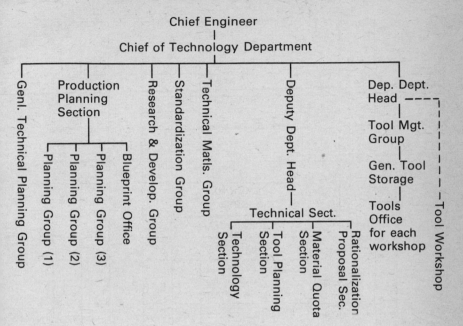

Chart 4   The Organization System of the Finance Department

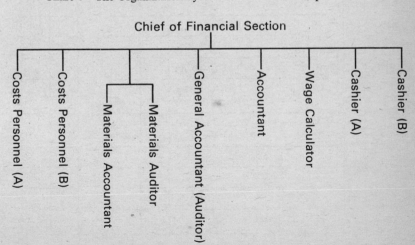

Appendix C

Workman's Job Record Card

Month 1961

Name: Type of Work: Equip. No. Name & Spec.:

Date		Order	Voucher No.	Name of Product	Name of Machine Accessory	Work Process	Thrown into plan		Production Working Hrs.								Actually Completed			Interrupted Working Hours						Causes
							No. of Art.	Working Hrs.	Fr.		To		Total			Work Hours	Nos.			Fr.		To		Total		
M	D								H	M	H	M	Regular Working Hours	Extra Working Hours	Re-making		Finished Products	Rejects		H	M	H	M			

Output Schedule

x x   shop   x x   section   M . . . . Ten-day period . . . 1961

Voucher No.	Name of Products	Name of Spare Part	Planned		Actually Completed	
			Quantity	Working Hours	Quantity	Working Hours
·						

The "working hours" column shown above is provided for those teams and sections which turn out multiple kinds of products which make it difficult to reflect the total progress of the fulfillment of team and section production plans. This column may be omitted in the case of those teams and sections that turn out single products.

Section Quality Register

xx shop xx section   M 1961

Date	Voucher No.	Name & Spec. of Product	Name of Spare Part	Quantity Delivered & Exam'd.	Quantity of Rejects		Working Hrs. Taken by Rejects		Name of Matls.	Unit Wgt. (kg)	Person Responsible	Causes of Reject
					Internal	External	Internal	External				

Section head ....   Quality examiner ....   Filled M .... D 1961

Section Delivery Orders

xx shop x x section   No. . . . .

Name of Materials	Specification	Unit	Quantity	Remarks

Storekeeper: . . . .   Received by: . . . .   M 1961

Section Materials Consumption Card

. . . . . . Section   M 1961   Page . . . .

Name of Material	Specif'ns.	Planned Quantity	1st 10 days				2nd 10 days				3rd 10 days				Total Quantity for the Month
			Planned Figure	Day	Day	Sub-total	Planned Figure	Day	Day	Sub-total	Planned Figure	Day	Day	Sub-total	

Section head: . . . .   Storekeeper: . . . .

Auxiliary Materials and Tools Consumption Card

.... Section   M 1961   P ....

Name	Specification	Plan		1st 10 days					2nd 10 days					3rd 10 days					Total Month		Consumption Compared With Plan	
		Quantity	Amount	Plan		D	D	Sub-total	Plan		D	D	Sub-total	Plan		D	D	Sub-total				
				Quantity	Amount			Quantity	Amount	Quantity	Amount			Quantity	Amount	Quantity	Amount			Quantity	Amount	Quantity	Amount	Over-spent (Y)	Sav-ing (Y)

Section head: ....   Store-keeper: ....

Attendance Records

..... Section   From .... to .... 1961 p.....
                 Day   Mo.   Day   Mo.

Series No.		On Duty	Off Duty	Extra Work	On Duty	Off Duty	Extra Work
Type of Work							
date	1						
	2						
	.						
	.						
	10						
date	11						
	.						
	.						
	20						
date	21						
	.						
	.						
	31						
1st 10 days	sick leave						
	casual leave						
	absent						
	extra work						
	present						
	total						
2nd 10 days	sick leave						
	casual leave						
	absent						
	extra work						
	present						
	total						
3rd 10 days	sick leave						
	casual leave						
	absent						
	extra work						
	present						
	total						
Total for the month	sick leave						
	casual leave						
	absent						
	extra work						
	present						
	total						

Symbols: Absent x   Sick leave o   Casual leave v

Notes

Introduction

1. Benjamin Schwartz, *In Search of Wealth and Power* (Harvard University Press: Cambridge, Mass.), 1966. *See also* Joseph Levenson, *Liang Ch'i-ch'ao and the Mind of Modern China* (Berkeley: University of California Press, 1966).

Chapter 1: Modernization in Historical Perspective: Capitalist Civilization and Developmental Convergence

1. For a similar approach to a study of the relationship between a dominant civilization and those constrained to operate within its aura of influence, Eugene Genovese, *Roll, Jordan, Roll* (New York: Pantheon, 1974).

2. For Hobbes' relationship to the ideological assumptions of later liberal capitalism, C.B. MacPherson, *Possessive Individualism* (London: Oxford University Press, 1962); Frank Coleman, "The Hobbesian Basis of American Constitutionalism," *Polity*, vol. 6, 1973–74.

3. Graeme Duncan, *Marx and Mill* (Cambridge, Eng.: Cambridge University Press, 1973), pp. 39–40.

4. For comments on centralization, concentration, and size of industrial enterprises in the industrialized capitalist countries and the USSR, Harry Magdoff "China: Contrasts With the USSR," *Monthly Review*, vol. 27, no. 3, July–August 1975, pp. 25–29. For more on concentration and centralization in capitalist economies, especially the U.S.A., John M. Blair, *Economic Concentration* (New York: Harcourt Brace, 1972).

5. Harry Braverman, *Labor and Monopoly Capital: The Degradation of Work in the 20th Century* (New York: Monthly Review Press, 1975).

6. For a review of the literature relating to how this process worked in relationship to the medical profession, Adrienne Rich, "The Theft of Childbirth," *New York Review of Books*, Oct. 2, 1975, pp. 25–30.

7. For the relationship between the needs of evolving capitalism and the changing educational system, Sam Bowles & Herb Gintis, *Schooling in Capitalist America* (New York: Basic Books, 1976).

8. See Gabriel Kolko, *The Triumph of Conservatism: A Reinterpretation of American History 1900–1916* (New York: Free Press of Glencoe, 1963).

9. The notion of "efficiency" is impossible to define without reference to goals. Weber's conception was clearly one that accepted the goals of cost minimization and maximum output. But even if maximum output is accepted as a goal there are three kinds of efficiency all of which contribute to maximization of output, but only one of which was used by Weber.

a. Allocational or "economic" efficiency would include the idea of allocating scarce resources (skilled manpower and natural resources) in a way such that the "opportunity cost" of the allocative decision is the lowest possible, or to put the matter another way, where the output generated by using a factor of production in one place exceeds its use in any alternative place. This was the concept of efficiency Weber used.

b. "Engineering" efficiency (a concept pointed out to me by William Snead of Hamilton College) concerns the technical problem of combining material in the most effective way in order to produce a desired effect. For example, platinum may be a better conductor of electricity than copper but it may also be far more expensive. Engineering efficiency, especially in its notion of sequential process, usually has a large influence on the division of labor in a modern factory as well as on the content and intensity of individual jobs, but it is not the same as cost efficiency.

c. Motivational efficiency, discussed in an essay by Harvey Liebenstein, "Allocative Efficiency vs. 'X' Efficiency," *American Economic Review*, June, 1966, p. 392, is of much greater significance in determining output than either allocational or engineering efficiency, providing the technical sequences of engineering efficiency are not violated. Not only is the motivation of the human worker able to overcome resource shortages or mis-allocation by means of improvisation or more intensified labor, but even the notions of engineering efficiency can be changed through technological innovation, reform, or invention.

10. H.H. Gerth and C.W. Mills, eds., *From Max Weber* (New York: Oxford University Press, 1958), pp. 204–208; 196 ff; 77–128.

11. *Ibid.*, pp. 230–235.

12. Robert Walker, ed., *Modern Technology and Civilization* (New York: McGraw-Hill, 1962), pp. 52–61. See also, Braverman, *Labor and Monopoly Capital.*

13. Robert Merton, *Reader in Bureaucracy* (New York: Free Press, 1952).

14. For the standard presentation of this neo-Weberian argument, see Ralf Dahrendorf, *Class and Class Conflict in Industrial Society* (Stanford: Stanford University Press, 1959).

15. Daniel Bell, *The Coming of Post-Industrial Society* (New York: Basic Books, 1973).

16. These concepts are associated with Bell, Jacques Ellul, and Zbigniew Brzezinski, respectively.

17. Elton Mayo, *The Human Problems of an Industrial Civilization* (New York: Macmillan Co., 1933).

18. H. Maslow, "A Theory of Human Motivation," *Psychological Review*, vol. L (1943), pp. 370–396; and *Motivation and Personality* (New York: Harper and Row, 1954).

19. Douglas McGregor, *The Human Side of Enterprise* (New York: McGraw-Hill, 1960).

20. See Walker, *Modern Technology*, pp. 41–136, pp. 223–269. Victor H. Vroom and Edward L. Deci, *Management and Motivation* (Baltimore: Johns Hopkins Press, 1970); George A. Litwin and Robert A. Stringer, Jr., *Motivation and Organizational Climate* (Cambridge, Mass.: Harvard University Business School, 1968); William G. Scott and Keith Davis, *Human Relations and Organizational Behavior*, 3rd ed. (New York: McGraw-Hill, 1969).

21. "The East India Company—Its History and Results"; "The Future Results of the British Rule in India"; "The Opium Trade"; "Revolution in China and Europe"; Marx and Engels, *On Colonialism* (Moscow: Progress Publishers, 1959).

22. Marx's classic refutation of the notion of a priori stages in historical analysis comes in an 1877 letter he wrote to the editors of *Otechestzennye Zapiski* (Fatherland Notes). Lewis Feuer, ed., *Marx and Engels, Basic Writings on Politics and Philosophy* (Garden City: Anchor Books, 1959), pp. 438–444.

23. Ardan Foster Carter, "Neo-Marxist Approaches to Development and Underdevelopment," *Journal of Contemporary Asia*, vol. 3, no. 1 (1973), pp. 7–33.

24. W. A. Williams, *The Great Evasion* (New York: Quadrangle Books), p. 19; Eric Fromm, *Marx's Concept of Man* (New York: F. Ungar Publishing Co., 1961), for a good description of the concept of freedom and liberation in Marxist thought. For a good discussion of Marx's concept of human nature and alienation, see Bertell Ollman, *Alienation: Marx's Concept of Man in Capitalist Society* (Cambridge, Eng.: Cambridge University Press, 1971), passim.

25. Jeremy Azrael, *Managerial Power and Soviet Politics* (Cambridge, Mass.: Harvard University Press, 1966), p. 16.

26. Engels, "On Authority," in Feuer, ed., *Marx and Engels*, pp. 483–485.

27. Azrael, *Managerial Power*, p. 14.

28. *Ibid.*, pp. 19–21.

29. Marx, "Civil War in France," in Feuer, *Marx and Engels*, p. 361.

30. Engels, "On Authority," *ibid.*, pp. 483–485.

31. Daniel Bell, "Two Roads from Marx," in *The End of Ideology* (New York: Free Press, 1960).

32. Azrael, *Managerial Power*, pp. 25–26.

33. The reasons that Japan was able to do this so quickly have as much to do with international politics as with the adaptability of Japan's own social system to the demands of capitalist based reform in the late 1860s. Both are crucial in understanding the Japanese transformation during the Meiji Restoration period. For a good discussion of this, John W. Dower, ed., *Origins of the Modern Japanese State: Selected Writings of E.H. Norman* (New York: Pantheon, 1975), Introduction. *See also* Jon Halliday, *A Political History of Japanese Capitalism* (New York: Pantheon, 1975).

34. Ronald Dore, *British Factory, Japanese Factory* (Berkeley: University of California Press, 1973).

35. See references cited in John Dower's "Introduction" to J. Halliday, *A Political History of Japanese Capitalism*, pp. xix and xxxiii. Recent studies of Japanese modernization such as Ronald Dore's *British Factory, Japanese Factory* have sharply criticized these theories of "marketplace convergence," and have even suggested that Japanese personnel policies may represent a more advanced form of bureaucratic rule, more nearly embodying the theories of the "human relations" school in the West. For a critique of Dore, see Joe Moore, "British Factory, Japanese Factory," *Bulletin of Concerned Asian Scholars*, vol. VI, #3, Oct. 1974.

36. *State and Revolution*, in V.I. Lenin, *Selected Works*, vol. II (New York: International Publishers, 1967), pp. 263–360.

37. Braverman, *Labor and Monopoly Capital*, p. 22.

38. Azrael, *Managerial Power*, p. 33. Charles Bettelheim, *Class Struggles in the U.S.S.R. First Period: 1917–1923* (New York: Monthly Review Press, 1976).

39. Azrael, *Managerial Power*, p. 153.

40. *Ibid.*, p. 250, n. 14.

41. Frederick and Lou-Jean Fleron, "Administrative Theory as Repressive Theory," *Telos*, No. 2, Summer, 1972, pp. 63–92; James Peck, "Revolution versus Modernization and Revisionism," in Victor Nee and James Peck, eds., *China's Uninterrupted Revolution* (New York: Pantheon, 1976).

42. Liberman Debates, in Myron Sharpe, ed., *Planning, Profit, and Incentives in the USSR*, 2 vols. (White Plains: International Arts & Sciences Press, 1966).

43. Peck, *op. cit.* Bell, *The Coming of Post Industrial Society*, pp. 99–112.

44. Azrael, *Managerial Power*, pp. 162–172.

45. Trotsky's opposition to Stalin based on workers'- self-management, while very important and real in terms of rhetoric, was never based on a realistic and

practical view of political process. As a result, when faced with actual administrative and political decision making, as for example in the Red Army, Trotsky proved to be as much an authoritarian, centralist, and elitist as Stalin ever was. Peck, *op. cit.*

46. For short summaries of a good portion of the social science literature on Soviet modernization in the West, Azrael, *Managerial Power*, pp. 1–11; Bell, *The Coming of Post Industrial Society*, pp. 86–99. The classic statement of the neo-Weberian perspective is Zbignew Brzezinski, *Ideology and Power in Soviet Politics*.

47. Peck, *op. cit.*, especially the section on Soviet criticism of American modernization theory.

48. Richard Hensman, *From Gandhi to Guevara* (London: Allan Lane, Penguin Press, 1969); Ian Clegg, *Workers Self Management in Algeria* (New York: Monthly Review Press, 1970).

49. Peck, *op. cit.*; Stephen Andors, *Factory Management in China: The Politics of Modernization in a Revolutionary Society*, Ph.D. dissertation, Columbia University, 1974, pp. 21–26.

50. Gilbert Rozman, "Soviet Reinterpretations of Chinese Social History: The Search for the Origins of Maoism," *Journal of Asian Studies*, vol. XXXIV, #1, Nov. 1974, pp. 49–55. Nee and Peck, *op. cit.*, especially "The Russian View of the Chinese Revolution."

Chapter 2: The Historical Setting

1. Etienne Balazs, *Chinese Civilization and Bureaucracy*, (New Haven: Yale University Press, 1964), p. 150. Balazs justifiably calls the attempt "presumptuous," and for a convincing argument of the dangers it exposes one to, see the review of Richard Solomon's book, *Mao's Revolution and the Chinese Political Culture*, in Fritz Mote, "China's Past in the Study of China Today," *Journal of Asian Studies*, vol. 32, No. 1, Nov. 1972, pp. 107–120. Others have attempted to deal with this broad theme in far greater detail and thoroughness that what is attempted here. See Joseph Levenson, *Confucian China and Its Modern Fate*, (Berkeley: University of California Press, 1966), and Mark Selden, *The Yenan Way in Revolutionary China*, (Cambridge, Mass.: Harvard University Press, 1972).

2. Mark Elvin, *The Pattern of the Chinese Past* (Stanford: Stanford University Press, 1973).

3. For an excellent summary of the various positions on this, *see* Carl Riskin, "Surplus and Stagnation in Modern China," in Dwight Perkins, ed., *China's Modern Economy in Historical Perspective* (Stanford: Stanford University Press, 1973), pp. 49–64.

4. John Fei, "The Standard Market of Traditional China," in Perkins, ed., *China's Modern Economy*, pp. 235 ff. G.W. Skinner, "Marketing and Social Structure in Rural China," *Journal of Asian Studies*, vol. 24, no. 1, 1964, pp. 3–43.

5. Mote, "China's Past."

6. Ho P'ing-ti, *The Ladder of Success in Imperial China* (New York: Columbia University Press, 1962).

7. Benjamin Schwartz, "The Reign of Virtue: Some Broad Perspectives on Leader and Party in the Cultural Revolution," *China Quarterly*, #35, July–September 1968, p. 16.

8. Balazs, *Chinese Civilization*, pp. 154–155.

9. *Ibid.*, Introduction.

10. *Ibid.*, p. xv. *See also* Edgar Snow, *Red Star Over China* (New York: Grove Press, 1961), pp. 121–188 and David Nivison, "Communist Ethics and Chinese Tradition," *Journal of Asian Studies*, vol. 16, November, 1956, p. 52.

11. Balazs, *Chinese Civilization*, p. 154.

12. *Ibid.*, pp. 9–10.

13. *Ibid.*, p. 10.

14. *Ibid.*, p. 16.

15. James R. Townsend, *Political Participation in Communist China* (Berkeley: University of California Press, 1967), p. 11.

16. Balazs, *Chinese Civilization*, p. 18.

17. *Ibid.*, p. 154.

18. Ch'ü T'ung-tai, *Local Government in China Under the Ch'ing* (Cambridge, Mass.: Harvard University Press, 1962).

19. Townsend, *Political Participation*, pp. 17–19.

20. John K. Fairbank, "The Nature of Chinese Society," in Franz Schurmann and Orville Schell, *The China Reader*, Vol. 1, *Traditional China* (New York: Vintage Books, 1967).

21. Balazs, *Chinese Civilization*, p. 159.

22. *Ibid.*, p. 42.

23. Albert Feuerwerker, "The Chinese Economy, 1870–1911," Michigan Papers in Chinese Studies, Ann Arbor, 1969 and "The Chinese Economy, 1912–1949," Michigan Papers in Chinese Studies, #1, Ann Arbor, 1968. Rhodes Murphy, "The Treaty Ports and China's Modernization: What Went Wrong?," Michigan Papers in Chinese Studies, #7, Ann Arbor, 1970.

24. Robert F. Dernberger, "The Role of the Foreigner in China's Economic Development," in Perkins, ed., *China's Modern Economy*, pp. 37–38.

25. James Morell, *Early Development of the Cotton Textile Industry in China*, unpublished Ph.D. dissertation, Harvard University, 1976.

26. For a description of the degree to which the surplus in the Chinese economy was made unavailable for investment because of these and other similar factors, see Carl Riskin, "Surplus and Stagnation in Modern China," in Perkins, *China's Modern Economy.*

27. Gunnar Myrdal, *Asian Drama* (New York: Pantheon, 1968), p. 468. Myrdal notes how rural emigration is a common trend in agricultural societies going through the first stages of industrialization.

28. Thomas G. Rawski, "The Growth of Producer Industries, 1900–1971," in Perkins, *China's Modern Economy*, pp. 209 ff.

29. Albert Feuerwerker, *China's Early Industrialization* (Cambridge, Mass.: Harvard University Press, 1958), pp. 8–9.

30. Leo Orleans, *Professional Manpower and Education in Communist China*, (Washington: U.S. Government Printing Office, 1961, NSF–61-3), p. 68.

31. Barry M. Richman, *Industrial Society in Communist China*, (New York: Vintage Books, 1969), pp. 478–479.

32. Len Adams and Al McCoy, *The Politics of Heroin in Southeast Asia* (New York: Harper and Row, 1970). *See also* the essay by Jonathan Marshall, "The KMT and the Opium Trade," *Bulletin of Concerned Asian Scholars*, forthcoming.

33. Paul Baran, *The Political Economy of Growth* (New York: Marzani and Munsell, 1960), p. 236.

34. Richman, pp. 228–229. Franz Schurmann, *Ideology and Organization in Communist China* (Berkeley: University of California Press, 1966), pp. 223–224.

35. Lynda Shaffer, "*Mao Tse-tung and the Hunan Labor Movement*," unpublished Ph.D. dissertation, Columbia University, 1974.

36. "Historical Materials on the Nanyang Brothers Tobacco Company," *Chinese Sociology and Anthropology*, vol. 6, nos. 1, 2, Winter, 1973–74; vol. 6, nos. 3, 4, Spring–Summer, 1974, International Arts and Sciences Press, White Plains, N.Y.

37. Shih Kuo-heng, *China Enters the Machine Age* (Cambridge, Mass.: Harvard University Press, 1944), pp. 57–58.

38. For excellent descriptions of the exactions made by gang bosses on the Shanghai Docks, "Changes at the Shanghai Harbor Docks," *Chinese Sociology and Anthropology*, vol. 5, no. 3, Spring, 1973 and vol. 7, no. 2, Winter, 1974–1975, International Arts and Sciences Press, White Plains, N.Y.

39. Shaffer, *The Hunan Labor Movement*, pp. 145, 151, 154, 220–225. John Gittings, *China and the World* (New York: Harper and Row, 1974), Ch. 1.

40. Shih Kuo-heng, *China Enters the Machine Age* (Cambridge, Mass.: Harvard University Press, 1944), pp. 117–118.

41. Shaffer, *The Hunan Labor Movement*, p. 138.

42. *Ibid.*, p. 148.

43. Ho Kan-chih, "The Rise of the Chinese Working Class Movement," in Franz Schurmann and Orville Schell, *The China Reader*, vol. II, *Republican China* (New York: Vintage Books, 1968), pp. 116–122.

44. For some graphic descriptions, see Schaffer, *The Hunan Labor Movement*; Jean Chesneaux, *A History of the Chinese Labor Movement*; and John Gittings, *China and the World*, Ch. 1.

45. Peter Schran, "On the Yenan Origins of Current Economic Policies," in Perkins, ed., *China's Modern Economy*, pp. 279–304.

46. Mark Selden, *The Yenan Way in Revolutionary China* (Cambridge, Mass.: Harvard University Press, 1972).

47. Jack Belden, "Goldflower's Story," in *China Shakes the World* (New York: Monthly Review Press, 1972); Delia Davin, "Women in the Liberated Areas," in Marilyn Young, ed., *Women in China*, Michigan Papers in Chinese Studies, no. 15, Ann Arbor, 1973.

48. John Gurley, "The Formation of Mao's Economic Strategy: 1927–1949," *Monthly Review*, vol. 27, no. 3, July–August, 1975, pp. 58–132.

49. John W. Lewis, *Leadership in Communist China* (Ithaca: Cornell University Press, 1963), pp. 38–45.

50. Selden, *The Yenan Way*, pp. 132–133, 150. William Hinton, *Fanshen* (New York: Monthly Review Press, 1967); Belden, *China Shakes the World*, pp. 174–189.

51. Townsend, *Political Participation*, p. 51; Gurley, "Mao's Economic Strategy," pp. 58–67.

52. Stephen Andors, "Mass Mobilization in Communist Controlled Areas of China: 1937–1945," unpublished East Asian Institute Certificate Essay, Columbia University, 1967.

53. Mao Tsetung, *Selected Works*, vol. IV, pp. 111–114.

54. T'ung Tsu-chü, *Local Government in China Under the Ch'ing* (Cambridge, Mass.: Harvard University Press, 1962), p. 195.

55. Schwartz, *Yen Fu and the West: In Search of Wealth and Power*; Levenson, *Confucian China and Its Modern Fate*; Chow Tse-tung, *The May Fourth Movement*; Marius Jansen, *The Japanese and Sun Yat-sen*; Maurice Meisner, *Li Ta-chao and the Origins of Chinese Marxism*; John Sari, "China's Special Modernity," in Bruce Douglass and Ross Terrill, eds., *China and Ourselves*, (Boston: Beacon Press, 1971), pp. 49–68.

56. Mary Wright, *The Last Stand of Chinese Conservatism* (New Haven: Yale University Press, 1960).

57. According to Richman, *Industrial Society*, and sources cited therein, I have calculated that approximately 46 percent of the graduates of Chinese universities were, in 1949, specialists in the fields of economics and finance, natural sciences or engineering. The percentage rises to 51 percent of all students enrolled,

since some enrolled students did not graduate. These figures do not include Chinese students in foreign universities, a group which was at its peak numbers during the mid-1930s, with a rapid decline during the 1937–1945 war years, only to rise again in 1947. For precise quantitative data, see Orleans, *Professional Manpower*, p. 78, and Richman, *Industrial Society*, pp. 169, 182, tables 3–17 and 3–19, respectively.

58. C. M. Wilbur and J. Howe, *Documents on Communism, Nationalism, and Soviet Advisers in China: 1918–1927* (New York: Columbia University Press, 1956).

59. Richman, *Industrial Society*, p. 404. James C. Thomson, *While China Faced West* (Cambridge, Mass.: Harvard University Press, 1970).

60. Thomson, *While China Faced West*, pp. 130–148, for details on the relationship between elite universities in China and the Rockefeller Foundation.

61. Franz Schurmann, *Ideology and Organization in Communist China* (Berkeley: University of California Press, 1968) for reference to criticisms of men like H. D. Fong who shared much of the liberal Western outlook on China's problems. These discussions went on in the *Nankai Social and Economic Quarterly* in the 1930s.

62. Shih Kuo-heng, *China Enters the Machine Age*, pp. 57–58.

63. For a fuller discussion of Mao's theories of education, Peter Seyboldt, *Revolutionary Education in Communist China* (London: Routledge & Kegan Paul, 1970).

64. Boyd Compton, *Mao's China, Party Reform Documents, 1942–1944* (Seattle: University of Washington Press, 1952), pp. xiii–xxiii. The campaign was called the *cheng-feng* or rectification campaign.

65. Mark Selden, "The Yenan Legacy: The Mass Line," in A. Doak Barnett, ed., *Chinese Communist Politics in Action* (Seattle: University of Washington Press, 1969), pp. 110–111, 135–140. Phyllis Andors, "K'angta: A Study in Revolutionary Education," unpublished essay, Columbia University, East Asian Institute, 1972.

66. Peter Seyboldt, "The Yenan Revolution in Mass Education," *China Quarterly*, no. 48, Oct.–Dec., 1971, pp. 641–670.

67. *Ibid.*, pp. 659–661; Selden, "The Yenan Legacy," pp. 145–148.

68. Belden, *China Shakes the World*; Richman, *Industrial Society*, pp. 478–479, 525.

Chapter 3: From Reconstruction to the Great Leap Forward: China's Industry in a Period of Transition

1. Mark Selden, *The Yenan Way* (Cambridge, Mass.: Harvard University Press, 1970); William Hinton, *Fanshen* (New York: Monthly Review Press, 1967); Stephen Andors, "Mass Mobilization in Communist Controlled Areas of China: 1937–1945."

2. Mao Tsetung, "Report to the Second Plenary Session of the Seventh Central Committee of the Chinese Communist Party," March 15, 1949, *Selected Works* (Foreign Languages Press: Peking, 1961), vol. IV, pp. 361–376.

3. Kenneth Lieberthal, "Tientsin," unpublished Ph.D. dissertation, Columbia University, 1973; Ezra Vogel, *Canton Under Communism* (Cambridge, Mass.: Harvard University Press, 1969). *See also* H. Arthur Steiner, "Chinese Communist Urban Policy," *American Political Science Review*, vol. XLIV, March 1950, pp. 47–63; and John W. Lewis, ed., *The City in Communist China* (Stanford: Stanford University Press, 1971).

4. Franz Schurmann, *The Logic of World Power* (New York: Pantheon, 1974), pp. 229 ff.

5. John Gittings, *The World and China, 1922–1972* (New York: Harper and Row, 1974), pp. 125–128, 169–170. *See also* Schurmann, *The Logic of World Power*, pp. 228–229.

6. Schurmann, *The Logic of World Power*, p. 229.

7. Mao Tsetung, "Report to the Second Plenary Session," *Selected Works*, p. 363.

8. Schurmann, *The Logic of World Power*, p. 232.

9. Harry Truman, "Proclamation," *American Foreign Policy, 1950–1955*, U.S. Department of State, Publication 6446, Superintendent of Documents (Washington: U.S. Government Printing Office, 1957), p. 2468.

10. Schurmann, *The Logic of World Power*, p. 233.

11. Mao Tsetung, "On the People's Democratic Dictatorship," *Selected Works*, vol. IV.

12. *Ibid.*

13. *Ibid.*

14. Schurmann, *The Logic of World Power*, p. 235.

15. Mao Tsetung, "On the People's Democratic Dictatorship," *Selected Works*, vol. IV.

16. John Gardner, "The 'Wu-Fan' Campaign in Shanghai," in A. Doak Barnett, ed., *Chinese Communist Politics in Action* (Seattle: University of Washington Press, 1969), p. 493.

17. Su K'o, "The Problem of Democratic Management of State-Private Enterprises Viewed in the Light of Workers Experience in Industrial Management," *KJJP*, Peking, Jan. 5, 1957, in *SCMP* #1491, March 18, 1957.

18. Gardner, "The Wu-Fan Campaign," p. 503.

19. For a good study of early mobility of skilled workers to management positions, Paul F. Harper, "Trade Union Cultivation of Workers for Leadership," in John Lewis, ed., *The City in Communist China* (Stanford: Stanford University Press, 1971).

20. "Democratic Reform in State Enterprises," *Ch'ang-chiang Jih-pao*, June 13, 1951 in *CB*, #115; Liu Tzu-chiu, "Democratic Reform in Factories and Mines," *K'ung-jen Jih-pao*, Sept. 12, 1951, in CB, #123, Oct. 5, 1951.

21. Gardner, "The Wu-Fan Campaign," p. 499.

22. Richman, *Industrial Society*, p. 134.

23. Richman, see chart, p. 899.

24. Gardner, "Wu-Fan Campaign," p. 493; Richman, *Industrial Society*, p. 433.

25. Leo Orleans, *Professional Manpower and Education in Communist China* NSF 61–3 (Washington, D.C.: U.S. Government Printing Office, 1961), pp. 125–127.

26. Gardner, "Wu-Fan Campaign," p. 482.

27. Richard Solomon, "Problems of Authority and Conflict in Chinese Social Process," in Barnett, *Chinese Communist Politics*, pp. 271–364.

28. NCNA, "The Case of the Shenyang Transformer Plant," *NCNA*, Peking, July 22, 1956 in *SCMP* #1344, p. 9–16.

29. Orleans, *Professional Manpower*, p. 43; Richman, *Industrial Society*, pp. 140–146.

30. An interview by K. S. Karol with an official in the Ministry of Higher Education in 1965 put the following percentages of students enrolled in universities as of working class or peasant background: 1952—20.46%; 1958—36.42%; 1962—42.34%; 1965—49.65%. Cited by Victor Nee, *The Cultural Revolution in Peking*

University (New York: Monthly Review Press, 1969), p. 13n. *See also* Richman, *Industrial Society*, p. 298.

31. Orleans, *Professional Manpower*, p. 130.

32. Richman, *Industrial Society*, pp. 126, 147, 169, 298. *See also* Orleans, *Professional Manpower*, pp. 46, 68–69.

33. See Appendix A, Tables 1 and 2.

34. Gardner, "The Wu-Fan Campaign," p. 503.

35. *NCNA*, Fukden, Sept. 21, 1952 and *Chuh-fang Jih-pao*, Shanghai, Sept. 7, 1952, both in *SCMP*, #421, pp. 14–16.

36. Richman, *Industrial Society*, p. 896; Gardner, "The Wu-Fan Campaign," pp. 493–494; Franz Schurmann, *Ideology and Organization*, pp. 246–247, 257.

37. Su K'o, "The Problem of Democratic Management of State-Private Enterprises Viewed in the Light of Workers' Experience in Industrial Management," *KJJP*, Peking, Jan. 5, 1957 in *SCMP*, #1491, March 18, 1957.

38. Schurmann describes the "one-man management" system and called the other one "plant manager responsibility under the collective leadership of the party." *Ideology and Organization*, pp. 255, 263. For a detailed survey of management during the 1949–1953 period, see William Brugger, *Democracy and Organization in the Chinese Industrial Enterprise* (New York: Cambridge University Press, 1976).

39. Su K'o, "The Problem of Democratic Management"; Gardner, "The Wu-Fan Campaign," p. 483.

40. Gardner, "The Wu-Fan Campaign," pp. 483, 485.

41. Su K'o, "The Problem of Democratic Management."

42. Liu Tzu-chiu, "Democratic Reforms in Factories and Mines," *KJJP*, Peking, Sept. 12, 1951, in *CB* #123, Oct. 5, 1951; "Democratic Reform in State Enterprises," *Ch'ang-chiang Jih-pao*, June 13, 1951; Gardner, "The Wu Fan Campaign," pp. 483, 497; Kenneth Lieberthal, unpublished Ph.D. dissertation, Columbia University.

43. Gardner, "The Wu-Fan Campaign," pp. 495–523.

44. Schurmann, *Ideology and Organization*, p. 263.

45. Gardner, "The Wu-Fan Campaign," p. 527; Paul Harper, "Trade Union Cultivation of Workers for Positions of Leadership," John Lewis, ed., *The City in Communist China*.

46. Gardner, "The Wu-Fan Campaign."

47. Liu Tzu-chiu, "Democratic Reform," in *CB*, #123.

48. *NCNA*, Peking, Sept. 14, 1955 in *SCMP*, #1134, sets Aug. 31, 1955 as the date of the State Council Decision to switch over to a wage system from the supply system. Ezra Vogel, "The Regularization of Cadres," *China Quarterly*, no. 29, January–March 1967, pp. 38–39.

49. Kojima Reitsu, "The Bearers of Science and Technology Have Changed," unpublished manuscript, Institute for Economic Development, Tokyo, Japan.

50. Roy Grow, "Liaoning," in Ed Winckler, ed., *A Provincial Handbook of China* (Stanford: Stanford University Press) [forthcoming].

51. Richman, *Industrial Society*, pp. 405–406.

52. *Ibid.*, p. 406.

53. Schurmann, *Ideology and Organization*, pp. 239–241. By 1952, sixty-eight of these had been completed according in E. L. Wheelwright and Bruce McFarlane, *The Chinese Road to Socialism* (New York: Monthly Review Press, 1970), p. 35.

54. Ibid., p. 241. See also *Ta Kung Pao*, Oct. 22, 1957, "Six Thousand Students Return to China from the Soviet Union" (Liu-ch'ien ming shih-hsüeh-sheng tsung su-lien hui-kuo).

55. "The Soviet Union Helps Our City to Train Large Numbers of Per-

sonnel" (Su-lien ch'uan-chia pang-chu wo shih p'ei-yang le ta-p'i jen-ts'ai), *Harbin Daily*, November 5, 1957.

56. For a good general essay defending the adoption of Soviet methods of planning and management, Ch'i Yün, "How China Proceeds With the Task of Industrialization" *JMJP*, Peking, May 22, 1953, in *CB*, #272.

57. Schurmann, p. 245.

58. *JMJP*, ed., "Learn the Use of Scientific Methods in Industrial Management," *JMJP*, Peking, June 19, 1953, in *SCMP* #601.

59. Schurmann, *Ideology and Organization*, pp. 242–262.

60. Ibid., pp. 251–252.

61. Charles Hoffman, *Work Incentives Practices and Policies in the Peoples Republic of China* (Albany: S.U.N.Y. Press, 1966).

62. Richman, *Industrial Society*, p. 314.

63. Vogel, "Regularization of Cadres," pp. 50–51.

64. *Ibid.*, p. 50.

65. Ibid., p. 51; Kojima Reütsu, "The Bearers of Science and Technology."

66. Ibid., p. 51.

67. Richman, *Industrial Society*, pp. 231–232, 314.

68. *JMJP*, ed., "Learn the Use of Scientific Methods in Industrial Management," *JMJP*, Peking, June 19, 1953 in *SCMP* #601; "No. 1 Ministry of Machine Industry Determines to Regard Operation Schedules as Central Task in Strengthening Planned Management," *JMJP*, July 28, 1953 in *SCMP* #639.

69. Mao Tsetung, "Reading Notes on the Soviet Political Economy."

70. Ting Tso-ch'eng, "Experiences Gained in Amalgamated Plants and Converting Them Into Jointly Operated Concerns," *Kung Shang Chieh* (*Industrial and Commercial Circles*), Peking, June 10, 1955, in *Extracts From China Mainland Magazines*, #11.

71. Richard Solomon, *Mao's Revolution and the Chinese Political Culture* (Berkeley: University of California Press, 1971), Part I.

72. Schurmann, *Ideology and Organization*, pp. 248–254.

73. "No. 1 Ministry of Machine Industry Determines to Regard Operation Schedule as Central Task in Strengthening Planned Management," *JMJP*, July 28, 1953 in *SCMP* #639.

74. Ibid. Also, Note 58 above.

75. "Strengthen Leadership Over Designing Work," *Chieh-fang Jih-pao*, Shanghai, July 8, 1954 in *SCMP* #900 Supplement.

76. NCNA reports for 1950–1953.

77. See Note 68.

78. "The Case of the Shenyang Transformer Plant," *NCNA*, Peking, July 22, 1956 in *SCMP* #1344, pp. 9–16.

79. *Ibid.*

80. William Brigger, unpublished paper, Contemporary China Institute, London, n.d.

81. *JMJP*, ed., "Eliminate the Evil Practice of Concealing Mistakes and Falsely Reporting Achievements in State Factories and Mines," *JMJP*, Oct. 18, 1953 in *SCMP* #676; also Note 78.

82. See Note 78.

83. Vogel, "The Regularization of Cadres," pp. 52–53; Schurmann, *Ideology and Organization*, p. 263.

84. See Note 58. *See also* "Shanghai Factories Obtain Preliminary Results in Promoting 'one-head' system," *Chieh-fang Jih-pao*, May 16, 1954 in *SCMP* #863, Supplement.

85. See Note 78.

86. Schurmann, *Ideology and Organization*, pp. 284–285.

87. *Ibid.*, pp. 285–286.

88. See Note 37.

89. For a detailed description of Lieberman's early proposal, see his "Cost Accounting and Material Encouragement of Industrial Personnel," in Myron E. Sharpe, ed., *Planning, Profit, and Incentives in the USSR*, 2 vols. (White Plains: IASP, 1966), vol. 1, pp. 3–19.

90. Sha Yi-mi, "After Reading Khrushchev's Report of February 1957," *TKP*, April 21, 1957.

91. *Nan-Fang Jih-Pao* editorial, "Resolutely Implement the System of Factory Manager Responsibility Under the Collective Leadership of the Party Committees," *NFJP*, Canton, Dec. 18, 1956 in *SCMP* #1495. *See also*, Schurmann, *Ideology and Organization*, pp. 288, 290–291.

92. Ibid.

93. For the English translation, *Survey of the China Mainland Press*, no. 1665, pp. 1–6.

94. Sharpe, ed., *Planning, Profit, Incentives*, pp. 10–12.

95. Schurmann, *Ideology and Organization*, p. 288.

96. *Ibid.*, pp. 290–291.

97. "Provincial Committee Convenes Industrial Political Work Conference" (Sheng-wei chao-k'ai kung-yeh cheng-chih kung-tso-hui), *Liaoning Daily* (*Liaoning Jih-pao*), April 24, 1957; *Shenyang Daily*, April 1, 1957.

98. "Party Leadership Is Not Just 'Strolling Across the Meadow' " (Tang-wei ling-tao ping-fei tsou 'Kuo ch'ang), *JMJP*, January 6, 1957.

99. Schurmann, *Ideology and Organization*, pp. 129, 291.

100. *Che-chiang Jih-pao* (Chekiang Daily), editorial, September 15, 1967.

101. "Engineering and Technical Personnel from Worker Background are Valuable" (Kung-jen ch'u-shen ti kung-ch'eng chi-shu-yuan ta kan-ming), *Shenyang Daily*, August 28, 1957.

102. Schurmann, *Ideology and Organization*, p. 291. *See also*, "How to Cultivate and Improve Basic Level Cadres" (Ju-ho p'ei-yang t'i-kao chi-ts'eng kan-pu) in *Coal Industry* (*Mei-t'an Kung-yeh*), September 19, 1957, and "Carry out Mass Line Education for Work-Section Chiefs" (Tui kung-tuan-chang chin-hsing ch'ün chung lu-hsien chiao-yü), *Liaoning Daily*, November 14, 1957.

103. *Chekiang Daily*, editorial, September 25, 1957; "How to Cultivate and Improve Basic Level Cadres," *Coal Industry*, September 19, 1957.

104. For an example of the complexity and detail of these regulations, see "Regulations Concerning the Responsibility of the Pit Director-Engineer" (K'ang chu-jen kung-ch'eng-shuai chih-tzu t'iao-liao) *Coal Industry*, September 19, 1957.

105. "Reduce the Number of Party Cadres in Enterprises Among the Masses Who Are Divorced from Production" (Chien-shao ch'i-yeh li-t'uo ch'an ti tang ch'ün kan-pu), *JMJP*, December 21, 1957.

106. "Honestly and Thoroughly Carry Out the Individual Responsibility System Under the Collective Leadership of the Party Committee" (Jen-chen kuan-ch'e tang-wei chi-t'i ling-tao-hsia ti jen-jen fu-tze-chih), *Inner Mongolia Daily* (*Nei-Meng-ku Jih-pao*), March 1, 1957. *See also*, "The Experience of the Swatow Waterworks in Carrying Out the System of Factory Manager Responsibility Under the Leadership of the Party Committee," (Sua-t'ou shui-ch'an shih-hsing tang-wei chi-t'i ling-tao hsia ti ch'an-chang fu-tse-chih ti ching-yen), *Southern Daily*, (*NFJP*), February 3, 1957.

107. Ibid., pp. 103–104 and Appendix A, Tables 1 and 2.

108. "Regulations Concerning . . . Pit Director-Engineer," *Coal Industry*, September 19, 1957.

109. "State Operated Enterprises Viewed from the Financial Viewpoint" (Ts'ai-cheng kuan-tien k'an kuo-ying ch'i-yeh), pp. 16–20. See Appendix B.

110. Mi Chin-tang and Li Miao-sheng, "The Administrative Meeting, the Mine Business Meeting, and the Arrangements Meeting Are Important Links in Organizing Leadership Work in Mines" (Hsing-cheng hui-yi, k'uang-wu hui-yi, ho tiao-tu hui-yi shih k'uang-ching tsu-chih ling-tao kung-tso ti chung-yao huan-chieh), *Coal Industry*, September 4, 1957.

111. For articles dealing with the powers of workers' congresses, see the following:

   a. "Kwangtung Provincial Party Committee Industrial Department Holds Industrial Meeting," *NFJP*, June 7, 1957.

   b. "Liaoning Provincial Party Congress Holds Meeting on Industry," *Liaoning Daily*, April 24, 1957.

   c. "Uncover Hidden Strength and Guarantee the Increase of Iron and Steel Production Plans" (K'ang chieh-li ting-ch'u ts'eng-ch'an kang-t'ieh chi-hua), *KJJP*, March 6, 1957.

   d. "A Workers' Congress in the Workshop" (Yi-ko ch'e-chien ti chih-kung ta-hui), *KJJP*, February 28, 1957.

   e. "The Workers' Representative Congress Develops Its Function" (Chih-kung tai-piao ta-hui lo tso-yung), *KJJP*, August 17, 1957.

   f. "Peking No. 2 State Cotton Textile Plant Settles on a Method for Beginning" (Pei-ching kuo-mien erh-ch'an ting-ch'u ch'u-pu pan-fa), *KJJP*, March 11, 1957.

   g. "Run Workers' Representative Congresses Well; Promote the Deep Development of the Production Increase and Economy Movement" (K'ai-hao chih-kung tai-piao ta-hui; t'ui-tung ts'eng-ch'an chieh-yueh yün-tung shen-ju k'ai-chan), *KJJP*, June 17, 1957.

112. Su K'o, "The Problem of Democratic Management," n. 37.

113. Mi Chin-tang, "The System of Leaders Meeting with the Masses Is an Important Method of Closely Relating to the Masses" (Ling-tao chieh-chien ch'ün-chung chih-tu shih mi-ch'ieh lien-hsi ch'ün-chung ti chung-yao fang-fa), *Coal Industry*, December 19, 1957.

114. Ibid., for these forms.

115. "Uncover Hidden Strength," *KJJP*, March 6, 1957.

116. Charles Hoffman, *Work Incentives, Practices and Policies in the People's Republic of China* (Albany: State University of New York Press, 1967) and "Work Incentive Policy in Communist China," in Cho Ming-li, ed., *Industrial Development in Communist China*; Peter Schran, "Unity and Diversity of Chinese Industrial Wage Policies," *Journal of Asian Studies* 23 (February 1964), 245–251; Richman, *Industrial Society*, pp. 311–314. Also Notes 64 and 65.

Chapter 4: Revolution and Modernization During the Great Leap Forward: "Politics in Command"

1. Alexander Eckstein, *China's Economic Development* (Ann Arbor: University of Michigan Press, 1975), pp. 23–27.

2. Soviet awareness of this weakness in China's international position and her willingness to take advantage of it could easily explain not only the real beginnings of the Sino-Soviet conflict, but the association between those who advocate a Soviet type development strategy with a pro-Soviet foreign policy line within China's political leadership after the Great Leap.

3. John Gittings, *The World and China*, pp. 239–241.

4. "Learn the Use of Scientific Methods in Industrial Management," *JMJP*, Peking, June 19, 1953, in *SCMP* #601.

5. Heilungkiang State Operated Chinghua Machine Tools Factory Party Committee, "A Preliminary Summing Up of the Experience of Cadre Participation in Production, Workers Participation in Management and Professional Reform" (Kuan-yu kan-pu ts'an-chia sheng-ch'an; kung-jen ts'an-chia kuan-li ho yeh-wu kai-ko ching-yen ti ch'u-pu tsung-chieh), *JMJP*, April 25, 1958. This article refers to the May 1957 directive.

6. The following analysis is taken from two sources written early in 1958: Li Hung-lin, "A Brief Talk on Bureaucracy," *Hsüeh-Hsi (Study)* #4, February 18, 1958; and "Take the Attitude of a Common Laborer," *JMJP*, ed., March 26, 1958, in *SCMP* #1755, pp. 6–9. Also, *Hung Ch'i (Red Flag)* published an article on the theory of the State and the problem of bureaucracy which was the same as the analysis in these two articles; see *SCMP* #1795, p. 4.

7. "Workers Representatives Talk About Workers Representative Congresses" (Chih-kung tai-piao t'an chih-kung tai-piao ta-hui), *KJJP*, Peking, January 22, 1957.

8. "The Way to Gradually Promote the Convening of Workers Representative Congresses in State Operated Enterprises" (Tsai kuo-ying ch'i-yeh chung ju-pu t'ui-kung chao-k'ai chih-kung tai'piao ta-hui ti pan-fa), *JMJP*, May 29, 1957.

9. The Trade union was generally responsible for convening workers' congresses, and many trade union cadres probably did not wish to see the practice eliminated. For example, see an article of the Shanghai Boiler Plant, "Utilize the Workers Representative Congress to Promote a Production High-tide" (Yün-yung chih-kung tai piao ta-hui t'ui-tung sheng-ch'an kao-ch'ao), *KJJP*, February 25, 1958; "Promoting Enterprise Reform and a High-tide in Production" (T'ui-tung lo ch'i-yeh cheng-kai ho sheng-ch'an kao-ch'ao), *KJJP*, February 26, 1958.

10. See the report on the Shihchingshan Iron and Steel Factory, *JMJP*, September 28, 1957. See also reports from other East China cities, including *Tientsin Daily*, October 20, 1957; *JMJP*, November 13, 1957; *Peking Ta Kung-pao*, October 18, 1957; *JMJP*, September 28, 1957; *Nanking Ta Kung-pao*, November 17, 1957; *T'aiyuan Shansi Daily*, November 6, 1957.

11. For articles dealing with this, see "Carry Out Education in the Mass Line for Section Leaders" (Tui kung-tuan-chang shih-hsing ch'ün-chung lu-hsien chiao-yü), *Liaoning Daily*, November 14, 1957; "Strengthen Leadership Work in Technical Studies for Young Workers" (Chia-ch'iang tui ch'ing-kung chi-shu hsueh-hsi ti ling-tao), *Chinese Youth*, (*Chung-kuo Ch'ing-nien*), January 23, 1958; "Engineering and Technical Personnel of Worker Background Number Over One Thousand" (Kung-jen ch'u-shen ti chi-shu kung-ch'eng jen-yüan to ch'ien-yü ming), *Shenyang Daily*, August 28, 1957; "Give Young Workers Basic Practice in Technique" (Hsiang ch'ing-nien kung-jen chin-hsing chi-pen chi-shu hsün), *Shenyang Daily*, January 18, 1957.

12. "Only Non-experts Can Lead Experts" (Chih-yu wai-hang tsai-neng ling nei-hang), *Wen-Hui-pao*, Shanghai, March 1958.

13. "The Situation Regarding the Changing Powers of Technical Personnel in the #8 Rubber Plant" (Hsing-chiao pa-ch'an kai-pien chi-shu jen-yüan yü chih-yüan ch'uan-li chuang-k'uang), *Changchun Daily*, June 2, 1957; "Democracy Can't Be Developed This Way" (Pu-neng che-yang fa-yang min-chu), *Heilungkiang Daily*, March 11, 1957.

14. "Industrial Departments Also Must Plant Experimental Fields" (Kung-yeh pu-men yeh-yao chung shih-yen-tien), *NFJP*, March 25, 1958. The relationships between industry and agricultural methods of experimentation was noted in an article in *JMJP*, "A New Experience in Planting Experimental Fields in Industry" (Kung-yeh chung chien-li shih-yen tien ti hsin ching-yen), *JMJH*, March 24, 1958.

15. Chang Chin-yu, "Foushin Central Machine Repair Plant's Leading Cadres Preliminary Experience in 'Planting Experimental Fields' " (Foushin chung-yang

chi-hsiu-ch'an ling-tao kan-pu kao 'shih-yen-tien' ti ch'u-pu ching-yen), *Coal Industry*, April 4, 1958.

16. "How We Plant Experimental Fields" (Wo-men tsem-yang kao shih-yen-tien ti), *KJJP*, Peking, March 14, 1958; Shanghai, *Wen-Hui-pao*, March 1, 1958.

17. "Carry Out 'Laboring With the Shifts'" (Shih-hsing 'ken pan lao-tung'), *JMJP*, March 14, 1958.

18. "Plant 'Experimental Fields' Well, Manage Production Affairs Well" (Chung-hao 'shih-yen'tien', Kuan-hao sheng-ch'an shih), *JMJP*, April 19, 1958; Yuan Cheng, "Leave the Offices," *JMJP*, April 1, 1958.

19. See Note 11.

20. "Cadres in Paint Factory Plant Experimental Fields and at First Reap a Bitter Harvest (Yu-tan-ch'an kan-pu chung-tien ch'u-t'ui hsin-shou), *Sheng-Ch'an-pao*, Dairen, April 14, 1958. *See also* "Only Non-experts Can Lead Experts," *Wen-Hui-pao*, March 1958.

21. "Divide Up Work and Send it Down to Small Groups" (Pu-fen kung-tso hsia-fang tao hsiao-tsu), *JMJP*, April 10, 1958. "Eliminate Red Tape to Improve Financial Management Systems" (Tan p'o-ch'u-ch'u kuei-kuei kai-chin ts'ai-wu kuan-li chih-tu), *Kuang-hsi Jih-pao*, February 15, 1958; "Plant Experimental Fields Well," *JMJP*, April 19, 1958; "Reform Interrelationships in the Production Process" (Kai-chin sheng-ch'an kuo-ch'eng chung ti hu-hsiang kuan-hsi), *JMJP*, April 24, 1958; Huang Shih-lin, "Leadership Workstyle Undergoes a Big Revolution, Production is Given a Big Push for a Great Leap Forward" (Ling-tao tso-feng ta ko-ming, Ts'u-chin sheng-ch'an ta yüeh-chin), *Ch'ang-chou Jih-pao*, March 29, 1958; Hui Hung-pin, "Labor With the Shifts: A Great Revolution in Leadership Method" (Ken-pan lao-tung: Yi-ko ling-tao fang-fa ti ko-ming), *Ch'ang-chou Jih-pao*, April 8, 1958; "The Results of the #2 Textile Plant's Experience Blossoms Forth" (Kuo-mien erh-ch'an ti ching-yen k'ai-hua chieh-kuo), *Hsin Wen-pao*, Shanghai, March 31, 1958.

22. "The 'Floating Office' Solves Problems Faster, Better, and More Economically" ('Liu-tung pan-kung-shih' chieh-chüeh wen-t'i tuo-k'uai-hao-sheng), *Lü-ta Jih-pao*, April 11, 1958.

23. For example, the beginning of the attempts to create workers who could do more than one job and handle both production and administration (called Jacks-of-all-trades or "to-mien-shou"), began in late 1957 but was accelerated in the first months of 1958. "Everyone Chooses to Become a Jack of All Trades" (Jen-jen cheng-ch'u ch'eng-wei "to-mien-shou", *JMJP*, March 31, 1958; "Production Increases Greatly While Personnel Are Fewer" (Sheng-ch'an ta-ts-'eng, kung-jen ta-chien), *JMJP*, April 19, 1958; "In Three to Five Years, People Can Become Red Experts" (San wu-nien-nei, jen-ch'eng-wei hung-ssu ch'uan chia), *NFJP*, March 30, 1958.

24. "Anshan and Other Units Actively Cultivate Technical Personnel (An-kang teng tan-wei chi-chi p'ei-yang chi-shu jen-yuan), *JMJP*, January 4, 1957. *See also* "Cadres of Worker and Peasant Status Drafted From Industrial System Given Intensive Course of Training in Secondary Trade Schools," *NCNA*, Peking, Feburay 15, 1958 in *SCMP*, #1716, 1958. These men "were in the main, veterans of the anti-Japanese War. Most had worked for more than two years in industrial systems and were under forty with an educational standard of junior middle school. *See also*, "Cultivate a Leading Backbone of Technicians Both Red and Expert" (P'ei-yang yu-hung yu-chuan ti chi-shu ling-tao ku-kan), *JMJP*, February 22, 1958.

25. Richman, *Industrial Society*, p. 435, notes that the "entire party leadership group" in Liaoning Province changed during the anti-Rightist Campaign of 1957.

26. Wang Hao-feng, "A Great Reform in Enterprise Management" (Ch'i-yeh kuan-li ch'ung-ta kao-ko), *JMJP*, April 26, 1958.

27. *ECMM*, #143, pp. 9–12.

28. "A Preliminary Summing Up of the Experience of Cadre Participation in Labor, Worker Participation in Management, and Functional Reforms" (Kuan-yu kan-pu ts'an-chia sheng-ch'an, kung-jen ts'an-chia kuan-li ho yeh-wu kai-ko ching-yen ti ch'u-pu ts'ung-chieh), *JMJP*, April 25, 1958.

29. *SCMP*, #1765, "Experience of a Machine Tool Plant in Industrial Management," *NCNA*, Peking, April 25, 1958.

30. Ibid.

31. *SCMP*, #1765.

32. *JMJP*, ed., "An Important Beginning for Reform of Industrial Management," May 7, 1958, in *SCMP*, #1774.

33. "Carry Out Big Investigations of Industrial Enterprise Reforms" (Tui kung-yeh ch'i-yeh cheng-feng sheng-ch'an chin-hsing ta chien-ch'a), *Nanking Daily*, May 25, 1958.

34. *Nan-fang Jih-pao* editorial, May 16, 1958.

35. "Push Forward A Double Great Leap in Production Reforms" (T'ui-tung cheng-feng sheng-ch'an shuang yüeh-chin), *Ch'ang-chiang Daily*, May 13, 1958.

36. *Chekiang Daily* editorial, May 28, 1958; *Kansu Daily*, October 22, 1958.

37. "Industrial Management Must Follow the Mass Line" (Ch'i-yeh kuan-li yao tsou ch'ün-chung lu-hsien), *Peking Daily*, June 9, 1958.

38. Ibid. *See also JMJP*, ed., May 7, 1958; Wang Hao-feng, "A Great Reform . . ."; "A Double Harvest in Production and Management" (Sheng-ch'an yü kuan-li shuang-feng-shou), *Inner Mongolia Daily*, August 17, 1958.

39. *Peking Daily*, June 9, 1958.

40. Fang Jung-k'ang, " 'Rural Work' and 'Guerilla Habit' are Orthodox Marxism" in *Cheng-chih Hsueh-hsi* (*Political Study*) #10, October 13, 1958, *ECMM* #150. *See also* Li Hsueh-feng, "The Question of the Mass Line in Industrial Management," *Hung Ch'i* (*Red Flag*) #4, August 2, 1958.

41. Lo Hsueh-feng, "The Question of the Mass Line in Industrial Management."

42. See Note 40.

43. Victor Li, "The Role of Law in Communist China," *China Quarterly* 44 (October–December 1970), pp. 100–101. *See also* Richman, pp. 278–279, 385–389; "Cooperative Meetings and Contracts Grow in Use" (Hsieh-tso-hui yüeh ch'i ta tso-yung), *KJJP*, May 9, 1958; "Systematize Regular, All-Around Cooperation" (Hsing-ch'eng hsi-t'ung ching-ch'ang ch'uan-mien ta-hsieh-tso), *Liaoning Daily*, June 17, 1958; "Three Areas in Canton Begin Production Cooperation Meetings (Kuang-chou san-ch'u k'ai sheng'ch'an hsieh-tso ts'hui), *JMJP*, June 30, 1958; "Promote Small-Scale Cooperation Meetings; Organize Each Factory to Check Inventory" (Yün-yung hsiao-hsing hsieh-tso hui-yi; tso-chih ko ch'an hu-t'ung yu-wu), *KJJP*, July 16, 1958; *CFJP*, Shanghai, April 29, 1958; *JMJP*, ed., August 6, 1958, "Mutual Assistance and Coordination—The Communist Working Style," *SCMP* #1831, pp. 1–4; "Use This Method To Do Accounting" (Yung che-tzu fang-fa chin-hsing ho-tzu), *Finance* (*Tsai-cheng*), July 5, 1958.

44. For examples of how this worked in practice, see reports on the Tientsin #4 State Cotton Textile Mill, "Reform Financial Work, Utilize Standards to Improve Production Management" (Kai-chin tsai-hui kung-tso li-yung chi-piao tsu-chin sheng-ch'an kuan-li), *Finance*, October 9, 1958; the Tientsin Hua-ta Dyeing Plant, "Finance System Set Up and Reformed in 20 Days" (Ku-chien erh-shih t'ien kai-pien tsai-hui kung-tso), *Finance*, October, 1958; The Liaoning High Voltage Switch Factory, "Production Can Be Increased Without Increasing

Floating Capital" (Pu-tseng liu-tung tzu-chin chiu-neng tseng-ch'an), *Ta Kung-pao*, n.d.; the Chengchow #3 State Operated Textile Plant by Sun Chin-Lua and Hsü Wei-hsiung, "The Management of Floating Capital Must Follow the Mass Line" (Kuan-li liu-tung tzu-chin pi-hsiu ch'ieh ch'ün-chung lu-hsien), *Finance*, June 5, 1958; and the Tairen Steel Mill, "Politics in Command, Rely on the Masses, Manage Floating Capital" (Cheng-chih kua-shuai, yi-k'ao ch'ün-chung, kuan-hao liu-tung tzu-chin), *TKP*, June 1958.

45. Jung Tze-ho, "Several Problems on the Improvement of the Financial Management System," in *Finance*, #1, January 1958, translation in *ECMM*, #126, pp. 48–57.

46. "Carry Out the 'Constitution' for Enterprises; Handle the Mass Movement in a Big Way (Kuan-ch'e ch'i-yeh 'hsien-fa'; ta kao ch'ün-chung yün-tung), *JMJP*, November 20, 1958; for a report on the Pao t'ou Machinery Plant, see *Inner Mongolia Daily*, August 17, 1958.

47. "Heilungkiang Experience Blossoms in Tientsin" (Hei-lung-chiang ching-yen tsai Tian-chien k'ai-hua), *KJJP*, Peking, May 18, 1958; "Everyone a Worker and Everyone a Manager" (Jen-jen shih sheng-ch'an che, jen-jen shih kuan-li che), *KJJP*, Tientsin, May 8, 1958. "Preliminary Experience of the Changchiang Electric Plant in Promoting Cadre Participation in Labor, Worker Participation in Management and Big Reform of Functional Work" *Szechwan Daily*, n.d. 1958.

48. "A Great Development in Socialist Enterprise Management" (She-hui chu-yi ch'i-yeh kuan-li chih-tu ti ch'ung-ta fa-chen), *Nanking Jih-pao*, May 12, 1958.

49. *KJJP*, Peking, May 8, 1958.

50. "Electron Tube Factory Has Inspection Personnel Participate in Labor in Shifts" (Tien-tzu-kuan ch'an shih-hsing chien-ch'a-yüan ken-pan lao-tung), *Nanking Jih-pao*, May 7, 1958.

51. Wu Wen-pin, "Unreasonable Regulations and Systems Must Be Reformed," *Che-hsueh Yen-chiu* (philosophical study) #4, August 10, 1958, in *ECMM*, #146, pp. 9–13. *See also* "Breakdown Superstition: Technical Work Follows the Mass Line" (P'o-ch'u mi-hsin; chi-shu kung-tso tsou ch'ün-chung lu-hsien), *Hopei Daily*, June 22, 1958.

52. *Nanking Daily*, May 12, 1958, article on the Chenkuang Machine Tool Plant.

53. Jao Pin, "Changchun Motor Car Works Strives for an Annual Output of 150,000 Motor Cars," *Hung Ch'i*, #12, November 16, 1958, in *ECMM* #156, pp. 43–48.

54. "Workers Take Part in Technical Management and the Triple Combination is Systematized" (Kung-jen tsan-chia chi-shu kuan-li; san-chieh-ho chic-tu-hua), *Liaoning Daily*, December 22, 1958.

55. Richman, *Industrial Society*, p. 129.

56. "Workers Take the Initiative in Running Technical Schools" (Chih-kung tung-shou pan chi-shu hsueh-hsiao), *KJJP*, Peking, June 15, 1958.

57. *NCNA*, August 11 and 25, 1958.

58. *NCNA*, November 13, 1958.

59. Peking, *NCNA*, October 31, 1958.

60. "How We Train Worker-Statisticians" (Wo-men shih tsem-yeng p'ei hsün kung-jen t'ung-chi-yuan ti), *Statistical Work*, December 29, 1958.

61. Wang Chin-sheng and Wang Lien-ch'un, "Many Talents, Many Techniques: If Something is Lacking, It is Learned" (Tuo-tsai tuo-yi, chueh-she, hsueh-she), *China Youth*, August 19, 1958.

62. "Cultivate and Uncover Workers' Experiences" (P'ei-hsün chueh-chin kung-jen ti ching-yen), *Coal Industry*, December 19, 1958.

63. Richman, *Industrial Society*, pp. 129–130.

64. *NCNA*, Peking, January 11, July 16, April 20, 1960.

65. "Anshan Steel Works and Other Units Actively Train Technical Personnel" (An-kang teng-tan-wei chi-chi p'ei-hsün chi-shu jen-yuan), *JMJP*, January 4, 1957.

66. "This Is the Way We Raise the Professional Level of Work Section and Group Leaders" (Wo-men shih che-yang t-i'kao pan-tuan-chang yeh-wu shui-p'ing ti), *Coal Industry*, November 19, 1957.

67. "Chungking Construction Machinery Plant Trains a Group of Cadres Both Workers and Technicians" (Ch'ung-ching chien-she chi'ch'uang ch'an p'ei-hsün ch'u yi-p'i kung-jen chi-shu kan-pu), *Szechwan Daily*, April 28, 1958.

68. *NCNA*, March 4, 1959.

69. "Training Technical Personnel for the Nation for Five Years" (Wu-nien-wei kuo-chia p'ei-yang chi-shu yüan), *Wen Hui-pao*, Shanghai, January 22, 1958.

70. "Technical Personnel of Working Class Background Increase Greatly" (Kung-jen ch'u-shen to chi-shu jen-yuan ta-tseng), *Wen Hui-pao*, May 25, 1958. For other evidence of the enormous increase in the number of basic level cadres, both Party and non-Party, with at least some technical and administrative talent during the years 1958–1959, see report from Chengtu, *China Domestic Service*, Peking, August 5, 1960; *NCNA*, Peking, October 12, 1959; *China Pictorial* #24, December 20, 1959, especially the article by Cheng Tien, "From Workers to Engineers." See also a report on the Heilungkiang Chia-ma-ssu Textile Mill, "Raise the Level of Worker-Managers (T'i kao kung-jen kuan-li-yuan kung-tso shui-p'ing), *KJJP*, Peking, September 17, 1960. Also, "Tientsin Introduces Worker-Engineers to the Repair Section" (Tien-chien chu-pan kung-jen kung-ch'eng-shai chin hsiu-pan), *JMJP*, September 17, 1960; and "Factories and Mines in Peking Train Large Number of Leading Cadres," (Pei-ching-shih ko ch'an-k'uang ch'i-yeh p'ei-hsun lo ta-p'i kung-jen ch'u-shen ti ling-tao kan-pu), *JMJP*, February 2, 1960; and "Providing a Backbone for the Frontlines of the Nation's Iron and Steel Industry" (Hsiang Kuo-chia kang-t'ieh chan-hsien yu-sung ku-kan li-liang), *JMJP*, February 27, 1960.

71. "Workers of Chi Shu Yen Locomotive and Vehicle Plant Do Away with Piece Wage System," *KJJP*, Peking, October 18, 1958, in *CB* #537, pp. 19–20.

72. Shih Ch'ing, "Don't Let Money Assume Command," *JMJP*, October 16, 1958, *CB* #537, pp. 5–8.

73. *NCNA*, October 21, 1958, *CB* #537, pp. 20–22.

74. *NCNA*, October 21, 1958, in *CB* #537, pp. 21–24.

75. Charles Hoffman, *Work Incentives, Practices and Politics in the People's Republic of China, 1953–1965* (Albany: State University of New York Press, 1967), pp. 97–100.

76. *JMJP*, October 13, 1958, *CB* #537, pp. 1–5.

77. Vogel, *The Regularization of Cadres*, pp. 49–50.

78. *JMJP*, October 17, 1958, *CB* #537, pp. 8–10.

79. Hoffman, *Work Incentives*, pp. 18–22.

80. Richman notes the average wage for a worker was 65y/m by the 1955 wage reform, with the minimum for a factory director or vice-director about 132y/m. Technicians and key specialists earned 2–3 times as much as an average worker, a remarkable low income differential ratio when compared to the U.S. or USSR or other countries. Richman, *Industrial Society*, p. 231; Hoffman, *Work Incentives*, p. 121.

81. Hoffman, *Work Incentives*, p. 17; Joyce Kallgren, "Social Welfare and China's Industrial Workers" in A. Doak Barnett, ed., *Chinese Communist Politics in Action* (Seattle: University of Washington Press, 1969), for a detailed dis-

cussion of the nature of social welfare programs in China. Wei Li, "The System of Wage Allowances Should be Radically Reformed" in *Planned Economy*, May 9, 1958, *ECMM* #135, pp. 29–32, for an argument to change the system of deducting a fixed portion of the wage bill of a given enterprise for welfare to a system of national standards, regardless of the enterprise wage bill. The purpose of this was supposedly to make welfare less a function of size and technical development and more a basic guarantee to all. This seems to have been the one approach to welfare during the Great Leap. There is no evidence to point to a movement toward abolishing basic social welfare insurance as being "non-revolutionary."

82. Richman, *Industrial Society*, p. 315; Hoffman, *Work Incentives*, pp. 58–79, 97–103.

83. Robert Walker, ed., *Modern Technology and Civilization*, pp. 114–118, 243–268.

84. Ibid., pp. 119–135. "Workers Want to Learn Many Techniques" (Kung-jen yao-hsüeh to-chung chi-shu), *JMJP*, July 28, 1958; Ch'en Chih-yen, "Continue Developing the 'Jack of all Trades' Trend" (Ch'ao-chao 'to-mien-shou' ti fang-hsiang fa-chen), *Political Study*, August 13, 1958; "Everyone Chooses to Become a 'Jack of all Trades' " (Jen-jen cheng-ch'u ch'eng-wei 'to-mien-shou,' " *JMJP*, March 31, 1958; Braverman, *Labor and Monopoly Capital*, pp. 35–38.

85. Ch'eng Feng, "Balance in the Financial Economic System and Planning" in *Hsin Chien-she* #8, August 1958, *ECMM* #146, pp. 40–47.

86. Shantung Provincial Party Committee, Industry and Communications Department, "The Combining of Manual and Mental Labor Promotes the Development of Production" (T'i-li lao-tung ho nao-li lao-tung hsiang chieh-ho tsu-chin sheng-ch'an ti fa-chan), *Construction*, 1958, (n.d.).

87. Yao Wen-yuan, "Disprove the 'Communism Breeds Laziness' Theory," *Shanghai Wen Hui-pao*, October 23, 1958, *SCMP* #1900, pp. 2–5. *Also see* Fan Ch'ang-chiang, "The Question of Motive Power of Intellectuals," *China Youth* #11, June 1, 1958, in *ECMM* #142, pp. 1–9.

88. "Rely on the Masses, Reform the System of Enterprise Management" (Yi-k'ao ch'ün-chung kai-ko ch'i-yeh kuan-li chih-tu), *JMJP*, November 27, 1958, translated in *SCMP* #1914, pp. 2–5.

89. "Promote the 'Fan-shen' Movement" (Ta-kao fan-shen yün-tung), *Liaoning Daily*, January 10, 1959.

90. Sun Yun-lung, "How to Consolidate and Develop the Work of Two Participations and One Reform" (Tsem-yang kung-ku ho fa-chan 'liang-tsan yi-kai' kung-tso), *KJJP*, Peking, January 20, 1959. *See also* Wang Shu-yen and Liu Shu-min, "How We Consolidate the Workers Participation in Management," *KJJP*, Peking, August 21, 1959, *SCMP* #2106, pp. 11–14.

91. "The 'Two Participations, One Reform and Triple Combination' System at Ch'-inghua Has a Big Development" ('Liang-tsan yi-kai san-chieh-ho'chih-tu yu ch'ung-ta fa-chan), *JMJP*, July 12, 1960; "New Management System, New Leadership Method" (Hsin-ti kuan-li chih-tu, hsin ti ling-tao fang-fa), *KJJP* editorial, Peking, July 5, 1960.

92. "Introducing the Experience of Heilungkiang Province's Chinghua Machine Tool Plant, Chienhua Machinery Plant, and Hua-An Machinery Plant" (Chieh-shao Hei-lung-chiang-sheng ch'ing-hua kung-chu-ch'an, chien-hua chi-hsieh ch'an, hua-an chi-hsieh ch'an ti ching-yen), *JMJP*, November 7, 1959.

93. Information on the Harbin Ballbearing Factory came from the following sources: "Harbin Ballbearing Plant Builds a Machine-Foreman System; Strongly Promotes Leap in Production" (Ho-erh-pin ch'ou-ch'eng-ch'an chien-li chi-t'ai-chang chih, yu-li t'ui-tung sheng ch'an yüeh-chin), *KJJP*, May 28, 1959; "Meeting

of Cadres at Four Levels in Harbin Ballbearing Plant Becomes a System"
(Ho-erh-pin ch'ou-ch'eng ch'an szu-chi kan-pu-hui hsing-ch'eng chih-tu), *JMJP*,
June 6, 1959; "Combine Professional Management with Participation of the
Masses in Management," *KJJP*, Peking, July 19, 1959, in *SCMP* #2080, pp. 11–16.

94. *Chinese Domestic Service*, Peking, July 3, 1959; "Changchun #1 Auto
Plant Re-orders Production Sequences and Firmly Grasps Functional Plans"
(Chang-ch'un ti-yi ch'i-ch'e-ch'an cheng-tun sheng-ch'an chih-hsu chin-kua tso-yeh
chi-hua), *KJJP*, August 18, 1959; "Tientsin #2 Heating Equipment Plant Unites
Production" (T'ien-chien ti-erh shui-huan ch'i-ts'ai-ch'an chieh-ho sheng-ch'an),
KJJP, July 5, 1959; *Chinese Domestic Service*, Peking, December 1, 1959;
"Strengthen Maintenance and Repair of Equipment to Guarantee Safety in Pro-
duction" (Chia-ch'iangshe-pei wei-hsiu pao-cheng an'ch'uan sheng-ch'an), *JMJP*,
June 6, 1959; "Ta-lien Diesel Engine Plant Strengthens Basic Level Management"
(Ta-lien ts'ai-yu chi ch'an chia-ch'iang chi-tseng kuan-li), *JMJP*, June 8, 1959;
"Everything Has Someone to Manage It and Someone Responsible for It" (Shih-
shih yu jen kuan-li, chien-chien yu jen fu-tse), *JMJP*, May 19, 1959.

95. Wang Hao-feng, "Consolidate and Develop the 'Two Participations, One
Reform, and Triple Combination System'; Raise the Standard of Enterprise
Management in All Respects," *Hung Ch'i (Red Flag)* #15, August 1, 1960, trans.
in *SCMM* #224, pp. 18–32.

96. "Harbin Measuring Instruments and Cutting Tools Factory Promotes
Small Group Economic Accounting" (Ho-erh-pin liang-chu-tao-chu-ch'an t'ui-hsing
hsiao-tsu ching-chi k'o-suan-chih), June 3, 1959; "Strengthen Financial Manage-
ment" (Chien-ch'uan ts'ai-wu kuan-li), *Tientsin Daily*, August 31, 1959; Tseng
Chih, "On the Mass Movement to Institute the Business Accounting System,"
Hung Ch'i, #14, July 16, 1960, trans. in *SCMM* #233, pp. 20–28; Li Hsien-nien,
"Text of Financial Report to NPC," *NCNA* English, Peking, March 31, 1960, in
CB #615, pp. 26–38.

97. "Shanghai #5 Printing and Dyeing Mill Factory Level Cadres Fix Time
to 'Serve in the Ranks' " (Shang-hai ti-wu yin-jan-ch'an ch'an-chi kan-pu ting ch'i
'tang-ping'), *JMJP*, February 25, 1959; "On the Question of Cadres' Participation
in Physical Labor," *Hung Ch'i* #2, January 16, 1960 in *ECMM* #200, p. 16;
JMJP ed., " 'Combination of the Three' Vital to Progress" *NCNA*, Peking, April
9, 1960.

98. "Conference of Industrial Secretaries of CCP Municipal and District
Committees in Shantung Urges All-Around Overfulfillment of State Plans," *Ta
Chung Pao*, Tsinan.

99. There seemed to be some retention of piece wage even during the Great
Leap period although the evidence does not suggest a good deal of this. See, e.g.,
"Intensively Develop the Labor Emulation Campaign at the Level of Work Squads
and Groups," *NCNA*, Peking, October 7, 1960. Po I-po noted in an article in
Hung Ch'i in May 1960 that the "time work wage system is the main foundation
of material reward, and piece rate wage system and 'bonus system' is the sub-
sidiary." See Po I-po, "New Development in Technical Revolution," *Hung Ch'i*
#10, May 15, 1960 in *SCMP* #2268, pp. 1–14. As early as January 1959, the
attitude toward piece wages seemed to be ambivalent. See Wang P'u "There is
No Negating the Principle of Material Interests," *JMJP*, January 20, 1959, in
SCMP #1947, pp. 1–5; *also* Sun Shang-ch'ing, "On the Nature and Destiny of
Our Current Piece Rate Wage System," *Ching-chi Yen-chiu* #4, April 17, 1959,
in *ECMM* #180, pp. 35–40.

100. "A New Form of Management System for Socialist Enterprises" (Hsin-
hsing ti she-hui chu-yi ch'i-yeh kuan-li chih-tu), *JMJP*, June 24, 1960, translated
in *SCMP* #2295, pp. 3–16.

101. Yang Lin, "Why Should Care Be Taken to Improve the Work of Party Teams," *JMJP*, December 17, 1960, in *SCMP* #2409, pp. 17–19; "Really Grasp the Work of Small Groups" (Cha-cha shih-shih kua hsiao-tsu kung-tso), *JMJP*, August 16, 1960; "Make Sure of Responsibility and Strength Systems" (Ming-ch'ueh ch'ing-jen ch'ien-ch'uan chih-tu), *JMJP*, May 16, 1959.

102. Cheng Tien, "From Workers to Engineers" and "What Mechanization Means to Shanghai Workers" *NCNA*, English, Shanghai, August 8, 1960 in *SCMP* #2316, pp. 18–20. See a report on the Peking #1 Machine Tool Plant, Chen Ch'i, "Ten Years Persistent Effort at Workers Spare Time Education in Peking's #1 Lathe and Machinery Plant," August 16, 1960 in *SCMM* #229, pp. 1–7.

103. "A Party Team that is Good at Carrying Out Ideological Work," *JMJP*, December 17, 1960, in *SCMP* #2409, pp. 13–16; Ku Ta-chen, "A Trade Union Must Take the Initiative and Active Steps to Play the Part of a Good Lieutenant to the Party," *Chinese Labor* #19, October 12, 1949, *ECMM* #198, pp. 40–44.

104. See series of articles in *Current Background* #640, pp. 16–12: "Work and Rest Must Be Combined in the Correct Proportions," *KJJP*, July 26, 1960; "Proper Rest for Workers of Tool Workshop of Chengchow Textile Machine Factory, *KJJP*, July 26, 1960; and "Coal Mine Workers Achieve Success in Production and Study and Have a Good Rest," *KJJP*, July 21, 1960.

105. Janet Goldwasser and Stuart Dowty, *Huan Ying: Workers China*, (New York: Monthly Review Press, 1975), pp. 65–66.

106. "Workers Dorms Generally Re-organized in Taiyuan" *JMJP*, April 15, 1960, in *SCMP* #2255, pp. 4–5.

107. "Admit Your Mistakes and Rectify Them" CCP Committee, Tsamkong Chemical Works, *NFJP*, Canton, November 13, 1960 in *SCMP* #2400, pp. 4–6.

108. "One Does the Work of Several Movement Energetically Developed in Fuhsun," *KJJP*, Peking, July 10, 1960.

109. Hsia Tun, "Investment Contract System, A Revolution in the Management of Capital Construction," *Hung Ch'i* #6, March 16, 1960, in *SCMM* #207, pp. 22–28; "Carry Out More Properly the Investment by Contract System," *JMJP* ed., March 12, 1960, in *SCMP* #2220, pp. 3–6.

110. Li Hsien-nien, "Several Problems in Finance and Banking Work," *Hung Ch'i* #1 January 1, 1960.

111. Yueh Kuang-ming, "Fully Mobilize the Mass of Workers" *KJJP*, August 23, 1959, in *SCMP* #2106, pp. 7–11; *Chinese Domestic Radio*, Peking, November 26, 1960, for report on Chungking Iron and Steel.

112. "How Strength Should Be Concentrated to Master the Major Links," *JMJP* ed., December 4, 1960, in *SCMP* #2400, pp. 1–4.

113. "Comprehensively Utilize the Available Materials and Develop Multiple Undertakings" *Hung Ch'i* #19, October 1, 1960, in *SCMM* #239, pp. 25–32.

114. Huang Hu-ch'ing, "Promote the Spirit of Communist Cooperation," *JMJP*, Peking, January 23, 1960, in *SCMM* #2201, pp. 1–16; "Improve Directing Methods by Industrial Control Authorities" *JMJP* ed., October 24, 1960, in *SCMP* #2378, pp. 19–22.

115. See Note 113, "Improve Directing Methods" and *NCNA*, Peking, December 4, 1960.

116. See Note 113, "Improve Directing Methods."

117. Shih Ching, "The Negation that Negates Everything," *JMJP*, Peking, August 30, 1959, in *SCMP* #2093, pp. 2–5; "Communique of the Eighth Plenary Session of the Eighth Central Committee of the CCP," *NCNA*, English, Peking, August 26, 1959, in *CB* #589, pp. 1–4.

Chapter 5: Industrial Enterprises in the Aftermath of the
Great Leap Forward, 1961–1963

1. This theory of cycles or oscillations in Chinese politics is a common one. Chinese politics, from this perspective, is analyzed in terms of how quickly "radicals" or "revolutionaries" are replaced by "moderates" and "pragmatists" after a mass mobilization campaign.

2. The evidence on this point is largely circumstantial. For members of the Central Committee, the Lushan Plenum and subsequent debates between individuals make it clear that high level party members, probably from the Provincial Level Party Committees on up, must have been sharply aware of differences over how to evaluate the Great Leap Forward. But the conscious awareness of this basic disagreement in lower levels are less easily ascertainable. Statements during the Cultural Revolution as to the "consciousness" over the struggle between the "two lines" suggest that the overwhelming majority of cadres were not aware of major political disagreements as long as the higher level party organs showed a façade of unity.

3. E. L. Wheelwright and Bruce McFarlane, *The Chinese Road to Socialism* (New York: Monthly Review Press, 1970), chap. 2. For two of the better evaluations of causation, see Audrey Donnithorne, *China's Economic System* (London: Allen and Unwin, Ltd., 1968), passim; Richman, *Industrial Society*.

4. *NCNA*, Peking, January 20, 1961, "Communique of the Ninth Plenum of the Eighth CCP Central Committee."

5. "Miscellany of Mao Tse-tung Thought: 1949–1968" in *JPRS* #61269–2, February 20, 1974; John Gittings, "New Light on Mao," *China Quarterly* #60, December 1974.

6. Po I-po, "For New Victories in Industrial Production and Construction in Our Country" *Hung Ch'i* #3–4, February 1, 1961, in *SCMM* #250, pp. 9–18.

7. *JMJP* ed., "All Enterprises Should Establish and Perfect the Responsibility System," *NCNA*, Peking, February 22, 1961.

8. "Perfecting Responsibility Systems," *Chieh-Fang* #7, Shanghai, June 5, 1961, in *SCMM* #312, pp. 16–20. For other articles which stress the same themes in great detail, see Hai Po, "On the Question of Authority in Socialist Economic Work: After Reading Engels' 'On Authority'," *Hung Ch'i* #1, January 1, 1962, in *SCMM* 298, pp. 24–30; "An Important Problem in Strengthening Enterprise Leadership Work" (Chia-ch'iang ch'i-yeh ling-tao kung-tso ti yi-ko chung-yao wen-t'i), *JMJP*, August 4, 1961 in *SCMP* #2561, pp. 7–10. *See also*, Fei Wu-wen, Kuei Shih-yung, and Liu Fu-yung, "On the Responsibility System of the Socialist State Owned Industrial Enterprises," in *Ching-chi Yen-chiu* #7, August 3, 1962, in *SCMM* #333, pp. 29–41.

9. See Notes 6, 8.

10. *Ibid.*

11. *Ibid. See also* Hsü Hsin-hsüeh, "Further Strengthen the Responsibility System in Industrial Enterprises," *Hung Ch'i* #20, October 16, 1961, in *SCMM* #298, pp. 25–30; *Chekiang Daily* ed., on Role of Party Committees, *Hangchow Domestic Radio*, April 8, 1962; *Nanking Domestic Radio*, April 15, 1962.

12. A. Doak Barnett, *Cadres, Bureaucracy and Political Power in Communist China* (New York: Columbia University Press, 1967), pp. 18–37, 203.

13. "Permanent Supply Relations Between Factories Established in a Number of Factories in Shanghai through Intensification of Cooperation," *JMJP*, January 18, 1962, in *SCMP* #2673, pp. 2–4; "Thoroughly Develop Rationalization Work for Material Utilization" (Shen-ju k'ai-chan wu-tzu ho-li-yung kung-tso), *KJJP*, January 20, 1961; Chi Ch'un, "In the Midst of Confusion, Grasp Firmly Material

Supplies" (Jang-san-kuan-ch'i-hsia, ta kua yuan-liao ts'ai-liao), *JMJP*, January 19, 1961; "Strengthen Economic Coordination," *JMJP*, April 2, 1963, in *SCMP* #2696, pp. 4–6.

14. Wen Yeh-ch'ing, "Why Is It Necessary to Carry out Team and Section Business Accounting," *KJJP*, September 5, 1961, in *CB* #673, pp. 1–2; Tso Ch'un-t'ai, "The Establishment and Development of an Economic Accounting System in China" April 1962 in *SCMP* #2767, pp. 1–9; Yang Jun-jui and Li Hsün, "A Tentative Discussion on Economic Accounting of Industrial Enterprises" *JMJP*, July 19, 1962, in *SCMP* #2817, pp. 13–20.

15. Wen Yeh-ch'ing, "The Contents and Methods of Team and Section Business Accounting," *KJJP*, September 7, 1961, in *CB* #673, pp. 3–4.

16. Tso Ch'un-t'ai, n. 23.

17. Tso-Hai, "Mass Accounting Must Be Correctly Combined With Specialized Accounting" *TKP*, July 12, 1961, in *SCMP* #2551, pp. 5–9.

18. Li Cheng-jui and Tso Ch'un-T'ai, "Several Problems Concerning Economic Accounting in Socialist Enterprises," *Hung Ch'i* #9, October 1, 1961; "Each and Every Enterprise Must Strengthen Economic Accounting," *JMJP*, December 24, 1961, in *SCMP* #2660, pp. 1–4.

19. "Tentative Regulations Governing Duties and Powers of Accounting Personnel," *JMJP*, January 9, 1963, in *SCMP* #2909, pp. 2–8. These regulations were first adopted by the State Council on November 24, 1962.

20. Hsü Hsin-hsüeh, "Strengthen Further Economic Accounting in Enterprises," *Hung Ch'i* #18, September 16, 1961 in *SCMM* #282, pp. 18–22; Li Ch'eng-jui, "On Socialist Economic Accounting," December 10, 1962.

21. Wen Yeh-Ch'ing, n. 24. *See also* Appendix C.

22. K'uang Jih-an, et al., "Tentative Views on the Question of Practice of Strict Economic Accounting by State Owned Industrial Enterprises," *CCYC* #8, August 17, 1963, in *SCMM* #388, pp. 30–42.

23. Ibid.

24. "Strengthen the Technical Management of Industrial Enterprises," *JMJP*, April 8, 1963, *SCMP* #2967, pp. 12–14.

25. Han Kuang, "Several Problems Concerning Technical Work in Industry," *Hung Ch'i* #24, December 16, 1961, in *SCMM* #295, pp. 1–8.

26. Wang K'ai, "Preliminary Understanding of Several Points," *KJJP*, June 19, 1962, in *SCMP* #2787, pp. 3–5.

27. Han Kuang, n. 25; "Technical Innovations Must be Repeatedly Tested," *JMJP*, November 25, 1961.

28. Kao Jun-chih, "How To Bring Up and Use Technical Personnel," *KJJP*, July 13, 1962, in *SCMP* #3789, pp. 11–13.

29. She Shu-tseng, "Management of Warehouses in Industrial Enterprises" (Kung-yeh ch'i-yeh ling-k'u kuan-li), *TKP*, May 28, 1962.

30. "Strictly Enforce the Inspection System," *JMJP,* September 6, 1961, in *SCMP* #2582, pp. 14–17.

31. "Carry Out Inspection and Repairs in a Planned Manner," *JMJP*, June 8, 1961, in *SCMP* #2521, pp. 17–19; "Thoroughly Perfect Maintenance and Repair of Metallurgical Equipment," *JMJP*, March 29, 1961, in *SCMP* #2476, pp. 20–22.

32. "Firmly Grasp and Go Deep Into the First Line of Production" (Chin-ch'ih shen-ju sheng-ch'an ti-yi-hsien), *JMJP*, January 11, 1961.

33. Wang Cheng, "Experience of the Chinghsi Coal Mines in Continued Leaps Forward of Production," *Hung Ch'i* #3–4, February 1, 1961, in *SCMM* #251, pp. 18–27.

34. "Take Production as Central; Beat the Drums" (Yi sheng-ch'an wei chung-hsin; Chi-hsi lo-ku), *JMJP*, February 1, 1961.

35. "Yutienpao Coal Mine Mobilizes the Masses to Manage Modernized Enterprises Well" (Yu-tien-pao mei-k'uang fa-tung ch'ün-chung kuan-hao hsien-tai-huah ch'i-yeh), *JMJP*, February 22, 1961.

36. "Consolidate the Work System of Cadres Moving Their Offices Down to the Shafts" (Kung-ku kan-pu hsia-ching pan-kung ti kung-tso chih-tu), *JMJP*, January 21, 1961.

37. "Improve Work Style, Strengthen and Perfect Systems" (Kai-chin tso-feng, chien-ch'uan chih-tu), *KJJP*, May 30, 1961.

38. "What We Have Learned From Our Experiment With the 'Four Fixings, Three Guarantees, and One Reward' System," *JMJP*, July 4, 1961, in *SCMP* #2539, pp. 3–7; "All Leadership Cadres in the Yutienpao Coal Mine Go Down Deep on the Spot to Make Investigations and Do Research" (Yu tien-pao mei-k'uang yi-ching ling-tao kan-pu shen-ju hsien-ch'ang tiao-ch'a yen-chiu), in *KJJP*, April 18, 1962.

39. *NCNA*, Peking, December 17, 1961.

40. "A Shanghai Factory Raises the Work Level of Basic Level Cadres" (Shanghai yi-ch'an t'i-kao chi-tseng kan-pu kung-tso shui-p'ing), *JMJP*, June 26, 1961.

41. *NCNA*, January 11, 1961; *NCNA*, September 19, 1962. *See also* "Anshan Steel Promotes a Batch of Management Cadres" (An-kang t'i-keng yi-p'i kuan-li jen-yüan), *Kuang-ming Jih-pao*, February 5, 1963; "Anshan Steel's Technical Ranks Grow Continuously" (An-kang chi-shu tui-wu pu-tuan ch'eng-chang chuang-ta), *KJJP*, September 27, 1963.

42. "Chungking Steel Workers Push Deeply Into Technical Research to Promote Production" (Ch'ung-kang kung-jen k'o-jo chien yen-chiu chi-shu t'ui-chin sheng-ch'an), *JMJP*, October 15, 1963.

43. "Leading Cadres of Worker and Peasant Background in Peking Industrial and Mining Enterprises Conclude One Year's Cultural Study" (Pei-ching yi-p'i kung-nung ch'u-shen ti ch'an-k'uang kan-pu chieh-su wei-ch'i yi-nien ti wen-hua hsueh-hsi), *KJJP*, August 8, 1963.

44. "Shensi Cadres in Machine Bureau and Departments Go to Factories and Are Tempered on the Shifts (Shen-hsi chi-hsieh chu ho pu-fen kung-ch'an chu-pan hsün-lien-pan), *JMJP*, August 11, 1961.

45. Carl Riskin, "Local Industry and the Chinese Model of Development," *CQ* #46, April-June 1971, p. 250.

46. *Ibid.*

47. "Shanghai Chemical Research Institute Trains Fertilizer Technicians for All Localities" (Shang-hai hua-kung yen-chiu-yüan wei ko-ti p'ei-hsün ch'u ch'eng-hui hua-fei chi-shu jen-ts'ai), *KMJP*, April 10, 1961; "Tientsin Chemical Plants Develop Worker Spare-time Technical Education" (T'ien-chien hua-kung ch'an k'ai-chan chih-kung yeh-wu chi-shu chiao-yü), *KMJP*, March 1, 1963; "Shanghai Chemical Research Institutes Train Technicians for Small-Scale Fertilizer Plants in Every Locality" (Shang-hai hua-hsüeh kung-yeh yen-chiu-yüan wei-ko-ti chi-chi p'ei-hsün hsiao-hsing hua-fei-ch'an chi-shu jen-ts'ai), *NCNA*, Chinese, April 14, 1961.

48. Yueh Kang-chao, "Fixed Personnel and Labor Norms of Industrial Enterprises," *JMJP*, November 18, 1961, in *SCMP* #2634, pp. 1–7; K'uang Jih-an, "Tentative Views on the Question of Practice of Strict Economic Accounting by State-Owned Industrial Enterprises," *Ching-chi Yen-chiu* #3, August 17, 1963, in *SCMM* #388, pp. 30–42.

49. Chou Hua, "Attend to Living Conditions of Workers and Call at Their Families," in *CB* #672, pp. 4–7; Lo Ting-fu, "Investigate and Study, Master the Laws, Put Out More Coal," *JMJP*, March 7, 1961, in *SCMP* #2464, pp. 8–12;

"Leading Cadres of Chungking #502 Factory Effectively Improve Their Work Style," *JMJP*, July 26, 1961, in *SCMP* #2555, pp. 4–6; Wang Cheng, "Experience of Chingshi Coal Mines," n. 37; Li Jun-chih, "On the Systems of Workers Congresses in State Operated Enterprises," *Hung Ch'i* #2; January 16, 1962, in *SCMM* #30, pp. 20–24; Ching Yu, "How Incentive Work Can Be Carried Out Well in Factory and Mining Enterprises," *JMJP*, July 4, 1961, in *SCMP* #2539, pp. 7–9.

50. Yang Lung, "It Is Not Right To Do Too Many Jobs Concurrently," *KJJP*, July, 7, 1962, in *SCMP* #2789, pp. 14–15.

51. Robert Dahl, *After the Revolution* (New Haven: Yale University Press, 1970) for a contemporary view of democratically controlled economic activity from a liberal perspective.

52. "Concerning the Question of Socialist Distribution According to Work," *TKP*, December 15, 1961, in *SCMP* #2656, pp. 1–14.

53. "Give Full Play to the Role of Workers Representative Conferences," *JMJP*, October 11, 1961, in *SCMP* #2604, pp. 15–16.

54. *Ibid.*

55. Li Jun-chih, "On the System of Workers Representative Congresses in State Operated Industrial Enterprises" (Kuan-yü kuo-ying ch'i-yeh chung ti chih-kung tai-piao ta-hui chih-tu), *Hung Ch'i* #2, January 16, 1962, in *SCMM* #300, pp. 20–24.

56. "Resolutely Convene Workers Representative Congresses" (Chin-ch'ih chao-k'ai chih-kung tai-piao ta-hui), *KJJP*, August 29, 1961.

57. "Really and Thoroughly Implement the Systems of Workers Representative Congresses" (Jen-chen kuan-ch'e chih-kung tai-piao ta-hui chih-tu), *NFJP*, June 16, 1961.

58. "Tayeh Mine Persists in Holding Workers Representative Conferences Regularly," *JMJP*, June 20, 1961, in SCMP #2530, pp. 19–20.

59. "How Hsiaokenshan Colliery Develops the Role of the Workers Representatives," *JMJP*, August 14, 1961, in *SCMP* #2564, pp. 6–7; "Help Advanced Producers Better Develop Their Functions" (Pang-chu hsien-chin sheng-ch'an-che keng-hao-ti fa-hui tso-yung), *KJJP*, December 7, 1962.

60. See Note 57; "Rely on the Masses to Perfect Enterprise Management and Improve the Livelihood of Mining Workers in Order to Boost Production," *JMJP*, July 20, 1961, in *SCMP* #2551, pp. 20–21.

61. "Resolutely and Regularly Do a Good Job on Workers Representative Congresses" (Chin-ch'ih ching-ch'ang k'ai-hao chih-kung tai-piao ta-hui), *KJJP*, November 11, 1961.

62. "A Suggestion" (Yi-chien t'i-an), *KJJP*, October 15, 1961.

63. See Note 61; "Shih ku Coal Mine, Kwangtung, Persists in Workers Congress System," *JMJP*, June 14, 1961, in *SCMP* #2525, pp. 9–10.

64. See Notes 57, 59; "Yumen Oil Refinery Calls Representative Conferences of Workers Quarterly, Thus Developing Democracy and Promoting Production," *NCNA*, Lanchow, July 24, 1961, in *SCMP* #2550, p. 15.

65. See Note 56.

66. Richman, *Industrial Society*, p. 315. Hoffman, *Work Incentives*, pp. 102–104. Ching Yu, "How Incentives Work Can Be Carried Out Well in Factories and Mining Enterprises," *JMJP*, July 4, 1961, *SCMP* #2539, pp. 7–9.

67. Hoffman, *Work Incentives*, pp. 105–106.

68. Richman, *Industrial Society*, p. 316.

69. *Ibid.*, p. 316, *NCNA*, December 1, 1963 gives a text of regulations for awards for technical innovations.

70. Hoffman, *Work Incentives*, p. 109.

71. "A Communist Education Supplement," *KJJP*, August 22, 1961, in *CB* 671, pp. 1–29.

72. Lo Keng-mo, "On the Two-Fold Character of the Principle of Distribution According to Work," *TKP*, April 4, 1962, in *SCMP* #2742, pp. 1–14.

73. Ho-Wei, "The Question of Relations Between Distribution According to Labor and Bourgeois Lawful Rights," *Ching-chi Yen-chiu* #4, April 14, 1962.

74. Hoffman, *Work Incentives*, p. 26.

75. *Ibid.*, pp. 105–106.

76. *Ibid.*, p. 106.

77. For some concrete examples of the multi-faceted nature of incentive systems being used at this time, see the following: "The Yangchün Coal Mines Strengthen Shift and Group Management Work" (Yangch'ün Mei-K'uang chia-ch'iang pan-tsu kuan-li kung-tso), *NFJP*, October 7, 1961; "Strengthen Enterprise Management" (Chia-ch'iang ch'i-yeh kuan-li), Kiangsi People's Radio, December 5, 1961; "Kunming Match Factory Reforms Wage Work" (K'un-ming huo-tsai-ch'an-kai-chin kung-tzu chih-tu), *TKP*, Peking, September 27, 1961; "How To Do Incentive Work Well in Industrial and Mining Enterprises" (Tsem-yang tsai ch'an k'uang ch-i'yeh chung tso-hao chiang-kung kung-tso), *JMJP*, July 4, 1961. Here, the importance of "rational and accurate" labor quotas was noted as the key link in the incentive system, thus implying the need for some authority other than the workers to set their own quotas when these quotas were the basis of calculating material rewards, rather than a means by which workers measured their contribution to the collective goal of increased production. For other examples of incentive systems, see "Leading Cadres Go Down Deep to Basic Levels and Into Mines (Ling-tao kan-pu shen-ju chi-tseng, shen-ju ching-hsia), *KJJP*, May 28, 1963; "Shanghai Steel Plant Builds Level by Level Responsibility and Shift by Shift Accounting System of Management" (Shang-hai-shih kang-ch'an chien-li tseng-tseng fu-tse, pan-pan ho-suan yung-mei kuan-li chih-tu), *JMJP*, June 14, 1961; "T'aiyuan Rolling Stock Factory Manages Production With Tests and Competitions" (T'ai-yüan ch'e-liang-ch'an k'o-tung k'o-chien ching-ying sheng-ch'an), *JMJP*, May 7, 1962.

78. Feng Ta-chih, "Handle Well the Relationships Among the Four Parties," *KJJP*, August 14, 1962, in *SCMP* #2809, pp. 8–10.

79. Ch'en Mao-li, "Fulfillment of Duties and Authority," *KJJP*, July 19, 1962, in *SCMP* #2792, pp. 6–8. *See also*, Chou Anhsi, "How to Protect the Authority of Technical Personnel," *KJJP*, July 13, 1962, in *SCMP* #2789, pp. 13–14.

80. Richman, *Industrial Society*, p. 296.

81. Shih K'o-chien, "Bringing the Strength of Technical Personnel Into Full Play," *Hung Ch'i (Red Flag)* #8–9, April 25, 1962, in *SCMM*, #314, pp. 47–50.

82. Li Ch'ao-po, "Unite and Contribute Greater Strength to Socialist Construction," *KJJP*, August 25, 1962, in *SCMP* #2823, pp. 7–9.

83. See above, chap. 4. Between 1957 and 1958, "23,500 spare time universities and part-time work part-study universities were established," cited from *NCNA*, September 1, 1959, by Orleans, *Professional Manpower*, p. 23.

84. *Ibid.*, p. 11.

85. Jao Pin, "Correctly Train and Use Engineers and Technicians," *KJJP*, August 30, 1962, in *SCMP* #2823, pp. 9–13.

86. "Further Develop the Role of Technical Personnel in Industrial Enterprises," *JMJP*, November 17, 1961 in *SCMP* #2635, pp. 4–7; Shih K'o-chien, "Bringing the Strength of Technical Personnel in Full Play," *Hung Ch'i* #8–9, April 25, 1962, in *SCMM* #314, pp. 47–50.

87. Wang Ch'ung-lin, "Make Friends With Engineers and Technicians," *KJJP*, June 19, 1962, in *SCMP* #2787, pp. 6–7.

88. Parris H. Chang, "Research Notes on the Changing Loci of Decision in the Chinese Communist Party," *CQ* #44, October–December 1970, pp. 164–194.

89. *Ibid.*, pp. 189–190; *NCNA*, International Service, August 25, 1967.

90. *Ibid., NCNA.*

91. "Further Promote Diversified Undertakings and Multiple Utilization," *NCNA*, Peking, January 19, 1961.

92. "Unfolding Economic Cooperation in a Well Planned Manner," *TKP*, January 30, 1962, in *SCMP* #2689, pp. 8–10; "Step Up Economic Coordination," *NCNA*, Peking, December 15, 1961.

93. "Develop the Revolutionary Spirit of Running Enterprises with Industry and Thrift and Carry Out a Strict System of Business Accounting," *JMJP*, July 7, 1963, in *SCMP* #3031, pp. 1–4.

94. "Correctly Handle the Relationship . . . ," *NFJP*, n. 110; Ouyang Ch'eng, "On Socialist Economic Cooperation," *TKP*; Richard M. Pfeffer, "The Institution of Contracts in the Peoples Republic of China," *The China Quarterly*, #14 and #15, April–June and July–September 1963.

95. Wen Chin, "Problems Concerning Fixing Targets in the Management of Industrial Enterprises," *TKP*, November 26, 1962, in *SCMP* #2921, pp. 15–20; Chih-ta and Ho Cheng, "The Profits of Socialist Enterprises; Their Significance and the Way to Earn Them," *Ching-Chi Yen-Chiu* #10, October 17, 1962, in *SCMM* #341, pp. 38–45; Sung Hsin-chung, "Acquire a Correct Idea of the Profit Problem of a Socialist Enterprise," *TKP*, July 13, 1962, in *SCMP* #2792, pp. 15–16.

96. "Retained profits" were allowed an enterprise in both of these positions, but in the second, there was much greater room for abuse. Retained profits were a fixed percentage of total profit, but when total profit was planned, as it was in the first position described above, then retained profits could only increase as actual efficiency in production increased. Moreover, retained profits would be used to meet needs of the enterprise or the locality in which it existed as these were determined politically. In the second position, there was little to prevent a large increase in total profit and hence of retained profit, and nothing but administrative controls to prevent their anti-social use. Sung Hsin-chung, "The System of Retaining a Percentage of Profits by Our Enterprises," *TKP*, May 12, 1961, in *SCMP* #2543, pp. 7–8. The retained profits made up a portion of the enterprise's "circulating funds"; the other portion being the enterprise's "finance funds" which was an amount given to the enterprise as part of the annual plan for capital construction, technical revolution, and the purchase of fixed assets (machinery, office equipment, etc.). The banks were to play a major role in regulating management's use of all circulating funds. *A decision to use these funds was the province of the Party Committee of the enterprise.* Another portion of the enterprise's finances, the credit fund, was to be loaned less rigorously by the banks for short term emergencies. *Presumably, the Factory Director had control over use of these funds*, with the bank's support or permission or the support or permission of a higher level economic body or Party organization. It is possible that many Party Secretaries and Directors used their power over these funds for self-enrichment or for special privileges (autos, expense accounts, etc.). An early attack on such practices came indirectly in mid-1961. See "Exposing the Truth About So-Called 'Self-Management of Enterprises' in Yugoslavia," *Hung Ch'i* #11, July 1, 1961, in *SCMM* #266, pp. 25–31. For a discussion of this system, see *TKP* editorial, "Satisfactorily Control and Use the Circulating Funds of Industry," *TKP*, Peking, June 20, 1961, in *SCMP* #2543, pp. 5–7. Also, Richman, *Industrial Society*, pp. 61–62, 107–110, 476 ff. In short, both retained profits and "credit funds" were open to fairly easy misuse by a management so disposed, and if the Party Secretary was also a manager, or at least close friends with one, the potential for trouble increased greatly.

97. "Down with 'Three Anti' Element and 'Big Renegade Po I-po,' Sinister

Despot on the Industrial and Communications Front," and "Forty Charges Against Po I-po" in *Current Background* #878, pp. 1–15, 16–20; Ho Li and Chu Chia-chen, "Refuting the Production Price Theory Formulated by Comrade Yang Chien-pa'i and Others," Shanghai, *Wen Hui-pao*, December 11, 1964. After October 1961, the First Ministry of Machine Building began to move in a direction that seemed to be in harmony with the idea of trusts. Economic relationships between enterprises in the machine industry, rather than handled through governmental departments at various levels, were handled by signing contracts directly between enterprises with no governmental planning other than price fixing, it seems. Moreover, specialization in the machine tool enterprises, another characteristic of "trusts", began to be advocated to replace multiple undertakings and comprehensiveness. See "First Ministry of Machine Building Adjusts Factory Relationships," *JMJP*, January 30, 1962, in *SCMP* #2681, pp. 14–15, and also articles on specialization in the machine industry beginning late in 1963, e.g., Fan Mu-han, "On Specialization in Industrial Production," *CCYC* #10, October 17, 1963, in *SCMM* #392, pp. 32–39. Interestingly, this argument in favor of specialization and, it seems, a "trust" organization concept came after the ideas of the technical economic managers began to come under the attack of the political-economic managers in June 1963. The attack on Po I-po, for example, accused him of trying to set up his own group in the Party which would try to influence enterprise level Party Committees to follow this type of management through their higher organizational position in industry and communications systems. Also, see below, chap. 6, for more on this controversy.

98. Ouyang Ch'eng, "On Socialist Economic Cooperation."

99. "Reading Notes on the Soviet Unions 'Political Economics'," in *Miscellany of Mao Tse-tung Thought, JPRS* #61269–2, February 20, 1974.

100. *Ibid.*, pp. 267 ff. and 279 ff.

101. Chang, "The Locus of Decision-Making," p. 191.

102. "Why Is the Steeling in Proletarian Consciousness More Important After Winning Political Power," *KJJP*, September 5, 1962, in *SCMP* #2382, pp. 11–12; Chu P'o and Chang Hui, "Lenin on Class Struggle in the Transition Period," *Hung Ch'i* #23–24, December 5, 1962, in *SCMM* #345, pp. 5–15.

103. Mu Tzu, "Class Struggle During the Transition Period and the Self Remolding of Industrialists and Merchants," *Hsin Kung-shan* #4, April 18, 1963, in *SCMM* #365, pp. 1–8; Chuang Fu-ling, "Criticizing the Fallacy of Bourgeois Sociology on the Question of Class and Class Struggle," *Hung Ch'i* #9, May 1, 1963 in *SCMM* #266, pp. 12–18; Chao Lin, "Some Problems Related to Class Struggle During the Period of Transition," *Hsin Chien-she* #11, November 20, 1963, in *SCMM* #399, pp. 5–15.

104. "The Great Revolutionary Significance of Participation in Labor by Cadres," *JMJP*, June 2, 1963, in *SCMP* #3006, pp. 14–18; "Participation in Collective Productive Labor by Cadres is of Fundamental Importance Under the Socialist System," *Hung Ch'i* #13–14, July 10, 1963, in *SCMM* #376, pp. 1–13.

105. "Cadres of Factories Must Also Do Manual Labor Seriously," *JMJP*, August 7, 1963, in *SCMP* #3040, pp. 5–6.

106. Hai Po, "Effectively Raise Labor Productivity in Industrial Enterprises," *Hung Ch'i* #17, September 1, 1962, in *SCMM* #332, pp. 6–15; "Take Production as Central; Beat the Drums," JMJP, February 1, 1961.

107. "Apply the 'Triple Combination' Method of Leadership More Properly," *JMJP*, February 11, 1963, in *SCMP* #2926, pp. 1–5.

108. "Develop the Revolutionary Spirit of Running Enterprises with Industry and Thrift and Carry Out a Strict System of Business Accounting," *JMJP*, July 7, 1963, in *SCMP* #3031, pp. 1–4; "Secretaries of Party Branches of Mining Enter-

prises Should Take Part in Labor," *JMJP*, August 17, 1963, in *SCMP* #3040, pp. 4–5.

109. Chang, "Research Notes," p. 191.

110. *NCNA*, March 7, 1963; Miao Tso-pin, "Ordinary Work and Great Ambition," *Hung Ch'i* #7–8, April 16, 1963, in *SCMM* #364, pp. 20–22.

111. "Factory Histories—Good Teaching Material for Class Education," *KJJP*, June 21, 1963, in *SCMP* #3022, pp. 7–10; Chang Ching-fu, "Study Lei Feng's Spirit and Correctly Handle the Relations Between the Individual and the Collective," *Chung-kuo Ch'ing-nien* #8, April 16, 1963, in *SCMM* #369, pp. 22–28.

112. "Intensify Activities to Compare With, Learn From and Catch Up With the Advanced and Help the Backward and Strive to Become '5 Good Workers," *JMJP*, February 2, 1964, in *SCMP* #3164, pp. 10–13.

113. Hoffman, *Work Incentives*, p. 109.

114. "The Mass Line is a Fundamental Guarantee for the Proper Management of Enterprises," *Hua-hsueh Kung-yeh* #15, August 6, 1963, in *SCMM* #384, pp. 17–24; Wang Shao-ch'uan and Chou Hsiao p'eng, "Class Education Must Be Conducted Firmly During the Production Increase and Economy Campaigns," *Chung-kuo Nung-yeh Chi-hsieh* #7, July 10, 1963, in *SCMM* #382, pp. 14–18.

Chapter 6: Ambivalence Becomes Confrontation: China's Industrial System from 1964 to 1966

1. Ma Wen-jui, "Discussion of the Characteristics, Objectives and Methods of Planning Socialist Enterprises," *CCYC* #7, 1964, trans. in *Chinese Economic Studies*, IASP, White Plains, Winter, 1967, Vol. 1, #4.

2. *Ibid. See also* Ma Wen-jui, "Several Problems in the Management of Socialist State-Run Industrial Enterprises" (She-hui chu-yi kuo-ying kung-yeh ch'i-yeh kuan-li ti chi-neng wen-t'i), *JMJP*, March 28, 1964.

3. Ibid., "Several Problems." *See also* Ma Wen-jui, "On the Nature and Tasks of State Operated Industrial Enterprises in Our Country," (Luen wo-kuo kuo-ying kung-yeh ch'i-yeh ti hsing-chih ho jen-wu), *JMJP*, March 3, 1964.

4. Ma Wen-jui, "Several Problems."

5. Ma Wen-jui, "On the Nature and Tasks."

6. Ma Wen-jui, "On Several Basic Systems in the Management of Socialist State Operated Industrial Enterprises" (Luen she-hui chu-yi kuo-ying kung-yeh ch'i-yeh kuan-li ti chi-ko chi-pen chih-tu), *JMJP*, November 23, 1964.

7. Ma Wen-jui, "Basic Principles Governing the Administration of Socialist State Operated Industrial Enterprises," *JMJP*, June 3, 1964, in *SCMP* #3245, pp. 7–14.

8. *Ibid.* and Ma Wen-jui, "China's State Owned Industrial Enterprises—Their Nature and Tasks," *Peking Review* #26, June 26, 1964, also in *SCMM* #424, pp. 27–33.

9. Ma Wen-jui, "On the Nature and Tasks."

10. Ma Wen-jui, "Several Basic Systems."

11. Ma Wen-jui, "Basic Principles."

12. Wu Hsing-feng, "A Question of Orientation in Relation to the Management of Socialist Enterprises," *JMJP*, May 12, 1964, in *SCMP* #3230, pp. 1–3.

13. *Ibid.*

14. Feng Tai, "The Need for Revolutionization as Well as Modernization," *TKP*, March 27, 1964, in *SCMP* #3206, pp. 10–14.

15. "Promoting Production by Paying Attention to Revolution," *NFJP*, July 21, 1964, in *SCMP* #3291, pp. 9–10.

16. Jung Wen-tso, "Handle Correctly the Relationship Between Political and Economic Work in Enterprise Management" (Ts'ai ch'i-yeh kuan-li chung cheng-ch'üeh ch'u-li cheng-chih kung-tso ho ching-chi kung-tso ti kuan-hsi), *JMJP*, September 2, 1964; "A Short Talk on the Basic Principles of Enterprise Management in Socialist State Owned Industrial Enterprises" (T'an she-hui chu-yi kuo-ying ch'i-yeh kuan-li ti chi-pen yüan-tse), *FMJP*, September 14, 1964.

17. Chung Huang, "Revolutionization and Modernization of Socialist Industrial Enterprises," *Ching-chi Yen-chui*, #12, December 20, 1964, in *SCMM* #459, pp. 18–30.

18. *Ibid.*

19. "Maintain a Firm Grip on Both Upper and Lower Levels," *JMJP*, April 2, 1964, in *SCMP* #3201, pp. 1–5.

20. "Departments Should Emphasize Service to the Production Front Line" (K'o-shih yao chu-tung sheng-ch'an ti-yi-hsien fu-wu), *KJJP*, April 14, 1964; "Let Us Remind All Once Again to Cut Down the Number of Unnecessary Reports and Statistical Forms," *JMJP*, April 21, 1964, in *SCMP* #3218, pp. 7–8.

21. *Ibid.*

22. *Ibid.*

23. "Genuinely Take Part in Labor Like an Ordinary Laborer," *JMJP*, September 22, 1964, in *SCMP* #3313, pp. 16–19. Slight grammatical correction inserted.

24. "Face the Shift Groups, and the Masses, and Serve Production" (Mien-hsiang pan-tsu, mien-hsiang ch'ün chung, wei sheng-ch'an fu-wu), *JMJP*, September 24, 1965, in *SCMP* #3555, pp. 2–8. *See also* the "23 points" of Mao, Baum and Teiwes, *The Socialist Education Campaign*, Columbia University, East Asian Institute, 1968. *See also* Mao Tsetung, "Reading Notes," pp. 270, 274, 283.

25. A Classroom Discussion by First Year Students, Dept. of Economics, Wuhan University, "How Do Capitalists Make Their Fortune? Can Their Supervision and Management of Production Be Regarded as Labor?" *KMJP*, March 1, 1965, *CB* #765, pp. 1–53; Pan Chen-te, "My Understanding of the Essence of Exploitation of the Capitalist," *KMJP*, March 15, 1965, in *SCMP* #3438, pp. 17–19; "Clarify the Distinction Between Labor and Exploitation," *KMJP*, March 15, 1965, in *SCMP* #3438, pp. 15–16; Ch'en Kuo-feng, "Should a Problem Be Studied on the Basis of Reality or Definition?" *KMJP*, March 15, 1965, *CB* #765, pp. 1–53; Ch'en Wen-hao, "Divest the Capitalist of His Mantle-Participation in 'Labor'," *KMJP*, March 15, 1965, *CB* #765, pp. 1–53.

26. Yün Hsi-liang, "Physical Labor and Mental Labor in Socialist Society," *Ching-chi Yen-chiu* #11, November 1965, in *SCMM* #507, pp. 4–18; Shih Hsiao-chu, "Two Melting Pots Before Young Students," *Chung-kuo Ch'ing-nien* #18, September 16, 1964, in *SCMM* #442, pp. 24–30.

27. See Note 24.

28. *Tung Fang Hung* [*East is Red*], February 15, 1967; "Down With the Three Anti-Element and Big Renegade Po I-po" in *CB* #878, pp. 1–15, p. 12.

29. Chang Ta-k'ai and Sung Chin-sheng, "A Basic Reform in Enterprise Management" (Ch'i-yeh kuan-li shang yi-ko ken-pen pien-ko), *JMJP*, December 25, 1964. Until otherwise noted, information on this Tsitsihar plant was obtained from this source.

30. "Stir Up the Revolution in Enterprise Management and the Face of Production is Transformed" (Ta-nao ch'i-yeh kuan-li ko-ming, sheng-ch'an mien-mao huan-huan yi-hsin), *JMJP*, December 26, 1964. *See also* Note 29.

31. *Ibid.* Actually about 75 to 82 percent of the plant were nonadministrative workers, with 17–25% in control departments.

32. Information of work-shop level functions from Wang Tso-chen and Miao

Shou-yeh, "A New Change in the Work of the Workshop Director" (Ch'e-chien chu-jen kung-tso ti hsin pien-hua), *JMJP*, December 25, 1964.

33. Sun Chung-ch'ing, "Materials Sent to Work Shift Groups to Serve Production" (Tsai-liao sung-tao pan-tsu wei sheng-ch'an fu-wu), *JMJP*, December 25, 1964.

34. Chang Shu-yüan, "A Reform in Cost Accounting" (Ch'eng-pen k'o-suan-shang ti yi-ko pien-ko), *JMJP*, December 25, 1964.

35. Hsü Ta-k'uei, "Talking From the Perspective of the 'Form King' " (Tsung 'chang-wang' t'an-ch'i), *JMJP*, December 25, 1964.

36. Szu Fu-wen, "Is Equipment Repair and Maintenance Begun in the 'Forest' or Is It Based on Reality" (She-pei chien-hsiu shih tsung 'lin' ch'u-fa hai-shih tsung shih-chi ch'u-fa), *JMJP*, December 25, 1964.

37. See Note 34.

38. See Notes 33–36.

39. In this plant, over 300 "non-production personnel" (Fei-sheng-ch'an jen-yüan) were released by February 1965. Five hundred production workers were also released. This phenomenon of drastic personnel retrenchment was not unique to the Tsitsihar Vehicles Plant. In fact throughout 1964 and 1965, reports from many factories on their re-organizations and management "revolutions" show a marked propensity to eliminate what would appear to be excessive workers from their ranks; not only in administrative or clerical positions, but in production as well.

40. See Note 28.

41. Unless otherwise noted, information on management at Ta-ch'ing came from Hsü Chin-ch'iang, "Raise High the Great Red Banner of the Thought of Mao Tsetung and Continuously Deepen the Revolutionization of Enterprises" (Kao-chü Mao Tsetung ssu-hsiang wei-ta ti hung-ch'i pu-tuan chia-shen ch'i-yeh ko-ming-hua), *Ching-chi Yen-chiu*, April 1966.

42. "Yingkuang Electro-plating Factory Establishes a Model for Revolutionizing Small Factories" (Ying-kuang tien-tu-ch'an wei hsiao-hsing ch'i-yeh ko-ming-hua shu-li p'ang-yang), *TKP*, Peking, October 23, 1965; CCP Committee, Kansu Metallurgy Co., "Reform Labor Organization with a Revolutionary Spirit," *JMJP*, July 7, 1965, in *SCMP* #3513, pp. 4–10. *See also JMJP*, June 18, 1965; "Department Personnel Leave Offices and Serve the Front Lines" (K'o-shih jen-yüan tsou-chu pan-kung-shih, wei ti-yi-hsien fu-wu), *KJJP*, December 17, 1964, "Breakdown the Old Management Framework; Factories in Canton Carry Out 2-Level Management" (Ta-p'o kuan-li t'i-chih ti chiu k'ua-k'ua; Kuang-chou yi-p'i ch'an-k'uang shih-hsing liang-chi kuan-li), *JMJP*, June 10, 1965.

43. "Chungking Water Turbine Works Adopts the 'Three Fixed and One Substitution System' for their Cadres to Take Part in Labor," "Take Part in Labor as an Ordinary Laborer," *JMJP*, September 22, 1964; n. 24.

44. "Canton Chemical Works Adopts 'Half-Day for Labor, Half-Day for Work' System for Cadres," *NFJP*, September 22, 1964, *SCMP* #3325, pp. 10–15. This system led the Plant Party Committee into conflict with higher level Party organs. Implementation of these systems was widespread. For example in Tientsin, one report noted that as early as January 1965, over 70 major enterprises tried, in one way or another, the "half-half" system. See *JMJP*, January 20, 1965. Other reports from Fuchow, Chengchow, Shansi Province, Chungking, Shanghai, Tsinan, Wuhan, and other places show similar patterns.

45. Tsai Shih-ying and Li Chang-pang, "A Meeting That's to the Point" (Chui-tzu hui), *KJJP*, December 12, 1964; "Kwangtung Pharmaceutical Plant Workers Liberate Thinking and Take New Path," (Kuang-tung chih-yao ch'an chih-kung chieh-fang ssu-hsiang chueh nao hsin-lu), *P'ing-ch'eng Wan-pao*, March 30, 1965.

46. "Taking Part in Labor Helps Improve Profession" (Ts'an-chia lao-tung tsu-chin yeh-wu), *P'ing-ch'eng Wan-pao*, April 1, 1965; Li Yeh, "Carry Out Well the Ideological Work of Workshops in Industrial Enterprises," *Hung Ch'i #5*, March 17, 1964, *SCMM #412*, pp. 8–10; "Party Branch of Dolomite Workshop of Shihchingshan Steel Company Brings Up a Staunch Army of Workers," *JMJP*, March 18, 1964, in *SCMP #3195*, pp. 5–6.

47. "Break Down Superfluous Rules; Do Department Work at Shift Groups" (Ta-p'o ch'u kuai, lien-hsi k'o-shih kung-tso tso-tao pan-tsu), *P'ing-ch'eng Wan-pao*, March 26, 1965; "Cadres Can Go Into the Ocean, Workers Can Depart from the Ordinary" (Kan-pu neng hsia hai, kung-jen neng li yu), *P'ing-ch'eng Jih-pao*, February 24, 1965.

48. "Cadres in People's Rubber Factory Dig In and Bow Their Heads" (Jen-min Chiao-ch'an kan-pu ch'u-yün kan-t'ou), *P'ing-ch'eng Wan-pao*, March 20, 1965; "Cadre Participation in Labor at People's Rubber Factory is Systematized" (Jen-min chiao-ch'an, kan-pu tsan'chia lao-tung chih-tu-hua), *NFJP*, September 19, 1965.

49. *NCNA*, April 27, 1964. *See also*, Party Committee, Chungking Iron and Steel Company, "Promote the Three Fix and One Substitution Labor System" (T'ui-hsing 'san-ting yi-ting' lau-tung chih-tu), *JMJP*, January 16, 1965; and an article on engineers in Chungking, "China's Qualified Engineers Learn Lathe Work," *NCNA*, English, Chungking, October 12, 1965, in *SCMP #3559*, pp. 17–18. *See also* an article on the Paot'ou Iron and Steel Plant, *NCNA*, Peking, September 15, 1964; Li Ch'ang-sung, Chu Jui-shang, and Hsü Chia-ch'eng, "To Supervise Production, It is First Necessary to Supervise Thinking," *KJJP*, August 20, 1964, in *SCMP #3293*, pp. 2–6. In other places, like the Canton's People's Rubber Plant, one-half of the cadres divorced from labor were former workers. See *NFJP*, September 19, 1965. Numerous other examples exist on the relationship between attitudes toward labor, and class, occupation, and education. See Stephen Andors, "The Politics of Modernization in a Revolutionary Society: Factory Management in China; 1958–1969," (Ph.D. dissertation, Columbia University, 1974), chapters 3 and 5.

50. See Note 24.

51. "A Great Reform in Accounting," *TKP*, Peking, December 19, 1965, in *JPRS #33,841* and *SCMP #3613*, pp. 3–5.

52. Ch'ai Shih-hsieh, "Improvements in Financial Regulations and Systems," *JMJP*, Peking, March 3, 1966, in *JPRS #34,980*.

53. Pien Yeh-chin, "The 'Wu Lan Shepherd Horsemen' in Enterprise Management," *JMJP*, Peking, February 21, 1966, p. 5, in *JPRS #34,840*, pp. 4–6. *See also* "A Precious Experience," *JMJP*, Peking, February 21, 1966, in *JPRS #34,840*, pp. 6–20.

54. Shu Chiang-p'o, "New Path in Revolutionizing Financial Work," *JMJP*, February 21, 1966, p. 5, in *JPRS #34,840*, pp. 22–30, pp. 23–24. Some grammatical changes made.

55. Ma T'ien-shui, "Intensify Mass and Foundation Work, Promote Technical Innovation and Revolution," *KJJP*, July 14, 1965, *SCMP #3521*, pp. 3–10.

56. "Resolutely Rely on the Mass Revolution for New Technology; Rely on Our Own Efforts to Carry Out Enterprise Reform" (Jen-chen yi-k'ao ch'ün-chung ko-ming hsin-chi-shu; tzu-li keng-sheng shih-hsien ch'i-yeh kao-tsao), *JMJP*, January 22, 1965; "Harbin Bearings Plant Raises Product Quality Without Increasing Costs," *NCNA*, December 10, 1964; report on Ch'angchün Motor Vehicle Plant, *NCNA*, September 28, 1966; "Enthusiasm the Greater the Need to Cherish It," *JMJP*, April 3, 1965, in *SCMP #3443*, pp. 11–13.

57. Ch'iao Jung-chang, "The Current Technical Innovation and Technical Revolution in China's Industry," *CCYC #10*, October 20, 1965, in *SCMM #502*,

pp. 1–10. *See also* reports on the Kansu Metallurgy Co. by Shen T'ien-chia, "Technical Revolution is a New Motive Force (Chi-shu ko-ming hsin tung-li), *JMJP*, July 7, 1965.

58. "Shanghai #1 Sewing Machine Plant Improves Sewing Machine Production" (Shang-hai fen-niu-chi-chan yi-ch'an kai-chin chi-chen sheng-sh'an), *TKP*, Peking, February 1, 1965. *See also* report on the Shenyang Tractor Factory, "Take the Good Experience of Workers and Assimilate It into Technical Rules" (Pa kung-jen ti hao-ching-yen na-ju kung-yi kuei-ch'eng), *JMJP*, March 29, 1965.

59. For evidence of the split and descriptions of opposition from factory level technical authority to the triple combination's extensive use, see *Hsin-min Wan-pao*, April 21, 1965, article on the Shanghai Shipbuilding Yard; *JMJP*, April 18, 1965, articles on the Wu Hsün Coal Mines, and Lao-Hui-Tai Coal Mine, and an article on the Taishan Sugar Refinery, *Hsin-min Wan-pao*, May 5, 1965.

60. Charles Bettelheim, *La Construction de la Socialisme en Chine* (Paris: Charrière, 1965, p. 55; Yeh Chih-chün, "Handle Properly '5 Good' Assessment and Comparison Work and Launch the '5 Good' Movement in a Penetrating Way," *KJJP*, June 26, 1965, in *SCMP* #3499, pp. 1–5.

61. Hua Lin, "Use the Revolutionary Spirit to Raise Product Quality" (Yung ko-ming ch'ing-shen t'i-kao ch'ang-p'in chih-liang), *P'ing-Ch-eng Wan-Pao*, August 30, 1964; Su Hsing, "A High Standard of Quality Stems From Thinking on a High Plane," *Hung Ch'i* #1, January, 1966, in *SCMM* #509, pp. 29–32; "Be Responsible to the State and to the People," *KJJP*, October 15, 1965, in *SCMP* #3561, pp. 8–14; "In Spreading Advanced Experiences, One Also Has to Grasp Thought" (T'iu-kuang kuang-chin ching-yen yeh yao kua ssū-hsiang), *KJJP*, January 17, 1965.

62. Ch'i Ch'i-sheng, "Some Problems Concerning the Principle of Distribution According to Work," *Hsin Chien-she* #8–9, September 20, 1964, in *SCMM* #451, pp. 21–33.

63. "More Extensively and Penetratingly Unfold the 'Compare Learn, Catch-Up and Help' Movement," *Hung Ch'i* #10, May 23, 1964.

64. *NFJP* series in *SCMP* #3320, pp. 4–14. *KJJP* series in April 1964, *SCMP* #3219, pp. 5–13; *See SCMP* #3576, pp. 5–10; *see also* "An Important Lesson in the Revolutionization of the Concept of Happiness," *NFJP*, April 15, 1964, in *SCMP* #2932, pp. 9–13. *See also* "Workers Enthusiastically Participate in the Discussion on 'What the Lessons of Ting Shao-ch'ien Are'," *KJJP*, July 22, 1964, in *SCMP* #3280, pp. 1–3.

65. "Propagate the 'Three-Eight' Working Style Throughout the Country," *JMJP*, February 23, 1964, in *SCMP* #3178, pp. 1–5; "Industrial and Communications Departments Must Master the Good Experiences of the PLA," *JMJP*, April 4, 1964, in *SCMP* #3200, pp. 4–7.

66. Report on Chiangchün Textile Mill, Hopei Province, January 1964, *Peking Domestic Radio*.

67. Hoffman, *Work Incentives*, p. 115; Bettelheim, *La Construction de la Socialisme en Chine*, p. 54; Richman, *Industrial Society*, p. 318.

68. Richman, *Ibid.*, p. 318, pp. 812–814.

69. Ibid., pp. 239–240, 318–320. Richman notes the strong possibility that in many enterprises bonuses for top level management personnel were never re-instated after the Great Leap, although they were legally abolished sometime around 1963–64. According to Bettelheim, *La Construction de la Socialisme en Chine*, p. 55, between a grade 1 and grade 8 worker, a ratio of 3 to 1 existed (120Y to 40Y) with an average of about 75Y. Technicians' salaries ranged from 60Y to 150Y, but some went much higher. Richman (p. 799) reported one director at the Shanghai Heavy Machinery Plant received 210Y per month, but

he was not a technician. Bettelheim reported a salary of 250Y for the chief engineer in the Shanghai fertilizer plant in 1965 (p. 54), and said that director's salaries ranged from 120Y to 180Y/m.

70. Hoffmann, *Work Incentives*, pp. 35–37; Joyce Kallgren, "China's Welfare System," in Barnett, ed., *Chinese Communist Politics in Action*, pp. 540–576.

71. Hoffmann, *Work Incentives*, pp. 37–39.

72. Temporary or contract labor began on a large scale in 1964, although the principle of part-time industrial work and part-time agricultural work seems to have begun during the Great Leap Forward. For a good brief description of this system, see Tung T'ai, "China's 'Be a Worker and a Peasant' Labor System," (Chung-kuo ti 'yi kung yi-nung' lao-tung chih-tu), *Chung-kuo Hsin-wen*, Canton, June 22, 1966. For a critique of the discrimination against these workers, see the Red Guard publication entitled "The Present Contract Labor System Is a Big Anti-Mao Tsetung Thought Poisonous Weed" (Hsien-ti ho-t'ung-kung chih-tu shih fan Mao Tsetung ssu-hsiang-ti ta-t'u-tiao), n.d.

73. "Use the Revolutionary Spirit to Reform Labor Organizations" (Yung Po-ming ch'ing-shen kao-ko lau-tung tsu-chih), *JMJP*, July 7, 1965; "Man's Ideological Transformation Changes a Factory," *Ching-chi Yen-chiu*, #4, Peking, April 20, 1966, pp. 44–48. Translated in *JPRS* #32,962.

74. Yang Fu-ch'eng and Kao Ku-yang, "Too Many People Are Really Not Good for Doing Things" (Jen to, k'ai-pu-hao pan-shih), *JMJP*, April 27, 1965; "Yuchuanwu Mine Uses Revolutionary Spirit to Reform Enterprise Management" (Yu-chan-wu-k'uang yung ko-ming ch'ing-shen kao-ko ch'i-yeh kuan-li), *JMJP*, April 27, 1965; "Loyang Tractor Factory Securely Builds a Post Responsibility System" (Lo-yang t'o-la'chi-ch'an t'a-t'a shih-shih chien-li kang-wei tse-jen-chih), *KJJP*, June 2, 1964; "How We Build and Perfect a Post Responsibility System" (Wo-men shih tsem yang chien-li ho chien-ch'uan kang-wei tse-jen-chih ti), *KJJP*, August 28, 1964; Tung Yang, "Construct a Post Responsibility System; Strengthen the Management Work of Industrial Enterprises" (Chien-li kang-wei tse-jen-chih; chia-ch'iang ch'i-yeh kuan-li kung-tso), *CCYC*, April 20, 1965, in *SCMM* #476, pp. 40–48. "Keep Lively Accounts, Not Dead Accounts," (Yao-suan huo-chang, pu-suan ssu-chang), *KJJP*, March 30, 1965.

75. *NCNA*, Peking, August 23, 1966.

76. See Note 73.

77. Walker, *Modern Technology*, pp. 119–135, 207–214, and bibliography, pp. 147–151.

78. "Metallurgical Workers of Shenyang Improve System of Workers Congresses," *KJJP*, October 13, 1965; "In the New Production Hightide, Look for Quality Amidst Quantity and Speed" (Tsai sheng-ch'an hsin-kao-ch'ao chung chin-ch'ih hao-chung ch'iu-to, hao-chung ch'iu-k'uai), *KJJP*, June 13, 1965; "Rectify Thought and Fully Develop Democracy" (Jui-cheng ssu-hsiang jen-shih, ch'ung-fen fa-hui min-chu), *KJJP*, November 28, 1965. See the report on the Yüeh-hua Textile Plant, Chungking, "Help the Shift Group Leader Master and Grasp Living Thought" (Pang-chu pan-tsu-chang hsueh-hui kua huo-ssu-hsiang), *KJJP*, February 19, 1965.

79. Po I-po, "Down With . . . ," *CB* #878, pp. 1–61, p .15; Baum and Teiwes, *The Socialist Education Campaign*, (Columbia University, East Asian Institute Monograph, New York, 1966).

80. "National Political Work Conference for Industry and Communications Resolves to Learn Firmly and Effectively from PLA," *NCNA*, Peking, April 3, 1964, in *SCMP* #3200, pp. 1–2. *See* a report on the Shantow Fruit and Vegetable Processing Plant, Kwang-tung, "Maintain 'Four-First' Good Cadres" (Chin-ch'ih 'szu ti-yi' tk hao kan-pu), *TKP*, September 7, 1965.

81. *Ibid. See also,* "Give Prominence to Politics, Promote Democracy and Make a Success of Summing Up, Assessment, and Comparison," *KJJP,* November 13, 1965, in *SCMP* #3590, pp. 3–10.

82. See Note 80.

83. See Note 16, *Ibid.,* p. 23.

84. "National Work Conference on Industry and Communications and National Political Work Conference in the Fields of Industry and Communications Set Basic Tasks for Industrial and Communications Departments this Year," *JMJP,* February 25, 1965, in *SCMP* #3414, pp. 1–4.

85. Chi Chung-wei, Li Lan-ch'ing and Lo Ching-fen, "Specialization and Cooperation Are Important Means of Achieving Greater, Faster, Better and More Economical Results in Developing Industrial Productivity," *JMJP,* February 20, 1965, in *SCMP* #3416, pp. 4–13; "Why Must Industrial Production Go the Road of Specialized Cooperation" (Kung-yeh sheng-ch'an wei-shem-mo yao tsou chuan-yeh hsieh-tso ti tao-lu), *TKP,* March 20, 1965; and "Certain Problems on the Specialization of Production in Light Industry," (Kuan-yü ch'ing-kung-yeh sheng-sh'an chuan-yeh-hua ti jo-kan wen-t'i), *CCYC,* March 20, 1965; Teng Chan-ming, "Several Problems in the Development of Economic Cooperation Between Industrial Enterprises" (Kuan-yü kung-yeh ch'i-yeh chih-chien k'ai-chan ching-chi hsieh-tso ti chi-ko wen-ti), *CCYC,* March 20, 1965; and also "Cooperation Among Specialized Factories—the Way to Develop the Processing Industry in China," *NCNA,* English, May 12, 1965, in *SCMP* #3458, pp. 16–17. Also Ching Sheng, "The Problem of Renovation of Fixed Assets and Technical Transformation," *TKP,* Peking, September 18, 1965, p. 5.

86. "Large Group of 'Small But Specialized' and 'Middle Sized But Specialized' Factories Set Up in Tientsin," *JMJP,* March 13, 1965, in *SCMP* #3427, pp. 1–3; Fan Jung-k'ang and Ch'en Ch'ih, "Effectively Combine the Large with the Medium and Small, Follow the Road of Specialized Production and Cooperation," *JMJP,* June 10, 1965, in *SCMP* #3492, pp. 1–11, "Large Scale Cooperation in Auto Production," *JMJP,* April 12, 1965, in *SCMP* #3453, pp. 1–3.

87. See Notes 85, 86.

88. *Ibid.* and Yang Cheng-min, "Organize Production of Machine-Building Industry on the Foundation of 'Small But Specialized' and 'Middle Sized But Specialized' Plants," *JMJP,* March 13, 1965, in *SCMP* #3427, pp. 3–9.

89. See Notes 85, 88.

90. See Note 85.

91. See Note 88.

92. "Promote Specialization and Cooperation in Processing Industries with the Revolutionary Spirit," *JMJP,* May 12, 1965, in *SCMP* #3473, pp. 4–7.

93. Peking Domestic Radio, November 15, 1964; speech by Shen Hung, Vice Minister of 1st Ministry of Machine Building, Peking Domestic Radio, April 21, 1965.

94. Shen Hung, "Let Us Become Revolutionary Promoters in Product Design Work," *KJJP,* April 8, 1965.

95. *JMJP* and *Hung Ch'i* joint editorial, "Attack on Sun Yeh-fang," *NCNA,* November 14, 1965.

96. The preceding argument combines an extrapolation of the logic of specialization in industry with direct polemics written specifically against the economist Sun Yeh-fang and his advocacy of profit incentives and "enterprise autonomy." For good examples of these arguments, all of which were published in 1966 when the Cultural Revolution began officially, *see*: Shih Chih, "Let Us See What Stuff Sun Yeh-fang's Theory of 'Enterprise Independence and Autonomy' Is," *Peking Daily,* August 10, 1966; see Note 28; *JMJP* ed., "Placing Politics in

a Prominent Position Is the Root of All Work," n.d.; Hsin Hsüeh-keng, "Article Attacks Sun Yeh-fang," *NCNA*, November 26, 1966 (original in *JMJP*); *JMJP* and *HC* ed., "Attack on Sun Yeh-fang," *NCNA*, November 14, 1966; Kung Wen-shang, "Sun Yeh-fang's Revisionist Economic Program Refuted," *JMJP*, August 10, 1966, in *SCMP* #3769, pp. 5–14.

97. Hsing, "Article Attacks Sun Yeh-fang."

98. See Note 28.

99. See Note 88.

100. The purpose of the enterprise, a theme since 1964, was consistently repeated until January 1967; "Enterprises Must Be Operated Like Tach'ing in Accordance with the Thought of Mao Tse-tung," *SCMP* #3760, pp. 7–10; Hsing Fu-lin, "Use Mao Tse-tung's Thought to Arm Your Brain" (Yung Mao Tse-tung ssu-hsiang wu-chuang t'ou-nao), *KJJP*, June 24, 1966.

101. Ouyang Ch'eng, "Is It Good to Have Excessive Stored Materials?" *TKP*, Peking, March 19, 1966, in *JPRS* #35, 262.

102. See Note 41.

103. See Note 41.

104. "National Conference of Industry and Communications and National Conference of Political Work on Fronts of Industry and Communications Held in Peking," *NCNA*, April 2, 1966, in *SCMP* #3676, pp. 21–25.

105. *Ibid.* It is impossible, given available evidence, to definitely state the role of Chou En-lai or Teng Hsiao-p'ing, but an interpretation is possible. Chou was probably trying to use his influence to persuade these industrial leaders and planners not to go along with Liu. Whether Teng backed Chou or Liu in this instance is equally unknown, but my guess is that Chou succeeded in getting his neutrality, since Chou probably helped Teng in his political rehabilitation after the Cultural Revolution.

Chapter 7: Politics, Planning, and Management in the Cultural Revolution: The Rebellion Begins and the Issues Are Clarified

1. "Decision of the CCP Central Committee Concerning the Great Cultural Revolution," *NCNA*, Peking, August 8, 1966, in *SCMP* #3761, pp. 1–8.

2. Glenn Tinder, *Political Thinking* (Boston: Beacon Press, 1971).

3. "All-China Federation of Trade Unions Notifies Trade Union Organizations at all Levels to Regard the Great Cultural Revolution as the Center of Trade Union Work," *KJJP*, June 10, 1966, in *SCMP* #3734, pp. 14–16.

4. *SCMP* #3650, pp. 9–11.

5. "Run Enterprises in Line with the Thought of Mao Tsetung," *JMJP*, April 3, 1966, in *SCMP* #3659, pp. 1–8.

6. "The Programatic Document on the Great Cultural Revolution of the Proletariat," *Hung Ch'i* #10, 1966, pp. 1–4.

7. "Grasp the General Orientation of Struggle, Realize Revolutionary 'Three Way Combination,'" *Hung Ch'i* #7, May 20, 1967; "How Factory's Leading Cadres Rebel Against Bourgeois Reactionary Line," *NCNA*, Tsinan, April 25, 1967, in *SCMP* #3927, pp. 30–31; "A Copy of the T'aoyuan Experience," Red Guard Group of Chukiang Paper Mill, in *Torch of Yenan* (*Yenan Huo-Chu*), *SCMP* #4062, pp. 3–9.

8. *NCNA*, July 29 and Sept. 30, 1966, Peking.

9. "Decision of the CCP Central Committee Concerning the Great Cultural Revolution," *NCNA*, Peking, September 6, 1966, in *SCMP* #3779, pp. 1–3.

10. *JMJP* ed., "Take Firm Hold of Revolution in Order to Stimulate Produc-

tion," *NCNA*, Peking, September 6, 1966, in *SCMP* #3779, pp. 1–3; "Conference of Workers in Canton to Call for Carrying Out 16-Point Cultural Revolution Decision," in *NCNA*, September 15, 1966, in *SCMP* #3786, pp. 11–15.

11. *Red Guard Reporter*, "Concerning the Twelve Directives on the Great Cultural Revolution in Factories" (Kuan-yü kung-ch'an wen-hua ta ko-ming shih-erh-t'iao chih-piao), November 17, 1966, East Asian Institute, Columbia University.

12. "Welcome the Upsurge of the Great Cultural Revolution in Industrial Mining Enterprises," *JMJP*, December 1966, in *SCMP* #3852, pp. 1–4; *NCNA*, Domestic Radio, Peking, December 26, 1966.

13. *Ibid.*

14. *NCNA*, Peking, December 31, 1966.

15. "China's Leading Steel Center Takes New Leap Forward," *NCNA*, English Shenyang, December 9, 1966, in *SCMP* #3840, pp. 15–17; "Sian Electrical Condenser Plant Makes Benzotrichloride Condenser and Fulfills Annual Plan Ahead of Schedule," *KJJP*, November 10, 1966, in *SCMP* #3826, pp. 15–16; Huang Jung-ch'ang, "Use the Thought of Mao Tse-tung to Defeat the Bourgeois Authorities," *KJJP*, October 18, 1966, in *SCMP* #3819, pp. 14–15.

16. "Making Revolution Depends on Mao Tse-tung's Thought—An Automatic Oxygen Top Blown Converter is Built in Shanghai in Record Time," *Peking Review* #44, October 28, 1966; also in *SCMM* #551, pp. 6–11; *Chiehfang Jih-pao* (*CFJP*) correspondents, "Thoughts of Mao Tse-tung Lights Up a New Path for Development of Science and Technology," *KMJP*, October 23, 1966, in *SCMP* #3819, pp. 6–11.

17. *NCNA*, Peking, September 21, 1966, on the Wuhan Iron and Steel Complex; "Electro-Plating Workers of Loyang Tractor Engine Factory Raise High the Great Red Banner of Mao Tse-tung's Thought, Defeat Bourgeois Technical Authorities, Blaze a China Type New Trail for Technology," in *Hung Wei-Pao*, Canton, September 14, 1966, in *SCMP* #3793, pp. 22–27. Also *NCNA*, Peking, September 19, 1966, for description of a split in the ranks of technicians in the Shanghai Machine Tools Plant.

18. "Mao Tse-tung's Thought Stimulates New Leap Forward in Central South China City," *NCNA*, English, Wuhan, September 28, 1966, *SCMP* #3793, pp. 27–28; "Loyang Bearings Plant Takes Its Own Road of Industrial Development," *NCNA*, English, Chengchow, September 27, 1966, *SCMP* #3792, pp. 35–37.

19. "Trust the Masses, Rely on the Masses," *Hung Ch'i* #9, July 1, 1966, *SCMM* #532, pp. 1–3; *NCNA*, Peking, November 21, 1966, for a description of the Shanghai Machine Tools Plant; "A New All-Round Leap Forward Situation Emerges," *Peking Review* #40, September 30, 1966; *SCMM* #545, pp. 5–11.

20. Richman, *Industrial Society*, p. 230; K. S. Karol, *China: The Other Communism* (New York: Hill and Wang, 1967), pp. 237–240.

21. Karol, *The Other Communism*, p. 239.

22. *Ibid.*, p. 239.

23. Richman, *Industrial Society*, p. 761.

24. *Ibid.*, p. 762; Karol, *The Other Communism*, p. 239.

25. "On Seizure of Power in China: An Interview with David Crook," *NCNA*, English, Peking, July 26, 1967, *SCMP* #3990, pp. 10–13. One of the first such power seizures came on January 10 in the Shanghai Glass Making Machinery Plant, *NCNA, Shanghai Domestic*, January 10, 1967.

26. James G. March, *Handbook of Organization* (Chicago: Rand McNally, 1965), pp. 4–5.

27. The following sources indicate the chief targets of the power seizures: San Fu-chun, Kai Kenshu and Ch'ai Feng-sheng, "We are Shouldering the Heavy

Burden of Revolution," *JMJP*, January 11, 1967, in *SCMP* #3865, pp. 15–16; "We Now Grasp Our Own Fate in Our Own Hands" (Ming-yun yu wo-men tzu-chi lai chang-wo), *Ching-chi Tao-pao*, Hong Kong, January 23, 1967; "Cadres Must Be Treated Correctly," *Hung Ch'i* #4, February 1967, *SCMM* #566, pp. 1–8; "Put Revolution in the First Place," *Hung Ch'i* #5, March 1967, *SCMM* #570, pp. 6–7; "Support Industry with Thought of Mao Tse-tung," *Hung Ch'i* #6, 1967, *SCMM* #577, pp. 18–23.

28. Richman, *Industrial Society*, pp. 814–815.

29. *Ibid.*, p. 797.

30. "32 Shanghai Workers' Revolutionary Rebel Organizations Issue 'Urgent Notice,' " *Wen Hui-pao* and *CFJP, NCNA*, English, Shanghai, January 11, 1967, *SCMP* #3861, pp. 1–4.

31. "Party Central Committee's Circular Concerning Opposition to Economism" (Chung-kung chung-yang kuan-yü fan-tui ching-chi chu-yi ti t'ung-chih), January 21, 1967, East Asian Institute, Columbia University.

32. Chengchow Municipal CP Committee and Provincial Committee of Honan Province, *Chengchow Domestic Service*, June 3, 1967; Sian #4 State Cotton Mill, *Sian Domestic Service*, January 17, 1967.

33. "A Copy of T'aoyuan Experience," *Yenan Huo-Chu* (*Torch of Yenan*) #15, October 5, 1967, *SCMP* #4062, pp. 3–9; "How Factory's Leading Cadres Rebel Against Bourgeois Reactionary Line," *NCNA*, English, Tsinan, April 25, 1967, *SCMP* #3927, pp. 30–31.

34. *NCNA*, Peking, October 4, 1967.

35. Political Department, CCP East China Bureau of Electricity Administration, "The Yangshupu Power Plant, a 'Red Citadel,' " *Shui-li Yü Tien-li* #8, April 25, 1966, *SCMM* #565, pp. 24–30. For description of this plant from a rebel view, see *Shanghai Domestic Radio*, January 18, 1967, and report by *NCNA*, "Shanghai Revolutionaries Use Self-Criticism to Resolve Contradictions among Themselves," English, Shanghai, June 13, 1967, in *SCMP* #3961, pp. 8–9.

36. "Peking #2 Lathe Plant Smashes Schemes of the Bourgeois Reactionary Line and Wins Victories in Revolution and Production," *JMJP*, January 18, 1967, in *SCMP* #3870, pp. 16–17; "Without Revolutionary Triple Combination, It Is Impossible to Guarantee Victory in the Struggle to Seize Power," *JMJP*, March 19, 1967, in *SCMP* #3907, pp. 19–25; Taiyuan Textile Mill, Peking Domestic Radio, March 29, 1967; Chungking Municipal Mining Machinery Plant, *NCNA*, Peking Domestic, February 17, 1967; Shanghai General Machinery Plant, Peking Domestic Service, January 17, 1967; Sian #4 State-operated Cotton Textile Plant, Sian Domestic Service, January 17, 1967.

37. Examples of exceptions, where the PLA was instrumental in power seizures (rather than in helping those who had already seized power) were in a report on the Lingtze Woolen Mill in Tibet where many workers wanted to go back to Shanghai, and this seemed to be the crux of their rebellion. *NCNA*, Peking Domestic Radio, April 17, 1967. *See* "Chinese Industrial Workers Honor May Day With New Achievements," *NCNA*, English, Peking, May 2, 1967, in *SCMP* #3932, p. 29; *see also* NCNA, English, Peking, March 18, 1967.

38. *SCMP* #3865, pp. 11–14.

39. Report on the Shanghai Diesel Engine Plant, Shanghai City Service, August 4, 1967.

40. My own belief is that it is impossible to say for certain who the rebels were, but previous and subsequent events seem to indicate that rebel leaders were very much part of the factories' history and development, at least in the early stages of power seizure. Even after the PLA stepped into the picture, the reality of struggle and emotion tends to lend credence to the view that rebel leaders of

many factions were primarily workers and cadres in the factories, and not "outside agitators."

41. *NCNA*, Domestic, Peking, February 17, 1967.

42. Peking Domestic Radio, February 9, 1967.

43. Peking Domestic, January 18, 1967.

44. "A Brand New Outlook Appears in Revolution and Production of Peking Stamp Printing Plant," *JMJP*, February 2, 1967, in *SCMP* #3881, pp. 7–8.

45. Kwieiyang Domestic Service, April 18, 1967.

46. "How a Revolutionary Three-Way Alliance is Formed After Seizure of Power," *NCNA*, Peking, March 17, 1967, in *SCMP* #3903, pp. 17–18.

47. Nanchang Domestic Service, February 13, 1967.

48. Shanghai Domestic Service, February 13, 1967.

49. Tsinan Domestic Service, March 3, 1967.

50. *NCNA*, Domestic Service, January 23, 1967.

51. "Experience of Kweiyang Cotton Mill in Forming Alliances Based on Administrative Units," *Peking Review* #12, March 17, 1967, pp. 19–20.

52. Nanking Domestic Service, February 20, 1967.

53. *Ibid.*

54. "PLA Strongly Supports Revolutionary Leftists of Auto Repair and Assembly Plant in Canton," *Kuang-chou Jih-pao*, April 2, 1967, in *SCMP* #3961, pp. 16–18.

55. "PLA Enthusiastically Helps Revolutionary Left Wing of Canton Power Plant," *Kuang-chou Jih-pao*, April 2, 1967, in *SCMP* #3961, pp. 13–15.

56. Shanghai Domestic Service, March 18, 1967.

57. "How Factory's Leading Cadres Rebel Against Bourgeois Reactionary Line," *NCNA*, English, Tsinan, April 25, 1967, in *SCMP* #3927, pp. 30–31.

58. Harbin Domestic Service, March 1, 1967.

59. Shanghai City Service, December 1, 1967.

60. "The More the Reactionary Bourgeois Line on the Cadres' Question is Criticized, the More Solid is the Base for Revolutionary and Three-Way Alliance," *JMJP*, May 9, 1967.

61. "Soochow Rebels Write Investigation Report on Laboratory," *Hsinhua News Bulletin*, October 31, 1968.

62. *Hsinhua News Bulletin*, October 31, 1968.

63. San Fu-chün, Kai Ken-hsün, and Ch'ai Feng-sheng, "We Are Shouldering the Heavy Burden of Revolution," *JMJP*, January 11, 1967, in *SCMP* #3865, pp. 15–16.

64. "Advance in the Storm of Class Struggle," *China Pictorial* #11, 1968; Li Chin-kuang, "Technical Power Is the Firm Grip of Us Workers," *Hung Ch'i* #3, September 10, 1968.

65. "Forging a Three-Way Alliance Is the Key to Ensuring the Victory of the Power Struggle," *JMJP*, February 13, 1967, in *SCMP* #3887, pp. 24–27.

66. "Red Rebels Unite Very Well with Revolutionary Leading Cadres," *JMJP*, February 19, 1967.

67. "Thoroughly Abolish the System of Temporary Labor and Outside Contract Labor," *Wen Hui-pao*, January 6, 1967.

68. For a rather detailed evaluation of the system of contract labor, *see* Red Rebel Team, Ministry of Labor and Revolutionary Rebel Team of Red Workers and Staff Ministers, Ministry of Labor, "Information about Liu Shao-ch'i in the System of Temporary Labor and Contract Labor," in *SCMM* #616, pp. 21–28, for a description of the discrimination. This article does not seem to distinguish between urban "contract" or "temporary labor," and seasonal labor in industry in local rural areas and agricultural related industry, which is also a form of contract labor. *See also*, "A Letter to Canton Municipal Rebels and Revolutionary

Worker Comrades," *Lao-tung Chih-pao*, February 3, 1968 (a Red Guard publication), Union Research Service, Hong Kong, for an analysis which does make this distinction between "contract labor" (ho-t'ung kung) and the "worker and peasant" labor system (yi-nung yi-kung, lao-tung chih-tu). For an interesting article attacking the contract labor system, *see* an unsigned Red Guard piece entitled, "The Present System of Contract Labor Is a Big Anti-Mao Tsetung Thought Poisonous Weed," Union Research Service, Hong Kong, n.d. *See note* 72, Chap. 6, above.

69. See Note 25; Victor Lippit, "Economic Development and Welfare in China," *Bulletin of Concerned Asian Scholars,* vol. 4, no. 2, pp. 76–87.

70. Li Ping, "Model Workers Must Stand at the Forefront of the Great Proletarian Cultural Revolution," *Hung Ch'i* #1, 1967, Peking Domestic Service, January 17, 1967, and an article on the dilemma of the model worker who has identified with management, Shanghai Domestic Service, March 19, 1967.

71. *See* a description of the Inner Mongolia Diesel Plant, Peking, Domestic Radio, September 19, 1968; also "Shanghai Steel Workshop Sets New Records After Seizure of Power," *NCNA*, English, Shanghai, February 19, 1967, in *SCMP* #3885, p. 16; also a report of the T'aiyüan Rubber Plant, "North China Rubber Factory Workers Make Important Technical Renovation After Seizing Power," *NCNA*, English, T'aiyüan, February 19, 1967, in *SCMP* #3885, pp. 16–17; also, "Industrial Production Moves Forward With Big Strides in Hainan District," *NFJP*, Canton, October 4, 1966, and "Industrial Production Leaps Forward in Chaoch'ing Municipality," *ibid.* Lynn T. White III notes the crucial importance of conflict between groups of technical and engineering decision-makers with different backgrounds during the power seizures in Shanghai. *See* "Shanghai's Polity in Cultural Revolution," in John W. Lewis, ed., *The City in Communist China* (Stanford: Stanford University Press, 1971), pp. 348–351. For a clear indication of early unhappiness over technical decision-making methods, *see* reports on Shanghai Printing Ink Factory and Shanghai Machine Tool Plant, *NCNA*, Peking, June 9, 1966.

72. "Red Rebels Enforce a New Order of Things in Chinese Factories," *NCNA*, Peking, February 21, 1967; "Bring Daring to the Fore, and Carry Two Loads, Revolution and Production," *JMJP*, January 24, 1967, in *SCMP* #3879, pp. 18–20; report on the Shanghai #2 Camera Factory, originally an editorial in *Wen Hui-pao*, Shanghai Domestic Service, February 13, 1967; report on Hung Ch'i Machine Building Plant in Wuhsi, Kiangsi Province, Nanking Domestic Radio, March 12, 1967, report on the T'aiyüan #1 Thermal Power Plant, *NCNA*, Peking, April 8, 1967; report on the Kweiyang Cotton Textile Mill, Kweiyang Domestic Radio, March 22, 1967.

73. Ch'ien Chun-pang, "Thoroughly Uncover the Big Conspiracy of Economism," *KMJP*, January 16, 1967, in *SCMP* #3870, pp. 1–5; report on the Kweichow Diesel Engine Plant, Peking Domestic Radio, February 9, 1967; report on the Peking #1 Machine Tool Plant by Ch'un Li, "Main Orientation of Struggle Must Never Be Altered," *JMJP*, January 16, 1967, in *SCMP* #3868, pp. 9–10.

74. "Shanghai Workers Promote Production in the Revolution," *NCNA*, Shanghai, December 30, 1967, in *SCMP* #4092, pp. 33–35. "Notice from CCP Central Committee, State Council, Central Military Commission and Central Cultural Revolution Group on Dealing Further Blows to Counter Revolutionary Economism and Speculative Profiteering Activities," Canton *Kang-t'ieh Tsung-ssu* (Canton Railway General Headquarters), #28, early February 1968, in *SCMP* #4129, pp. 1–4.

75. Report on the Shanghai Instrument and Hair Spring Factory, which emphasizes the issue of status symbols and working conditions as a concern of the rebels, Shanghai Domestic Radio, March 8, 1967; also a report of different motives

for rebellion on the part of leaders who wanted changes in managerial power, and some workers who wanted more money in the Taiyüan Textile Plant, "PLA's Fine Traditions Prevail in Taiyüan Factory," *NCNA*, English, Taiyüan, March 15, 1967, in *SCMP* #3901, pp. 23-24. For reports where economist motives were not crucial in the power seizure stage, see "Revolution Stimulates Production in Northeast China Steel Mill" (The Peimen Steel Plant), *NCNA*, English, Peking, March 2, 1967; and another report on the Kwanghua Wood Products Factory, "Mao Tse-tung Thought Is a Basic Guarantee of Promoting Production," *KMJP*, March 20, 1967. *See also* a description of how resentment at leadership style led to sharp criticism of leading cadres, Yang Shu-te, "A Factory Superintendent Joins the Brigade," *Chieh-Fang-chün Wen-yi* (*PLA Literature and Art*), #3, March 25, 1967, in *SCMM* #575, pp. 34-37.

76. The information on the Shanghai Glass-Making Machinery Plant was obtained from the following sources: "In Praise of the 'Revolution and Production' Committee," *JMJP*, January 24, 1967, in *SCMP* #3869, pp. 1-3; "Another New Product Nurtured by the Great Thought of Mao Tse-tung," *ibid.*, pp. 8-11; "Revolutionary Workers of Shanghai Factory Set Up Revolution and Production Committee,'" *NCNA*, English, Peking, January 23, 1967 in *SCMP* #3869, pp. 1-3; "Founding of Revolutionary Production Committees in Shanghai Factory Marks New Victory," *NCNA*, English, Shanghai, January 15, 1967, in *SCMP* #3863, pp. 2-3; Shanghai Domestic Service, *FBIS*, January 10, 1967; *NCNA*, Peking, January 15, 1967; and Shanghai Domestic Service, *FBIS*, February 1, 1967.

77. Information on the Kweiyang Cotton Mill was obtained from the following sources: "*JMJP* Commends New Form of Proletarian Revolutionaries Alliance," *NCNA*, English, Peking, March 1, 1967; "Kweiyang Cotton Mill Introduces Revolutionary Management System," *NCNA*, English, Kweiyang, March 30, 1967, in *SCMP* #3910, pp. 24-25. Kweiyang Cotton Mill, Revolutionary Committee, "Experience of Kweiyang Cotton Mill in Forming Alliances Based on Administrative Units," *Peking Review* #12, March 17, 1967, pp. 19-20.

78. Information on the Kwanghua Wood Products Factory came from the following sources: Red Rebels of Peking Kwanghua Timber Factory, "After the Seizure of Power," *Hung Ch'i* #3, February 1, 1967, in *SCMM* #564, pp. 11-16; *NCNA* Domestic Service, February 4, 1967, carried the same article: also Anna Louise Strong, "How Rebels Seize Power in a Factory," *China Report*, Box 326, Cathedral Station, New York, March 1967.

79. "Put Revolution in Command of Production," *Hung Ch'i* #5, March 1967, in *SCMM* #573, pp. 7-13.

80. Red Rebel Group of Harbin Boiler Plant, "Without Revolutionary 'Triple Combination' It Is Impossible to Guarantee Victory in the Struggle to Seize Power," *JMJP*, March 23, 1967, in *SCMP* #3907, pp. 19-25; *NCNA*, Peking, March 23, 1967.

81. Information on the Peking #2 Machine Tool Plant was gathered from the following sources: "Revolutionary Masses in Peking #2 Lathe Plant Smash Schemes of the Bourgeois Reactionary Line and Win Victories in Revolution and Production," *JMJP*, January 18, 1967, in *SCMP* #3870, pp. 16-17; *NCNA*, Peking Domestic Service, January 18, 1967; "After Revolutionary Rebels Assume Power, A Double Victory is Achieved in Revolution and Production," *JMJP*, February 2, 1967, in *SCMP* #3881, pp. 9-11; *NCNA*, Peking, Domestic Service, March 9, 1967; "Peking Machine Workers Combat Bourgeois Reactionary Line," *NCNA*, Peking, English, April 14, 1967, in *SCMP* #3921, pp. 26-27; Revolutionary Rebel General Headquarters, Peking #2 Machine Tool Plant, "Grasp the General Orientation of the Struggle, Realize Revolutionary 'Three Way Combination,'" *Hung Ch'i* #7, May 20, 1967, in *SCMM* #580, pp. 1-7.

82. Information on the Loyang Tractor Works was obtained from the follow-

ing sources: Honan Provincial Radio, Chengchow, September 11, 1968; "Advance in the Direction of Independence, Self-Determination, and Regeneration Through Self-Reliance," *JMJP*, May 20, 1969, in *SCMP* #4433, pp. 6–14; "Loyang Tractor Plant Advanced Along the Road of Self-Reliance," *Peking Review*, June 20, 1969.

83. Other factories, not included in the survey above, but for which information is available, also followed these same general patterns. *See* reports on the Coking Chemical Plant of the Penki Steel Company, *NCNA*, October 31, 1968; the Hsingtai Municipal Knitting and Dyeing Factory, Tientsen Domestic Service, April 15, 1967; the Tsingtao #1 Furniture Factory, *NCNA*, Peking, April 11, 1967; the Harbin Bicycle Factory, "Cultural Revolution Brings Big Changes to a Harbin Factory," *NCNA*, English, Harbin, April 11, 1967, in *SCMP* #3918, pp. 30–32; Wheelwright and McFarlane, *The Chinese Road to Socialism*, pp. 118–120.

84. Tien An-Men, Observer, "Unite More than 95% of the Cadres, Make Revolution to the End," *T'ien An-Men* (A Red Guard periodical) #2, March 1967, in *SCMM* #576, pp. 8–10.

85. For a discussion of factionalism, *see* Andrew Nathan, "A Factionalism Model for CCP Politics," *China Quarterly* 53 (January–March 1973): 34–67.

86. The situation above the enterprise was extremely complex. In some places, government departments gave help to the rebels. For an example of this, *see* a report on the Kiangsi Insecticide Plant, *NCNA*, Peking, January 15, 1967. At other times, higher level government organs seemed quite willing to go along with party organs at that level. *See* report on the Chengtu Tungfanghung Paper Mill, Szechwan Provincial Service, Chengtu, February 28, 1968. And in Shanghai, the "January Revolution" was aimed not only at the municipal party organs. A "Frontline Command for Grasping Revolution and Stimulating Production" was established to "replace the leading economic organ of the former *municipal people's council*." *See* "Shanghai Economic Life Thrives Under Control of Revolutionary Rebels," *NCNA*, February 10, 1967, in *SCMP* #3880, p. 25. For the way in which the army offered alternatives to both party and governmental higher level authority, *see* "Support Industry with the Thought of Mao Tse-tung," *Hung Ch'i* #6, 1967, in *SCMM* #577, pp. 18–23, and K'ang Wei-chung, "Teach Her to Stand on the Side of the Proletarian Revolutionaries," *JMJP*, February 24, 1967, in *SCMP* #3893, pp. 39–41.

87. Report on Shansi Province's activities of the PLA for how the chain of command worked, *Peking Domestic Service*, March 28, 1967.

88. Report on PLA representatives from municipal and provincial levels performing administrative or ceremonial tasks at the founding of the Revolutionary Committee at the Akosai Colliery, Kansu Province, Kansu Provincial Radio, Lanchow, November 17, 1967.

89. For some of many examples of this function, *see* reports on the Taiyüan Textile Mill, *NCNA*, Peking, March 15, 1967; the Kailan Coal Fields, *NCNA*, Peking, May 15, 1968; the Tatung Coal Field, "North China Colliery Establishes New Revolutionary Order," *NCNA*, English, Peking, May 5, 1967, in *SCMP* #335, pp. 30–31; the Ssufang Rolling Stock Plant, "Tsingtao Railway Workers Develop Revolutionary Great Alliance," *NCNA*, English, Peking, October 31, 1967, in *SCMP* #4054, pp. 12–14; and the North China Metal Structure Plant, "Creatively Study and Apply Chairman Mao's Writings Correctly and Handle Contradictions Among the People," *Hung Ch'i* #10, 1967, in *SCMM* #585, pp. 6–11. *Also see* reports on the Tsingtao Chemical Fertilizer Plant, "Revolutionary Alliances in China's Factories," *SCMP* #4047, pp. 16–18; report on the Anshan Iron and Steel Complex, *NCNA*, Peking, December 8, 1967; report on the Lanchow Tungfanghung Glass Factory, Kansu Provincial Service, Lanchow, November 13, 1967; report on the Wuhan Iron and Steel Corporation, Wuhan

Domestic Service, March 21, 1967; "PLA Propaganda Team Helps Mine Cadres to Come Out and Make Revolution," *NCNA*, Peking, July 16, 1967, in *SCMP* #3992, p. 5; and a report on the Shih-chiachuang #3 State Cotton Mill, *JMJP*, April 23, 1968.

90. "Helping Workers Study Chairman Mao's Works Is the PLA's Main Task in Aiding Industry," *NCNA*, English, Peking, April 11, 1967, in *SCMP* #3918, pp. 28-29; report on Tatung Colliery, Shansi Province, Peking Domestic Service, April 18, 1967; reports on Nanking Factory #3503, Nanking Electronic Tube Factory, and Chenkuang Machine Plant, Kiangsu Provincial Service, July 16, 1968.

91. Another report on the Tatung Colliery shows how PLA helped in organizational reform, *NCNA*, Peking, May 5, 1967. *See also* a good detailed study in *NCNA*, Trends in the Cultural Revolution, "The Experience of the PLA in the Peking Hsinhua Printing Plant in Mobilizing the Masses to Carry Out Struggle Against the Enemy" (Pei-ching hsin-hua yin-shua-ch'an chün-kuan-hui fa-tung chün-chung k'ai-chan tui-ti tou-cheng ti ching-yen).

92. Report on Tungya Woolen Textile Mill where Liu Shao-ch'i made his infamous visit in 1949, now called Tientsin #3 Woolen Textile Mill, *NCNA*, Peking, April 15, 1967.

93. Ch'i Yi-ch'i, "Influence of the Cultural Revolution on Communist Industrial and Mining Enterprises," *Fei-ch'ing Yueh-pao* (*Bandit Monthly Report*), vol. II, #2, April 1968, pp. 63-71, in *JPRS* #45741-19, June 1968.

94. Mao mentioned this revolutionary "three-in-one" combination in an undated "instruction" sometime early in 1967. Wheelwright and McFarlane, *The Chinese Road to Socialism*, p. 228. Another central "instruction" from Mao in later 1967 said that the setting up of "revolutionary committees" should become the goal of power seizures. (*Ibid.*, p. 231.)

95. Hangchow Radio, Chekiang, September 23, 1967.

96. "Zest for Great Alliance Steadily Spreads in China," *NCNA*, English, Peking, September 23, 1967, in *SCMP* #4090, pp. 12-13.

97. "Peking Workers Win New Victories in Cultural Revolution," *NCNA*, English, Peking, December 28, 1967, in *SCMP* #3090, pp. 12-13.

98. "Peking Garrison Commends Exemplary Units and Individuals for Their Contributions to the Cultural Revolution," *NCNA*, English, Peking, October 23, 1967, in *SCMP* #4090, pp. 23-24.

99. "A Brilliant Victory for Chairman Mao's Latest Instructions Hailing the New Upsurge of Shanghai Revolutionary Great Alliance," *JMJP*, September 18, 1967, in *SCMP* #4031, pp. 10-11, 23-24.

100. "Excellent Situation in China's Leading Steel Center," *NCNA*, English, Anshan, December 8, 1967, in *SCMP* #4078, pp. 33-34.

101. "Textile and Other Light Industries Thriving," *NCNA*, English, Peking, December 24, 1967, in *SCMP* #4089, pp. 29-30.

102. McFarlane and Wheelwright, *The Chinese Road to Socialism*, pp. 119-121. I have estimated, in a survey of 180 plants and mines, that in at least 25 percent of these the PLA was specifically mentioned as present, and it can safely be assumed that this is a very gross underestimate. One study of the machinery industry, for example, has a sample of 44 factories and mentions a PLA presence in about one-half of these (23 out of 44 by rough count). *See* Ch'i Yi-ch'i, "Influence of the Cultural Revolution in Communist Industrial and Mining Enterprises," (n. 93), pp. 21-29.

103. *Ibid.*, pp. 123, 231,

104. The information presented in this table was obtained from the following sources:

1. My own files which list over 200 factories, obtained from a thorough survey

of the Chinese press in the files of the Union Research Institute, Hong Kong, and the translation services of the United States government (*SCMM, SCMP, JPRS,* and *CB*).

2. A copy of a diary kept by Bruce McFarlane on a trip to China in 1969 where he did extensive interviews in various factories. The diary was made available to me by Dr. Benedict Stavis, a research associate at Cornell University.

3. Ch'i Yi-ch'i, "The Influence of the Cultural Revolution on Communist Industrial and Mining Enterprises," pp. 21–29.

4. Richman, *Industrial Society,* pp. 726–737.

5. *A General Survey of Industrial and Mining Enterprises in Bandit Areas of the Mainland* (Ta-Lu fei-ch'u ch'an-k'uang tsung-chien), Taiwan, 1968, in 5 vols., courtesy of Richard Sorich, Lehman Library, Columbia University.

6. *A Survey of Industry and Mining in China,* Tokyo, 1965, East Asian Library, Columbia University.

105. Richman, *Industrial Society,* pp. 726 ff., and McFarlane, *Diary.*

106. Wheelwright and McFarlane, *The Chinese Road to Socialism,* pp. 123–124. For reports of how rapidly revolutionary committees were set up after March 1968, *see NCNA,* Peking, May 14, 1968. For a report on Anshan, *see NCNA,* Peking Domestic, April 16, 1968; "Central China Coal Mine Greatly Steps Up Production," *NCNA,* Chengchow, June 17, 1968, in *SCMP* #4204, pp. 20–21. For a report on Wuhan, *see* "Increased Industrial Output in Central China City," *NCNA,* English, Wuhan, April 24, 1968, in *SCMP* #4166, p. 24. In Heilungkiang, over 90% of factories and mines established revolutionary committees by June; *see* "Northeast China Province Makes Progress in Cultural Revolution and Industrial Production," *NCNA,* English, Harbin, June 29, 1968, in *SCMP* #4211, pp. 23–24.

107. For a brief discussion of the origins of the "70 Articles" in 1961 in the aftermath of the Great Leap Forward, *see* Chap. 5 above. The date of origin of the "70 Articles" is given as September 1961 by a Japanese correspondent Samejima in *Nihon Kezai,* April 19, 1968. Chinese Communist sources date the 70 Articles in 1961 (for example, *see* Shanghai City Service, June 24, 1967) while a Chinese Nationalist Intelligence source, "Seventy Articles on Industrial Policy," dates them in the first third of December 1961, a date which seems rather late ("Seventy Articles on Industrial Policy," East Asian Institute, Columbia University).

108. For a brief though somewhat superficial description of the "bourgeois line" as opposed to Mao's "proletarian line," *see* "Two Diametrically Opposed Lines in Building the Economy," *JMJP,* August 25, 1967, translated in *Chinese Economic Studies,* International Arts and Sciences Press, White Plains, New York, Winter 1967–68. For greater detail and a very important article, *see JMJP* and *Hung Ch'i,* joint editorial, "Along the Socialist or Capitalist Road," *JMJP,* August 15, 1967.

109. Samejima, *Nihon Kezai,* Tokyo, April 19, 1968, translated in *Survey of the Japanese Press,* U.S. Embassy, Tokyo.

110. Liaoning Provincial Radio, Shenyang, June 30, 1968.

111. Shanghai City Radio, June 14, 1967, as monitored by FBIS, June 1967.

112. See Note 109; "What Are the Ulterior Motives of Advocating that Factories Should Be Run By Experts—3rd Comment on the 70 Articles Industrial Program," *CFJP* editorial, Shanghai City Service, June 13, 1967.

113. Richman, *Industrial Society,* pp. 767, 789.

114. *Ibid.,* pp. 753–760.

115. *NCNA,* Peking Domestic, June 25, 1967, original in *Hung Ch'i* #10, 1967.

116. Kweichow Provincial Service, Kweiyang, July 21, 1968.

117. Shanghai Domestic Service, May 9, 1967. *See also*, "Cultural Revolution Releases Productive Forces in Clock Factory," *NCNA*, English, Shanghai, July 15, 1968, in *SCMP* #4222, pp. 18–20; *NCNA*, Peking, July 15, 1968; "China Clock Factory Carries Out Chairman Mao's Policy on Cadres," *NCNA*, English, Shanghai, April 7, 1967, in *SCMP* #3916, pp. 34–35; and "Shanghai Clock Makers Fight Revisionist Practices in Their Factory," *NCNA*, English, Shanghai, January 24, 1968, in *SCMP* #4108, pp. 20–24. Numerous other examples exist of how factory formal organizational structure had led to over-staffing, exacerbation of the division between mental and manual labor, and to cumbersome rules and regulations. *See* Stephen Andors, "Factory Management in China", Ph.D. dissertation, Columbia University, 1974, Chap. 7, Note 121.

118. Shanghai Domestic Service, June 4, 1967, originally an editorial in *CFJP*; Wheelwright and McFarlane, *The Chinese Road*, pp. 162 ff.; "A Machine Enterprise Which Takes the Road of Independence and Self-Reliance" (Yen-chih tu-li tzu-chu tzu-li keng-sheng ti tao-lu ou-chin ti chi-hsieh kung-yeh) in "Special Supplement for the Autumn Chinese Expert Fair 1969," *Economic Reporter*, October 10, 1969, Hong Kong, pp. 32–33; "Advance in the Direction of Independence, Self-Determination, and Regeneration Through Self-Reliance," *JMJP*, May 20, 1969, in *SCMP* #4433, pp. 6–14.

119. "Working Class Must Always Exercise Power of Leadership in Socialist Enterprises," *NCNA*, English, May 28, 1969, for a report on the Machinery and Power Equipment Plant of the Penki Iron and Steel Company; *Lin Tehching*, "The Working Class Must Hold Power in Industry," *China Reconstructs*, January 1969, pp. 9–10; "Workers Mount the State of Designing," *China Pictorial* #1, January 1969.

120. "The Road for Training Engineering and Technical Personnel Indicated by the Shanghai Machine Tools Plant," *Peking Review* #31, August 2, 1968, pp. 9–14; "How the Shanghai Machine Tools Plant Turned Out Grinding Machines Up to World Standards," *NCNA*, English, Peking, July 30, 1968, in *SCMP* #4232, pp. 31–34.

121. *NCNA*, Peking, May 11, 1968.

122. *NCNA*, October 31, 1968.

123. Kweichow Provincial Service, Kweiyang, August 4, 1968.

124. Liaoning Provincial Service, Shenyang, July 2, 1968.

125. *JMJP*, August 4, 1968.

126. Shanghai Domestic Service, June 9, 1967.

127. The incentive system of the Seventy Articles was attacked in *CFJP*, Shanghai Domestic Service, June 9, 1967. *See also*, Samejima, *Nihon Kezai*, April 19, 1968.

128. Hoffman, *Work Incentives*, pp. 103–104.

129. Shanghai Domestic, June 9, 1967. The same theme was repeated a year later in a *Jen-min Jih-pao* article in July 1968, "Newspaper Article Repudiates Material Incentives Advocated by China's Khrushchev," *NCNA*, English, Peking, July 13, 1963, in *SCMP* #4221, pp. 15–19.

130. Samejima, *Nihon Kezai*, April 18, 1968.

131. The Yangshupu plant in Shanghai may have been an exception because of its pre-1949 history and the probability that pre-1949 technicians and engineers stayed on in some management posts and were receiving comparatively high remuneration. Richman, *Industrial Society*, pp. 318–319. Hoffman, *Work Incentives*, p. 26.

132. For one among numerous examples of this, "Textile Workers Repudiate China's Khrushchev," *China Reconstructs*, vol. XVIII, no. 2, February 1968, pp. 40 ff.

133. For interesting comments on the relationship between goals and organizational performance, *see* Amitai Etzioni, *Complex Organizations* (Glencoe, Illinois: Free Press, 1961), pp. 71–72, especially on the relationship between "process" and "goals." This dynamic certainty influenced the nature of party leadership in the enterprise.

134. Samejima, *Nihon Kezai*, April 19, 1968.

135. Stephen Andors, "Revolution and Modernization: Man and Machine in Industrializing Society, The Chinese Case," in Mark Selden and Edward Friedman, eds., *America's Asia* (New York: Pantheon, 1970).

136. For evidence of the phenomenon of collusion between lower and higher party officials, all the way down to the enterprise level, in implementing the 70 Articles, *see* "Workers Mount the Stage of Designing," *China Pictorial* #1, 1969; Samejima, *Nihon Kezai*, April 18, 1968; "Peking Factory Reports Record Output," *NCNA*, English, Peking, August 26, 1967, in *SCMP* #4012, p. 27. *See also* a report on Anshan municipality, "Revolutionary Committee Established in China's Biggest Steel Center," *NCNA*, English, Anshan, April 17, 1968, in *SCMP* #4162, p. 12; and a report on Heilungkiang Province where the collusion of enterprise level personnel was not clear: *See* Kirin Provincial Radio, Changchün, July 29, 1967. *Also see*, "The Cultural Revolution in Canton Factories," in *SCMP* #4208, p. 13; and "A History of Crimes of Opposing the Party Socialism and the Thought of Mao Tse-tung," *Pa-San Hung-wei-ping* #68, May 13, 1967, in *SCMM* #585, pp. 25–34. The great publicity given to the collusion between factory level managerial personnel and higher party officials in attacks on Liu Shao-ch'i's activities in the Tientsin #3 State Cotton Mill, formerly a capitalist enterprise called the Tung-ya Woolen Textile Mill, seems to be significant as a symbol of what probably was more than an isolated instance: Revolutionary Rebels Joint Committee of Finance and Trade Office of the State Council, "Struggle Between the Two Lines in the Transformation of Capitalist Industry and Commerce," *JMJP*, April 15, 1968, in *SCMP* #4159, pp. 13–19; "Tientsin Workers Condemn Top Party Person in Authority Taking the Capitalist Road," *NCNA*, English, Tientsin, April 15, 1967, in *SCMP* #3922, pp. 27–30, and "Comments on the Reactionary Bourgeois 'National Reconstruction Program': The Tientsin Speeches of Liu Shao-ch'i, a Counter-Revolutionary Revisionist," Canton *Pa-erh-wu Chan-pao*, February 7, 1967, in *SCMM* #574, pp. 8–14.

137. "Down With the Reactionary Docile Tool Theory," *Peking Daily*, in *JMJP*, April 10, 1967, *NCNA*, Peking, April 10, 1967. *Also see* descriptions of Wuchang Carriage Factory in "Wuchang Carriage Factory Purifies Its Class Ranks," Hopei People's Radio, October 11, 1968, Union Research Service, vol. 53, #10, November 1, 1968; and *see* "Peking General Knitwear Mill Takes the Great Task of Liberating All Mankind to Unite and Educate Cadres Who Make Mistakes," *Selected Essays on Six Factories and Two Schools in Peking*, San Lien Bookstore, Hong Kong, 1970; *see also*, "A Report on the Peking Printing Plant Rectifying and Building the Party" (Pei-ching hsin-hua yin-shua-ch'an cheng-tang chien-tang tiao-ch'a pao-kao), *ibid*.

138. In the Peking General Knitwear Mill, the minutes of a meeting of the revolutionary committee quote the former deputy director of the mill as saying that of 300 Party members in the mill, about 80% opposed the rebels at the beginning of the Cultural Revolution, but did so because they "did not understand Chairman Mao's line" not because they understood and opposed it. The deputy director himself claimed that he "didn't know there were two headquarters in our Party." (Source for minutes: Richard Sorich, East Asian Institute, Columbia University.)

139. "Shanghai Workers Criticize Liu at a Mass Meeting," *SCMM* #592, pp. 11–16.

140. Ching Hung, "The Plot of the Top Ambitionist to Operate 'Trusts' on a Large Scale Must be Thoroughly Exposed," *KMJP*, May 9, 1967, in *SCMP* #3948, pp. 1–9.

141. "Seventy Articles on Industrial Policy," East Asian Institute, Columbia University.

142. Ouyang Cheng, "On Socialist Economic Cooperation," *Ta Kung Pao*, February 9, 1962, in *SCMP* #2689, pp. 1–6.

143. Peking Domestic Radio, January 29, 1962; "Strengthen Economic Cooperation," *JMJP* editorial, April 12, 1963, in *SCMP* #2966, pp. 4–6; "Correctly Handle the Relationship Between the State and Enterprises," *NFJP* editorial, April 7, 1962; "Four Industrial Systems in Shenyang Practice Extensive Economic Cooperation Under Unified Leadership," *SCMP* #2689, pp. 6–8; "Deeply Develop the Work of Cooperation," *JMJP*, January 20, 1961; "Permanent Supply Relations Between Factories Established in a Number of Factories in Shanghai through Intensification of Cooperation," *JMJP*, January 18, 1962, in *SCMP* #2673, pp. 2–4; and "Get Things Together, Make Use of All Resources," *JMJP*, January 19, 1961.

144. "Satisfactorily Control and Use the Circulating Funds of Industry," *TKP* editorial, Peking, June 20, 1961, in *SCMP* #2543, pp. 5–7; *JMJP* editorial, "Correctly Develop the Supervisory Role of Banks," *NCNA*, May 10, 1962, a study of the Hsingki Combustion Engine Plant; report of the Taiyüan Locomotive and Carriage Repair Works, "All Around Tightening of Control Over Funds to Promote Production," *TKP*, June 20, 1961, in *SCMP* #2543, pp. 1–2.

145. Sung Hsin-chung, "The System of Retaining a Percentage of Profits by Our Enterprise," *TKP*, May 12, 1961, in *SCMP* #2543, pp. 7–8; and "Acquire a Correct Idea of the Profit Problem of a Socialist Enterprise," *TKP*, July 13, 1962, in *SCMP* #2792, pp. 15–16; Ko Chih-ta and Ho Cheng, "The Profits of Socialist Enterprises, Their Significance and the Way to Earn Them," *Ching-chi Yen-ch'iu* #10, October 17, 1962, in *SCMM* #341, pp. 38–45; Ouyang Cheng, "On Socialist Economic Cooperation"; Chi Ch'eng, "Understand the Role of State Taxation Correctly," *TKP*, Peking, August 11, 1961, in *SCMP* #2569, pp. 1–6; *JMJP* ed., "Step Up Economic Coordination," *NCNA*, Peking, December 15, 1961; Wang Ling, "Handle Economic Contracts Correctly," *KJJP*, November 26, 1961, in *SCMP* #2639, pp. 3–5; "Unfolding Economic Cooperation in a Well-Planned Manner," *TKP* editorial, January 30, 1962, in *SCMP* #2689, pp. 8–10; "Further Promote Diversified Undertaking and Multiple Utilization," *JMJP* editorial, January 19, 1961, in *SCMP* #2434, pp. 9–10; "First Ministry of Machine Building Adjusts Factory Relationships,"*JMJP*, January 30, 1962, in *SCMP* #2681, pp. 14–15; and Fan Mu-ken, "On Specialization in Industrial Production," *Ching-chi Yen-ch'iu* #10, October 17, 1963, in *SCMM* #392, pp. 32–39. For an interesting article which very early forecasts the attack which came on the "trust system" some six years later, *see* Liao Yuan, "Exposing the Truth About the So-Called 'Self-Management of Enterprises' in Yugoslavia," *Hung Ch'i* #11, June 1, 1961, in *SCMM* #266, pp. 25–31. For other surveys of this dispute, *see one by Dwight* Perkins, "Incentives and Profits in Chinese Industry: The Challenge of Economics to Ideology's Machine," *Current Scene*, vol. 10, May 15, 1966, and "The Short-Lived Liberal Phase in Economic Thinking in Communist China," Central Intelligence Agency, U.S. Government, Office of Research and Reports, CIA/RR ER 63–14, 1963.

146. I have reconstructed the essential criticisms leveled at the trust system from the following sources: Wheelwright and McFarlane, *The Chinese Road to Socialism*, pp. 162–179, especially pp. 168–170; the Tungfanghung Corps of the Economic Research Institute, "The Fallacy Advocated by the Top Ambitionist in

Economic Work Refuted," *KMJP*, April 22, 1967, in *SCMP* #3928, pp. 21–26; The Red Guards of Mao Tse-tung's Thought of the East Is Red Commune of the Shantung Finance and Economic College, "Abolition of Socialist Planned Economy Means Capitalist Restoration," *KMJP*, July 19, 1967, in *CB* #836, pp. 20–24; Ching Hung, "The Plot of the Top Ambitionist . . . ,"; "Completely Settle the Heinous Crimes of China's Khrushchev and Company in Undermining Agricultural Mechanization," *Nung-yeh Chi-hsieh Chi-shu* (*The Technology of Agricultural Mechanization*), #5, August 8, 1967, in *SCMM* #610, pp. 17–31; The Writing Group of the Kirin Provincial Revolutionary Committee, "Class Struggle in the Field of Socialist Construction and Economics—Criticizing the Revisionist Economic Theory of Sun Yeh-fang," *Hung Ch'i* #2, January 30, 1970, in *SCMM* #673–674; "Newspaper Article Repudiates Material Incentives Advocated by China's Khrushchev," *NCNA*, English, Peking, July 13, 1968, in *SCMP* #4221, pp. 15–19; "JMJP Article Refutes Counter-Revolutionary Revisionist Line in Workers' Movement," *NCNA*, English, Peking, June 13, 1968, in *SCMP* #4201, pp. 17–24.

147. The French economist Charles Bettleheim refers to this group as a "state bourgeoisie." Paul Sweezy, "The Transition to Socialism," *Monthly Review*, vol. 23, #1, May 1971, p. 13.

148. For a graphic description of how this process worked, see a report on the Shanghai Odd-Shaped Steel Tubing Factory, Shanghai Domestic Service, April 1967; report on the Shanghai Printing Ink Plant, Shanghai Domestic Service, May 9, 1967.

149. "Comments on the Reactionary Bourgeois 'National Reconstruction Program'; The Tientsin Speeches of Liu Shao-ch'i, a Counter-Revolutionary Revisionist," *Canton Pa-erh-wu Chan-pao*, February 17, 1967, in *SCMM* #574, pp. 8–14; "Liu Shao-ch'i Befriends Reactionary Capitalist Wang Kuang-ying," *Canton Pa-erh-wu Chan-pao*, February 17, 1967, in *SCMM* #574, pp. 1–3; "Looking at Liu Shao-ch'i's Counter-Revolutionary Revisionist Face Through His Crimes in Tientsin Tungya Woolen Textile Mill," *Ching Kang Shan*, Tsinghua University, Peking, #17, February 15, 1967, in *SCMP* #3898, pp. 11–14; "Tientsin Workers Condemn Top Party Person in Authority Taking the Capitalist Road," *NCNA*, English, Tientsin, April 15, 1967, in *SCMP* #3922, pp. 27–30; "A History of Crimes of Opposing the Party, Socialism, and the Thought of Mao Tse-tung," *Pa-San Hung-wei-ping* #68, May 13, 1967, in *SCMM* #587, pp. 24–34; and Revolutionary Rebels Joint Committee of Finance and Trade Office of the State Council, "Struggle Between Two Lines in the Transformation of Capitalist Industry and Commerce," *JMJP*, April 15, 1968, in *SCMP* #4159, pp. 13–19.

150. Joint editorial by *Hung Ch'i* and *JMJP*, "Reference Material for 'A Great Historic Document,' " *Hung Ch'i* #7, 1967, in *SCMM* #577, pp. 28–32.

151. The matter of examining and debating over the issue of individual attitudes embodied in individual behavior became known as a process of "taking stock of class ranks" or sometimes "purifying class ranks." The task of organizational change was called a move toward "better troops and simpler administration." Kiangsi Provincial Radio, Nanchang, July 15, 1968.

Chapter 8: "Taking Stock of Class Ranks" and "Better Troops and Simpler Administration"

1. Kiangsi Provincial Service, Nanchang, July 15, 1968.

2. Report on the Tsingtao #9 Cotton Mill, Peking, December 15, 1967; the Shanghai #3 Iron & Steel Plant, in "How We Differentiate, Educate and Make Use of Revolutionary Cadres," *JMJP*, April 14, 1967; report on the Tsing-tao

Chemical Fertilizer Plant, "Proletarian Revolutionaries in Tsingtao Municipality Earnestly Implement Chairman Mao's Policy of Cadres," (*sic*), *NCNA*, Peking, October 22, 1967, in *SCMP* #4050, pp. 20–24.

3. "How the Shanghai Machine Tools Plant Turns Out Grinding Machines Up to World Standards," *NCNA*, English, Peking, July 30, 1968, in *SCMP* #4232, pp. 31–34; "Revolutionary Criticism Pushes Scientific Experiments in Chinese Factory" (in this case, the Machinery and Electric Equipment Plant of the Penki Iron & Steel Works), *NCNA*, English, Shenyang, July 8, 1968, in *SCMP* #4217, pp. 23–24.

4. *JMJP* Commentator, "The Most Fundamental Requirement," *JMJP*, April 3, 1968, in *SCMP* #4161, p. 8; "The Lowly Are the Most Intelligent; The Elite are Most Ignorant," *Peking Review* #47, November 22, 1968.

5. "Minutes of the Meeting of the Revolutionary Committee," Peking General Knitwear Mill for March 1969. Courtesy Richard Sorich, Lehman Library, Columbia University.

6. *Ibid.*

7. *Peking Review* #45, November 8, 1968 report on this type of cadre in the Shukuang Electric Motor Plant, Peking.

8. "Represent the Masses in a Still Better Way," *JMJP*, April 22, 1968, in *SCMP* #4172, pp. 22–23.

9. Joint *JMJP* and *Hung Ch'i* editorial, "Develop the Party's Working Style of Forging Close Links with the Masses," *NCNA*, English, Peking, June 30, 1968, in *SCMP* #4212, pp. 11–16.

10. "Peking General Knitwear Mill Takes the Great Task of Liberating All Mankind to Unite and Educate Cadres Who Made Mistakes," in *Six Factories*.

11. Richman, *Industrial Society*, p. 127.

12. *Ibid.*, pp. 148–149.

13. *Ibid.*, p. 203.

14. The percentage in 1965 was 51.35%; *see also* Richman, *Industrial Society*, p. 301.

15. *NCNA*, Peking, July 26, 1968.

16. "The Road for Training Engineering and Technical Personnel Indicated by the Shanghai Machine Tools Plant," *Peking Review* #31, pp. 9–14, p. 11; *Peking Review* #40, October 4, 1968, for the Shihchiachuang Printing and Dyeing Mill.

17. Wang Teh-fa, "Live Up To Chairman Mao's Expectations," *China Pictorial* #12, 1968.

18. Report on the Shanghai Machine Tools Plant, "The Road for Training . . . ," *Peking Review* #31, p. 13 (n. 16); the Penki Iron & Steel Company's Machinery and Power Equipment Plant, *NCNA*, English, Peking, May 28, 1969; the Loyand Tractor Plant, *Peking Review*, June 20, 1969, pp. 3, 4, 11; Li Hsin-kung, "Technical Power Is In the Firm Grip of Us Workers," *Hung Ch'i* #3, September 10, 1968, in *SCMM* #629, pp. 25–26; Richman, *Industrial Society*, p. 300. Also see report on the Shanghai Compressors Works, "Shanghai Workers Criticize Revisionist Line in Management," *SCMM* #592, pp. 11–16. *See also* McFarlane, *Diary*, on the Shanghai Diesel Pump and Motor Factory.

19. See Note 16.

20. Richman, p. 142, *Industrial Society*, pp. 129–153.

21. "Shanghai #17 State Cotton Mill Adopts a Realistic Method of Cultivation" (Shang-hai kuo-mien shih-ch'i ch'an tsai-ch'u ch'ieh-ho shih-chi ti p'ei-hsiu fang-fa), *KJJP*, May 16, 1962.

22. "Shanghai #17 Cotton Mill—'Red Bulwark' of Shanghai's Proletarian Cultural Revolution," *NCNA*, English, Peking, June 2, 1969; John Gittings, "The

Millers Tale," *Far Eastern Economic Review*, Hong Kong, (July 31, 1969), pp. 283–286.

23. Gittings, *ibid.*, pp. 284, 286.

24. "Worker Technicians Play Vanguard Role at Anshan Plant," *NCNA*, English, Shenyang, August 12, 1968, in *SCMP* #4241, pp. 26–27.

25. Reports on the Shanghai Heavy Machine Tools Plant in *NCNA*, Peking, October 2, 1967, in McFarlane, *Diary*, pp. 24–34.

26. For information on the "February Seventh" Rolling Stock Plant at Changhsintien, see "New Record in Monthly Output by Peking Rolling Stock Plant," *NCNA*, English, Peking, September 17, 1967, in *SCMP* #4025, pp. 22–23; *NCNA*, Peking, September 7, 1969; "A Very Good Revolutionary Situation Promotes the Development of Flying Leaps in Production," in *JMJP*, December 7, 1969, and reprinted in *Six Factories*; and "The Peking 2–7 Rolling Stock Factory Really Implements the Party's Policy of Struggle for Dealing with the Enemy" (Pei-ching erh-ch'i ch'i-ch'e ch'e-liang kung-ch'an jen-chen lo-shih tang ti tui-ti tou-cheng cheng-tze), in *JMJP*, December 8, 1969; and *Six Factories*. Japanese correspondents visited this plant in late 1967 and their reports were carried in *Asahi*, Tokyo, November 6, 1967, and the correspondent Samejima, in *Nihon Kezai*, November 6, 1967, reported on this plant in *Translations from the Japanese Press*, U.S. Embassy, Tokyo, November 1967. The Changhsintien "February Seventh" plant was clearly an illustration of what was a general problem. At the First Plenary Session of the Ninth Party Congress, Mao himself noted that many factories faced similar problems. For Mao's comments, see the files on the Ninth Party Congress at the East Asian Institute, Columbia University. For a very similar report concerning cadres with pre-1949 KMT connections, see "The Experience of the PLA in the Peking Hsinhua Printing Plant in Mobilizing the Masses to Carry Out Struggle Against the Enemy," *NCNA*.

27. "Wuchang Carriage Factory Purifies Its Class Ranks," Hopei Radio, translated in URS files, vol. 53, #10.

28. "The Workers in the Shihchiachuang Printing and Dyeing Mill Fully Play Their Leading Role," *Peking Review* #40, October 4, 1968.

29. Shanghai City Service, June 24, 1968.

30. Kiangsu Provincial Service, Nanking, July 11, 1968.

31. *NCNA*, Peking Domestic, June 25, 1967.

32. *NCNA*, Peking, May 13, 1968.

33. See "Shanghai Workers Criticize Revisionist Line in Management," *SCMM* #592, pp. 11–16.

34. Elitism and careerism can be taken as a working definition of "bourgeois." For a clear statement of the crucial importance of attitude as a variable in determining behavior characteristics attributed to class phenomena, see a statement of a young rebel worker in the No. 2 Woolen Textile Plant, Inner Mongolia, "We are workers and we are now in power. Two alternatives lie ahead of us. One is to indulge in showing off and in extravagance, sitting high above the masses and divorcing ourselves from them; the other is to preserve the true color of the proletariate, to lead a life of plain living and hard struggle, devoting ourselves to wholeheartedly serving the people. That is to say, we are likewise faced with the test of the struggle between two classes, two roads, and two lines," in *SCMP* #3985, pp. 14–18.

35. "Participation by Representatives of Revolutionary Masses Bring Vigor to Revolutionary Committees," *NCNA*, English, Shanghai, June 23, 1968, in *SCMP* #4208, pp. 17–19, on the Shanghai Ko Hsin Electric Motor Plant.

36. Richman, *Industrial Society*, p. 163.

37. *Ibid.*, p. 134.

38. Joint *JMJP* and *Hung Ch'i* editorial, "On the Question of Re-educating Intellectuals," *NCNA*, Peking, September 11, 1968.

39. The following list should not be taken to mean that *only* those people mentioned are on the revolutionary committee. However, the table is not meant to be an analysis of the make-up of the committees, but rather an analysis of the patterns of representation changes that occurred in management. The difference is crucial, and while our data is not even complete enough to do a thorough job on the latter, it is sufficient, I believe, to suggest patterns. Sources for the data are in my files based on surveys of Chinese and English language publications available at the Union Research Service, Hong Kong, and in *SCMM*, *SCMP*, and *JPRS*.

The personnel survey does not cover the presence of military men on factory level revolutionary committees. The data is simply not available. Even where the PLA was active in the political and ideological conflict, it was not clear if a member of the PLA would be on the revolutionary committee on a permanent basis. See "Minutes of Revolutionary Committee Meeting of Peking General Knitwear Mill," Columbia University, East Asian Institute, 1969. *Also see* report on the Nan K'ou Rolling Stock Machinery Plant, "A New Problem in the Building of Political Power," *Hung Ch'i* #8, 1969, in *Six Factories*.

40. Richman, *Industrial Society*, p. 296.

41. *Ibid.*, p. 438.

42. *Ibid.*, pp. 300–301.

43. *Nihon Kezai*, November 6, 1967, in *Translations from the Japanese Press*, U.S. Embassy, Tokyo, November 6, 1967.

44. "The Present State of the Movement in Some Factories in Canton," *Kuang-chou Kung-jen* #34, in *SCMP* #4208, pp. 7–16.

45. *JMJP*, April 23, 1968.

46. "Peking General Knitwear Mill Takes the Great Task of Liberating All Mankind to Unite and Educate Cadres Who Made Mistakes," in *Six Factories*.

47. See Note 5. It is interesting that the Peking General Knitwear Plant received so much publicity for the way it handled the "cadre question," thus suggesting not only that this problem was widespread, but that the preferred solution was re-integration. For other examples of re-integration, see reports on the Tsingtao Chemical Fertilizer Plant (n. 2), the Shanghai #3 Iron and Steel Plant (n. 2), The Shenyang #2 Agricultural Machinery Parts Plant, *JMJP*, May 25, 1968, and the Peking Hsinhua Printing Plant, in *Six Factories* (n. 10). Also, see report on Tsingtao Foundry Machine Plant, *NCNA*, Peking, July 15, 1968.

48. The fact that many of the new leading cadres seemed to be either former workers, or former workers who had become technicians and engineers, is seen, for example, in the Shanghai #17 State Cotton Mill where 80% of the twenty-three man revolutionary committee were workers (see *NCNA*, June 2, 1969), or in the Peking Lightweight Aluminum Factory where nine out of sixteen revolutionary cadres were former workers (*KMJP*, October 9, 1968), or in the Shanghai Seamless Steel Tube Factory where five out of nine revolutionary committee members were workers, (*JMJP*, June 16, 1968). The evidence, however, is fragmentary and not conclusive.

49. Richman, *Industrial Society*, p. 300.

50. Shanghai City Service, October 28, 1967; report on the Revolutionary Committee in the Anshan #1 Steel Mill, *NCNA*, Domestic, March 20, 1968, Peking #3 Chemical Plant, "Grasp Ideological Education; Do Work Meticulously" (Chang-wo ssu-hsiang chiao-yü, kuo-hsi tso-hao kung-tso), *JMJP*, January 6, 1970.

51. The dates of references used here are August 1966 for the start of the Cultural Revolution, and June 1969 for the end, those dates being the publication

of the "Sixteen Points" and the convening of the Ninth Party Congress respectively. Two main sources were used to obtain data on the names of people who held party or government position before and after the Cultural Revolution. For the names of people who held official positions in government before the Cultural Revolution, I used the *Directory of Chinese Communist Officials*, Department of State, Intelligence Research Aid, A 66–8, March 1966, Washington, D.C. For the list of officials on revolutionary committees as of the end of 1969, I used *Directory of Chinese Communist Officials: Party, Provincial, Municipal and Military*, Department of State, Reference Aid A 70–13, May 1970, Washington, D.C. The list of factory managerial and technical personnel workers and other employees was obtained from my own files after exhaustive listing of the name of every factory employee manager or party official that I came across in the course of my research. In addition, where Chinese characters were available for the names of personnel, I checked those against the international Standard Telegraphic Codes for those characters using *Tsui Hsin Piao-Chün Tien-Ma-Pen* (China Publishing Bureau, n.d.), so that, insofar as possible, the names of officials and factory personnel referred to the same person. When obvious discrepancies occurred even when the Chinese name was exactly the same, I assumed that two different people had the same name, and simply did not use that person in the data. While I have compiled a fairly exhaustive list of factory personnel, I obviously do not have the names of all the important people in China's factories. Nor does the post-Cultural Revolution directory of officials contain the names of everyone on every Revolutionary Committee. Therefore, the conclusions drawn from this table must of necessity be considered tentative until more complete quantitative data are available.

It should be noted that this personnel study is only an attempt to see how *the pattern of representation of industrial enterprises on organs of higher political authority changed as a result of the Cultural Revolution*. It is *not* an attempt to analyze the changes in the organs of authority above the enterprise except insofar as indirect inferences from increases or decreases in the number and type of representative from industry on those organs justify such conclusions. Information on and analysis of the make-up of municipal and provincial revolutionary committees and government organs is very sparse and, at any rate, is not the subject of concern here. For one study of the impact, in a purely quantitative personnel sense, of the Cultural Revolution on the economic organs of authority at the national level, see Richard K. Diao, "The Impact of the Cultural Revolution on China's Economic Elite," *China Quarterly* #42, April–June 1970, pp. 65–87.

52. This is not to imply that party membership had no meaning. But very often, attitude and organization were simply *not convergent*. For example, a member of the party organization could have more in common with a nonmember than with another member.

53. The larger number of managerial personnel in our sample should not be taken as a final judgment about the relative number of workers vs. managers in government in China before the Cultural Revolution. These numbers are, to an undetermined degree, influenced by the frequency of appearance in the press, and the fact was that in surveying factory personnel, the names of managerial personnel appeared more conspicuously than did the names of workers. However, since the names of *prominent* workers were frequently printed and can safely be assumed to be those workers who did hold government positions, I do not feel that the numbers are without significance. In other words, if a worker's name did not appear, the chances are he or she was not a prominent worker at the time and, hence, *probably* not in government.

54. This accounts for the doubt about the identity of the person in question.

55. See n. 53.

56. *NCNA*, Peking, May 9, 1967.

57. "Conscientiously Carry Out Struggle-Criticism-Transformation in Factories," Shanghai City Service, September 4, 1968. The exact same theme was sounded earlier in a *Hung Ch'i* article on the AiMin Confectionary Factory, *NCNA*, Peking, Domestic, June 25, 1967. *See also* a report on the situation in the Tsitsihar Railway Works, "Revolutionaries at Tsitsihar Railway Works Help Revolutionary Committees," *NCNA*, English, Peking, April 4, 1968, in *SCMP* #4155, pp. 18–20.

58. For examples, some rather detailed, of new management organization, see the following: The Tientsin Ssuhsin Yarn Mill, *JMJP*, August 24, 1968. The Tsitsihar Railway Works, "Revolutionaries at Tsitsihar Railway Works Help Revolutionary Committee," *NCNA*, English, Peking, April 4, 1968, in *SCMP* #4155, pp. 18–20; The No. 1 Mine, Tatung Coal Field, *NCNA*, Peking, June 21, 1968; The Kweiyang Cotton Textile Mill, *Kweiyang Domestic Service*, March 22, 1967, and *NCNA*, Peking, March 30, 1967; The Tsingtao Foundry Machinery Works, *NCNA*, Peking, July 15, 1968, and *SCMP* #4222, pp. 13–15; Kweiyang Iron and Steel Plant, *Kweichow Provincial Service*, Kweiyang, July 14, 1968; Peking Foreign Languages Printing House, *Peking Review* #15, April 12, 1968, pp. 7–9; The Harbin Tractor Accessories Plant, *NCNA*, Peking, July 11, 1967; The Shanghai #17 State Cotton Mill, *NCNA*, June 3, 1969; The Peking Peichiao Timber Mill, *JMJP*, December 28, 1969, in *Six Factories*, and *NCNA*, July 22, 1969; "New Revolutionary Administration in Shanghai Printing Ink Factory," *NCNA*, English, Shanghai, November 21, 1967, in *SCMP* #4066, pp. 21–23. "The Shanghai #3 Iron and Steel Works Forges Ahead in Production," *Peking Review* #43, October 25, 1968.

59. *Minutes*, Richard Sorich, Columbia University; "Peking General Knitwear Mill Simplifies Administration," *SCMP* #4231, pp. 16–18, *NCNA*, English, Peking, July 28, 1968. *See also* Charles Bettelheim, *Cultural Revolution and Industrial Organization in China* (New York: Monthly Review Press, 1974).

60. "Ninyang Chemical Fertilizer Plant Unfolds the Mass Movement of Struggle-Criticism-Transformation," Kwangtung Radio, October 9, 1968, translated in Union Research Service, vol. 53, #10, November 1, 1968.

61. *SCMP* #4108, pp. 20–24; "China Clock Factory Reforms Old Management Structure; Joyously Revives the Production Atmosphere," (Chung-kuo chung-ch'an kao-ko chiu ti kuan-li chi-kou jen-jen chuan-pien tso-feng sheng-ch'an hsi-hsi hsiang-jung), *NCNA*, Hong Kong, Chinese, July 15, 1967.

62. *Shanghai City Service*, September 5, 1968.

63. "Changing Irrational Rules and Regulations is a Revolution, says Journal *Red Flag*," *NCNA*, July 22, 1969. The original "Kai-ko pu-ho-li ti kuei-chang chih-tu shih ch'ang ko-ming," *Hung-Ch'i* #6–7, 1969.

64. *China Reconstructs*, April 1969, pp. 28–29.

65. For some further examples, see reports on the following enterprises: The Power Equipment Plant of the Penki Iron and Steel Company, *NCNA*, May 28, 1969; The Shanghai #17 State Cotton Mill, *NCNA*, June 2 and June 3, 1969; The China Clock Factory, Shanghai, "Cultural Revolution Releases Productive Forces in Clock Factory," *NCNA*, English, Shanghai, July 15, 1968, in *SCMP* #4222, pp. 18–20.

66. Wheelwright and McFarlane, *The Chinese Road*, p. 198.

67. "An Important Question in the Struggle-Criticism-Transformation Campaign in Industrial and Mining Enterprises," *JMJP*, November 29, 1970, translated in *Chinese Economic Studies*, International Arts and Sciences Press, White Plains, N.Y., Winter 1971–72, vol. 5, #2, pp. 131–142.

68. "Rely on the Working Class to Institute Rational Regulations and Systems," *Chinese Economic Studies*, International Arts and Sciences Press, Vol. V, #2, pp. 162–192.

69. Richman, *Industrial Society*, p. 318.

70. *Nihon Kezai*, Tokyo, April 19, 1968; Tadashi Nogami and Sochi Miyoshi, "After Visiting Peking" in *Summaries of Selected Japanese Magazines*, January 1–8, 1968, U.S. Embassy, Tokyo. *Nihon Kezai* reported the elimination of piece wage and bonus payments in the Changhsintien "2–7" Rolling Stock Plant as early as November 1967. See "Visit to a Peking Factory," *Nihon Kezai*, November 6, 1967. *See also* "Trade Unions in China," *Broadsheet*, Vol. 8, #6, June 1971, China Policy Study Group, 62 Parliament Hill, London. *Also*, McFarlane, *Diary*. The factories he visited which had abolished material stimulus and kept the wage grade system included the Double Rhomb Clock and Meters Factory, Peking; the Hsinhua Printing House, Changsha, Hunan; the Peking Steel Works Steel Rolling Mill; and the Shanghai Docks and the Shanghai 555 Clock Factory. And, Tillman Durdin, "Wage Levels Problem for China," *The New York Times*, Thursday, April 29, 1971.

71. McFarlane report on the Shanghai Docks in *Diary*, p. 10; "Textile Workers Repudiate China's Khrushchev," *China Reconstructs*, February 1968, p. 43.

72. See Note 70.

73. Seymour Topping, "China: New Dogma, New 'Maoist Man,' " *New York Times*, Friday, June 25, 1971, p. 2; Carl Riskin, "Maoism and Motivation: A Discussion of Work Incentives in China," in Nee and Peck, *China's Uninterrupted Revolution*.

74. Committee of Concerned Asian Scholars, *China! Inside the People's Republic* (New York: Bantam Books, 1972), pp. 135–136, 189.

75. Sources for the following table are the following: For factories #1–38, Barry Richman, *Industrial Society*, pp. 800–801; for factories #39–41, Karol, *China: The Other Communism* (New York: Hill and Wang, 1967), pp. 446–448; for factories #42–47, McFarlane, *Diary*; for factories #48–52, Committee of Concerned Asian Scholars, *China*, p. 189; for factories #53–55, Seymour Topping, "China: New Dogma . . . ," *New York Times*, June 25, 1971, p. 3.

76. Rosemary Stewart, "Managers Under Mao," *Management Today*, April 1967, pp. 66–72, 71.

77. McFarlane, *Diary*; Richman, *Industrial Society*, p. 239; *see also* Riskin, "Maoism and Motivation," in Nee and Peck, *China's Uninterrupted Revolution*.

78. Karol, *China: The Other Communism*, p. 446; Stewart, "Managers Under Mao," p. 71; Richman, *Industrial Society*, p. 804.

79. Richman, *Industrial Society*, p. 804.

80. *Ibid.*, p. 805.

81. McFarlane, *Diary*, p. 38.

82. The degree of inequality in Chinese industry is not the same as the degree of inequality in Chinese society generally, at least as measured by the wage-grade system. For an interesting and polemical discussion of the wage-grade system in the society as a whole, see "Why Can't High Salaries Be Lowered," *Shang-ch'en-yueh* (*Moonlight on a Frosty Morning*, a Red Guard publication), January 10, 1968, in *SCMM* #616, pp. 16–20.

83. Tillman Durdin, "Wage Levels Problem for China," p. 2. Durdin later reported that sometimes the elimination of bonuses was followed by an across-the-board wage-grade increase. *See* "Report on a Visit to China: Stability Seems to Reign," *New York Times*, May 9, 1971, p. 1.

84. Report on the Shenyang Mining Bureau in "Anarchism Must Be Regu-

larly Criticized and Again Criticized," (Tui wu-cheng-fu chu-yi yao ching-ch'ang p'i-fan fu-p'i), *JMJP*, August 5, 1969; Peking General Knitwear Mill, in *Six Factories*: Investigation Report of the Peking Peichiao Lumber Products Factory, "Reform of Irrational Rules and Regulations is a Revolution," *Hung Ch'i* #6, 7, 1969; *NCNA*, June 2, 1969, report on the Shanghai #17 State Cotton Mill.

85. Chao Shu-tseng and Li Ching-hsia, "Heed What Chairman Mao Says, Operate Machines for the Proletarian Revolution," *Hung Ch'i* #3, September 19, 1968, in *SCMM* #629, for a report on the model Peking General Knitwear Mill. *See also* a report on the Penki Iron and Steel Company's Power Equipment Plant, *NCNA*, May 28, 1969.

86. "Shanghai Workers Criticize Revisionist Line in Management," *SCMM* #592, pp. 11–16. *See also* Shanghai City Service, September 12, 1968.

87. *NCNA*, Peking, October 4, 1967.

88. "The Working Class is Master of Technical Revolution," *China Reconstructs*, April 1969, p. 29.

89. *SCMP* #4013, pp. 20–23.

90. Shanghai City Service, June 14, 1968, report on the Shanghai Machine Tools Plant and *SCMP* #4013, p. 22, report on the factories in Tsingtao.

91. Durdin, "Wage Levels Problem For China," p. 2.

92. Samuel Bowles, "Unequal Education and the Reproduction of the Social Division of Labor," *Review of Radical Political Economics*, Fall–Winter 1971, #3, pp. 1–30; Herb Gintis, "Education, Technology, and the Characteristics of Worker Productivity," *American Economic Review*, May 1971, 61, pp. 266–279.

93. *Peking Review* #43, October 25, 1968, report on the Shanghai #3 Iron & Steel Works; *NCNA*, International, Peking, July 30, 1968, report on the Tatung Coal Mines in Shansi Province; "Jem-min Jih-pao Acclaims Revolutionary Worker-Cadres," *NCNA*, English, Peking, May 9, 1967, in *SCMP* #3937, pp. 21–22, report on the Peking Jade Factory; Richman, *Industrial Society*, pp. 753–760.

94. "Ningyang Chemical Fertilizer Plant," Kwangtung Radio, October 9, 1968, in *URS*, vol. 53, #10, November 1, 1968.

95. Topping, "China: New Dogma . . . ," p. 2.

96. Report on the Kweiyang Bearings Factory, *Kweichow Provincial Service*, Kweiyang, August 31, 1968.

97. Joint *JMJP* and *Hung Ch'i* editorial, "Develop the Party's Working Style of Forging Close Links With the Masses," *NCNA*, English, Peking, June 30, 1968, in *SCMP* #4212, pp. 11–16. Walter Sullivan, "Swedes Will End Assembly Lines," *New York Times*, December 28, 1971.

98. *"Jen-min Jih-pao* Acclaims . . . ," *SCMP* #3937, pp. 21–31, report on the Peking Jade Factory.

99. Richman, *Industrial Society*, p. 233.

100. Peking General Knitwear Mill, *Minutes of Revolutionary Committee Meeting*.

101. Jon Sigurdson, "Rural Industrialization in China—A Travel Report," *China Quarterly*, #50, April–June 1971. *See also* Joint Investigation by Kiangsu Provincial Revolutionary Committee, Ministry of Light Industry, *NCNA* Correspondent and *JMJP* Correspondent, "Relying On Our Own Efforts and Adopting Indigenous Methods to Develop 'Small-Scale Fibre Plants,'" *Chinese Economic Studies*, Winter 1971–72, pp. 122–130. Joint Investigation Group of the Kwangtung Provincial Revolutionary Committee and Ministry of Light Industry, "Develop Production in Depth and Breadth," *ibid.*, pp. 150–161. *See also*, Committee of Concerned Asian Scholars, *China*, pp. 150–156.

'102. "Workers of Northeast China Machine Building Plant Combine Industry with Agriculture," *NCNA*, English, Peking, May 6, 1968, in *SCMP* #4175, pp. 15–19.

103. Wheelwright and McFarlane, *The Chinese Road*, pp. 164–168.
104. *NCNA*, October 31, 1968.
105. Karol, *China: The Other Communism*, p. 217; Wheelwright and McFarlane, *The Chinese Road*, p. 200.
106. Karol, *ibid.*, p. 217.
107. Tsingtao Municipal Revolutionary Committee, *NCNA*, Peking, Domestic, August 10, 1968; Chukiang *Hsien* Revolutionary Committee, Kwangtung, *JMJP*, September 1, 1968.
108. *NCNA*, Peking, Domestic, February 8, 1968.
109. In the matter of using "trusts" as a method of inter-enterprise coordination, Mao is purported to have said, "Trusts (cartels or monopolies) should not all be overthrown. An old name may have a new content. We should chiefly criticize and repudiate the capitalist road followed by a trust." *See* "Chairman Mao's Instructions on Mass Criticism and Repudiation," Canton, *Wan Shan Hung P'ien* (Myriad Red Hills) #1, September 26, 1967, in *SCMP* #4057, p. 2. "Trusts" remained largely in the commercial sector (marketing and supply) rather than production (planning and investment). See Wheelwright and McFarlane, p. 132, for a short and rather clear explanation of the "trust" in China's planning system. *See also* McFarlane, *Diary*, p. 33 ff. for a report on the Shanghai State Silk Factory #1.
110. This factory was a model for this type of education. Committee of Concerned Asian Scholars, *China*, pp. 178–180; "Contingent of Engineering and Technical Personnel in the Shanghai Machine Tools Plant Grows," *China Pictorial* #11, 1969, or *NCNA*, July 21, 1969.
111. *Shanghai City Service*, August 16, 1968.
112. "A School Where the Working Class Holds Power," *China Pictorial* #3, 1969.
113. *NCNA*, Peking, May 8, 1968.
114. Mark Gayn, "China's Schools," *New York Post Magazine*, December 9, 1968, p. 5; Committee of Concerned Asian Scholars, *China*, Chap. 7.
115. This was the argument made for example, in the Peking General Knitwear Mill and publicized widely. See *Six Factories*.
116. For descriptions of how the new Party Committees were created, see reports on the Peking Hsinhua Printing Plant, *Six Factories*; the Peking General Knitwear Mill, *ibid.*; and the Shanghai #17 State Cotton Mill, *NCNA*, June 2, 1969. For a description of how the new Party Committees operated, see report on the Crane Workshop of the Shenyang Locomotive and Rolling Stock Plant, *Chinese Economic Studies*, pp. 162–172, plus the three previous sources. Also see "The Communist Party in the Factory," *Broadsheet*, vol. 7, #2, February 1970.

Chapter 9: "One Divides into Two": China's Industry Since the Cultural Revolution

1. "Party Committee of Hengyang Metallurgical Machine Repair and Manufacturing Plant Strengthens Line Education," *Kuang-ming Jih-pao*, November 14, 1972, in *SCMP* #5262; Lu Ching-wu, "Study Dialectical Materialism and Historical Materialism," *JMJP*, March 16, 1971, in *SCMP* #4870.
2. "Shanghai Diesel Engine Plant Puts Politics in Command of Production and Achieves Outstanding Results," *NCNA*, Shanghai, January 4, 1970, in *SCMP* #4573; "First Chinese-Built 3,200 Ton Ice-Breaker Launched in Shanghai," *NCNA*, January 2, 1970, in *SCMP* #4575; "China's Metallurgical Workers Repudiate Liu Shao-chi's Slavish Compradore Philosophy," *NCNA*, Peking, January 16, 1970, in *SCMP* #4582; *see also* a story on the Chingkangshan Motor Vehicle Plant in Nanchang, Kiangsu Province, in *SCMP* #4606, February 1970.

3. "Revolutionary Committee Members of Central China Rolling Stock Plant Forge Close Links With the Masses," *NCNA*, Changsha, February 16, 1970, in *SCMP* #4603; Nanking Hungwei Machine Works, "There are Good Prospects For Factories to Undertake Scientific Research," *KMJP*, February 28, 1971, *SCMP* #4857.

4. "Educate Engineering and Technical Personnel With Mao Tse-tung's Thought," *JMJP*, January 10, 1970, in *SCMP* #4580.

5. "Anarchism Must be Regularly Criticized and Criticized Again" (Tui wu-cheng-fu chu-yi yao ching-ch'ang p'i-fan fu-p'i), *JMJP*, August 5, 1969.

6. "Setting Up an Economic Supervisory Group in a Factory is a Good Method," *JMJP*, March 4, 1970, in *SCMP* #4615; "An Important Matter for Running Socialist Enterprises Well," *JMJP*, February 28, 1971, in *SCMP* #4857; news release on the Wuchang Railroad Car Factory, *NCNA*, February 26, 1971, in *SCMP* #4853; Investigation Group of Kirin CCP Provincial Committee, Investigation of the Changchun #1 Auto Foundry Branch, "Strengthen the Party's Leadership, Tightly Grasp Production Management," *JMJP*, December 31, 1971, in *SCMP*, #5044; "Promote the Role of Veteran Cadres in the Three Great Revolutionary Movements," *JMJP*, March 29, 1972, in *SCMP* #5113.

7. "Profit Principle is a Capitalist Principle," *Kuang-ming Jih-pao*, January 23, 1970, in *SCMP* #4595; other articles dealing with an on-going critique of the economist Sun Yeh-fang in *SCMP* #4596; Investigation Team of Ch'angchün Municipal Revolutionary Committee, "Ch'angchün Municipal General Glass Works Develops an Upsurge in Comparing Revolution and Frugality," *Jen-min Jih-pao*, January 5, 1970, in *SCMP* #4579; "An Important Question in the Struggle-Criticism-Transformation Campaign in Industrial and Mining Enterprises," *JMJP*, November 29, 1970, in *Chinese Economic Studies*, Vol. V, #2, Winter 1971–72, pp. 131–142. "Put Mao Tse-tung Thought in Command of Economic Accounting," *ibid.*, pp. 142 ff.

8. Hung Hang-hsiang, "Basic Law of Operation of Enterprises by the Proletariat," *KMJP*, March 21, 1970, in *SCMP* #4627.

9. *Ibid.*

10. Sam Bowles and Herb Gintis, *Education in Capitalist America* (New York: Basic Books, 1976.

11. See note 8.

12. "Closely Relying on the Masses For Successful Running of Socialist Enterprises," *JMJP*, February 10, 1971, in *SCMP* #4852.

13. *Ibid.*

14. "Seriously Carry Out the Party's Policy Toward Intellectuals, Bring the Positive Role of Technicians Into Full Play," *JMJP*, May 24, 1971, in *SCMP* #4913.

15. "Unfold Penetrating Revolutionary Mass Criticism and Raise Line Consciousness Continuously," *JMJP*, March 21, 1972, in *SCMP* #5106.

16. Chang Mei-hua, "Train a Technical Contingent of the Working Class," *Hung Ch'i*, #2, February 1, 1971, in *SCMM* #700.

17. "Implement Party Policy Conscientiously, Unite With Everyone Who Can Be United With," *JMJP*, March 3, 1972; in *SCMP* #5092; "Fully Mobilize the Revolutionary Actionism of the Masses," *KMJP*, March 21, 1972, in *SCMP* #5105; "Show Concern Politically For Technical Personnel and Support Them in Their Work," *JMJP*, March 10, 1972, in *SCMP* #5098; "Unfold Penetrating Mass Criticism and Raise Line Consciousness Continuously," *JMJP*, March 21, 1972, in *SCMP* #5106; "Prevent One-Sidedness in Grasping Enterprise Management," *JMJP*, October 24, 1972, in *SCMP* #5251.

18. Kung Hsiao-wen, "We Must Have Figures in Mind," *JMJP*, October 29, 1971, in *SCMP* #5014.

19. Suo Kang, "We Must Establish a New Production Order," *JMJP*, August 29, 1971, in *SCMP* #4973; "Fully Mobilize the Masses to Reform Regulations and Systems," *JMJP*, August 29, 1971, in *SCMP* #4973; "Closely Relying on the Masses For Successful Running of Socialist Enterprises," *JMJP*, February 10, 1971.

20. See note 17.

21. "Prevent One-Sidedness in Grasping Enterprise Management," *JMJP*, October 24, 1972, in *SCMP* #5251; "With the Line as the Key Link, Manage a Socialist Enterprise Conscientiously," *JMJP*, July 19, 1972, in *SCMP* #5187.

22. Shanghai Municipal Radio broadcast on Shanghai #19 Radio Plant as monitored by FBIS, May 24, 1975.

23. "Number One Men Take the Lead in Going Deep Into Reality to Conduct Investigation and Study," *KMJP*, August 30, 1971, in *SCMP* #4972. For an interesting account of how cadre participation in labor worked in favor of worker initiated technical innovation, even as control became more centralized within a factory, "Grasp Well This Fundamental and Important Matter," *JMJP*, July 26, 1971, in *SCMP* #4957.

24. "Let Technical Personnel Play Their Parts to the Full," *JMJP*, March 5, 1972, in *SCMP* #5094; "Some Experiences in Conducting Line Education Among Technicians," *Hung Ch'i* #6, June 1, 1972, in *SCMM* #732.

25. See Note 12.

26. *Ibid.*; Lu Ching-wu, "Study Dialectical Materialism and Historical Materialism, Raise Initiative in Implementing Chairman Mao's Revolutionary Line," *JMJP*, March 16, 1971, in *SCMP* #4870; Kung Hsiao-wen, "We Must Have 'Figures' in Mind," *JMJP*, October 29, 1971, in *SCMP* #5014.

27. "Heighten Revolutionary Sense of Responsibility," *JMJP*, November 11, 1971, in *SCMP* #5015.

28. Yün Wen, "Raise Understanding, Strengthen Enterprise Management," *JMJP*, August 28, 1972, in *SCMP* #5211.

29. Stephen Andors, "Factory Management and Political Ambiguity, 1961–63," *China Quarterly*, July–September, 1974; Hung Ch'i, "Grasp Revolution and Promote Production," *Hung Ch'i* #5, May 1, 1974, in *SCMM* #776.

30. Liu Chin-t'ang, "Chairman Mao's Revolutionary Line is Our Life-line," *Hung Ch'i*, #11, October 1, 1971, in *SCMM* #715; "New Cadres From Among Workers are Growing Up With Vigor," *JMJP*, February 27, 1972, in *SCMP* #5089.

31. See Notes 6, 25, 26.

32. "Use Technical Personnel Boldly and Strengthen their Education," *KJMP*, January 20, 1972, in *SCMP* #5066; "Workers and Staff Members of Anshan Iron and Steel Company Perseveringly Carry Out Technical Innovation," *KMJP*, April 30, 1973.

33. "Arouse Workers to Take Part in Management, Run Socialist Enterprises Well," *JMJP*, March 4, 1972; "Make a Success of Enterprise Management in a Down-to-Earth Manner," *JMJP*, March 2, 1972, in *SCMP* #5093; "How Chinese Workers Take Part in Factory Management," *NCNA*, Shenyang, April 28, 1973, in *SCMP* #5370.

34. Carl Riskin, "Maoism and Motivation: Work Incentives in China," in Victor Nee and James Peck, eds., *China's Uninterrupted Revolution* (New York: Pantheon, 1976).

35. Yang Hsüeh-p'ing, "Material Incentive is Reaction to Bringing Proletarian Politics to the Fore," *KMJP*, February 26, 1970, in *SCMP* #4612.

36. "Report of the Yale Economists' Visit to the PRC," December 1, 1973, mimeo. Copies may be obtained "within reason" from Dr. Bruce Reynolds, Department of Economics, Union College, Schnectady, New York. *Also see*

Charles Hoffman, *The Chinese Worker* (Albany: SUNY Press, 1974); Carl Riskin, "Worker Incentives in Chinese Industry," in *China: A Reassessment of the Economy*, U.S. Congress, Joint Economic Committee, Washington, D.C., 1975.

37. See Note 12; Suo Kang, "We Must Establish a New Production Order," *JMJP*, August 29, 1971, in *SCMP* #4973.

38. *Ibid*.

39. "Boldly Arouse the Masses, Grasp Demarcation Line of Policy," *Hung Ch'i* #3, March 3, 1974, in *SCMM* #772; "Be the Master of the Wharf, Not the Slave of Tonnage," *JMJP*, February 1, 1974, in *SCMP* #5561; "The Masses of Workers Must Be Relied On To Make Technical Innovations," *Hung Ch'i* #11, November 1, 1974, in *SCMM* #800.

40. "Grasp Well Major Issues of a Fundamental Nature Under the Socialist System," *KMJP*, November 24, 1974, *SCMP* #5782; "Where are the Party Committee Members' Hammers?" *JMJP*, March 31, 1974, in *SCMP* #5596; article on Hangchow Paper Mill, Chekiang Provincial Radio, August 7, 1975, in *FBIS*.

41. "Grasp Well This Fundamental and Important Matter," *JMJP*, July 26, 1971, in *SCMP* #4957.

42. "A Profound Discussion," *JMJP*, July 21, 1974, in *SCMP* #5663.

43. "Reliance on the Working Class is a Basic Experience in the Building of Socialism," *JMJP*, December 25, 1973, in *SCMP* #5538.

44. See Note 39.

45. "Worker Cadres in East China Coal Mine," *NCNA*, Tsinan, June 13, 1973.

46. See Note 40; "Grasp Revolution and Promote Production," *Hung Ch'i* #5, May 1, 1974, in *SCMM* #576; "No. One Men Take Lead in Going Deep Into Reality to Conduct Investigation and Study," *KMJP*, August 30, 1971, in *SCMP* #4972; "Shanghai Factory Cadres Labor; Selected Workers Manage," Shanghai City Radio, July 18, 1975, as monitored by *FBIS*, July 22, 1975.

47. See Notes 37, 39.

48. "The Participation of Workers in the Management of Enterprises is a Major Matter in Strengthening the Dictatorship of the Proletariat," *KMJP*, July 10, 1975; "An Illustration of Worker's Role in Management," *NCNA*, Shenyang, February 26, 1975, in *SCMP* #5807.

49. For information on the labor unrest in Hangchow, *see* the *FBIS* monitoring of Chekiang Provincial Radio, July and August 1975. I pieced this analysis together from admittedly fragmentary, but quite real bits of information contained in articles on various factories.

50. Chekiang Provincial Radio, August 22, 1975, as monitored by *FBIS*, August 25, 1975; Phyllis Andors, "Economic Development and Women's Emancipation in China During the Great Leap Forward," *Bulletin of Concerned Asian Scholars*, vol. 7, no. 1, pp. 33–42.

51. "Training the Workers Theoretical Force in the Struggle to Criticize Lin Piao and Confucius," *JMJP*, March 11, 1974, in *SCMP* #5596.

52. "Link the Criticism of Confucius With the Criticism of Lin Piao," *Hung Ch'i* #12, December 1, 1973, in *SCMM* #766.

53. "Lin Piao and the Doctrines of Mencius and Confucius," in *Hung Ch'i* #2, February 7, 1974, in *SCMP* #5555; "The Means By Which to Bring Enthusiasm for Production into Play," *JMJP*, May 15, 1975, in *SCMP* #5871, "Consolidate the Dictatorship of the Proletariat and Restrict Bourgeois Right," *KMJP*, February 28, 1975. *See also* Po Ch'ing, "On Lin Piao's 'Principle of Material Allocation'," *KMJP*, July 31, 1975, in *SCMP* #5922.

54. Carl Riskin, "Self-Reliant System or Independent Kingdoms?"

55. *Ibid*.; "Our Country's Machine Industrial Front Shows Thriving Development," *JMJP*, December 25, 1971, in *SCMP* #5051.

56. "Iron and Steel Industry in Peking Municipality Basically Achieves Self Sufficiency in Iron Ore," in *SCMP* #5324.

57. "Develop the Variety of Metals to Achieve Greater, Faster, Better and More Economical Results Under the Guidance of Chairman Mao's Revolutionary Line," *JMJP*, August 9, 1971, in *SCMP* #4961; "Strengthen Party Leadership over Economic Work in a Down-to-Earth Manner," *JMJP*, November 2, 1971, in *SCMP* #5014.

58. *Ibid.*; "Maintain Placing Proletarian Politics in Command, Strengthen Technical Management in an All Around Manner," *JMJP*, April 5, 1972, in *SCMP* #5116.

59. "Operate Small Chemical Fibre Industry Well," *Hung Ch'i* #9, August 8, 1970, in *SCMM* 609; "Central China City Develops Local Industry Through Self-Reliance," *NCNA*, Changhow, March 22, 1970, in *SCMP* #4626; "Our Country's Machine Industrial Front Shows Thriving Development," *JMJP*, December 25, 1971, in *SCMP* #5051.

60. "Let Us All Go Into Action and Regenerate By Our Own Efforts," *JMJP*, April 26, 1970, in *SCMP* #4650; "Shanghai Municipality Scores Tremendous Achievement in Unfolding Socialist Cooperation," *JMJP*, November 28, 1970, in *SCMP* #4794.

61.

62. "Simultaneous Development of Large Sized, Medium Sized and Small Sized Enterprises," *JMJP*, August 24, 1970, in *SCMP* #4731; "Shanghai Develops Neighborhood Factories," *NCNA*, Shanghai, April 25, 1972, in *SCMP* #5128; "New Changes in China's Biggest Motor Vehicle Plant," *NCNA*, Changchün, July 19, 1971, in *SCMP* #4946.

63. "Peking Factory Workers Help Spring Farming," *NCNA*, Peking, April 15, 1974, in *SCMP* #5602; "Industry in Major Chinese Cities Gives Powerful Support to Agriculture," *NCNA*, Peking, March 17, 1970, in *SCMP* #4622.

64. See Notes 60–62.

65. "Rapid Development of Local Industry in Northeastern China City," *NCNA*, Shenyang, April 8, 1970, in *SCMP* #4636; "Shanghai Workers Turn Three Wastes into Three Treasures," *JMJP*, February 20, 1970, in *SCMP* #4606; "Multi-purpose Utilization on the Industrial Front Scores New Achievements," *JMJP*, February 28, 1972, in *SCMP* #5090.

66. *Ibid.*

67. "Dialectics of Paupers Turning Out One-Thousand Motor Cars," *KMJP*, November 21, 1970, in *SCMP* #4729. Other examples appeared in *JMJP* on November 19 and 20, in *SCMP* #4729; "Shanghai Plant Uses Small Machines to Make Heavy Equipment," *NCNA*, March 20, 1970, in *SCMP* #4625.

68. "New Changes in China's Biggest Motor Vehicle Plant," *NCNA*, Changchün, July 19, 1971, in *SCMP* #4946.

69. Riskin, "Self Reliant Systems . . . ;" "Develop Commune and Brigade Industry and Maintain 'Four Not Competing'," *JMJP*, February 14, 1973, in *SCMP* #5321.

70. "Fuksün Extracting Machine Building Factory Fulfills State's Contract and Plan," *JMJP*, November 26, 1971, in *SCMP* #5029.

71. Investigation Team of Ministry of Finance, Fuksien Municipal Revolutionary Committee and Fuksün Military Sub District, "Carry Out the Great Principle of 'Developing the Economy and Insuring Supplies'," *Hung Ch'i* #2, February 1, 1971, in *SCMM* #700; Tsai Cheng, "Establish the Idea that Financial Work Must Serve the Development of Production," *JMJP*, February 11, 1971, in *SCMP* #4847.

72. "Strengthen Leadership Over Mass Scientific Experiment Movement," *KMJP*, June 13, 1973, in *SCMP* #5401; "Mass Technical Activities in North-

eastern China City," *NCNA*, Harbin, September 24, 1973, in *SCMP* #5469; "Northeastern China City Popularizes Technical Cooperation," *NCNA*, Shinyang, January 20, 1973, in *SCMP* #5307.

73. "Socialist Cooperation in Shanghai's Industry," *NCNA*, Shanghai, June 15, 1974, in *SCMP* #5642; "Shanghai Cadres Take Part in Physical Labor Regularly," *NCNA*, Shanghai, November 13, 1974, in *SCMP* #5742; "Socialist Relationships Among Factories in China," *NCNA*, Shanghai, August 14, 1973, in *SCMP* #5435.

74. "Revolution and Production on Shenyang's Industrial and Communications Fronts in Even Better Situation," *NCNA*, Shenyang, October, 1971, in *SCMP* #5032; "T'angshan Municipal Party Committee Strengthens Leadership Over Key Enterprises," *JMJP*, July 24, 1973, in *SCMP* #5430.

75. Dwight Perkins, ed., *Rural Small Scale Industry in the People's Republic of China*, forthcoming.

76. "Operate All Enterprises Industriously and Thriftily and Strive to Serve the People," *KMJP*, March 14, 1973, in *SCMP* #5341.

77. K'o Hsueh, "Protect and Improve the Environment to Benefit the People," *KMJP*, November 4, 1973, in *SCMP* #5499; "Medium Sized Chinese City Develops Industry," *NCNA*, Nanking, March 22, 1975, in *SCMP* #5824; "China's Heavy Industrial Base Develops Light Industry," *NCNA*, March 23, 1975; "Tach'ing Oilfield: Industrial Area Combining Industry and Agriculture, Town and Country," *NCNA*, Peking, March 22, 1975, in *SCMP* #5824; "Northwest China City Develops Light Industries," *NCNA*, Sian, January 10, 1975, in *SCMP* #5777; "Diversified Economy Thrives on Peking's Outskirts," *NCNA*, Peking, October 18, 1974, in *SCMP* #5727; "Chinese Factories Equip Themselves," *NCNA*, Shenyang, September 19, 1975, in *SCMP* #5946.

78. "Shanghai Municipality Extensively Carries Out Activities of Running Schools By Factories," *JMJP*, July 27, 1973, in *SCMP* #5432.

79. "Vigorously Promote Technical Education and Train a Technical Force of the Working Class," *KMJP*, December 24, 1973, in *SCMP* #5538.

80. "Train Workers Technical Force," *JMJP*, July 21, 1971, in *SCMP* #4950.

81. "Unswervingly Take the Road of Training Technicians From Among Workers," *KMJP*, December 16, 1973, in *SCMP* #5531.

82. "First Group of Worker Students Graduated from Talien Engineering College," *JMJP*, April 30, 1973, in *SCMP* #5371.

83. "First Group of Students Graduate from July 21 Workers College," *KMJP*, July 23, 1971, in *SCMP* #4950.

84. See Note 81.

85. "Insist on Training Technicians From Among Workers," *JMJP*, December 16, 1973, in *SCMP* #5531.

86. See Note 80.

87. P'ei Yü, "Establish Good Link-Up Between Factory and School in an Earnest Way," *Hung Ch'i* #9, September 1, 1972, in *SCMM* #738.

88. *Ibid.*; "Factories and Mines in Peking Form Ties With Schools," *JMJP*, May 4, 1973, in *SCMP* #5375.

89. *Ibid.*

90. *Ibid.*; Shihchiachuang Municipality Energetically Promotes Operation of Schools By Factories, Mines, and Enterprises," *KMJP*, September 21, 1973; "Vigorous Development of Workers' Spare-time Education in Heilungkiang Province," *KMJP*, August 21, 1973, in *SCMP* #5450.

91. See Note 8.

92. Mass Criticism Group of Peking University and Tsinghua University,

"Lin Piao and Doctrines of Mencius and Confucius," *NCNA*, February 7, 1974, in *SCMP* #5555. The essay also appeared in *HC*, February 1974.

93. See Note 87.

94. "How China Trains Technical Force," *NCNA*, Peking, March 19, 1975, in *SCMP* #5822.

95. "Consolidate and Raise the Ranks of Worker Theorists in the Struggle to Criticize Lin Piao and Confucius," *JMJP*, November 21, 1974, in *SCMP* #5772.

96. *Ibid.* Kan Ko, "Strengthen the Build-up of the Ranks of Workers Toward Revolutionization," *JMJP*, May 17, 1975; "Seize Upon the Special Topic: Deepen Study," *JMJP*, May 25, 1975; Workers Theorist Group, Nanning Machinery Co., Kwangsi, "The Means By Which to Bring Enthusiasm For Production Into Play," *JMJP*, May 15, 1975, in *SCMP* #5871.

97. See Note 95.

98. "Over 100 July 21 Workers' Colleges Established in Peking," *NCNA*, Peking, July 24, 1975, in *SCMP* #5908.

99. See Note 94.

100. *Ibid.*

101. See Note 83.

Bibliography

By coincidence, yet certainly not without significance, the final manuscript for this book was completed within days of Mao Tsetung's death. My own personal sense of having completed a long task was strengthened by the realization that so much of what I had analyzed and described was the result of Mao's vision and his methods of political struggle; his ability to understand, capture, and direct the forces at work in Chinese society and the imagination of the Chinese people. Through his bold and consummate sense of timing, he was able to launch massive political movements which gave energy to people's own efforts to continuously transform themselves and the world they live in.

Most of the sources I used to reconstruct the evolution of revolutionary industrialization and to describe what has so far resulted from Mao's legacy of Marxist vision, analysis, and struggle have all been listed in great detail in the footnotes to each chapter. There have, however, been some particularly important works which have shaped my own understanding of how contemporary society operates, and, because I found their arguments particularly persuasive or provocative, these works are noted below and annotated appropriately.

Other Western works on China's modernization and industrialization have also been useful in providing information and pointing to problems. The quality of these works varies greatly and unfortunately is not what one would expect from the great number of them available. I have listed only those which I think are good or which bear directly on industrialization and planning.

Chinese newspaper and magazine articles, if read judiciously and with the understanding that their avowed purpose is political communication as well as objective description, are excellent sources of information. Readers must also be familiar with the Marxist intellectual categories with which they are infused, and with the meaning of Chinese political slogans. Not all important essays are translated into English, however, and most that are are found in a relatively few university libraries or in libraries and offices in Washington, D.C. The problem of access is not so much legal or procedural as geographical and logistical.

Chinese-language articles can be found in newspapers and magazines imported from China into the United States and other Western countries, but aside from the obvious language problem, there is the same distribution problem as with English-language translations. I have listed some of the articles which are particularly comprehensive, theoretically important, or descriptive, but the bulk of these sources are cited in the appropriate notes to the text.

A more complete bibliography of Chinese sources, either in the original Chinese or in English translation, from the period 1958 to 1969 can be found in the bibliography to my Ph.D. dissertation, "The Politics of Modernization in a Revolutionary Society: Factory Management in China, 1958–1969," Columbia University, New York, 1974.

WESTERN SOURCES

GENERAL

Almond, Gabriel, and Coleman, James. *The Politics of the Developing Areas*. Princeton: Princeton University Press, 1960. An example of Western modernization theory and its application to area studies.

Azrael, Jeremy. *Managerial Power and Soviet Politics*. Cambridge, Mass.: Harvard University Press, 1966.

Baran, Paul. *The Political Economy of Growth*. New York: Marzani and Munsell, 1957. An analysis of the process of economic growth and development in global perspective, with especially penetrating chapters on the third world.

Bell, Daniel. *The Coming of Post Industrial Society*. New York: Basic Books, 1973. A good presentation of the neo-Weberian argument that predicts a modified form of societal convergence and the rule of a technocratic elite.

Bettelheim, Charles. *Class Struggles in the U.S.S.R.: First Phase, 1917–1923*. New York: Monthly Review Press, 1976. An analysis of the historical roots of class stratification and growing inequality in the Soviet Union in the light of Marxist thought on socialist development. Bettelheim's comparisons with China are provocative, especially his discussion of the relationship between production and social transformation.

Bowles, Samuel, and Gintis, Herb. *Schooling in Capitalist America*. New York, Basic Books, 1976. An excellent discussion of the history of and relationships between the educational system, the division of labor, and class stratification in the United States.

Braverman, Harry. *Labor and Monopoly Capital: The Degradation of Work in the Twentieth Century*. New York: Monthly Review Press, 1975. A brilliant theoretical and empirical investigation of how the contemporary division of labor has been influenced not by technological development but by the class structure of capitalism.

Burnham, James. *The Managerial Revolution*. Bloomington, Ind.: Indiana University Press, 1959. An account of how "modern society" makes the distinction between capitalism and socialism meaningless, with the development of a technocratic and bureaucratic stratum of managers. Along with Bell and Ralf Dahrendorf (*Class and Class Conflict in Industrial Society* [Stanford: Stanford University Press, 1959]), Burnham is one of the major neo-Weberians.

Djilas, Milovan. *The New Class*. New York: Praeger, 1957. How the communist parties in the Soviet Union and Eastern Europe have become a privileged and bureaucratic elite.

Dore, Ronald. *British Factory, Japanese Factory*. Berkeley: University of California Press, 1973. A very interesting comparative study of British and Japanese industrial organization and labor-management relations. Dore tries to deal with the larger political implications of industrial organization and with the conclusions of convergence theorists.

Ellul, Jacques. *The Technological Society*. New York: Alfred A. Knopf, 1964. A pessimistic prediction of technocratic rule.

Etzioni, Amitai, ed. *Complex Organizations*. New York: Holt, Rinehart, and Winston, 1966. A reader on the behavior of people in bureaucratic organizations and the structural and organizational causes of different kinds of behavior.

Gerth, Hans H., and Mills, Charles W. *From Max Weber: Essays in Sociology*. New York: Oxford University Press, 1968. A very convenient collection of Weber's major writings on politics and social organization.

Huneryager, S. G., and Heckman, I. L. *Human Relations in Management*, 2nd ed. Cincinnati: Southwestern Publishing Company, 1967. A good reader with essays on the theory of human relations in industrial organization and with interesting descriptions of actual experiments.

LaPalombara, Joseph, ed. *Bureaucracy and Political Development*. Princeton: Princeton University Press, 1963. Along with the works of Almond, Coleman, Lucian Pye, and others, this book is part of the very influential Princeton modernization series. It is instructive to read these works with a good reader in industrial management, especially one from the human relations school, in order to better see the underlying philosophical assumptions of the modernization theorists. For an excellent critique of this school, see John W. Dower, ed., *Origins of the Modern Japanese State: Selected Writings of E.H. Norman* (New York: Pantheon Books, 1975), especially Dower's introduction, "E. H. Norman, Japan, and the Uses of History."

Lenin, V.I. *Selected Works*, 3 volumes. New York: International Publishers, 1967. The last essays reveal his unsuccessful but still active search for an antidote to the bureaucratic tendencies that his previous policies had created.

McGregor, Douglas. *The Human Side of Enterprise*. New York: McGraw-Hill Book Co., 1960. A classic work presenting the foundations of the human relations school of management in American industry, building on the work of Elton Mayo (*The Human Problems of an Industrial Civilization*, New York: Macmillan Co., 1933). Both these works postulate that workers are happier when treated as adults capable of working independently and cooperatively rather than under tight supervision for monetary incentives alone. Neither challenges management's ultimate prerogatives.

Maslow, Abraham. *Motivation and Personality*. New York: Harper and Row, 1954. Maslow's theory of a hierarchy of human needs is a basic psychological premise of the human relations school of management.

Marx, Karl. *Capital*. New York: Random House, Modern Library ed.

————. *The Grundrisse.* Translated and with an introduction by Martin Nicolaus. New York: Random House, 1974. These two very difficult works are not only excellent critiques of capitalist society but excellent examples of Marx's own analytical methodology. In view of distortions of the Marxist intellectual heritage prevalent in most Western, particularly American, social science, the best place to get a good understanding of Marxism is from the originals. Robert Tucker, in a reader called *The Marx-Engels Reader* (New York: W. W. Norton, 1972), has well-chosen excerpts from the major works of Marx and Engels. Bertell Ollman, in *Alienation: Marx's Concept of Man in Capitalist Society* (New York: Cambridge University Press, 1971), gives an excellent analysis of the Marxian view of human beings.

Merton, Robert, K. *Reader in Bureaucracy.* Glencoe, Ill.: Free Press, 1949. An uneven collection of essays on all aspects of bureaucracy and its relationship to the wider social and political context within which it functions.

Sennett, Richard, and Cobb, Jonathan. *The Hidden Injuries of Class.* New York: Random House, 1972. A sensitive study, based on interviews of American working-class people, of how the class structure in the United States limits people's confidence and shapes their sense of identity.

Terkel, Studs. *Working.* New York: Pantheon Books, 1975. Terkel is not only a great journalist, but a brilliant "social scientist" able to get to the reality of people's lives and visions.

Walker, Robert. *Modern Technology and Civilization.* New York: McGraw-Hill Book Co., 1962. Fascinating essays and descriptions of the implications of modern technological development on human relationships.

BOOKS ON CHINESE INDUSTRY AND INDUSTRIAL PLANNING

Bettleheim, Charles. *La Construction de la Socialisme en Chine.* Paris: Maspero, 1965.

————. *Cultural Revolution and Industrial Organization in China.* New York: Monthly Review Press, 1974.

Brugger, William. *Democracy and Organization in the Chinese Industrial Enterprise.* New York: Cambridge University Press, 1976. This book treats the first years of Communist power, showing the impact of the Soviet type of planning and management in China. It discusses the political problems of worker-management relations and the role of the Communist party in the factories.

Cavendish, Patrick, and Gray, Jack. *Chinese Communism in Crisis.* New York: Praeger, 1968. A good survey of economic development strategy, the causes of the Cultural Revolution, and its impact on that strategy.

Committee of Concerned Asian Scholars. *China: Inside the People's Republic.* New York: Bantam Books, 1971. An eyewitness account by the first group of Asia scholars to visit China from the United States since 1949, including much data on factory wages, welfare, and management.

Donnithorne, Audrey. *China's Economic System.* New York: Praeger, 1967.

Goldwasser, Janet, and Dowty, Stuart. *Huan Ying: Workers' China.* New York: Monthly Review Press, 1975. This book has much hard information on welfare expenditures, wages, and living conditions for the Chinese working class.

Hoffman, Charles. *Work Incentives Practices and Policies in the People's Republic of China, 1953–1965.* Albany: State University of New York Press, 1967.

————. *The Chinese Worker.* Albany: State University of New York Press, 1974.

Howe, Christopher. *Wage Patterns and Wage Policy in Modern China: 1919–1972.* New York: Cambridge University Press, 1973.

Karol, K. S. *China: The Other Communism.* New York: Hill and Wang, 1967. Some very good data on wages and decision-making in factories.

Lewis, John, ed. *The City in Communist China.* Stanford: Stanford University Press, 1971.

Lifton, Robert J. *Revolutionary Immortality.* New York: Vintage Books, 1968. A very influential but seriously flawed work which interprets the Cultural Revolution as Mao's own personal search for immortality. Lifton's view of the imperatives of technological development is a simplistic Weberian one.

Nee, Victor, and Peck, James, eds. *China's Uninterrupted Revolution.* New York, Pantheon Books, 1976. The essay by James Peck, "Revolution vs. Modernization and Revisionism," is an excellent discussion of both mainstream American modernization theory as applied to China and Soviet analysis of the Chinese revolution. Carl Riskin's essay on work incentives is also very useful.

Orleans, Leo. *Professional Manpower and Education in Communist China.* Washington, D.C.: U.S. Government Printing Office, 1961.

Perkins, Dwight, ed. *China's Modern Economy in Historical Perspective.* Stanford: Stanford University Press, 1975. Some excellent essays on the historical legacy with which the revolutionary government had to deal in industrializing and modernizing the economy.

Richman, Barry. *Industrial Society in Communist China.* New York: Random House, 1970. The first work of significance on China's industrialization, filled with important data.

Seyboldt, Peter. *Revolutionary Education in China: Documents and Analysis.* White Plains, N.Y.: International Arts and Sciences Press, 1973.

Wheelwright, E. L., and MacFarlane, Bruce. *The Chinese Road to Socialism.* New York: Monthly Review Press, 1970. A good, comprehensive survey of Chinese economic development, with separate treatments of agriculture and industry.

ARTICLES AND ESSAYS

Donnithorne, Audrey, and Lardy, Nicholas. "Comment: Centralization and Decentralization in China's Fiscal Management." *China Quarterly* 66 (June 1976).

Gardner, John. "The 'Wu-Fan' Campaign in Shanghai. In *Chinese Communist Politics in Action,* edited by A. Doak Barnett. Seattle: University of Washington Press, 1969.

Kalgren, Joyce. "Welfare in Communist China." In *Chinese Communist Politics in Action,* edited by A. Doak Barnett.

Riskin, Carl. "Small Industry and the Chinese Model of Development," *China Quarterly* 46 (April–June 1971).

————. "Worker Incentives in Chinese Industry." In *China: A Reassessment of the Economy*. Washington, D.C.: U.S. Congress, Joint Economic Committee, U.S. Government Printing Office, 1975.

————. "Maoism and Motivation." In *China's Uninterrupted Revolution*, edited by Victor Nee and James Peck. New York: Pantheon Books, 1976.

Schwartz. Benjamin. "Modernization and the Maoist Vision: Some Reflection on Chinese Communist Goals." *China Quarterly* 21 (January–March 1965).

CHINESE SOURCES

WORKS BY MAO

Mao Tsetung. *Selected Works*, 4 vols. Peking: Foreign Languages Press. 1964.

————. "Reading Notes on the Soviet Union's Political Economy." In *Miscellany of Mao Tse-tung Thought*. Washington. D.C.: United States Technical Information Service, February 20, 1974, *JPRS* 61269–2.

Schram, Stuart, ed. *Chairman Mao Talks to the People*. New York: Pantheon Books, 1974.

NEWSPAPER ARTICLES

JMJP, editorial, "Learn the Use of Scientific Methods in Industrial Management." *JMJP*, Peking, June 19, 1953, translated in *Survey of the China Mainland Press* (*SCMP*) #601.

Ting Tso-ch'eng. "Experiences Gained in Amalgamating Plants and Converting Them into Jointly Operated Concerns." *Kung-Shang Chieh* (Industrial and Commercial Circles), Peking, June 10, 1955, translated in *Extracts from China Mainland Magazines* (*ECMM*) #11.

"The Case of the Shenyang Transformer Plant." *New China News Agency*, Peking, July 22, 1956, in *SCMP* #1344.

Su K'o. "The Problem of Democratic Management of State-Private Enterprises Viewed in the Light of Workers' Experience in Industrial Management. *Kung-jen Jih-pao* (*KJJP*, Workers' Daily), Peking, January 5, 1957, in *SCMP* #1491.

Wang Hao-feng. "An Important Reform in the Management of Industrial Enterprises." *JMJP*, April 26, 1958, in *SCMP* #1774. This essay sets out, in comprehensive fashion, the Great Leap Forward's approach to industrial management and is a major document in the history of Chinese industrialization.

Fan Jung-k'ang. " 'Rural Work Style' and 'Guerrilla Habit' Are Orthodox Marxism." *Cheng-chih Hsueh-hsi* (Political Study) #10 (October 13, 1958), in *ECMM* #150.

CCP Committee of the Harbin Bearings Factory. "Combine Professional Management with the Participation of the Masses in Management." *KJJP*, Peking, July 19, 1959, in *SCMP* #2080, pp. 11–16.

CCP Committee, Measuring Instruments and Cutting Tools Factory, Chengtu.

"The New Socialist System of Enterprises Management." *JMJP*, June 24, 1960, in *SCMP* #2295, pp. 3–16.

Wang Hao-feng, "Consolidate and Develop the 'Two Participations,' One Reform and Triple Combination System, Raise the Standard of Enterprise Management in All Respects." *Hung Ch'i* (*AC*, Red Flag) #15 (August 1, 1960), in *Survey of China Mainland Magazines* (*SCMM*) #224, pp. 18–32.

JMJP editorial, "Further Promote Diversified Undertakings and Multiple Utilization." *JMJP*, January 19, 1961, in *SCMP* #2434, pp. 9–10.

Li Ch'eng-jui and Tso Ch'ien-jui. "Several Problems Concerning Economic Accounting in Socialist Enterprises." *HC* #19 (October 1, 1961), in *SCMM* #274, pp. 20–30.

Hsü Hsin-hsüeh. "Further Strengthen the Responsibility System in Industrial Enterprises." *HC* #20 (October 16, 1961), in *SCMM* #286, pp. 1–6.

"Concerning the Question of Socialist Distribution According to Work." *Ta Kung Pao* (*TKP*, Impartial Daily), December 15, 1961, in *SCMP* #2656, pp. 1–4.

Yüeh Kuang-chao. "Fixed Personnel and Labor Norms of Industrial Enterprises." *JMJP*, November 18, 1961, in *SCMP* #2634, pp. 1–7.

Li Jen-chih. 'On the System of Workers' Congresses in State Operated Enterprises." *HC* #2 (January 16, 1962), in *SCMM* #300, pp. 20–24.

Fei Wu-wen, Kwei Shih-yung, Liu Fu-yung. "On the Responsibility System of the Socialist State-Owned Industrial Enterprises." *Ching-Chi Yen-Chiu* (*CCYC*, Economic Research) #7 (August 3, 1962), in *SCMM* #333, pp. 29–41.

Chu P'o and Cheng Hui. "Lenin on Class Struggle in the Transition Period." *HC* #23–24 (December 5, 1962), in *SCMM* #346, pp. 5–15.

Chuang Fu-ling. "Criticizing the Fallacy of Bourgeois Sociology on the Question of Class and Class Struggle." *HC* #9 (May 1, 1963), in *SCMM* #366, pp. 12–18.

HC editorial. "Participation in Collective Productive Labor by Cadres Is of Fundamental Importance Under the Socialist System." *HC* #13–14 (July 10, 1963), in *SCMM* #376, pp. 1–13.

Chao Lin. "Some Problems Related to Class Struggle During the Period of Transition." *Hsin Chien-She* (New Construction) #11 (November 20, 1963), in *SCMM* #399, pp. 5–15.

Fang Tai. "The Need for Revolutionization as Well as Modernization." *TKP*, March 27, 1964, in *SCMP* #3206, pp. 10–14.

Sun Chien-te. "The Path of Thought Remolding for Young Technicians." *Chung-Kuo Ch'ing-Nien Pao* (*CKCNP*, Chinese Youth Report) #16, August 16, 1964), in *SCMM* #440, pp. 15–18.

"Chungking Water Turbine Works Adopts the 'Three Fixed and One Substitution' System for Their Cadres to Take Part in Labor." *JMJP*, September 22, 1964, in *SCMP* #3313, pp. 12–16.

Ma Wen-kuei. "On Several Basic Systems of Management of Socialist State Industrial Enterprises." *JMJP*, November 23, 1964, in *SCMP* #3355, pp. 1–7.

Ho-li and Chu Chia-chen. "Refuting the Production Price Theory Formulated by Comrade Yang Chien-pai and Others." *Wen-hui Pao*, Shanghai, December 11, 1964.

Chung Huang. "Revolutionization and Modernization of Socialist Industrial Enterprises." *CCYC* #12 (December 20, 1964), in *SCMM* #459, pp. 18–30.

Chi Ch'ung-wei, Li Lan-ch'ing, Lo Ching-fen. "Specialization and Cooperation Are Important Means of Achieving Greater, Faster, Better, and More Economical Results in Developing Industrial Productivity." *JMJP*, February 20, 1965, in *SCMP* #3416, pp. 4–13.

JMJP editorial, "Turning to Work-Shifts and Groups, Turning to the Worker Masses for the Purpose of Serving Production." *JMJP*, September 24, 1965, in *SCMP* #3555, pp. 2–8.

Ch'iao Jung-chang. 'The Current Technical Innovation and Technical Revolution in China's Industry." *CCYC* #10 (October 20, 1965), in *SCMM* #502, pp. 1–10.

Yün Hsi-liang. "Physical Labor and Mental Labor in Socialist Society." *CCYC* #11 (November 1965), in *SCMM* #507, pp. 4–18.

JMJP editorial, "Penetratingly Develop Revolution in Product Designing, Rapidly Raise the Technical Level of China's Industrial Production." *JMJP*, December 22, 1965, in *SCMP* #3611, pp. 8–12.

Jen Yung-chiang. "Some Relationships in Industrial Management." *CCYC* #1 (January 20, 1966), in *SCMM* #525, pp. 28–33.

"Carry Out Ideological Revolution, Send Doctors and Medicine to Workshops, Integrate Prevention With Medical Treatment, Promote Production." *Liao-ning I-hsüeh* (Liaoning Medicine) #2 (February 1, 1966), in *SCMM* #595, pp. 11–19.

Pien Yeh-chin. "The 'Wu Lan Shepherd Horsemen' in Enterprise Management." *JMJP*, February 21, 1966.

"A Precious Experience." *JMJP*, February 21, 1966.

JMJP editorial, "Run Enterprises in Line with the Thought of Mao Tse-tung." *JMJP*, April 3, 1966, in *SCMP* #3679, pp. 1–8.

Kung Wen-shang. "Sun Yeh-feng's Revisionist 'Economic Program' Refuted." *JMJP*, August 10, 1966, in *SCMP* #3769, pp. 5–14.

Shih Chieh. "Let Us See What Stuff Sun Yeh-feng's Theory of 'Enterprise Independence and Autonomy' Is." *Pei-ching Jih-pao*, August 10, 1966.

Tungfanghung Corps of the Economic Research Institute. "The Fallacy Advocated by the Top Ambitionist in Economic Work Refuted." *KMJP*, April 22, 1967, (good example of argument against vertical integration), in *SCMP* #3928, pp. 21–26.

Ching Hung. 'The Plot of the Top Ambitionist to Operate 'Trusts' on a Large Scale Must Be Thoroughly Exposed." *KMJP*, May 9, 1967, in *SCMP* #3948, pp. 1–9.

Chieh-fang Jih-pao editorial, "The Seventy Articles." *Shanghai Domestic Service*, June 4, 1967.

Wen Hui Pao editorial, "The Seventy Articles." *Shanghai Domestic Service*, June 6, 1967.

Chieh-fang Jih-pao editorial, "The Seventy Articles." *Shanghai Domestic Service*, June 9, 1967.

Chieh-fang Jih-pao editorial, "The Seventy Articles." *Shanghai Domestic City Service*, June 13, 1967.

Chieh-fang Jih-pao editorial, "Comment on the Seventy Articles." *Shanghai City Service*, June 13, 1967.

Shanghai City Service editorial, "On the 70 Articles." *Shanghai City Service*, June 14, 1967.

"The Road for Training Engineering and Technical Personnel Indicated by the Shanghai Machine Tools Plant" (Report of an Investigation). *Peking Review* #31 (August 2, 1968), pp. 9–14.

"Down With 'Three Anti' Element and Big Renegade Po I-po, Sinister Despot on the Industrial and Communications Front." *East Is Red*, February 15, 1967, in *Current Background* #878, April 28, 1969.

The Writing Group of the Kirin Provincial Revolutionary Committee. "Class Struggle in the Field of Socialist Construction and Economics—Criticizing the Revisionist Economic Theory of Sun Yeh-fang." *HC* #2 (January 30, 1970), in *SCMM* #673–74.

Suo Kang. "We Must Establish a New Production Order." *JMJP*, August 29, 1971, in *SCMP* #4973.

Yeh Yen. " 'Anshan Steel Constitution Radiates Forever." *JMJP*, March 23, 1974, in *SCMP* #5599.

Worker Theorist Group, Peking Hsinhua Printing Plant. "Consolidate the Dictatorship of the Proletariat and Restrict the Bourgeois Right." *KMJP*, February 28, 1975, in *SCMP* #5827.

"The Participation of Workers in the Management of Enterprises Is a Major Matter in Strengthening the Dictatorship of the Proletariat." *KMJP*, July 10, 1975, in *SCMP* #5917.

CHINESE-LANGUAGE SOURCES

"Kuo-wu yüan kuan-yü kai chin kung-yeh kuan-li t'i-chih ti kuei-ting" [The state councils regulations for improvement of industrial management systems]. *TKP*, November 18, 1957.

Ch'en Chin-yu. "Fou-hsin Chung-yang chi-hsiu ch'an ling-tao kan-pu kao 'shih-yen tien' ti ch'u-pu ching-yen" [The preliminary experience of the Fouhsin Central Machinery Repair Plant in "planting experimental fields"]. *Mei-t'an Kung-yeh* (Coal Industry) #8 (April 4, 1958).

Heilungkiang State Operated Chinghua Machine Tools Factory, CCP Committee. "Kuan-yü kan-pu tsan-chia sheng-ch'an, kung-jen tsan-chia kuan-li, ho yeh-wu kai-ko ching-hen ti ch'u-pu tsung-chieh" [On the preliminary summing up of the experience of cadre participation in production and worker participation in management, and professional reform]. *JMJP*, April 25, 1958.

Shanghai Diesel Oil Engine Plant, Party Committee. "Yi-k'ao ch'ün-chung kai-ko ch'i-yeh kuan-li chih-tu" [Rely on the masses to reform the system of enterprise management]. *JMJP*, November 27, 1958.

"Kung-jen ts'an-chia chi-shu kuan-li, 'san-chieh-ho' chih-tu-hüa [Workers take part in technical management, the 'Triple Combination' is systematized]. *Liaoning Jih-pao*, December 22, 1958.

Ma Wen-jai. "She-hui chu-yi kuo-ying kung-yeh ch'i-yeh kuan-li to chi-neng wen-t'i" [Several questions in the management of socialist state-operated industrial enterprises]. *JMJP*, March 28, 1964.

Jung Wen-tso. "T'an she-hui chu-yi kuo-ying kung-yeh ch'i-yeh kuan-li ti chi-pen yuan-tse" [A short discussion on the basic principles of management in Socialist state-operated industrial enterprises]. *KMJP*, September 14, 1964.

Chiang Ch'uan-kuei and Li Shih-ch'uan. [Are average profit and production price objective economic categories reflecting the specific economic relations of socialism?]. *Wen-hui Pao*, November 12, 1964.

Chang Ta-k'ai and Sung Chin-sheng. "Kuan-yü k'ai-chan ch'i-yeh kuan-li ko-ming-hua ti wen-ti" [A problem in the revolutionization in enterprise management]. *CCYC*, March 20, 1965.

Teng Chan-ming. "Kuan-yü kung-yeh ch'i-yeh chih-chien k'ai-chan ching-chi hsieh-tso ti chi-ko wen-t'i" [On several problems concerning the unfolding of economic cooperation among industrial enterprises]. *CCYC*, March 20, 1965.

Tung Yang. "Chien-li kang-wei tse-jen-chih, chia-ch'iang kung-yeh ch'i-yeh ti kuan-li kung-tso" [Build up the post responsibility system, strengthen the work of industrial enterprise management]. *CCYC*, April 20, 1965.

Hsü Chin-ch'iang. 'Kao-chü Mao Tsetung ssu-hsiang wei-ta hung-ch'i pu-tuan chia-shen ch'i-yeh ko-ming-hua" [Raise high the big red banner of Mao Tsetung Thought and continuously deepen the revolutionization of enterprises]. *CCYC*, April 20, 1966, in *SCMM* #538.

An Investigation Report on the Peking Peichiao Timber Mill. "Kai-ko pu-ho-li ti kuei-chang chih-tu shih yi ch'ang ko-ming" [Changing irrational regulations and systems is a revolution]. *HC* #6, 7 (June–July 1969).

About the Author

Stephen Andors graduated from Lafayette College, and received his M.A. from the Fletcher School of Law and Diplomacy and his Ph.D. from Columbia University in political science and Chinese studies. He is the editor of *Workers and Workplaces in Revolutionary China* and a contributor to *America's Asia* (Pantheon, 1970). From 1973 to 1976 he was editor of *The Bulletin of Concerned Asia Scholars*. From 1970 to 1975, he taught at the State University College in Oswego, New York. He has been in Thailand with the Peace Corps and traveled across Southern Asia and the Middle East. At present, he is a Research Associate at the East Asian Institute of Columbia University.